Then
I Was Black

Then I Was Black

South African
Political Identities
in Transition

Courtney Jung

Yale University Press
New Haven and London

Designed by Mary Valencia.
Set in Bembo type by Keystone Typesetting, Inc.,
Orwigsburg, Pennsylvania.
Printed in the United States of America.
Library of Congress Cataloging-in-Publication Data
Jung, Courtney Elizabeth.
Then I was Black : South African political
identities in transition / Courtney Jung.
   p.   cm.
Includes bibliographical references and index.
ISBN 0-300-08013-1 (cloth : alk. paper)
1. Democracy—South Africa.   2. Ethnicity—
Political aspects—South Africa.   3. South Africa—
Politics and government—1978–1989.   4. South
Africa—Politics and government—1989–1994.
I. Title.
JQ1981 .J85 2000
305.896′8—dc21   99-059628
A catalogue record for this book is available from
the British Library.
The paper in this book meets the guidelines for
permanence and durability of the Committee on
Production Guidelines for Book Longevity of the
Council on Library Resources.
10 9 8 7 6 5 4 3 2 1

For my parents, Ann and Clark,
and for my brother
Craig

We were disgusted with the label Coloured *and we would say, in disgust—as a way of saying this is not how it is or how it is supposed to be—we would say "so-called Coloured people." "So-called" meaning we didn't call ourselves Coloured people. It was others calling us that. It was the name given us by our oppressors, the colonialists, and the Afrikaner nationalists. And people didn't see themselves, I didn't see myself, as Coloured. Then I was Black. I saw myself as a Black person fighting for the interests of the Black people. . . . [Now] I would say I'm a Coloured. I would say I'm a Coloured. And I wouldn't have said that ten years ago.*

—Eugene Paramoer

Contents

Acknowledgments

This project was born from speaking. It was generated by hundreds of hours of interviews among South African political elites and ordinary people. I owe a great debt to the many people who gave of their time and insight to allow me to see the "new South Africa" refracted through multiple prisms.

Unlike many books, this one is not the result of onerous fieldwork, tedious note taking, and agonizing writing. The worst I can say about the research and writing is that it did not take long enough, and that I would be pleased to spend another couple of years working on this project. On the other hand, it seems that I have probably written enough, and perhaps said too much.

Like most books, this one is a collaborative effort which has benefited tremendously from the sage advice of people in both the United States and South Africa. I thank William Foltz, without whose good offices I never would have written so much. I thank David Cameron, without whose friendship and willing ear I never would have written so long. Jim Scott has encouraged me and prompted me to think the deep thoughts. I am immensely grateful for the extensive and insightful comments of Crawford Young. Anthony Marx continues to give me sound and helpful advice, even as I drift afield. Arun Agrawal has provided guidance and inspiration, and has more than once helped me to remember my point and to locate it. I thank Dan Heaton, the excellent editor at Yale University Press who ushered the manuscript through drafts to completion with some patience and much perspicacity. Among other things, I thank these seven people profoundly for having read it all, at least once.

Alex Wendt, who it must be said agrees with almost nothing written here, has nevertheless made a deep mark in the substance of my arguments. So has Mike Ebeid, who has read little but heard much, and has interpreted what I tried to say. Casiano Hacker Cordon has helped to carry a couple of nascent arguments over the threshold. Clarissa and Adam Hayward have been a bulwark of clarity and reason as we have navigated together the shoals of graduate school. I thank also John Kane, whose insights into things of which he ostensibly knows nothing make him a good person to ask about anything. And I am indebted to Leonard Wantchekon, who agrees with me, which is an unmitigated good for a person vulnerable with such a massive undertaking. I thank Kevin MacLean for walking every step, and reading every word, with grace and humor.

My greatest debt is to Ian Shapiro, who listened (skeptically) to me when the ideas that inspired this book sounded like the incantations of sorcerers, but not so clear. His confounding questions, methodological rigor, suggestions about further work to be done, and analytical insights have been essential in guiding a sense of possibility toward hundreds of pages of book. I practice vainly to achieve his clarity of thought, and am indebted to him for his generosity of time and spirit.

In South Africa I have to thank first of all Mark Stevenson and Miles Oates, without whose friendship and collusion this project would never have been conceived, and Julie Stevenson and Lianne Oates, without whose good sense and humor it would never have gone beyond conception. I thank also Philip Hunter, to whom I am indebted beyond what is reasonable and without whom my fieldwork would have been, if not impossible, certainly diminished. I am grateful to Mike Courtenay for his occasional but worthy translation of unfathomable speeches. I thank Jeremy Seekings, who also read and commented on the entire text, and without whose wisdom, guidance, and prodding I would have foundered more often. I thank Nicoli Nattrass for friendship and encouragement, but probably most for her undercurrents of inherent doubt. And I am grateful to Mike Morris for subtle analysis in an unsubtle climate.

Many other people have played a role in making my world a better place in the years I have spent writing. I thank Christa Clarke, Jack and Dolores Clarke, Lucy Cobby, the Davidsons, Dave DeGroot, the Duggans, Griffin Eaton, Adam Edwards, Kelli Farnham, Roberto Garcia, Meg Garlinghouse, Lynn Harris, Hannah Hotchkiss, the Kanes, Alisa LaGamma, Fred Lee, Dara Levine, Brendan Magrab, Kristin and Tom Meagher, the Morgenthaus, the Ozimeks, Thom Pak, the Shapiros, Matt and Jamie Smith, Deb Stevenson, Kim and Paul Vessa, Peter Waszkis, Peter Watson, and Todd Wiener. I am grateful to my brother, without whom I would be a very different person, and to my parents, for their belief. I thank Ben Morgenthau for being always on the side of goodness and light.

Finally, I gratefully acknowledge the fiscal and institutional support I have received in this endeavor. I thank everyone at the Centre for Social and Development Studies at the University of Natal for their help and hospitality. I am grateful for the support of the Jill Nattrass Fellowship at the Centre for Social and Development Studies, the Enders Fellowship, the Harold K. Hochschild Fellowship for African Studies, and the Arthur M. Leland Dissertation Fellowship.

Introduction

The Permanence of Change

There is nothing permanent except change.
                                                Heraclitus

The last decade of the twentieth century has been marked by tremendous and unexpected political tumult. One of the world's two dominant political ideologies collapsed under the weight of practice, leaving the institutions and ideological tenets of the other to race like prairie fire across the globe. Between 1975 and 1990 the number of democracies in the world increased from 40 to 76.[1] Between 1990 and 1996 the number leaped from 76 to 118. Most countries in the world today either are democratic or make democratic claims.

But this development should not precipitate congratulatory backslapping on the part of democrats everywhere. As the term and its institutions have spread beyond their more familiar habitat in "advanced Western" societies, they have come to mean many things to many people. There is sufficiently wide variation in what counts as democracy that its internal differences may be greater than some of its comparative ones. The terms and parameters of democracy are renegotiated as they travel. The institutions of democracy and the commitment of its local proponents also appear vulnerable. Whether many new democracies will be consolidated, or whether they will further mutate into new and unpredictable forms of political organization, is an open question.[2]

At the same time, the politics of identity has proliferated almost as rapidly. The international spread of democracy has been accompanied by a significant increase in the salience of ethnicity as a marker of political affiliation and cleavage. The decline of Cold War–era national and regional identities has been countered by an apparent increase in the salience of mostly subnational ethnic and other allegedly communal identities. Ethnicity, race, language, and religion stand at the center of political engagement in country after country on continent after continent. Naturally, the politics of identity is not new. In this century alone, ethnicities have surged, submerged and resurged, infused with varying degrees of political significance. Nevertheless, the engagement of ethnicity and politics seems different this time, for three reasons. First, ethnicity last played a prominent political role in the postcolonial era. This context generated the abiding impression that ethnicity was a symptom of political affiliation in the former colonies of the underdeveloped South.[3] Faced with the reality of identity politics in Canada, Northern Ireland,

Belgium, and Bosnia, this framework of difference no longer seems plausible. Second, in some places the politics of identity has taken a nasty turn, generating what appear to be impenetrable cycles of violence and destruction. As a result, whereas the diffusion of democratic ideals is heralded as a practical good, ethnicity and its visible effects are viewed with trepidation.

Third, the simultaneous rise of both democracy and ethnicity has meant, practically, a great deal of new interaction between politically mobilized ethnic groups and the institutions of democracy. More and more countries that include highly politicized ethnic groups are attempting democratic consolidation, prompting a new round of questions regarding the ability of "normal" democratic institutions to process identity politics. Even in established democracies, "the political salience of the ethnic and collective divisions of a country arguably has become the new fulcrum of the politics of liberal democracy." Whereas the language of rights has traditionally supported the claims of individuals, it is now employed on behalf of groups.[4] The claim for group recognition, or group equity, is a modern claim. The question is whether a liberal democracy, premised in our imagination on individual rights, freedom, and equality, can entertain the competing claims of groups.

Whether we believe it can depends on the way we understand the human social condition. This book is about the interaction of individuals with cultural groups and the interaction of cultural groups with politics. How, when, why, and among whom are collective identities mediated by ethnicity, language, race, and religion politicized, and what are the implications for democracy?

Human beings exhibit a universal tendency toward group affiliation. People are northerners, southerners, Black, union members, environmentalists, feminists, Serbs, Republicans, Catholics, campesinos, Tutsis, clan members, Klan members, Indonesians, Hatfields, Africans, pro-life activists, Asian Americans, businessmen, Californians, communists, and a practically infinite number of other things. Empirical evidence demonstrates that groups are ubiquitous and often in conflict. Experimental evidence suggests that the pull toward affiliation with a group is innate—part of human nature.[5] Identities, which derive in part from temperament and personality, are also filtered through group membership. Who we are is mediated in part by where our commitments lie and how we distinguish between "us" and "them."

Identities are in fact centrally bound by the distinction between "us" and "them." Experiments with human subjects have demonstrated that group membership entails comparison and discrimination. In the 1970s a team of social psychologists conducted a series of studies on group dynamics. Subjects were divided arbitrarily into separate groups, A and B. No effort was made to instill positive in-group or negative out-group evaluations among group members. Group members experienced no face-to-face interaction with either in-group or out-group members. Nevertheless, people divided randomly into separate groups quickly developed in-group loyalties and a tendency to discriminate against out-groups in experiments involving the allocation of rewards.[6] Group members went so far as to reduce their own profits if in so doing they could maximize the difference between their profits and those of the out-group. Psychologists conclude that, as members of groups, people strive to achieve positive social identity through competition with other groups.

Furthermore, the basis of group discrimination may be minimal or even nonexistent. Subjects were divided on the basis of trivial differences, no differences, or a coin toss. The tendency to discriminate in favor of in-group members was not affected by the standard used to assign membership. Even groups not united by any common attribute quickly developed group loyalty. In another experiment, people not assigned to any group were given the opportunity to apportion rewards among other subjects with similar artistic preferences, dissimilar preferences, and no known preferences. This produced no statistically significant tendency to discriminate on the basis of similarity. What counts is group membership, not demonstrated affinity.[7] Because anything, and even nothing, can serve to distinguish people as members of one group but not another, the possibilities of group formation and affiliation are practically infinite. Groups need not be distinguished from each other by any social, physical, practical, or material markers. They need only to be named.

That group-based identity is universal and innate suggests that we should not take the existence of groups as an aberration to be attenuated, manipulated, or wished away. Identities mediated by distinct and separate groups are here to stay. The evidence of experiments in social psychology also indicates that groups may form around anything, or even nothing. The symbols that are used to generate group identity do not affect in-group loyalty, out-group discrimination, or the desire to harm members of another group. Groups are universal precisely because they may form around anything and do not rely on objective difference.

Although the tendency to form groups may be innate and universal therefore, the meanings, goals, boundaries, and symbols of group identity are constructed and particular. Some characteristics are transformed into symbols with public meaning and the power to bind groups, while others remain unsignified. This is what is meant by the claim that group identities are socially constructed. The process by which potential loyalties and affiliations actually do organize the social, psychological, political, and economic grid of people's lives is neither natural nor automatic. It is the socially constructed result of specific contextual and historical forces operating in a unique temporal space.

The universality of the tendency of human beings to form group allegiances is filtered through the particularity of human experience. The implications of distinct and separate identities for peace, stability, democracy, and the possibility of respect for universal human rights depends on how groups form, how they derive political content, why symbols develop resonance, and among whom mobilization succeeds. Furthermore, as Henri Lefebvre puts it, "Insofar as the science of man exists it finds its material in the 'trivial,' the everyday."[8] Because the meaning, salience, and boundaries of identity are not universal but particular, they must be investigated through the "trivial," the everyday.

In April 1995 I was in the eighth month of what would eventually be fifteen months of field research in South Africa. I had just acquired a fourteen-year-old Land Rover, and I was traveling from Johannesburg to Durban to begin interviewing Zulu political leaders of the Inkatha Freedom Party (IFP) and the African National Congress (ANC). About ninety miles outside of Durban, in the Valley of a Thousand Hills, my Land Rover broke down. I was on a major highway, so this was not necessarily a big problem, and I was soon towed to a garage. It turned out, though, that the garage was not as useful as one might anticipate; the mechanic was away, and there was no telephone. The gas station ordinarily had telephone service, but twelve miles of copper cable had recently been stolen from the poles, and the phone had not worked for a week or so. The station manager suggested that his brother-in-law might be able to help me out, and that I should wait until he could reach him. So I waited.

I had been waiting about three hours when one of the gas station attendants approached me during a break and began to talk. His name was Philemon Ndebele, and he was about sixty years old. Philemon told me that he was a Zulu and that he lived with his three wives in a nearby village. His children were grown. He told me that in his village the chief was well respected and responsible, and looked out for his people. He said his chief had no affiliation to any of the dominant political parties, and Philemon believed that this was appropriate for a chief. In the context of violent conflict between political parties in Natal during the 1980s, the political affiliation of chiefs "only brought trouble" to the village.[9]

Philemon considered himself a traditional Zulu. He lived in the village he grew up in. He had worked on the gold mines near Johannesburg when he was younger but had come home earlier than most, and had stayed. He followed Zulu marriage custom by taking more than one wife. In an era when it was not uncommon to hear complaints about the authority of chiefs, Philemon purposely professed loyalty to a controversial institution. As a rural-dwelling Zulu firmly embedded in a traditional ethnic hierarchical and psychic framework, Philemon's political identity might be expected to have remained essentially stable throughout his life. Yet his personal history of political affiliation and sympathies belies this assumption, demonstrating what seems intuitively a surprising degree of change over time.

Philemon was a strong supporter of the ANC in the 1950s. Although he did not recall participating in any political actions, he remembered that discussions about ANC goals and campaigns, and admiration for the movement's leaders, were pervasive. Most of the people in his village, as well as in the mines, supported the ANC at that time. After the ANC was banned in 1961, Philemon continued to support its ideals, though he was not politically active. In 1975 Zulu homeland leader Gatsha Buthelezi launched Inkatha as the political party of the KwaZulu homeland. Philemon then joined Inkatha. He did not however, relinquish support for the ANC. He said he "followed Inkatha, but also the ANC." In the 1970s Inkatha membership entailed little other than paying occasional dues, and Philemon identified it as simply a party "for the Zulus," without further ideological content. Philemon's apparent dual political commitment remained mostly latent and held no internal contradiction in the 1970s.

In the 1980s the ANC-aligned United Democratic Front (UDF) tried to establish a political stronghold in Natal. Competition for support and serious ideological disagreements between Inkatha and the UDF precipitated a decade of bloody interparty violence among Zulus in Natal. The possibility for dual allegiance was erased, and Philemon became "more strong for Inkatha." His chief remained neutral, though aligned ostensibly with Inkatha for pragmatic reasons. Philemon's swing toward Inkatha was explicitly accompanied, and partly driven, by rejection of the UDF, which he perceived as consisting of radical, communist youth. Philemon did not equate the ANC that he had supported in the 1950s with the UDF, even though the UDF identified itself, and was commonly perceived as, the internal wing of the ANC during the 1980s.

Philemon's affiliation with Inkatha in the 1980s affected the salience of his ethnic identity, as well as his public expression of it. He believed that Inkatha acted as the explicit representative and protector of the Zulu people, and he said that he had been "more Zulu" then. As an Inkatha member, he had gone to political rallies wearing traditional Zulu skins that he was not otherwise in the habit of wearing, and carrying the "traditional weapons" that became a symbol of Inkatha affiliation in that period. He was an ardent supporter of the Zulu monarch in the

1980s, although he did not remember the king as an important figure of ethnic leadership in his youth.[10] He had attended three annual Reed Dance celebrations at the ancestral home of the Zulu king in the mid-1980s, but none since 1987.[11]

By 1995 Philemon was again unsure of the place of the king in Zulu cosmology. The king had switched allegiances, joining in alliance with the ANC, and Philemon felt that perhaps he should not play a political role at all. He was also unsure of the place of Zuluness in politics. Philemon had begun to feel that neither the ANC nor Inkatha was particularly "for the Zulus" anymore, and that parties should be open to everyone in the "new South Africa." In South Africa's first democratic election, in April 1994, Philemon voted for Inkatha. He said that he would consider voting for the ANC in the next election, however. He had "not made up [his] mind."

Philemon's everyday experience of his own identity has changed significantly during his political life. His claims about shifting identities are striking in part because he lives in the village in which he grew up. His identities have not changed in response to migration to an urban area, or because of exposure to new ideological or organizational frameworks.[12] He himself has remained physically stable, while meaning and salience have shifted around him. He perceives that his political and ethnic identities have been more or less intertwined at different points in time, and that, although Zulu identity has been politically pivotal at some times, it recedes at others. Philemon has made political choices based on his Zulu identity. More often, though, ethnicity has not mediated his political affiliation.

Not only do the political meaning, salience, and boundaries of Zuluness shift over time for people who identify as Zulu, but so do they shift in different ways for different people. Philemon's political identity and its engagement with the symbols of Zuluness have exhibited considerable change over time. The relation between Zulu identity and politics also demonstrate heterogeneity across space. Philemon himself recognized the fluidity and variable political salience of Zulu identity when he described his relationship with his son and his son's engagement with politics.

Philemon bemoaned the fact that young people, including his own children, were leaving the villages and moving to urban areas. His son had gone to work in Durban in 1984. There he became a member of the UDF, which Philemon explained "was against Zulus." His son lived in KwaMashu, one of the most heavily contested and violent townships of Durban during the war. Philemon was not sure about his own son's involvement in violence, but he did say they were "using guns," which "is not the Zulu way." He claimed that, as a member of the UDF, his son had renounced his Zuluness. He did not carry a stick, or "behave in the Zulu way."[13] Father and son fought bitterly over politics, and Philemon forbade his son from returning to the village. He told him that he was not a Zulu. His son did not come home at all for many years. Philemon did not see him again until 1993.

By 1995 their relationship had improved. When the UDF was disbanded in 1991, Philemon's son joined the ANC, the movement's ideological parent. For Philemon, the ANC lacked the anti-Zulu baggage of the UDF. He said "The ANC [was] for Zulus, not against them; not like the UDF," and he did not see a problem with his son's joining the ANC. He laughed, "No, it's okay, it's okay," in response to my insistent questioning regarding his feelings about the ANC. After 1993 his son started to come home again, and he moved to Pietermaritzburg, which is closer to the village than Durban. In 1994 Philemon's son was married, and he complied with the Zulu practice of paying *lobola,* bride wealth, to the bride's family. Philemon said that his son was a Zulu again. "Yes of course. I am a Zulu, my son is Zulu. My wife also Zulu."

Philemon clearly described changes in his own political identity, in the political salience of his ethnic identity, in the boundaries of ethnicity, and in the links between his ethnic group and organized politics. He experienced no apparent crisis of identity as he described the variety of political affiliations and meanings that had been compatible with Zuluness over his lifetime, how political affiliations affected who could properly count as a Zulu, and how his performance of Zulu identity had changed in a shifting political context. He also perceived that other members of his ethnic group, and even family unit, are involved in a similar process, and that they may be affected differently. Though he identified the hereditary quality of ethnicity ("I am a Zulu, my son is Zulu"), he also patiently described the mutability of blood ties. Zuluness ebbs and flows at different times for different people and can be distinctly navigated. To the extent that it is, it divides the family and ethnic groups in which Philemon feels membership.

Zulu identity was less politically salient and divisive in the 1990s than in the last decade of the apartheid era. Nevertheless, the retreat of the political significance of Zuluness is not accompanied by a similar diminution of its importance in other spheres. Philemon introduced himself to me as a Zulu, and he was clearly pleased that his son had followed Zulu marriage custom. Philemon's Zuluness is performed differently depending on context, however. As a political identity, it was manifest in his attendance at rallies, his commitment to the king, and his use of traditional weapons. Otherwise, Zulu identity is expressed variously in the language he speaks, in the customs he follows in his home, in his choice of wife (or wives), and in his decision to remain in the village under "traditional" rule. Whether Zulu identity is politically salient does not affect Philemon's commitment to Zuluness, or its performance in social, cultural, and personal interactions.

When identity is politicized, however, as it was for Philemon during the 1980s, it is contested. As a result, it becomes more "tightly scripted."[14] In its public form, Zuluness acquired a particular set of identifying markers. Those Zulus who failed to appropriate the standards of the public articulation of Zulu identity, who failed to attend Inkatha rallies or carry traditional weapons, were denied Zulu identity. Philemon's own son, the son of two Zulu parents, "lost" his Zuluness when he joined the UDF, even as his father's own Zulu identity became "more strong." The politicization of identity potentially renders its definition, boundaries, and expression more singular and less permeable. Harnessed to a particular political agenda, Zuluness was temporarily unavailable to those who failed to perform their identity in the manner prescribed by the party that claimed to be the standards bearer of Zulu culture.

How and when are ethnic identities politicized and depoliticized, and what are the implications for democracy? In this book I seek to expose and explore the multiple and fluid nature of political identities mediated by race and ethnicity for the purpose of reconceptualizing the nature of politics in societies that have been dubbed "divided." I shall move beyond the now-commonplace assumption that ethnic identity is socially constructed, and I shall explore the conditions under which it is constructed as *political,* how and when ethnicity is mobilized for the purpose of gaining power and access to resources located in government, when such mobilization succeeds, and among whom it succeeds. The experience of Philemon, and his personal narrative, is incompatible with dominant assumptions regarding the organically derived, practically permanent, and politically over-determining character of communal identities. The theoretical argument is built on detailed comparative study of changes in the political meanings, goals, and boundaries of Afrikaner, Zulu, and Coloured political identities in South Africa between 1980 and 1995. Findings suggest that such political institutions as electoral laws have only a limited role to play in the manipulation of ethnic identities. In addition, because ethnicity is constructed and potentially fluid, not primordial and permanent, it bears a closer resemblance to political identities mediated by class and ideology than to the static and overdetermining pillars of a divided society. As a result, whether societies are organized primarily along ethnic, ideological, or class lines should not represent a fundamental distinction that sets some societies apart from others and predicts their inability to sustain democracy.

In Chapter 1 I investigate the question of political identity. I propose an analytical distinction between political identity—that part of identity which emerges as salient in the organized struggle for control over the allocation of resources and power residing in the state—and other identities that people hold in other spheres. Any identity may be politicized, but none is inherently political. Zuluness, for example, mediates political identity in a way that is both inconstant over time, for any one individual, and over space for different members of the Zulu group. Moreover, it is not possible to derive political identity from objective characteristics or qualities a person might possess. In Chapter 1 I shall introduce and preliminarily explore five factors that are likely to affect whether, when, and among whom ethnicity will be politicized: political institutions, mobilizing discourse, material conditions, organization, and available ideology. Resonance is the conceptual category that describes political identity as the result of that which is organized and mobilized by political institutions and entrepreneurs, refracted through the lens of those who are being mobilized. I explore how these variables interact, and which are most crucial to the politicization of ethnicity, in the following chapters.

Empirical case studies in Chapters 2 through 7 demonstrate that the political meaning, salience, and boundaries of Afrikaner, Zulu, and Coloured identities, which have had varying degrees of resonance in South African politics at different times, shifted in politically relevant though not necessarily predictable ways between 1980 and 1995. Although discursive shifts in the tactics of political entrepreneurs resulted partly from changes in the structure and scope of South Africa's political institutions, whether political entrepreneurs succeeded in politicizing ethnic identities depended primarily on material conditions, organization, and available ideology. Zulu identity, which divided Zulus politically in the 1980s, has grown less politically salient in the postapartheid era. Afrikaner identity is more politicized now than a decade ago, yet primarily mediates the political identities of only a minority of Afrikaners. Coloured identity, shunned politically as well as socially in the 1980s, has remained politically dormant in the 1990s, despite the efforts of some political elites to mobilize support around Colouredness. So too, however, has Black identity, which dominated "Coloured politics" in the 1980s, and Whiteness, despite the best efforts of the National Party to forge a single racially based identity among its constituents. Despite their foundation in ethnicity, the political meanings and boundaries of each of these three identities has changed sufficiently that they must be clearly recognized as fluid in the transitional era at least.

In Chapter 8 I present a critique of the literature on electoral laws to demonstrate that those options that have been proposed as "solutions" to the problems of "divided societies" are not likely to work. Although political institutions play a role in shaping identity, their effect is diluted by an indirect relationship to resonance. Political elites respond to incentives generated by material conditions, organization, and ideology, as well as political institutions. Moreover, their success, whether or not their attempts at mobilization resonate, depends primarily on the conditioning variables that frame the political lives of their potential constituents. Democracy, stability, and equality may be better supported by attention to conditioning than to proximate factors.

In Chapter 9 I present an alternative conceptual paradigm of ethnically mediated political identities based on evidence and analysis drawn from the South African case studies. Politicized ethnic identities are constructed around such symbols as race, ethnicity, ideology, and class in ways that make them more or less politically enduring, under conditions in which members will have varying capacity for exit. The character of the group depends not on the symbols of its constitution but on the manner of its construction. There is no a priori reason to believe that groups mediated by race and ethnicity are more likely to be static, homogeneous, and overdetermining than groups mediated by class and ideology. This conclusion has implications for the way we think of "divided" societies, for democratic consolidation, and for ethnic conflict.

This project was originally motivated by a reaction against the divided-society paradigm. "Divided societies" are those in which two or more politically salient racial, ethnic, religious, or linguistic groups are presumed to determine the possibilities of politics. Ethnic and racial groups are considered permanent, and group-based political affiliations are assumed to be stable over time and across space among a consistently bound group of people. As a result, elections are nothing more than a "racial census." Moreover, because communal groups apparently command a primordial and passionate attachment, politics are expected to be conflictual in societies that are dubbed "divided." The vast majority of supposedly divided societies are in the underdeveloped societies of the East and South, juxtaposed against the "advanced democracies" of the West.

Any survey of the literature reveals that the paradigmatic case of a divided society is South Africa. An unfortunate combination of historical, political, ideological, institutional, social, and economic factors has made many of South Africa's racial and ethnic cleavages highly salient politically. As a result, almost every piece of scholarship on South Africa refers to the "fact" that South Africa is a divided society.[15] South Africa is a clear case of a society in which multiple racial and ethnic groups are engaged politically, and in which the possibilities of democracy are presumed to be limited by the politics of identity.

It is in the interaction of individuals with groups and the interaction of groups with politics that this book takes place. If South Africa's racial and ethnic groups are not permanent and homogeneous, if they are unevenly politicized, and fluid in terms of commitments and boundaries, then there are good reasons to think South Africa is not a divided society. If South Africa is not a divided society, there are good reasons to think there are no divided societies, in the sense the term has been used. And if groups in South Africa do not behave in the fixed and over-determining ways we have imagined, then there are good reasons to believe that groups elsewhere will not either.

Between 1948 and 1990 South Africa's apartheid government systematically divided South Africans into racial and ethnic categories reinforced through ideology, political institutions, laws, and economic rights. All South Africans carried identity books in which they were defined by race and, if they were Black, further by ethnic group. Such classifications determined where they could live, where they could work, how much they would be paid, whom they could marry, how far they could travel, what areas they could enter, what schools they could attend, where they could eat, whom they could hire, whom they could work for, what legal recourse they had, whether they could vote, whom they could vote for, what bus they could take, and a thousand other details, large and small, of everyday life. With the possible exception of Nazi Germany, allegedly ascriptive characteristics were more completely determining in South Africa than anywhere else in the modern era.

Apartheid ideology was based on the concept of separation. It was rooted in an understanding of a world divided into "peoples" with irreconcilably different languages, cultures, religions, customs, working habits, mores, aspirations, temperaments, histories, and traditions. Individuals naturally sought fulfillment within their own group, befriending, marrying, working with, and voting for "their own" people. Each people, or *volk,* represented a distinct political unit which ultimately should have self-determination. Groups, especially those defined in racial terms, should be kept separate to prevent the boundaries between them from blurring. To "mix" people was a sin against God, a betrayal of the group, and a travesty against the natural order of things. "After all, the buffalo does not mix with the giraffe" is one analogy often used by conservative Afrikaners to underscore the logic of apartheid ideology.

Despite the considerable psychological, military, institutional, economic, and coercive resources dedicated to the enforcement of the apartheid vision, the political project foundered from the start. The architects of apartheid should have had an inkling of the misguided premise of their endeavor when they defined the groups into which South Africans would be divided. The Population Registration Act defined a White person "as someone who in appearance is obviously a White person and who is not generally accepted as a Coloured person, or who is generally accepted as a White person and is not obviously in appearance not a White person. This definition is not applicable to a person who, for the purposes of his classification, freely and voluntarily admits that he is by descent a Black or Coloured person, unless it is proved that the admission is not based on fact." By contrast, "a Black person is one who is a member of any aboriginal race or tribe of Africa or who is generally accepted as such," and "a Coloured is a person who is not a White or a Black person."[16]

In cases of doubt, "general acceptance" as a member of a particular group took legal precedence over descent to determine racial group membership. During the 1940s White government census takers resorted to differentiating Whites from Coloureds on the basis of the individual's own demeanor toward the official. If he was deferential and called the official *Baas,* he was classified as Coloured rather than White.[17]

Problems with the substance and boundaries of these definitions, which were strictly enforced and yet subjectively interpreted, bedeviled apartheid administration. "A person's first or initial classification need not be his final classification: the director general [for] internal affairs may reclassify him, or a race classification board may order a reclassification." Thousands petitioned for reclassification every year—to marry someone in another racial category, to improve their employment opportunities, or to improve their children's chances of favorable race classification. Each case was investigated, and many people succeeded in changing race. Others were reclassified by the internal affairs department, "to ensure that the population register is kept up to date and correct."[18]

The South African government was forced to legislate membership in racial categories; categories that by definition should have been obvious and natural to the individuals themselves; categories over which there is allegedly no room for choice. Legislation was necessary precisely because people might not *choose* the "appropriate" category. People made choices about their identities for personal, material, strategic, and ideological reasons. By conscious design, South Africans often failed to self-categorize according to prescribed definitions.

The fact that such subjective indicators as "general acceptance" and deference to Whites trumped ancestry and physical markers as final tests of racial classification further undermines the "natural" and biological underpinnings of apartheid ideology. In many cases, families, even brothers and sisters, were classified differently.[19] The frequency of reclassification, and the permeability of categories specifically designed to be binding and mutually exclusive, made it obvious that such classifications were not permanent, nor ultimately dependent on (presumably stable) blood ties or racial characteristics.

Apartheid ideology never achieved hegemony. The forced segregation of racial and ethnic groups into separate categories, in separate areas, with separate rights and resources, was always contested and never gained legitimacy among the majority of South Africans.[20] The oppositional ideology of Black Consciousness undercut apartheid's racial divisions by denying the validity of racial classifications that split the oppressed.[21] It rejected separate classifications for Africans, Coloureds, and Asians and united them politically as Blacks. Blackness was explicitly rooted not in color but in an experience of common oppression.[22] In the 1980s the Tricameral Parliament, in which Coloureds and Asians were represented in separate chambers by "their own" representatives at central government level, was shunned by most of those it intended to represent—not only because it denied representation to Africans but because separate representation on a racial basis had by then been thoroughly delegitimized.

Apartheid was based on the untenable premise that South African society comprises discrete biological and cultural groups that act as homogeneous units for political purposes. If racial and ethnic groups had been the natural and permanent affiliative categories envisioned by the architects of apartheid, the state would have faced much less opposition than it did, and it could have channeled political expression more efficiently.

Although there is no question that some racial and ethnic categories are politically salient in postapartheid South Africa, there is abundant evidence they do not constitute a divided society. The majority of South Africans reject sectional appeals and have a common attachment to the South African nation. Surveys conducted in 1995 found that more than 90 percent of respondents were "proud" or "very proud" to be South African.[23] Only two parties explicitly mobilize an ethnic power base. Between them, the Freedom Front (FF) and the Inkatha Freedom Party (IFP), garnered only 13 percent of the vote in South Africa's first democratic election. In local government elections eighteen months later, both parties fared worse. Each party has the support of less than half of its ostensible ethnic base.

In 1994, eighty-three percent of South Africans voted for either the African National Congress (ANC) or the National Party (NP). Along with the Democratic Party (DP), the ANC and the NP occupy the moderate center (particularly in racial/ethnic terms) of the South African political spectrum. Divided societies are ostensibly dominated by ethnic parties characterized primarily by particularistic and exclusive interests inimical to the common good.[24] The ANC and NP however, both articulate a vision for South Africa that includes the society as a whole. The NP and ANC are in fact best classified as catch-all parties that appeal to a wide range of interests and individuals. Both include multiracial, multiethnic leaderships. The NP has a multiracial support base; the ANC's is multiethnic. Although the popularity of most parties dropped between 1994 and 1997, support did not appear to be moving toward ethnic parties. Among the major parties, only the moderate DP, which calculated in 1997 that 24 percent of its supporters were African, has increased its support base.[25]

Although most Blacks voted for the ANC and most Whites voted for the NP, South Africans did not obviously vote because of race. In 1994 fewer than 1 percent of de Klerk supporters and only 7 percent of Mandela supporters claimed to vote on the basis of the communal identities that would presumably be politically determinant in a divided society. Most respondents to a postelection poll were able to place themselves and the parties on a left-right ideological continuum and made clear connections between their own ideological position and that of their preferred party.[26] Voters' ideological positions mirrored their political choices. Black NP voters were more conservative, more concerned about law and order, and of higher socioeconomic status, than ANC voters. Polling data indicates that the primary concerns of most South Africans are employment, housing, education, access to resources such as electricity and water, and crime. The ANC campaigned for the 1994 national election under the slogan "A Better Life for All." During the local government election campaign eighteen months later, the ANC focused attention on its record of providing housing, water and electricity, and on its efforts to decrease unemployment. The party presented itself as "tough on crime." Since 1994 ANC campaigns have been built around the issues that most concern South African voters, and most voters appear to believe that the ANC is the party most likely to address those issues that concern them.

In addition to most Whites, most Coloureds also voted for the NP in the first democratic election, which turns the racial divide on its head—people of different race groups may vote together. Divided-society theorists leap to the conclusion that this alliance is based on linguistic affinity (most Coloureds also speak Afrikaans) or was racially motivated by fear among both Coloureds and Whites of *swartgevaar*, "black danger." In fact, polling data demonstrates that Coloureds do not generally feel closer to Whites than to Blacks, and in any case their perceived closeness to one group or the other does not conclusively determine political affiliation.[27] Better-educated, wealthier, urban Coloureds were more likely to vote for the ANC than the NP. Ultimately, the Coloured vote exhibited a plethora of cross-cutting cleavages (a phenomenon explicitly lacking in a "divided society") that proved more relevant to political affiliation than Colouredness.[28]

Researchers also tried to measure the potential and direction of voter fluidity by asking respondents to rate their second party choice. The results show that ANC voters' second choice was the more radical Pan Africanist Congress (PAC) and to a lesser extent the more centrist DP and the NP. For NP supporters, the liberal DP and the Zulu-based Inkatha Freedom Party were the most popular second choices, with the ANC slightly lower. IFP voters chose the Afrikaner nationalist FF, the NP, and DP in that order, and for DP voters the overwhelming second choice was the IFP. These results suggest that voters perceive South African politics as operating along an ideologically, not racially or ethnically, structured spectrum. South African parties are organized from left to right as follows: PAC, ANC, DP, NP, IFP, FF. Voters choose a second party based on its ideological proximity to their first choice on this spectrum, not on the party's racial composition. The PAC and ANC are predominantly Black, the DP and NP are mostly White, Coloured, and Indian, the IFP is mostly Zulu, and the FF is almost exclusively Afrikaner. It is for this reason that R. W. Johnson and Lawrence Schlemmer believe that if the ANC were "to lose its symbolic grip on its supporters, an extremely fluid situation would develop in the new South African polity."[29] The potential for an "extremely fluid situation" is not what we should expect of a divided society.

Although the ANC won the second election in 1999 with an even greater majority than it achieved in 1994, the apparent consistency of the first two elections masks some important shifts in South African electoral politics. The ANC increased its share of the vote by 4 percent, (from 62 percent to 66 percent) even though it had the support of almost two million fewer voters. Turnout in South Africa's second democratic election was roughly three-fourths what it had been in the first, with important effects for party fortunes. There was a tremendous shakeup among opposition parties. Whereas the National Party formed the official opposition in 1994 with more than 20 percent of the vote, the New National Party (NNP) dropped to fourth place in the second election, garnering only 6 percent of the vote and losing the Western Cape province. The Inkatha Freedom Party also lost support, slipping from 10 percent to 9 percent, though the party maintained its third-place position. The biggest surprise of the election was the DP, which moved from fifth place, with 1 percent of the vote, to official opposition with just less than 10 percent. The DP appears to have picked up support from NNP, IFP and Freedom Front/Conservative Party voters. Although the ANC vote remains secure, it lost a fair amount of support to the newly formed United Democratic Movement, especially in the Eastern Cape, where the UDM became the official opposition by siphoning off more than 10 percent of the ANC's support base there. In the Northwest province Lucas Mangope's United Christian Democratic Party (UCDP) also garnered 10 percent of former ANC votes to become the official opposition. The results of the second election demonstrate that ANC electoral dominance is not inviolable, and that the party may be vulnerable to regional challenges even if no national contender appears capable yet of taking it on.

The nation's history suggests that if ever there were going to be a divided society, South Africa would be it. It is apparent that some of the racial and ethnic categories into which the apartheid government divided the population have resonated in varying degrees at different times.[30] Nevertheless, the political legitimacy of racial and ethnic group identity in South Africa has always been contested. Race and ethnicity certainly emerge as salient features of postapartheid politics. But close inspection reveals that South African voters exhibit a number of tendencies, including an overarching national identity, interests, concerns, and ideological positions that inform political identity, as well as cross-cutting cleavages, that place them closer to voters in Western democracies than to the prototypical "divided society" voter.

The South African case studies reveal that politically mobilized ethnicity and race include significant capacity for change over time and heterogeneity across space. The boundaries, goals, meaning, and salience of politicized ethnic groups shift in dialectic engagement with a changing context. In addition, ethnicity and race distinctly mediate the identities of different members of objectively identifiable groups at different times, so that each apparent communal group is likely to contain significant internal variation. It is the change and movement of politically mobilized ethnic and racial groups that I seek to explore and explain.

1 Born from Speaking

The Construction of Political Identity

In this chapter I introduce the paradigm, vocabulary, and preliminary assumptions that guide the research and analysis of political identity in this book. I propose a way of thinking that is intended to capture and explain more of the complexity and indeterminacy of political identity than standard models and assumptions have permitted. I aim in particular to explain change over time, differential levels of identification and affiliation among members of the same ostensible group, and the failure, as much as success, of mobilizing discourse to resonate.[1]

Political identity must be treated as an analytical category, distinct from identities people hold in personal, social, spiritual, or economic spheres. As a result, the behavior of political identity cannot be conflated with commitments that compel cultural, religious, or linguistic action or beliefs. Political identity is not innate, and does not spring from characteristics and ties determined by birth. It is the complex and multilayered result of that which is mobilized by political elites refracted through the memories and networks of those who are mobilized. It is constructed in reciprocal engagement with a series of variables that make some identities and affiliations more salient and accessible than others. All individuals have multiple characteristics, commitments, and connections. Which develop political significance, and which of their potential identities individuals recognize, are contingent. I propose that salience and meaning are functions of the interaction, over time, of political institutions, mobilizing discourse, material conditions, organization, and available ideology. Political identity emerges as the presumptively indeterminate, fluid, and heterogeneous result of constant negotiation and renegotiation between subject and context.

The Possibilities of Construction

An investigation of the construction of political identities is based on the premise that political identity is neither inherent nor essential. Recent work in the fields of history, anthropology, and political science demonstrates that identities—political and otherwise, ethnic and otherwise—are derived rather than innate and, for the most part, recent rather than timeless.[2] Wide-ranging surveys show that many of the ethnic groups that form part of the demographic, and in some cases political, landscape of southern Africa today were constructed in the colonial and postcolonial eras of the past century.[3] They have not existed since time immemorial, regardless of the predilection of group elites to retrieve ancient origins and histories for the group.

New social movement theory approaches the study of political and sociological phenomena from a similar nonessentialist and partly contingent perspective. Collective identities are built around symbols and ideas that are given content and meaning by political elites who seek to construct a common groupness. Political entrepreneurs, behaving more or less strategically, mobilize collective identities through "frames"—a story, an analysis of a situation—which resonate to the extent that they fit the lived experience of the individual.[4] Far from being inherent, political identity emerges as an indirect result of mobilization refracted through the frames of those who are mobilized. Social movement theory treats political meanings, boundaries, and identities, who "we" are and where "we" stand, as well as who "they" are and where "they" stand, as perceived, subjective, and elastic. Although this theoretical perspective was developed to explain and explore such "new" social movements as environmentalism and nuclear disarmament, its vocabulary and perspectives shed interesting light on the behavior of such apparently "old" social movements as ethnic groups.

Any effort to ascertain the conditions and extent of change in collective political identities must proceed in two parts. First, how is political identity constructed? What factors affect the relative salience of different identities? How do these factors interact, both with each other and with identity? Are some more crucial than others? Some may simply define parameters of possibility, while in some moments perspectives telescope to make a single identity dominant.

Second, to what extent do those variables that affect political identity themselves change? Some will probably appear relatively stable, perhaps even fixed over time, while others are always at least potentially in flux. Under some circumstances they may change quite quickly, at other times slowly. Usually one or two will change; only rarely will all of the variables that affect political identity change at once. Where two or more variables change simultaneously, they may behave at cross-purposes and negate a presumed effect, or they may act to reinforce movement in a particular direction. If political identity is a function of the interaction of five or six variables and some or all of them change, we should expect identity itself to change. This perspective opens the door to a conception of collective political identities in a state of at least potential semiconstant flux.

A mechanism of change must therefore be incorporated into a theoretical proposition about the construction of political identity. Much of what has been written about political identity, however, explores how it is constituted, not constructed.[5] Constitution involves unraveling the package of attributes that accompany a particular identity. Identity is partly constituted in opposition, for example. There is no possibility for an identity without a common understanding of what that identity stands apart from: without women there would be no men, only people. Constitution is essential to the construction of the meaning, substance, and boundaries of political identities.

Constitution, however, cannot explain how identities emerge as salient or remain latent, or what is mobilizable and what ultimately fails to resonate. Constitution is still inherently static, relying on impetus external to the model to explain variation over time. An explanation of the embedded construction of political identity, on the other hand, assumes change through the constant interaction of changing variables. Political elites affect such variables as political institutions, which in turn redefine the parameters within which people are able to act, causing them to act in new ways, all the while figuring and reconfiguring political identities in a potentially shifting arena. Change over time is inherent in the concept of construction, so that to acknowledge that political identities are constructed is to imply that they are also fluid. It is not the same thing to say that identities are constructed and that identities are fluid, but the former assumes the possibility of the latter. The constructivist approach to political identities establishes a methodological presumption of flux.

The Parameters of Political Identity

Political identity is that portion of identity which emerges as salient in the organized struggle for control over the allocation of resources and power residing in the state. An individual's political identity determines what group or groups he aligns himself with, and against, in that struggle. The group may be defined in terms of race, class, region, ideology, special interests, or virtually any other category of affiliation that could become politically salient. Because any individual has multiple interests, and multiple identities informing those interests, it is partly a matter of choice which identities become salient. People's options for political identification are at the same time partly circumscribed by a realm of political possibility they do not control. Although "Catholic" is a loaded and salient political identity in Northern Ireland, for instance, it has practically no political substance or meaning at all in South Africa. It nevertheless clearly exists as a religious identity in both places. Political identity also determines group membership in ways that may be more or less stark. In some contexts political identity may simply place an individual on a spectrum; in a polarized or conflictual political environment, group membership may be essential for survival.

Political identity is at least partly dependent on context.[6] Different issues trigger the politicization of different identities. If the state begins to make decisions about language rights, for example, language may be (more or less suddenly) politicized and may begin to inform political identity. Under some circumstances, a person whose political identity had been primarily mediated by his occupational role as a farmer might begin to think of himself, politically, as a Spanish speaker. One identity need not eclipse another, however. This same Mexican farmer may retain an agricultural political identity in his role as a farmworker union organizer but feel a strong linguistic identity when he joins other parents to lobby for Spanish-medium instruction at his daughter's school. To the extent that these respective identities bring him into alliances with different people, the polity may be said to have cross-cutting cleavages.

Political identity must be self-conscious; it is not the equivalent of any latent objective marker of group membership. Individual characteristics that apparently mark a person as Coloured, or middle class, or female, do not necessarily tell us anything about her political identity. None of these characteristics need be relevant to the political decisions a person makes or to the political groups a person affiliates with, even if in salient moments they constrict the parameters of political possibility.

Political identity exists at both the collective and individual levels. Collective identity is "the shared definition of a group that derives from members' common interests, experiences, and solidarity."[7] Collective identity exists only at the point where some catalyst has converted an "ascriptive category into an ascriptive group," in the same way that Marx distinguished "class in itself" from "class for itself."[8] To the extent that an objectively defined group member internalizes the groupness of his categorization, he appropriates a group-mediated political identity.[9] The political salience and "shared definition" of the group include the potential to change over time under circumstances where one, some, or all of the variables that affect political identity change. Who is included in the collective, why the collective exists, and who the collective exists in opposition to are fluid in ways that renegotiate the political space and salience of the group over time. Collective political identity is constantly reconstructed in more or less radical ways.

The collective is, in turn, made up of individual identities.[10] Although change at the level of the group is more easily perceived and measured, strict attention to the collective risks reification, and limits our capacity to explore, or even see, the potentially unstable and permeable boundaries of the group. The group comprises individuals who have separately negotiated relationships with, and commitments to, the collective. If it is true that "individuals see themselves as part of a group when some shared characteristic becomes salient and is defined as important," why is it that some people who share a language, for example, perceive themselves as part of a collective mobilized around the issue of language, and others do not?[11] Why is it that an objective marker, such as skin color, cannot determine a person's political identity, though it may in some cases affect it?

This presents a level-of-analysis problem. Analysis that occurs at the level of the group tends to take the collective as a given and to focus on the activities of the group as a unit. Although the activities of the group provide insight into the meaning and goals of the group, the behavior of the collective represents only one prong of an investigation into the relative salience of particular identities. The other prongs involve how it is constructed as a collective, who is constructed in or out, and how identity is constituted, for individuals as for the group, within the shifting parameters of the collective. It is at the level of the relationship between the individual and the collective that the primary questions explored in this book are located.

Questions about how, and how much, political identities change are most usefully addressed at the "meso" level, between the individual (micro) and the collective (macro).[12] Such a focus incorporates both poles, posits neither as primary, and focuses attention on the interaction between the two. Political identity is constructed at both the collective and individual levels and is constituted in part on the plane of intersection. Neither is inherent or static. Both may be more or less stable over time. Although individual political identity outside of the group is not a focus of this project, it may exist. On the other hand, collective identity has no substance without the individuals who make up the group. Once it becomes a collective, however, it negotiates and renegotiates meaning for, and in interaction with, its own members, and sometimes for relevant others.[13]

At this point it may be appropriate to flesh out the meaning of political identity with a clear statement of what "political" is intended to stand apart from. Political identity is that aspect of a person's identity that manifests itself in, and is relevant to, political action. The political is here narrowly defined as that which has to do with governance and government, state allocation of resources, and the organization of public (political) space. It does not involve all relations of power. A distinction between the broadly and narrowly political is drawn on the understanding that the identities that govern power relations between husband and wife, or between employer and employee, differ qualitatively from those that mediate political action. Political identities drive, and result from, the organized struggle for power and resources residing in the state.

This understanding of "political" identifies the parameters of this project. Anthropologists and historians have recently dedicated themselves to the task of demonstrating how ethnic groups are constructed over time in ways that generate new groups in response to new situations. South African "Zulus," for example, have only recently come to include all people whose languages have been standardized as "Zulu." Earlier this century, people who lived south of the Tugela River would not have identified themselves, or been identified by Zulus, as Zulu. Today they are.[14]

Political identity, however, is conceptually more circumscribed. Although it appears to be the case that Zulus today need not be Zulus tomorrow, the fluctuation of Zulu political identity is not dependent on correspondent changes in the cultural meanings and boundaries of the ethnic group. The political salience and significance of Zuluness are separate from their manifestation in other spheres. If political identity is treated as a discrete category of identity, not automatically contingent on ethnic, racial, or other identities held in other spheres, then Zulus may remain Zulus for a relatively long period of time. Zulu political identities may change even if an ethnic Zulu cultural or linguistic identity remains more or less constant. Identities are politically mobilized, reinforced, transformed, and suppressed in a manner not necessarily related to their operation outside the political realm. Identities held in cultural, linguistic, or religious domains are not relevant to identities held in the political domain unless and until they are infused with political content. Although political identity is by no means "the only identity game in town," it nevertheless merits treatment as a distinct phenomenon.[15]

An analogy may serve to illustrate the premise, as well as to explore the relation between identities and what apparently count as objective characteristics. I have blue eyes. The fact that my eyes are blue is objectively true, and barring any fancy use of contact lenses or unexpected physiological developments, I will always have blue eyes. The fact that I have blue eyes, however, is in no way relevant to me in the political arena (although in fact my eye color probably does form part of my personal identity). I make no political decisions based on the color of my eyes, and I perceive no political identity tied to my eye color, or to that of others. Nor does my eye color affect how people perceive me in the political world. Today, in the United States, eye color is not politically salient.

In theory, though, eye color could develop resonance. The state might begin to make decisions about the allocation of resources based on eye color, and political entrepreneurs might begin to mobilize people of particular eye colors to make claims over access to resources and power. If that happened, I might fairly rapidly develop a political identity based on eye color. I would probably be a blue-eye. On the other hand, I might not identify myself as a blue-eye under such circumstances. Because I have relatives and close friends who are brown-eyes, I might not buy into the new cleavage structure that separated them from me. Blue-eye leaders might express interests I did not perceive as congruent with my own, or they might construct an identity that did not resonate with my lived experience. Just because I objectively am blue-eyed does not mean that I would necessarily identify as such for political purposes.

At the same time, if somebody asked me what color my eyes were, I would probably still say blue. I might not, though. Blueness might have become so fraught with political meaning as to make any statement about the color of one's eyes replete with symbolism. I might resort to saying "light," or aggressively confront anyone who asked me such a question. I might even say "brown," to make the point that politically I identified with brown eyes, regardless of the objective color of my eyes.

At some point, however, the option of refusing to identify as a blue-eye, of saying I was a brown-eye or abstaining from defining myself along that cleavage line at all, might become unavailable to me. For one thing, blue eyes are a relatively obvious and objectively definable physical marker. Regardless of what I say, it would be evident to people that I do in fact have blue eyes. People might classify and treat me as a blue-eye regardless of my preferences. If benefits accrued from blue-eye status, it might be difficult for me to resist taking advantage of that which has been newly defined as "my right." If, conversely, blue-eyes lost status and power, and brown-eyes discriminated against me on the basis of their perception of my eye color, it might be impossible for me to continue to identify with them. At an extreme, if the politics of eye color took a violent turn and I was attacked by brown-eyes because I have blue eyes, my capacity to identify as anything but a blue-eye would likely be erased.[16]

This simple analogy usefully illustrates many points that emerge as complex, and less obviously malleable, when the same issues are raised with regard to identities which are already politicized. If instead of eye color, for instance, we examined the possibilities of Serbian identity, it would be less obvious that such an identity is also available to interpretation. Today it appears that people either are or are not Serbian and that their Serbian identity corresponds with an entire package of historical legacy, meaning, ideology, political preferences, perceptions of friends and enemies, and leaders. Election results show that this condition is more complex and less straightforward today than it appears, and it certainly was not nearly this clear as recently as 1990.[17]

Another thing that political identity is not, or at least is not necessarily, is cultural identity. Cultural or communal groups may be constituted by the symbols of language, religion, skin color, common culture and norms, a myth of common ancestry, or all or any combination of these. Communal identity may inform interaction on some levels. An Afrikaner might adhere to some or most Afrikaner customs and norms. He or she might interact predominantly with other Afrikaners and might even think twice about marrying someone who was not an Afrikaner. An Afrikaner would probably speak Afrikaans at home and might prefer Afrikaans-medium instruction for her children. An Afrikaner would probably also attend one of the three traditionally Afrikaner sister churches. This represents the package of affiliations that make up Afrikaner cultural identity.

This identity need not pervade all aspects of life, however, and it is not automatically relevant, or available, for political purposes. Cultural identity is not a political factor unless it is also political identity. Individuals hold many identities, sometimes strongly, which remain nevertheless irrelevant to political identity and action. Many Scandinavian Americans who live in Minnesota retain Swedish or Norwegian cultural practices and hold a common ancestral identity based on group membership, but identities that are culturally relevant to them are apparently not politically salient. Although Zulu is a highly politicized identity in South Africa, Pedi is not. It would be dangerous to conclude from this evidence that Pedis feel their ethnic identity less strongly than Zulus, however. Ethnic identity may inform, and in particular moments constrain the possibilities of, political identity, but there is no natural correlation between communal and political identities in the same way that eye color could become, but is not naturally, politically relevant.

The process of politicization involves the mobilization of symbols and the (re-)negotiation of meaning. In the everyday expression of cultural Zuluness, for example, the Zulu king is irrelevant, barely known to most people who would count themselves Zulu before his political revival in the 1970s.[18] Zulu political identity and claims about Zuluness, however, centrally revolved around the symbol of the monarchy in the 1980s. For Afrikaners, the *Volkstaat,* an ethnic Afrikaner state, is similarly part of the political, but not necessarily cultural, project of Afrikanerdom. Furthermore, under normal circumstances a political entrepreneur is unlikely to be able to transfer an entire ethnically bound group into the political sphere. Only in moments of extreme mobilization, normally associated with violent and inescapable conflict, are most members of an ethnic or racial category likely to perceive their political interests in common. More likely, like Afrikaners, Bosnian Muslims, or Kurds, ethnic and religious groups will split politically.[19] People do not necessarily perceive cultural affinity as politically relevant, and an apparently culturally homogeneous group may be as likely to divide as it is to maintain political unity.

Political identity, in short, is mobilized in the particular context of the struggle for resources and power located in the state. It may be based on some objective characteristic that pertains to an individual, such as the language she speaks, or it may be an identity that is salient only in the political arena, such as Republican. Political identity cannot be derived from observed characteristics or social location, as if there were some automatic correlation between class or ethnicity and political identity. Nevertheless, social, cultural, or economic position may make some identities more available than others, and more likely to resonate.

The Construction of Political Identity

It is tempting to try to reduce an explanation of political identity to one or two crucial variables, and to end up with an equation which reads something like "if X, then Y." Such parsimony is applauded in science, and appears to explain much. Grand theory, in which all the world can seemingly be explained by a single variable—material conditions, for example, or political institutions—can change paradigms. It may, however, forfeit explanatory capacity. Explanations that rely on one or two independent variables are notoriously criticized for missing other important factors, or for reducing what should be a subtle portrait to bold and brash lines on canvas. It may be that different types of questions lend themselves to different types of explanations. There may be only one reason that states levy taxes or that nations go to war. Political identity, on the other hand, does not lend itself to reductionism. Causal models that depend upon a single variable produce a more determinate analysis than identity can sustain. There is no single variable that determines which identities emerge as salient for political purposes and which remain latent, none that can predict among whom identities will resonate. These are more likely the result of the partly interdependent operation of multiple variables.

Empirical evidence suggests that political identity emerges as the result of the complex interaction of five variables: political institutions, mobilizing discourse, material conditions, available ideology, and organization. In the remainder of this chapter, the definitions, parameters, and roles of each of these factors are placed in the context of their relationship to political identity. Comparative case studies of Zulu, Afrikaner, and Coloured identities in South Africa explore the function and importance of each in shaping those political identities which ultimately emerge as salient. In Chapter 8 I shall attempt a more definitive statement of the importance of each factor in the determination of resonance, and the relation among factors that operate in conjunction to condition political possibility.

The Independent Variables

Political institutions play a role in the mediation of political identity to the extent that they organize political space. The institutions of governance are at some point designed by people with more or less interest in how those institutions will subsequently order power.[20] They are not permanent, nor are they generated by an "unseen hand." Once they are put into effect, however, and embedded in a legal or constitutional system that provides for their reproduction over time, opportunities to change them diminish noticeably. They attain a quality of permanence that imbues them with characteristics of structure. As elements of structure, political institutions partially govern political possibility and, in turn, may situate identity. Both elites and masses acting politically perceive politics as operating within boundaries that circumscribe what counts as reasonable and relevant behavior in the struggle to maximize their share of the vote or their access to resources residing in the state. Political institutions are therefore likely to affect identities if they structure politics in such a way that some identities seem more relevant to the organization of power than others.

This reasoning informs the argument, for example, that South Africa's apartheid system, which ordered politics (in particular among Blacks) along ethnic lines, played an important role in politicizing some forms of ethnic identity during the apartheid era. The system created tangible incentives for people to identify as members of an ethnic group by allocating resources through "traditional" ethnic elites. The creation of "homelands," in which designated ethnic group members were required to have permanent residence and in which they were permitted to exercise some secondary political rights, was intended in part to reinforce ethnic identity and undermine the development of a common Black opposition to the White minority government.[21] Whether political institutions can actually play a definitive role in determining the salience of identities, and whether governments succeed in manipulating identities in the way they plan, are empirical questions. Suffice to say that it is possible to imagine the circumstances under which political institutions would suggest some, but not other, political identities.

Electoral systems in particular are assigned an important role in structuring political possibility.[22] A first-past-the-post electoral rule for example, in which the candidate with the most votes wins a district's single seat, is presumed to create disincentives for political elites to mobilize any group or coalition of groups that is not potentially numerically larger than all other groups or coalitions. Fringe or minority groups therefore remain unmobilized, and majority rule tends toward a two-party system. Conversely, a proportional representation system elects representatives in relation to the percentage of the vote their parties receive. This system is more likely to generate incentives for the mobilization of marginal groups, for any party that attains the threshold can expect access to the legislature. Most democratic systems use variations of one of these two systems to translate votes into leadership, and the system they choose is expected to have implications for the development of group identities.

In consociational systems, members of previously designated (ethnic, religious, or racial) or self-selecting groups vote for leaders of their own group, who then form coalitions with other group leaders. Consociationalism is based on group, not individual rights. It presumes group identity, and thus may act to produce or reinforce, it. Political elites have an apparent incentive to consistently mobilize the group that constitutes its power base and whose group identity affords it a position in government. Consociationalism may also set the stage for ordinary individuals, acting politically, to organize the political world into the groups designated as politically salient. Any political act requires that the voter establish first which group she or he belongs to and which political arena she or he can therefore legitimately act in. In this system, group membership must be salient for every individual who engages in a political act.

A federal system devolves some degree of power to the state or provincial level. It may create incentives for political elites to mobilize regionally based groups. Even if they cannot expect to win any support outside of the region, state government itself provides a base of power and jurisdiction. A strong federal system also establishes territorial parameters from which a group may launch, or legitimate, secessionist demands. Once a regional identity is constituted, probably as against an out-group defined as central government or other states, demands for self-determination may follow.

Federalism may be the apparent result of seemingly strong regional identities, as in the case where constitutional engineers believe that they must devolve power to regional elites to avoid civil war or secession. It may also lay the groundwork for the development of a regional identity at the grassroots, however. In this regard, political institutions may play a role in bounding the realm of possibility for ordinary voters. Provinces or states may acquire tangible political meaning if the tax base is regional, if education is local, and if real decisions about people's lives are made at the provincial level. In particular, if the party or group that dominates provincial government differs from the party or group that controls national government, it may attain an oppositional quality that imbues provincial identity with greater political salience. Individuals do not necessarily identify regionally, but federalism may foster the objective conditions that might ground such identities.

Mobilizing discourse is the language used by political elites in the attempt to construct a worldview that makes a particular set of identities and affiliations more accessible and apparent than others.[23] Elites at all levels of the political hierarchy are engaged in this project. Dominant or opposition leaders may have more or less power, and local leaders close to the ground may be more influential in particular communities than nationally recognized leaders. An individual may have more or less influence over his own or other people's political identities. Some people, such as leaders of political parties or social movements, may have the ability, by virtue of their position of authority and probable legitimacy, to constitute meaning for an entire group of people. Perhaps they have the charisma to inspire people, or a network that binds people, or an argument that convinces people, or an army that coerces them.

At any rate political elites, be they national or local, dominant or oppositional, and more or less influential, construct a constituent base through the use of a discursive repertoire that defines and activates the substance of a particular identity. They may do so more or less self-consciously and more or less strategically. Political entrepreneurs, for example, may make strategic calculations regarding which identity is likely to resonate most among a particular group. They may purposefully choose the characteristic or identity that they feel will mobilize the largest group or catalyze the most extreme sentiments. They may tailor their discourse to particular audiences, assuming that what resonates with one constituency may strike out with another. Other political elites are true believers. They articulate a particular position regardless of its popularity and are more likely to garner a following through a happy coincidence of circumstance than through rational calculation of options.[24] Some political elites behave instrumentally, and some do not.

Discourse may be one of the most powerful tools that political elites, both calculating and coincidental, have at their disposal. Unlike an argument or a position, a discursive repertoire is meant to invoke an entire world of meaning. It is not simply the articulation of already existing ideas, identities, understandings, or worldviews.[25] Discourse plays a prior role in the actual construction and constitution of meaning actively and continuously renegotiated through speech.[26] An event or situation is translated through discourse into an episode that people can understand in the context of salient meaning. Meaning is itself transformed in the process, as political elites interpret events to give them broader significance. The process of fitting moments into a historical trajectory may operate to create a sense of threat, or to suggest a particular set of boundaries, or to link the group to a piece of land. It is through mobilizing discourse that elites construct a sense of who the political "we" are, where "we" belong, who "we" are with and who "we" are against. Afrikaners, for example, descended of Dutch, French, German, and English ancestry, are bound into a single ethnic group through the retrieval of such moments as the Battle of Blood River, the Great Trek, and the Boer War.

In the effort to create meaning, political entrepreneurs draw on existing events, fears, and discriminations, but they are not always constrained by objective conditions. The power of discourse is that threats, boundaries, claims, and character traits may be "born from speaking." The perception of difference may exist both when difference is objectively identifiable and when it is not. The discourse used to construct a politicized ethnic identity includes a more or less identifiable historical lineage, a set of critical moments, a myth of common ancestry, a claim to territory, a construction of outsiders and insiders, and a description of group attributes.[27] Each is variably grounded in what we might call truth. Little is apparent without the stories that give substance to the myth. Without the persistent retrieval of the legend of Shaka, Zulus are not a warrior nation.

Differentiation is part of the process of mobilizing group identity through discourse. If the only difference between Hutus and Tutsis is that they have been called by different names, it is harder to generate a commitment to one identity over another. If, on the other hand, one is imbued with qualities, by dint of group membership, that distinguish one group from another—if being Tutsi suggests height, cunning, intelligence, and superiority, as it reputedly does—then Tutsi identity is invested with meaning and difference.

The construction of threat plays an important role in the constitution of group identity through differentiation. No threat is unmediated. What is perceived as threatening is dependent on (a) what is actually threatening, such as an advancing army, and (b) how the threat is constructed. No truth is unmediated. The advancing army may be made up of the proletariat, it may be Scottish, it may be anti-Semitic, or it may be communist. Whatever "it" is crucially affects the possibilities for who "we" are, and this is not simply a matter of objective observation. "It" is constructed and interpreted by its leaders, and also by our leaders. The majority of people involved in the 1991 Los Angeles riots were male, unemployed, young, African-American, inner-city dwellers. Despite their multiple characteristics, however, they were understood, possibly by themselves and certainly by others, as African Americans. Their constitution in racial terms signified something different politically than would their constitution in gender or economic terms. In the determination of political identity, the manner in which a threat is constructed is more important than the objective conditions of the threat itself.

Threat may be more or less available and may play a greater or lesser role in affecting identity. Recent experience of threat is likely to affect what a group recognizes as threatening. Some threats appear to emerge and reemerge constantly and can be reinvigorated with fairly little effort or objective impetus. New threats, however, such as a perceived threat against the Afrikaans language, can emerge and be made salient in relatively short periods of time. Where collective political identity is constituted in relation to external threat, old or new, it may be stronger and more cohesive than identity simply constituted around common interest or a description of the internal attributes of the group. For the purposes of tracking the potential for change over time, a shifting perception of the source of the threat is likely to affect the boundaries and meaning of the group. And the perception of the source of threat is mediated by discourse.

Material conditions partly structure the place of the individual in society, in the economy, and in relation to other individuals and groups. In any economic system some people are workers of greater or lesser skill, some are farmers, others are farm laborers, others are unemployed, while still others may be managers or businessmen, and these roles partly determine, or at least affect, their places in the economic system. Although economic status is not automatically politically relevant, material differences do exist and may contribute to a person's understanding of self, place, and, potentially, membership.

Class differences may lead to distinct and occasionally conflicting sets of interests. Under some circumstances the interests of individuals in one position are likely to clash with those of individuals in another position. When the economy is bad, for instance, certain groups bear the brunt of inflation or falling export prices more than others. If the price of agricultural commodities drops, or if there is a drought, other things being equal the economic position of farmers will fall more precipitously than that of businessmen in nonagricultural sectors. Both farmers and businessmen are likely to notice this turn of events, although farmers are likely to notice it more because their fortunes are changing for the worse. Farmers may begin to develop some animosity toward businessmen who benefit from lower food prices in the cities and who sit in plush offices unaffected by weather. Such animosity may manifest itself in vague grumbling about particular individuals who enter the orbit of the farmer. Individual farmers may feel some solidarity with other farmers in the same plight. These are the types of objective conditions that economic systems generate.

Such identities will probably remain latent, however, unless mobilized by agents. The "fact" that there are businessmen and farmers with ostensibly opposing interests does not mean that they will organize into separate groups with any political relevance. But objective conditions and positions do form part of a person's lived experience, and if political entrepreneurs try to mobilize identities and form groups that are incompatible with such structural constraints as material conditions, they may be less successful than if they are able to tailor their rhetoric to lived experience. What counts as lived experience, however, may not always be obvious, and objective markers need not determine how a group will be constituted. A group whose identity derives from common occupational status as farmers may be mobilized as farmers; but they may also be organized along ethnic, regional, or other lines. Groups apparently rooted in class or occupational ties may be constituted as ethnic, and vice versa. Afrikanerdom, for example, has emerged as a salient political identity primarily among farmers and those of lower socioeconomic status. What is apparently class and occupational identity finds ethnic expression.

Such policies as affirmative action have repercussions which are material and, because they take as a starting point the existence and rights of a group, may reinforce those identities they assume exist to begin with. Affirmative action is intended to redress past wrongs against a group of people. If one group has historically been discriminated against, affirmative action prescribes that discrimination must now favor them. Members of the group should be hired, accepted to schools, and promoted, for example, over nonmembers. Under such circumstances it is wise to proclaim membership in the in-group, if at all possible, rather than let one's membership lapse or become secondary. Non–group members, probably the previously discriminated-for, are in turn threatened by what they translate as sudden discrimination against them and may develop animosity against the new in-group. Such animosity may or may not become politically salient, but where benefit or discrimination accrues on the basis of what people believe is group identity, and not what people believe is individual desert, group identity is poised to become stronger as people assert their membership in one group or another—to receive benefits, or to mobilize against perceived discrimination.

Material conditions may affect identities in another way. Unequal access to material resources leads to competition, and competition may take violent form. Such material conditions as unemployment, poverty, housing backlogs, and overcrowding, coupled with massive and disorganized influx into urban areas, may create a situation of apparent anarchy. In poor areas, where new people are constantly moving in and crowding the space and resources of prior tenants, and where there is no legitimate structure of appeal and enforcement, sporadic violence is likely to break out. Initially it is likely to be criminal violence that will probably not generate collective identity. But real experiences of violence can divide, and may define identities more starkly once groups are named.

Organization appears also to play an important role in the construction of political identity. Political entrepreneurs lend substance to discourse through organizational networks that bind members to each other and to the ethos of groupness. Collective identity becomes more tangible and real to an individual once he is connected to other members of the group through an organizational network.

How political elites choose to organize, how well they organize, and how encompassing are their networks are factors likely to affect the types of meanings that are possible and the success of the mobilization effort. Political parties or opposition movements may organize along ethnic lines through traditional leaders, on the shop floor around work-related issues, or through religious institutions, to name just a few choices. Each one of these options will open up different possibilities for the construction of identity. The American Christian right, for example, articulates the concerns of people who are predominantly white, downwardly mobile, and socially conservative. The fact that they are (partly) organized through the church, and mobilized from the pulpit, plays a role in delineating their identity as primarily religious, rather than racial or economic.

It may be true that the more encompassing a political identity, the more often it is reinforced in different spheres, the easier it is to mobilize. Organization that takes advantage of preexisting lines of affect may be more successful than that which attempts to create links where none existed before. It may be easier, and more effective, to tap into prior organizational networks, such as ethnic hierarchies or religious communities, than to generate party organization from scratch. It is nevertheless true, however, that groups with no previous history of group identification may be mobilized successfully through effective organization.[28] So-called new social movements, constructed around such issues as the environment and abortion rights, are examples of newly constructed political groups whose members have no obvious preexisting ties but who nevertheless exhibit a strong drive toward group identity and have even been moved to violence and acts of terror. Conversely, organizational networks outside the political sphere may never be politicized.

Political elites have some control over how they choose to organize. They have leeway to devise an organizational structure that they hope will maximize their access to, and influence over, a potential constituency. But they do not have infinite freedom. Their choice is partially constrained by what has gone before and by how political society is structured. In the run-up to the 1994 election, South Africa's African National Congress, for example, was constrained to organize support among Coloureds in a way that conformed with its own organizational history but clashed with organizational patterns familiar to Coloureds. Once a party organizes along particular lines, the existing organization itself acts to constrain the ability of agents to make strategic choices and to further reconstruct identity. At some point the parameters of political possibility and the choices they or their predecessors have already made may force political elites to mobilize a particular identity that fits, or at least does not conflict, with the way people are already organized politically. Organization may operate to create a tangible basis of group affinity and, further, to build a rationale for the mobilization of some identities over others.

Available ideology exists on multiple levels. Ideology is at some point that which is constructed by political entrepreneurs for purposes of legitimating (existing or alternative) power relations. In this sense, ideology is indistinguishable from mobilizing discourse. It stands as a separate variable, however, once ideologies become symbolic resources. Through acts of circulation and reiteration, ideologies develop currency that allow them to in turn more or less shape the realm of further discursive possibility.

An ideology operates at the level of accepted habit once it achieves legitimacy as a worldview. At this level, ideologies are more or less coherent sets of ideas, such as Marxism or libertarianism, which are available to political entrepreneurs in greater or lesser degrees. Ideologies orient the political spectrum. In the United States, for instance, one major spectrum is liberal/conservative. Liberal and conservative ideologies differ mainly over how to allocate the resources that accrue to the state. The two dominant parties line up along this spectrum, and third parties find a space somewhere along the line, taking a partly distinct position on the same issues. At this level, ideology is an "articulated worldview" within and against which people position themselves, and through which political beliefs are negotiated.[29] Ideologies orient what is salient and how salient issues are framed.

Ideologies may be more or less hegemonic to the extent that they form patterns of political possibility that more or less constrain the realm of ideas available to aspiring politicians. Ideologies are available when they resonate among some section of the population because they are perceived as legitimate, or at least familiar. Ideologies may, on the other hand, be simply unavailable. Ethnic mobilization was mostly unavailable to Black political entrepreneurs in the apartheid era because Black Consciousness and nonracialism, both of which denied a political role to ethnicity, were hegemonic among the extraparliamentary opposition. In part because democracy is the hegemonic ideology in South Africa today, ideologies that fall outside the parameters of democracy have become unavailable. Communism, for example, a primary oppositional ideology during the apartheid era, has been marginalized—rendered virtually unavailable in the postapartheid era.[30]

Ideology is likely to affect identity to the extent that it structures ideas and frames possibility. It may bound what is possible to imagine. There is no ideology which privileges blue over brown eyes, or in which eye color is politically relevant, and it is partly for this reason that the potential for the politicization of eye color appears so remote to us today. Ideology has historical roots in that it appears that what has been mobilized before may be mobilized again. Fascism is politically possible in Italy, for example, but probably not in Great Britain. It often seems as if the ideologies that condition a society are fairly stable and tend to continuously bubble to the surface. Ideologies may change quite quickly, however, and capsize what is politically imaginable. This was the case with Black Consciousness in South Africa, which converted "non-White" Africans, Asians, and Coloureds into "Blacks" and thus reinvented political identity for an entire generation of activists.[31] That Blackness was the constitutive feature of oppositional identity was, however, also a function of the salience of Black identity in the context of a racially organized ideological space dominated by apartheid.

The Dependent Variable

Resonance is the extent to which individuals internalize the political meanings and boundaries that elites mobilize. It functions as a gauge of political identity at the mass level. Resonance operates on the plane of interaction between political elites and their potential constituents. It presumes that individuals do not mobilize spontaneously around any issue, or "naturally" organize into discrete units for political purposes. Resonance assumes that political identities do not emanate from people but that they are rather shaped and mobilized by political elites. Conversely, however, it also presumes that political elites do not have infinite freedom to mobilize whichever identities they choose. It includes the possibility, and even likelihood, of their failure. Those political identities that do ultimately, but not permanently, emerge as salient for political purposes, are the result of the refraction of the mobilizing discourse of political elites through the cognitive frames of those they are trying to mobilize.

Political identity is constructed though the complex interaction of independent variables that play more or less proximate or conditioning roles. Proximate variables are political institutions and mobilizing discourse—those which operate self-consciously in the political arena and appear to directly affect the organization of political society. Political institutions play a direct role in structuring the political arena and in shaping the incentives of political elites. Acting within boundaries partly prescribed by political institutions, political elites use mobilizing discourse in an attempt to give political content and direction to identities that preexist in social, religious, or economic spheres, or they try to generate a sense of common purpose among individuals not previously constituted as a group. At any rate, based on incentives that derive in part from the institutional structure of the political system, political entrepreneurs, acting more or less strategically, use mobilizing discourse in an attempt to construct identities that they hope will resonate and, in turn, maximize their share of power.

Other things (such as the charisma and resources of the entrepreneur) being equal, their success or failure—whether and when the identities they attempt to mobilize resonate—depends on conditioning variables. Available ideology, material conditions, and organization condition possibility in the sense that they make up the lived (political) experience of potential constituencies. Individuals undergoing mobilization preexist in a fabric of networks, exchanges, commitments, and beliefs patterned by their embedded interaction with conditioning variables. People filter the discourse of political entrepreneurs through their own experience. Cognition is not static, however. It is in constant negotiation and renegotiation as both conditioning and proximate variables change. The successful mobilization of a particular identity, for example, may change available ideology, material conditions, and/or organization, as well as the incentives of political entrepreneurs, such that another identity, which might not otherwise have been mobilizable, will resonate. Discourse that failed to mobilize a constituent base at time X may succeed at time $X+1$.

In addition to providing the scaffolding of political possibility on the ground, conditioning variables affect the incentives of political elites trying to construct political identity. People's lives are structured by material conditions, organizational patterns, and available ideologies which make some alliances and identities more "real" or likely than others. People occupy apparently objective positions—they are either poor or rich, white or black—which condition their perception of the world, and in turn perhaps their political possibilities, depending on what those things mean in their society. Although it seems true that political entrepreneurs respond to incentives generated by political institutions, their behavior is also influenced by incentives generated by material conditions, organizational patterns, available ideology, and the cleavages they suggest.

Conditioning and proximate variables should not be considered either discrete or impermeable categories of factors, however. Political identities are also "conditioned" by proximate variables to the extent that these are entrenched and appear to circumscribe possibility. Mobilizing discourse, for example, is deployed in a background of prior discourse that has been more or less successful in constructing previous identities. New efforts by political elites to interpret events and to mobilize and organize particular political identities are read in the context of previous efforts. People filter today's experience through yesterday's experience and are more or less likely to respond to political entrepreneurs through the prism of personal political history. To the extent that people have been mobilized or organized in certain ways before, the memory of such political identities and affiliations as have previously existed serves to make new identities and alliances more or less plausible.

This dependence on historical precedent places limits on the malleability of political identities. Political identity is not infinitely fluid, and some identities may consistently fail to resonate. The history of a society's salient conditioning and proximate variables may even make it possible to partly anticipate the likely success or failure of some identities to resonate. It is nevertheless impossible to state categorically that some identities will never emerge as politically salient, or that some identities will always constrain the possibilities of political identification. As structures, practices, and relative positions shift, so will the prism through which historical precedent is translated and retrieved. History itself does not remain static.

In the following chapters, resonance, captured by the concept of interaction between proximate and conditioning variables, is used to read political identity at the mass level. Conditioning and proximate variables are likely to work in reinforcing or conflicting ways to create identities that people perceive as politically relevant. Which identities do people internalize, which make sense to them, which prompt them to identify with particular groups and to act in certain ways? In other words, which resonate?

The measurement of resonance is a complicated business that involves the use of various types of data.[32] Voting patterns, for example, provide a rough sketch of political identity. Parties mobilize certain identities, and party supporters might be expected to internalize, to some degree, the identity commonly associated with the party. Voting patterns can give us a good broad idea of what the political landscape looks like. If most people are voting for parties that are moderate, that do not mobilize exclusive nationalist or radical religious political identities, then we can fairly assume that most people do not hold those political identities. If a political system is extremely polarized, political support can also be indicative. Where voting has taken place, it is a good preliminary indicator of political identity.

Sometimes though, voting patterns may provide a fairly indirect extrapolation that relies too heavily on inferences that presume certain identities. A political party may encompass several groups or may inexactly reflect or shape political identities. Different people vote for parties for different reasons. While some people may vote for a party because it appears to endorse their economic interests, others may support the same party because they hope it will protect whites, and others still because it is tough on crime. A single party may appeal simultaneously to identities mediated by class, race, and ideology. People also act strategically in response to their perception of the political structure. Where there is a double ballot, and people vote separately for regional and national governments, people are more or less likely to split their vote depending on how they perceive the local and national balance of power and their own place within it. Voting for different parties at different levels of politics does not mean that one's political identity has changed in the time it takes to move from the national to the regional ballot in the polling booth. It is possible for political identity to remain stable but to be reflected differently in different domains. Thus voting behavior only imperfectly expresses political identity.

Polls that ask questions about how people register their own identity also provide some insight. One might assume that a person who says she identifies first as an Afrikaner might hold an Afrikaner political identity. And she might. In a context in which Afrikanerdom is politicized, Afrikaner identity appears to encompass an entire package of ideological and political positions, as well as affiliation to some parties and rejection of others. This indicator is also imperfect though, though, because the respondent may be expressing a cultural or linguistic identity that she does not perceive as politically relevant. Many Coloureds who said they identified more closely with Blacks than with Whites also said they voted for the NP.[33] This appears incongruous unless the respondents were (a)lying, (b)expressing a historical or cultural and not political (Black) identity, or (c)identifying the NP as a party that expressed/embodied Blackness. Any of these three possibilities underscores the very elusive quality of political identity.

In-depth interviews that focus on specific questions of political identity provide a more usefully complex portrait. People tell a story, and the story provides insight into the political and social worldview of the respondent. A respondent may describe the order of her political world, the relative salience of various groups and identities, and the relevant aggregation of friends and foes. Interviews entail a portrait of a cosmos as well as an individual within a cosmos, adding depth and breadth to the quantitative evidence derived from voting results and polling data. A single interview, however, cannot give an accurate representation of change over time. People tend to remember events, commitments and their own responses to them in a way that maximizes coherence. They are likely to explain past identities in a way that coheres with current identities. The political project may conversely entail a demonstration of the extent of change. Many White South Africans, for example, are now eager to show how far they have come and how much they have changed. In this case, interviews suggest that nothing is as it was, and respondents may be expected to try to demonstrate proof of a complete break with the past. Either way, an interview should be treated as evidence of the present, and present feelings about the past, not of the past itself.

A picture of resonance that most closely approximates apparent reality relies on all three types of data—voting patterns, polls, and personal interviews. Interviews supplement polling data and election results to paint a more accurate, and accurately complex, picture of political identity. The following case studies use all three types of data to try to capture the evolving features of political identities over time.

Many of the factors that are credited with shaping political identity changed between 1980 and 1995. South Africa's new constitution has upended the structure of politics and transformed the terms of engagement, primarily through the expansion of the franchise. The discourse of new, and old, political elites has changed, adapting in part to the politics of nonracial democracy. For some, material conditions have actually changed; for most, there is a perception that they will change, for better or worse. Many of the organizational patterns that bound people into groups in the apartheid era continue to structure lives; some of the ties, and what supported them, have disappeared. Some of the ideologies that structured political possibility in the 1980s continue to influence what resonates; many have been virtually eclipsed. The factors that interact to construct political identity have changed in more and less important ways, to greater and lesser extents, in the transition period.

We should therefore expect the political salience, meanings, and boundaries of political identities to shift, in more and less important ways, to greater and lesser extents, in the same period. The six cases examined here trace the partial transformation of the political content and boundaries of Zulu, Afrikaner, and Coloured identities in two periods over the course of South Africa's transition from apartheid. These identities, which include racial and linguistic as well as ethnic markers, have been highly politicized, both in the apartheid and postapartheid eras. Moreover, as groups occupying different racial designations in a society organized hierarchically by race, people in separate racial and ethnic categories have had unequal access to, and control over, the conditioning and proximate variables that ordered their political lives. Groups in different positions may exhibit distinctive patterns of transformation, in which some factors may be more important than others, depending on their dominant or subordinate position with relation to the variables that shape their cognition: political institutions, mobilizing discourse, material conditions, organization, and available ideology. Only by comparative analysis is it possible to ascertain whether the relative effect of each variable differs depending on social, economic, and political status. Finally, even though each of these collective identities is highly politicized, none commands the allegiance of all, or even a majority, of those people who might objectively be considered members of the group. Thus they afford the opportunity to explore why identities may have political resonance among some, but not other, members of a group.

2 Black Against Zulu

The Politics of Zulu Identity, 1975–1990

At least since the period of Shaka in the early nineteenth century, "Zulu" has represented an explicit ethnic category with which varying numbers of people identified at different times. But it has not always been salient, and it has usually not been politically relevant for most of the people living in KwaZulu Natal, the majority of whom are today called Zulus.

Until the 1980s Zulu identity coexisted easily with affiliation to the African National Congress (ANC). Inkatha, the political party of the KwaZulu homeland, claimed to represent the "Zulu nation," even as it maintained a connection with the liberation struggle, and in particular with the banned ANC. After the ANC broke with Inkatha in 1979 and its ideological successor, the United Democratic Front (UDF) was launched in 1983, however, it became almost impossible for Inkatha to continue to articulate a national liberation identity. At the same time, Inkatha was locked in a fierce battle with the UDF for political control over a mainly Zulu constituency in Natal. Inkatha retreated to an ethnic Zulu discursive base while the UDF embraced a national workerist identity that denied political legitimacy to "parochial" ethnic identities.

Party identities were polarized and entrenched in the context of a violent civil war between Inkatha and the UDF in Natal. Inkatha appropriated the symbols of Zuluness in such a way that Zulu identity became synonymous with Inkatha affiliation. Although almost everyone involved in the conflict on either side was Zulu, Inkatha members identified as Zulu whereas UDF supporters called themselves Black. Material conditions, organizational patterns, and available ideology combined to draw the boundaries between "Zulus" and "Blacks," as political institutions combined with them to create incentives for the mobilization of these, and not other, identities. The political cleavage between Zulus in Natal has been the most violent and deadly since the Anglo-Boer War at the turn of the century.

Historical Precedent: 1818–1975

The Zulu kingdom was first consolidated by Shaka in a series of wars against neighboring groups in northern Natal between 1818 and 1828. Shaka enlisted young men from his own Usuthu clan and from conquered chiefdoms to establish a strong centralized state with a permanent force deployed in the service of the Zulu kingdom. Shaka's military regiments ensured the kingdom a monopoly of regional force, which enabled him to extract taxes from local chiefs, as well as to protect and expand his domain.[1] Shaka exerted control through chiefs who had traditional jurisdiction over the clans and villages that structured social organization in Natal. Chiefs and their followers owed work or goods to the king, according to his demands, and could in turn expect favors and protection.[2] Throughout most of the 1800s Zulu social, economic, and political systems remained relatively stable and comparatively underpenetrated by the colonial state and economy.

During the Anglo-Zulu war of 1879, the Zulu kingdom enjoyed some initial success against the English, a fact passed down through South African mythology to contribute to the modern perception of the Zulus as a "warrior nation."[3] They were soon defeated by superior colonial firepower, however, thus undermining the internal legitimacy of the kingdom. Over the next decade, KwaZulu was wracked by a civil war that pitted the royal house against various chiefs disloyal to the king.[4]

The integrity of the Zulu monarchy was again undercut by the British colonial government when it became convinced that the kingdom's network of centralized control inhibited state capacity to penetrate northern Natal to collect hut taxes and recruit Zulu labor. In 1887 King Dinuzulu and his immediate family were arrested for treason and exiled to the island of St. Helena.[5] Dinuzulu was returned to Natal in 1897 and reinstated as chief of the Usuthu clan only, with no legal jurisdiction over any other clan.[6] He was later blamed for the 1906 Bambatha Rebellion and exiled again to the Transvaal, where he died in 1913.

By 1900 Zululand was firmly integrated into the colonial system. Zulu men migrated regularly to the mines. The British colonial government, and later the South African government, integrated the hierarchical structure of Zulu politics into official administration, using a standard colonial system of indirect rule.[7] Chiefs were made responsible for administering and enforcing central government laws in their areas and acted as the local representatives of the government. They in turn were remunerated by the government, and granted recognition that increased their prestige and served to further entrench their position. At the same time, though, chiefs became dependent on the government for official sanction— a chief's successor had to be vetted by the government before he could officially become a chief—thus severely circumscribing their capacity for independent action. For example, although a chief retained the right to appoint his own *izinduna* (headmen or lieutenants), an *induna* would strive to increase his political power through the government-appointed district magistrate, not through the chief or his subjects.[8]

The balance of evidence suggests that by 1913 Zulu political life was no longer characterized by a sense of Zulu national unity, with the Zulu monarchy at its core. Zulus were divided, and even the Buthelezi clan, whose hereditary leader had acted as traditional adviser to the royal house, failed to send a representative to the funeral of King Dinuzulu in 1913.[9]

In the meantime, more secular political forces emerged to contest Black politics in South Africa. In 1912 the South African Native National Congress (later renamed the ANC) was formed in Bloemfontein to represent the interests of the Black middle class. Among its founding members were Pixley ka Isaka Seme and John Dube, two prominent, well-educated Zulus who formed part of a small class of African landowning petit-bourgeoisie. Dube was elected the first president-general of the ANC.

Dube was also the publisher of the Zulu language newspaper *Ilanga laseNatal* and had long cultivated a relationship with the Zulu royal house. As early as 1908 Dube used his newspaper to champion the right of the monarch to official government recognition as the Zulu king.[10] In 1917 Dube was ousted from ANC leadership by a more radical middle- and working-class alliance frustrated by the "go slowly" approach of the more conservative middle and upper classes. Dube then left the national ANC to head the provincial-level Natal Native Congress, which acted as a conservative antiworkerist parallel to the ANC in Natal until his death in 1946.

In 1920 the government passed the Native Affairs Act, which provided for African political participation through local institutions in rural African areas. This, and the fact that the 1913 Land Act stipulated that Blacks could purchase land only through a "tribal structure," set the conservative wing of aspirant landowners on a course toward a more formal alliance with the Zulu hierarchy. In 1924 leaders of the Natal Native Congress formed an organization named Inkatha. Inkatha was to act as a trust to buy land for the Zulu nation (though in fact the transactions were exploited by the petit bourgeoisie), as a repository of funds to maintain the king, and as a platform from which to demand government recognition for Dinuzulu's son Solomon.

Although the "traditional" Zulu political structure, of *amakhosi* (chiefs) and *izinduna*, taxation and collective responsibility, continued to govern political and social organization in rural Natal, the secular ANC was well-embedded in provincial politics by the 1930s.[11] The ANC and other liberation organizations were well known in rural areas, in part because patterns of regular rural-urban-rural migration broke down information barriers which may otherwise have existed between urban and rural areas. By the 1940s the bulk of the ANC's rural branches were in KwaZulu. The ANC was nevertheless a predominantly urban organization, though, and most of its membership was concentrated in the area around Johannesburg in the Transvaal.

In this period, there was no contradiction between "tribal" allegiances and an allegiance to the national liberation movement. The ANC itself cultivated traditional leaders in order to gain legitimacy and access to certain sectors of the population. Until the 1970s the Black liberation movement had a fairly ambiguous relation with the tribal system, on the one hand concerned lest ethnic particularism undermine pan-African antiapartheid solidarity, and on the other hand searching for roots, African identity, and independence from White ideology and institutions, all of which they believed could be moulded from the context of the "tribal" heritage.

In 1952 Zulu chief Albert Luthuli was elected president of the ANC. Under Luthuli, the ANC became more radical and expanded its mass base. The 1952 Defiance Campaign drew thousands of people into the ranks of the ANC as they joined in burning their passes, sitting on Whites-only park benches, riding in Whites-only buses, daring the government to imprison so many thousands, and hoping to overwhelm the system. The system was unfortunately up to the test, but the campaign served to raise the consciousness of a generation of Black South Africans. Membership in the ANC rose from four thousand to one hundred thousand by the end of the pass campaign in 1953.[12]

The government still retained control over the installation and remuneration of chiefs, however. The secretary of native affairs demanded that Luthuli, a chief in the Groutville mission area, make a choice between the chieftancy and the ANC. Luthuli refused to resign either position and was subsequently removed by the government from his hereditary role. He continued to use the title of Chief in defiance of the regime and its claim of control over traditional Zulu leadership.[13] Chief Luthuli was the last president of the ANC before the organization was banned in 1961.

During this period, the official position of the ANC on the subject of ethnicity was spelled out in the Freedom Charter.[14] The ANC's founding document appears to be less nonethnic than multiethnic. It does not deny a place to ethnicity, but it denies a place to the preeminence of any particular ethnicity over any other, or to ethnic chauvinism. The Freedom Charter states: "This will encompass the equality of all ethnic groups—large or small, black or white—the satisfaction of their national rights and feelings, traditions and customs, aspirations and emotions, characteristics and features and the development of their language and culture and inter-ethnic contact."

The personal political history of Mangosuthu Gatsha Buthelezi was intertwined with the ANC during this period. Buthelezi studied at Fort Hare University in the Eastern Cape from 1948 to 1951. Fort Hare University was attended by many of the liberation leaders of southern Africa, including Robert Mugabe, Kenneth Kaunda, Nelson Mandela, and Walter Sisulu, and it has long been the intellectual home of Black liberation ideology, and the ANC, in southern Africa. Buthelezi studied Bantu administration under Professor Z. K. Matthews, a prominent member of the ANC and later a member of its executive committee.[15] In the 1940s Fort Hare was a hotbed of ANC radicalism, and Buthelezi was a member of the ANC Youth League from 1948 to 1950.

After he left Fort Hare, Buthelezi spent two years with the Department of Native Affairs, ostensibly to "clean the slate" of his earlier political involvement with the ANC.[16] He returned home in 1953 to become an adviser to Zulu King Cyprian and eventually, in 1957, chief of the Buthelezi clan. Although he steered clear of the ANC and radical politics in order to secure his chieftanship, Buthelezi appeared to retain a commitment to the liberation movement in this period. He resisted the imposition of bantustan policy in Zululand, initially thwarting government plans to allocate a series of separate parcels of territory for Zulus. By the time the government changed the legislation to make self-government mandatory in the late 1960s, Buthelezi had gained a reputation for defending the rights of Africans against the government and enjoyed considerable political stature and legitimacy among Black South Africans.[17]

A majority of Zulu chiefs agreed to the establishment of a Zulu Territorial Authority in 1970. In 1972 it was replaced by the KwaZulu Legislative Assembly, adding limited legislative powers to highly circumscribed executive authority. Buthelezi became the first chief minister of the KwaZulu homeland, paid by the South African government, in 1972. He nevertheless continued to refuse independent status for the homeland that constituted only 38 percent of the land of Natal, in forty-four separate segments, for more than 70 percent of the population of that province.

The launch of the Inkatha National Cultural Liberation Movement in 1975 marks the beginning of a new era of Black politics in Natal. This second Inkatha, modeled on the first, was designed to mobilize support for the KwaZulu government and to promote a spirit of unity "among the people of KwaZulu throughout Southern Africa, and between them and all of their other African brothers in Southern Africa."[18] Over the next fifteen years, it was Inkatha that mobilized Zulu identity for political purposes, with mixed success.

Homeland politics were additionally intertwined with internal power struggles between Buthelezi and his nephew King Goodwill Zwelithini. Buthelezi insisted from the outset on the supremacy and importance of the Zulu monarchy. As "traditional prime minister" to the Zulu king, Buthelezi's own place within the ethnic (but not homeland) hierarchy derived from the importance of his connection to the king. At the same time, though, he denied the king a political role, relegating him to the status of constitutional monarch, lest he gain political leverage and contest control over KwaZulu. Because Buthelezi continued to refuse independent status for KwaZulu, the South African government tried in the 1970s to sideline him and to induce the king to accept "Zulu independence." Thus there was reason for Buthelezi to be wary of the king and to try to marginalize him politically. The two finally consolidated an alliance, which appeared for a time unbreakable, in 1980.

Political Institutions

As envisioned in the 1950s by South African president H. F. Verwoerd, apartheid aimed at carving the territory of South Africa into ethnic homelands in which ascriptively bound groups could exercise separate political, social, and cultural self-determination. The vision never progressed much beyond establishing homeland territories for African ethnic groups; plans for Coloured, Indian, or Afrikaner homelands were never seriously explored, for example. At any rate, after the Promotion of Bantu Self Government Act was passed in 1959, the government began to carve up land for different ethnic groups and to devolve self-governing status to "tribal governments."

The homeland system was the primary pillar of what was known as grand apartheid. The intention behind homeland legislation was to allow Africans to exercise political rights in their "own areas" and thus to dilute the strength of demands for the franchise in the same places, and on the same level, as Whites. One secondary goal was to remove millions of Africans from the ostensible responsibility of the White government. South African unemployment, poverty, literacy, malnutrition, and infant mortality figures always excluded the homelands, for example, making South Africa seem a more prosperous and less inegalitarian place than in fact it was. The homeland system also devolved responsibility for meeting African demands to the woefully inadequate homeland governments, which had few resources and even fewer mechanisms for acquiring resources. The final goal was to rekindle ethnic nationalism in an attempt to undermine African solidarity, which appeared increasingly dangerous to White South Africa in the 1950s and 1960s.[19]

From the beginning, the government was keenly focused on plans for a Zulu homeland. Zulus make up the largest single ethnic group in South Africa, accounting for approximately 27 percent of the African population in 1986.[20] By creating an independent Zulu homeland, South Africa could rid itself of responsibility for six million Africans. Zulus, moreover, remained concentrated in Zululand and Natal, where there was some reason to believe that they would be occupying their ancestral lands, unlike some other groups, for whom territories were randomly allocated with less apparent legitimacy or historical justification.

Buthelezi resisted independence until 1972, however, and the Zulus were one of the last of the originally envisaged ethnic groups forced into "self-government." The Transkei, for example, accepted self-governing status in 1963. Initially, KwaZulu was allowed to establish an executive council, but it was prohibited from exercising such powers as governing townships or appointing and dismissing chiefs. The KwaZulu constitution provided that September 24 would be an official holiday known as King Shaka Day. The KwaZulu Legislative Assembly (KLA) would comprise one representative of the king, three chiefs appointed by each of the twenty-two regional authorities, and fifty-five elected members.[21] Buthelezi was allowed to select his own executive council.

Buthelezi revived Inkatha as a political party in 1975 and officially linked it to the KwaZulu government. The Inkatha constitution stipulated that the party president must be the chief minister of KwaZulu. Most legislators were members of Inkatha. Civil servants in KwaZulu were eventually forced to pledge allegiance to Inkatha, as were teachers and doctors in the homeland. In some areas, Inkatha membership became a prerequisite for receiving a pension or gaining access to schools and housing.

It was not until the late 1970s, however, that Inkatha gained an institutional power base. In response to a request from the KLA, the South African government significantly increased the status and power of the KwaZulu government in 1978. Without ever accepting independence, the KLA, and hence Inkatha, eventually gained control over an independent police force; the appointment, dismissal, and remuneration of chiefs; pensions; educational syllabi and access to schools; provision of township services and housing; distribution of development funds; some employment opportunities; a large civil service; and such infrastructure elements as roads, bridges, clinics, hospitals, and schools. Inkatha's extensive powers obviously derived from its position as the political party of an ethnic homeland government in an apartheid state organized on an ethnic basis.

Inkatha, however, also occupied an ambiguous space, operating within the context of the homeland structure as well as within the broader antiapartheid movement. Although the details are murky and have probably been further submerged by subsequent events, the ANC initially condoned and fostered the creation of Inkatha. ANC members referred ruefully in the 1980s to the role of the ANC in "creating the monster." Until 1979 some ANC leaders believed that Inkatha could play an internal oppositional role and that the homeland government might be a viable political platform if used by someone with a commitment to "the struggle." The ANC may also have hoped (vainly, as it turned out) that it would be able to use KwaZulu to train and infiltrate Umkhonto we Sizwe (MK) soldiers into South Africa.[22]

Buthelezi himself seemed eager to project a national identity for his organization, imagining that Inkatha, as a political organization, could take on a national role in a way that the KwaZulu homeland could not. Speaking in the KLA, for example, Buthelezi claimed that Inkatha was "the base from which to plan our liberation."[23] On one level, Inkatha was the political party of the KwaZulu homeland. Simultaneously, it claimed to embody Zulu political expression. On still a third plane, Inkatha aspired to be a national liberation movement based in an ideology of African self-help and Black Consciousness. The homeland structure gave Inkatha a base of support and a tangible source of power. But the same political institutions also limited its ability to break out of its regional, ethnic base to become a national liberation movement, despite aspirations toward this end.

While Inkatha was operating within the context of the homeland structure, radical opposition to apartheid, and to the KwaZulu homeland, evolved in a separate institutional setting. In the late 1970s the National Party government, under the leadership of P. W. Botha, began a process of liberalization. In 1979 trade unions were legalized. Government-appointed Urban Bantu Councils (UBCS), known popularly as Useless Boys Clubs, were replaced by locally elected community councilors with some limited powers to collect rents, allocate houses, and issue trading licenses. The 1983 Constitution, which included provision for the Tricameral Parliament in which Coloureds and Indians, but not Africans, were represented separately at national level, was part of the reform process. The fact that such institutions continued to exclude Africans provided the impetus for a new wave of political activism in the 1980s, under circumstances in which political space was opened sufficiently that greater levels of political mobilization and organization were possible.

The KwaZulu government took on a politically and socially conservative ideology in the period of Black political radicalism at the start of the 1980s. After a period of relative quiescence in the 1970s, especially in Natal, which was mostly unaffected by the 1976 student unrest that spread through the rest of the country, radical political opposition began to emerge in the early 1980s. Inkatha had by then become part of the system, complicit as it was in local level administration, so antigovernment militancy in Natal, which extended into the homeland, was perceived as a direct threat to the KwaZulu as well as South African governments. Antiapartheid activists were harshly repressed by both. When students in the KwaMashu township of Durban joined a nationwide school boycott in 1980, for example, they were attacked by Inkatha *izimpi* (military regiments), setting the tone for conflict between at least some township residents and the homeland government.

Opposition to Inkatha began to develop in urban areas starting in 1980. Most of the Durban townships were placed under the jurisdiction of the KwaZulu government after 1978. The homeland, however, had little money to dispense for development. What is more, it tended to use what it did have for patronage and personal enrichment. Living under homeland jurisdiction in the townships of KwaMashu or Umlazi provided no benefit over South African governance in Clermont or Lamontville for most Africans. In fact, the KwaZulu townships were often less developed, with fewer services, and were certainly disadvantaged by their greater distance from the city center, where most people worked.

The townships that remained under the jurisdiction of the White government, Clermont, Chesterville, and Lamontville, were run by the Port Natal Administration Board (PNAB) in the late 1970s. After the UBC was abolished, The Ningizimu Community Council was elected by residents to run the Durban townships.[24] For ideological reasons, because councilors were considered government collaborators, very few "progressive" Africans stood for election to community councils. As a result, the councils were dominated by conservatives, most of whom were either then or later aligned with Inkatha, in particular as the decade progressed and political affiliations grew more stark and polarizing.

Confrontations between community councilors and township residents often erupted in violence. A 1982 bus fare hike was blamed on the failure of councilors to represent the interest of their constituents against the government. In 1983 the PNAB announced a rent increase. When councilors failed to take action against the government or to represent the community's grievances, community activists organized bus boycotts and protests. These were initially organized on an ad hoc basis, but the leadership and networks that emerged to coordinate protests were soon structurally embedded in permanent community organizations called civic associations. These civic associations arose in ideological opposition to community councils but came to operate as competing power structures, vying for control of the townships.

The UDF was a Charterist movement organized in opposition to the Tricameral

Parliament system. The UDF was launched in 1983 and was immediately involved in mobilization against elections for the Tricameral Parliament. After the 1984 election, which it failed to prevent but certainly helped to delegitimize, the UDF was momentarily at a loss for a motivating purpose. In Durban the organization eventually became the linchpin uniting radical opposition to the South African and KwaZulu governments. Political organization and mobilization against the system, which had already begun at the grassroots level, was soon embedded in a greater political and ideological battle between Inkatha and the UDF that ultimately divided Natal politically.

Black politics in Natal were clearly situated in, and responsive to, the apartheid political structure. Inkatha's political space and possibilities were partly circumscribed by its position, within the system, as the political party of an ethnic homeland government. The UDF was defined in large part by exclusion from, and mobilization against, South Africa's political structures. It was cooperation and collaboration with the institutional structure of apartheid, versus opposition and noncollaboration, which most crucially defined the Black political spectrum in South Africa, and particularly in Natal, in the 1980s. And it was Inkatha and the UDF that most obviously anchored each extreme of the spectrum.

Mobilizing Discourse

In one sense it is inaccurate to characterize the entire period between 1975 and 1990 as a single era of "Zulu politics." The shifts that occurred within this period were at least as important as the shifts that occurred on either side of it. An analysis of the entire Inkatha era, however, tells a more complete story of the emergence of Zuluness as a relevant political identity. This section focuses on the discursive changes that took place within this period, in particular before and after 1983.

Inkatha partly defined itself and identified its perceived constituency through the statement of objectives published at its inception. Inkatha's goals included "liberating Africans from White domination, abolishing racial discrimination, advancing the cause of Zulu self-determination, and bringing about a national convention to devise a program for power sharing and progression to majority rule."[25] In this statement, Inkatha simultaneously constructed a pan-African identity against a dominating White Other, a possibility for negotiating and sharing power with Whites, and a narrower Zulu identity in search of self-determination separate from Whites and from other Africans. Inkatha sought multiple strands of legitimation.

From its inception Inkatha portrayed itself as a Zulu nationalist organization, the political embodiment of Zuluness. "In other words, all members of the Zulu nation are automatically members of Inkatha if they are Zulus. There may be people who are inactive members as no one escapes being a member as long as he or she is a member of the Zulu nation."[26] In July 1975 Buthelezi was accepted at the first national council and general conference meeting of Inkatha as "the unchallenged leader of the four and a half million Zulus in their struggle" and was empowered, by the council, to speak on behalf of all Zulus.[27]

At the same time, though, Buthelezi was focused on carving a national political base for himself and for Inkatha. Although his attempts to engage in narrow ethnic politics and broader African politics later seemed contradictory, because the two became antithetical and mutually exclusive in the context of subsequent ideological divisions, the realm of possibility was less constricted in 1975. For Buthelezi, Zulu nationalism could form the basis of African nationalism, and Black Consciousness, a progressive liberation ideology with unassailable credentials, could serve the reification of African tribal traditions and hierarchies:

We must accept regional politics as a reality which existed long before we were conquered. The danger comes only when some people allow themselves to be blinded by regional involvement to the exclusion of participation in the cause of all Blacks. . . . It is so much poppycock . . . for people to imply that, being involved in regional politics one is necessarily undermining Black unity. The people in these Reserve areas have to exist and they should be helped by us, and we by them, in our attempts to eke out an existence, even within our dreary circumstances. This means that we have to face the fact that we have day-to-day goals, as we have to live for 365 days each year and every year. On the other hand we must have long term goals which are in the interests of our common Black struggle in the whole of South Africa. I have never been confused about the line between these two phases of our Black struggle.[28]

Buthelezi wove together strands of Zulu and Black consciousnesses, claiming that the origins of the Black Consciousness Movement (BCM) lay within Zulu history, that Black Consciousness derived from the assertive nationalism of Shaka.[29] Buthelezi created a long and ethnically rooted political tradition to prop up the relatively more recent BC ideology, dominant in South Africa only after 1972. In this period Buthelezi was also able to present Inkatha as the ideological descendant of the ANC. Buthelezi managed to combine Zulu nationalism with ANC nonracialism by amalgamating "a disparate range of ethnic histories which he found malleable enough to mould together into an argument which exerted the existence of an historically derived black multi-ethnic political union under the banner of the ANC."[30]

Buthelezi's national political ambitions and liberation discourse were somewhat circumscribed by the public break between Inkatha and the ANC in 1979. He was nevertheless able to continue to articulate a national vision for several years after the split. Buthelezi resorted to calling the ANC the "Mission in Exile" during this period, denying the legitimacy of external opposition and claiming for himself the mantle of Chief Luthuli: "Inkatha claims that in a symbolic meeting between Chief Luthuli and the Hon. Chief M. G. Buthelezi in the 1960s the heritage of the leadership of the liberation struggle was passed on to the Hon. M. G. Buthelezi."[31] A leading Inkatha ideologue explained in 1984: "Inkatha was founded in response to the political vacuum that had been created after the African National Congress and Pan Africanist Congress were banned, and it was formed on the principles of the founding fathers of the ANC."[32]

Buthelezi has consistently reinforced his own connection to the ANC:

Inkatha is Black South Africa undivided, standing together, pursuing the time-honoured traditions of Black South Africa. For us, Black South African political traditions go back to 1912 when the African National Congress was formed. I stand boldly before you and say that those are the traditions which Black South Africa serves. Those are the traditions which Inkatha serves. The struggle for liberation in our country started with history itself. . . . I am rooted in this tradition, Dr. Pixley ka Isaka Seme was my uncle. He was one of the founding fathers of the ANC. I grew up at my mother's knee learning what he and others did. When I became older I joined the ANC. . . . I knew people like Nelson Mandela, Robert Sobukwe and Oliver Tambo personally. I know what their faces looked like.[33]

This dual representation remained available to Buthelezi and to Inkatha during this period partly because the ANC's position on ethnicity was still fairly ambiguous. The ANC and ANC-aligned organizations, including most trade unions and civic associations, opposed the homeland system and any type of ideological construct or identity which might divide the "oppressed," constituted as simultaneously poor and broadly Black. Marxist ideology and a workerist base also led them to support class over ethnic identification because the latter undercut broader cross-ethnic class affiliations. At the same time, they resisted explicitly undermining ethnic identity. Through the early 1980s unions in Durban were careful not to make anti-Inkatha remarks or to take an anti-Inkatha stance, for fear of alienating Zulu workers.[34] After Elijah Barayi, president of the Congress of South African Trade Unions (COSATU), promised in 1985 at a mass rally in Durban to "bury Buthelezi," a union coordinator stated that Barayi "gave the impression that COSATU's major aim was to oppose Buthelezi and the homeland system. His speech ignored the major lesson learnt by Natal unionists over the years: winning workers in the region to progressive positions was achieved by hard organizational work, and not by attacks on Buthelezi."[35] COSATU tried to define its constituency as "workers" rather than as "non-Zulus": "It is important that the politics of the working class eventually become the politics of all the oppressed people of this country. We must combat the divisions amongst the workers of South Africa and unite them into a strong and confident working class. When we speak of people, we do not speak of individuals but of groups of people that have the same basic problems, needs, and inspirations. The most basic of these defining features is that of class position, for us it is this that defines people's place and role in society."[36]

After 1983, however, the UDF grew increasingly prominent in Natal, competing with Inkatha for the Zulu constituency that Inkatha considered its own and undermining Inkatha's claim to national prominence. It is unclear whether the UDF first took a distinctly antiethnic and apparently anti-Zulu position in Natal and forced Inkatha to defend an increasingly ethnic stance, or whether Inkatha tried to solidify its support base by firing up ethnic sentiment, thus compelling the UDF to define its own antiethnic position more clearly. What is clear is that Inkatha did mobilize a conservative, confrontational political identity that it defined as embodying Zuluness, and that the UDF at the same time mobilized a "modern," urban, class-based and antitraditional identity. Furthermore, the position of the UDF in Natal was more clearly antiethnic than that of the organization elsewhere in the country. As the power struggle between the two sides assumed a violent dimension, ideological and discursive differences were solidified and exacerbated.

One way in which Buthelezi sought to strengthen his ethnic base was by raising the profile of the king within the framework of Inkatha. Buthelezi was careful not to allow the king to gain political ascendancy or to assume an independent role from which he could muster his own power base. Thus the mythology of the king was intertwined with Inkatha in the popular perception, making support for the king synonymous with support for Inkatha. After 1982 the king began to appear with Buthelezi at Inkatha events, thus legitimating Inkatha's claim to represent all Zulus. King Zwelithini echoed Inkatha rhetoric, defined Zulus and their political place, and identified the enemies of the Zulu: "Those who want to drive the Zuluness out of the souls of the people of Durban will be eradicated one by one. We are the people of warrior blood, forged as a people in war and peace."[37] On another occasion, the king declared: "We have always rooted out Zulus who turn against Zulus and in so doing we have kept our honour. It does not shame the whole nation when traitors emerge amongst us as a people."[38]

Inkatha also buttressed the place of Zulu identity in the 1980s by establishing a Zulu cultural base through museums. At the opening of the Nodwengu Museum of Zulu history in 1983, Buthelezi spoke "of the reconstruction of the Zulu nation through the process of refurbishing cultural roots and inspiring a rediscovery of our pride and our identity as Zulus and as South Africans." Buthelezi represented the 1980s as the period of the political rebirth of the Zulu nation. He described the construction of the KwaZulu legislative buildings as "the fulfillment of centuries of Zulu history" (rather than the fulfillment of the bantustan policy). Even the conflict between the UDF and Inkatha was described as the "birth pangs of the new Zulu nation, reborn after its defeat in 1879 by the British."[39]

During the 1980s Inkatha articulated a worldview that located the traditional Zulu hierarchy at its center. Thus it strengthened the position of thousands of chiefs and headmen who might otherwise have felt their status eroding as more and more people moved to cities outside the traditional purview of the chief. Inkatha also strengthened the position of chiefs by dispensing important resources through them at a time when their control over access to resources was otherwise diminishing.

The UDF, on the other hand, ideologically opposed ethnic politicization because it believed that ethnic divisions were created and strengthened by the apartheid state, through the homeland system, to divide Black opposition. Its Black Consciousness legacy denied divisions among the Black oppressed. Its Marxist legacy denied the legitimacy of ethnic political affiliation. Apartheid was understood as a particularly ruthless form of capitalist exploitation in which the relevant political cleavages existed between workers and the owners of capital. Ethnicity was false consciousness. Ostensibly, the UDF also faulted the Zulu hierarchy because it was undemocratic—chiefs are hereditary and male, and they exercise absolute and often arbitrary control. The UDF was thus ideologically predisposed against the mobilization of ethnic nationalism. The movement's position became more extreme, however, as the 1980s wore on and the conflict in Natal escalated. In other parts of South Africa, for example, the UDF cooperated with, and even worked through, traditional leaders and networks.[40] Fighting in KwaZulu, however, was articulated as a battle between *amabutho,* the title given to the traditional Zulu regiments organized by Shaka, and *amaqabane,* "comrades." The "comrade" moniker has a fairly obvious Communist derivation, which included a connection to the broader international struggle against oppression and highlighted the revolutionary possibilities of the antiapartheid movement: "Bantustan leaders are going up and down the world saying that Black people would suffer if the companies disinvested. I have got a message for the puppets of the bantustans: the blood of the black people and the tears of the black people will be asked from you. We believe that the 'rulers' of the Bantustans are doing their master's calling."[41] A UDF pamphlet charged, "Inkatha calls for unity, but up until 1979, only Zulus could be members of its central committee. Buthelezi speaks about the superiority of Zulus."[42]

The conflict between Inkatha and the UDF nevertheless did not originate in esoteric ideological differences over whether or not to mobilize ethnic identity for political purposes. Many other homeland leaders were engaged in the same pursuit and had even gone farther down the road of collaboration by accepting independence from the South African government, without ever becoming involved in a conflict with the liberation movement over this or any other issue. But the ways in which the parties to the conflict constructed the boundaries and issues that divided them paved the way for violence.

Until 1983 there was no threat to Inkatha's regional power base in Natal. Inkatha was the ruling party of the Zulu homeland government, propped up and sanctioned by Pretoria, and any potential organized opposition was either banned, exiled, or both. Such popular opposition to Inkatha as existed, mainly in the urban townships, was disparate, unorganized, and fairly easily, albeit harshly, quashed by Inkatha amabutho. The growth of the UDF after 1983, and its focus on African politics after 1985, changed the political landscape of KwaZulu, in part by presenting a clear threat to Inkatha's power base. The UDF portrayed itself as a national liberation movement and sought to amass a national support base throughout South Africa, including Natal, to bolster its claim to represent Black South African opinion and the position of the "moral majority."

The relevant threat to Inkatha, then, was the UDF in Natal. The socioeconomic and demographic bases of Inkatha and the UDF were, initially at least, quite different. The bulk of Inkatha's support came from rural areas and from informal settlements in the urban areas. UDF support was based in the townships. UDF supporters tended to be better educated, younger, and more established than Inkatha members, with lower rates of unemployment. In Natal, however, both groups were made up overwhelmingly of Zulus who account for more than 90 percent of the African population of that province.

Nevertheless, the threat that the UDF represented to Inkatha was articulated in ethnic terms: "You know that the UDF and COSATU have come into your midst to turn you against Inkatha. Why? Is it because Inkatha is led by a Zulu? I am not being party political. . . . Does the ANC encourage you to be Zulu, to do your Zulu thing and play your Zulu role? . . . What does the UDF say about your Zuluness?"[43] The UDF was explicitly constructed as a threat to Zulu identity, thus reinforcing the place of Inkatha as the defender of Zuluness, the "natural" political home of the Zulu people. Buthelezi said at a mass rally, for example, "I want to make it quite clear that ANC attacks are not only attacks against Inkatha. They are attacks against Zulu people just because they are Zulu."[44]

In addition, the UDF was described as a party dominated by people of other ethnic groups, foreign to Zulu people, and threatening to their traditions. In Natal there is some history of animosity and violence between Indians and Africans.

Inkatha leaders tried to retrieve and capitalize on potential tensions between these racial groups by claiming that the UDF was controlled by Indians or foreigners. In the context of violence between Inkatha and members of a grassroots affiliate of the UDF in 1983, Buthelezi claimed repeatedly that UDF leaders were Xhosas.[45]

Material Conditions

After decades of uninterrupted growth, South Africa's gross domestic product (GDP) began to fluctuate in the late 1970s. An increase in the gold price stabilized the economy for a short time, but in 1981 the price of gold dropped and the nation sustained severe balance-of-payments shortfalls. South Africa was forced to turn to the International Monetary Fund (IMF) in 1982.[46] The South African economy continued to weaken throughout the 1980s as a result of increasing unrest, international sanctions after 1986, the declining price of minerals and the increasing cost of extracting them, and global recession.

In the old provincial system, which divided South Africa into four provinces, Natal occupied 8.1 percent of South Africa's total land area. Natal's population density is more than twice as high as the national average, though, as 20 percent of all South Africans live in Natal. Ninety percent of the African population of Natal is Zulu, and 75 percent of all Zulus live in Natal. Most of the remainder live in the townships surrounding Johannesburg and Pretoria.

Until the 1960s Natal's economy was dominated by sugar farms, which still cover most of the province's north coast. Starting in the 1960s, however, Natal, drawn into a national policy drive to stimulate capitalism, began to develop industry. The growth of manufacturing created a need for a stable, longer-term, and better-skilled workforce, in Natal as in the rest of South Africa. People employed in this way were better off economically than most of the Black population, but fewer workers were needed, creating a large and growing sector of chronically unemployed. During the 1980s some thirty thousand new job seekers entered the employment market every year in Natal alone. In 1980 Natal had the second-highest unemployment rate of any province, at 12 percent, and the population in Natal is generally poorer than the national average.[47]

Seventy percent of those people who live in Natal inhabit the former KwaZulu homeland. Fifty-six percent of the economically active population of KwaZulu was employed outside the bantustan in 1976. During the 1980s, on average, 70–80 percent of families had members away as migrant workers. Moreover, more than one-third of the population of KwaZulu is landless and almost totally dependent on migrant remittances, which represented 75 percent of total household incomes in the early 1980s.[48] In 1982 and 1983 the Natal Provincial Administration spent four times as much as the KwaZulu government on health facilities for all race groups.

Part of the reason for South Africa's balance-of-payments deficit in the early 1980s was that manufacturing had begun to replace mining and agriculture as the backbone of the economy. South Africa was forced to spend much of its foreign exchange on machinery and equipment imports for the manufacturing sector. Durban is South Africa's busiest port, largely because it is closest to the north of the country and to the nation's industrial center in the Pretoria-Witwatersrand-Vereeniging triangle. Most equipment imports, as well as many mineral and agricultural exports, went through the port at Natal. Dockworkers therefore suddenly found themselves in a position of unprecedented strength and embarked on a number of strike actions throughout the 1970s, eventually forcing the South African government to legalize and recognize Black trade unions in 1979. In the 1980s the trade unions formed the organizational backbone of the UDF.

Other material changes affected living patterns in the province. The structure of settlement and economic differentiation in Durban can be divided into distinct periods. Between the 1940s and 1960s most Africans seeking work in Durban moved from rural areas to Cato Manor, where they found relatively cheap accommodation as tenants or subtenants on Indian-owned or vacant land. During the 1960s Urban Areas and Group Areas acts led the government to enforce residential segregation and influx control and to embark on mass forced removals. By the mid-1960s most of the residents of Cato Manor had been removed, leaving open a large tract of land to the west of Durban.[49]

Most Africans were resettled in housing projects in KwaMashu and Umlazi. Many, however, were unable to afford rent in the new housing schemes or were ineligible to receive housing because they were "illegal" migrants from other countries, or had moved from rural areas without proper documentation. Many of these people moved to freehold areas in Inanda and Clermont, where they rented rooms or erected their own dwellings. Others sought permission to live in the areas of amakhosi or izinduna abutting the townships.[50]

The 1960s was a period of political stability and economic growth. By the end of the decade, however, the government had halted its large state-funded housing programs. A new stage of urbanization and apartheid spatial planning began in the 1970s. When KwaZulu gained self-governing status in 1974, all of the Black townships of Durban except Clermont, Lamontville, and Chesterville were included in the the KwaZulu territory. Although the supply of housing was fixed, migration to the cities was not, and new migrants were forced to build informal settlements around the townships.

Whereas the South African government was willing and able to control squatting with repressive influx control and forced removals in South Africa's other major urban centers, KwaZulu's control over areas that were practically inside Durban wrested demographic control of the city from the hands of White officials. Traditional leaders were reluctant to enforce influx control in their areas, particularly when squatters were paying them, and the KwaZulu government had no incentive to stop squatters. Durban's hilly terrain and dense vegetation also allowed squatting to progress for a long time almost unnoticed by Whites.

Apartheid population controls thus began to disintegrate in Durban about a decade before they did in the rest of the country. At the same time, in the early 1980s there was some effort to introduce economic liberalization into the framework of residential apartheid. Such liberalization benefited relatively better-off and more permanent township residents, allowing some people to buy homes and to exercise greater control over services. It also exacerbated socioeconomic divisions within the townships and between townships and adjacent squatter areas. Squatter camps were for the most part completely underdeveloped, with limited or no access to services such as running water, electricity, public transport, sewage, or waste disposal. As an unprecedented number of people fled drought and flocked to the city in search of work in the early 1980s, an increasingly overwhelming number of squatters vied with township residents for access to services and facilities.

Thus in the early 1980s material conditions played an important role in dividing urban dwellers into socioeconomically differentiated and competing categories. The two groups were further divided spatially. Township residents were generally longtime urban dwellers who were steadily employed. Many owned their own homes and were tied into urban community networks. Shack dwellers were generally recent arrivals to the city who retained primary ties to rural areas. Many were unemployed, and they tended to be less educated and less skilled than township dwellers. The shacks sprung up around the periphery of the townships, and squatters routinely entered the townships to use outside water taps, public transport, and other facilities. Competition for scarce resources had begun to erupt in random violence by the early 1980s.

Organization

Inkatha has a strict and hierarchical organizational base. The leadership, dominated by Buthelezi himself, embraces several top decision-making bodies: the national council, the general conference, and the central committee. The national council is the policy-making organ. It includes roughly three hundred members drawn from the central committee, the KLA, representatives of the regions and affiliated organizations, and brigade members. The general conference meets annually and includes all national council members and two or three representatives from every branch. The central committee, which was initially envisioned as a small, elite unit, grew unwieldy in the 1980s as Inkatha tried to co-opt powerful and potentially wayward local leaders by appointment to the central committee. As a result, an inner council of the central committee became Inkatha's key decision-making body during the 1980s.

Below the national council is the regional level, and below the regions are the branches. Individual members affiliate at the branch level. In rural areas a branch constituency coincides with the chief's area of authority. Inkatha regions have the same boundaries as the regional authorities established by the 1951 Bantu Authorities Act in Natal. Chiefs act as patrons and, according to Buthelezi, "are expected to exercise a watching brief over local branches." Lawrence Schlemmer, an Inkatha spokesman for part of the 1980s, claimed that Inkatha's spectacular growth, to one million members by 1985, could be ascribed "in large measure to the active cooperation of tribal chiefs."[51]

Chiefs, their networks, and their representatives constitute the primary level of politics in rural KwaZulu.[52] A headman may be appointed by the chief, or he may inherit his position from a father or an uncle. He is generally responsible for a village, while a chief presides over a larger area, probably including several, or even many, villages. Some, like Chief Mathaba of Mthunzini, control large areas of KwaZulu. A person who has a problem—a conflict with another person or group, a missing pension payment, or another domestic or even legal matter—is likely to turn first to his or her induna. The induna might resolve the issue himself or seek help from the chief or homeland official.

The chief's main source of power is land. He controls the allocation of land and decides which land may be cultivated and when. Young men, who need to establish their own homesteads in order to marry, are particularly vulnerable to the whim of the chief in allotting land on which they can build and farm. The chief also controls movement into and out of his area. If an individual or family seeks to move into his area, a chief will ask why they left the area they were in. He will ask the previous chief for references, and if the family left because of a conflict with the old chief, they are likely to be refused asylum in the area of another chief. Movement between rural areas is thus difficult and rare. In the event of conflict between chief and subject, "exiting the system" is a strategy unavailable to most rural dwellers unless they move to an urban area.[53]

At Inkatha's height of power, chiefs also derived power from their connection to Inkatha and to the KwaZulu government. They formed an important link in the vast network of patronage that partly sustained (and partly destroyed) the KwaZulu economy. A chief on good terms with Inkatha (and through the 1980s, most were) could expect such benefits as roads and hospitals to come to his area. One Inkatha-affiliated chief on the south coast of KwaZulu Natal, for example, boasts a two-story school and a new clinic in his area, while the more densely populated adjacent area, the domain of a chief who opposes Inkatha, has neither school nor clinic.[54] Access to valuable resources can reasonably be expected to increase the power and prestige of a chief.

At the same time, a chief in KwaZulu was essentially a political hostage to Inkatha. He had very little room for independent action or affiliation. Besides controlling the allocation of development resources, the homeland government assumed the right to appoint, remove, and pay chiefs. Although the position of chief is hereditary, succession is often open to interpretation. Some people say that the eldest son should be the chief, but the eldest son of the wife married by Christian rites may also inherit the position. Some degree of ambiguity was probably built into the system to allow the chief's subjects a say in who became chief.[55] A handicapped, drunk, or despotic heir could be passed over without any apparent break with tradition. There is almost always some debate about the rightful heir to the deceased chief, and factions supporting different contenders are likely to emerge in the interim. In the context of generalized UDF-Inkatha violence in the 1980s, factions sometimes aligned themselves with the parties to the larger conflict, both feeding into and reinforcing locally, Natal's civil war by embedding the broader conflict in local disputes.

In urban areas Inkatha's organizational network and control were somewhat attenuated. Urban dwellers have more freedom of movement and are less reliant on local authorities for favor and patronage. Particularly if they are employed, people are able to exercise more control over their own lives and spaces. In the KwaZulu townships, Inkatha nevertheless maintained considerable influence and authority through government structures. Civil servants in KwaZulu were required to pledge allegiance to Inkatha.[56] The government and administration of most Durban and all Pietermaritzburg townships were also under Inkatha control. The homeland system provided Inkatha with a number of pressure points, including pensions, work seekers' permits, housing, land, and jobs, to ensure party membership and allegiance. By 1977 Inkatha claimed to have three hundred branches, including one hundred in urban areas near Durban.[57] In the 1980s Inkatha also began to recruit support in the squatter camps, and for a time the conflict between Inkatha and the UDF, which dominated the townships, exhibited clear socioeconomic and spatial dimensions.

As early as 1980 Inkatha was also able to call on young men to form fighting regiments to quash opposition to the KwaZulu government. Along with the KwaZulu police, which operated essentially as the armed wing of Inkatha, the regiments enforced Inkatha policy. Young men armed with "traditional weapons" were often bused in from rural areas to quell urban "radicalism" and, later in the decade, to ambush UDF funerals and meetings and to attack UDF supporters. The Inkatha Youth Brigade served in part as an organizing and mobilizing base for Inkatha fighting units.

Inkatha gradually gained control in the 1980s of those township councils that remained under the jurisdiction of Natal, as well as those in KwaZulu. Very few Africans aligned with the UDF or other progressive organizations stood for election in the town councils because the liberation movements opposed collaboration with the system. This left those councils wide open for people who were conservative, even if initially unaligned, or for Inkatha members. Because the councils controlled rents and housing allocation, they had significant leverage over many township residents. Eventually most people who did serve on those councils affiliated to Inkatha, in part because Inkatha condoned working within the system and in part because council members came under attack as collaborators from radicalized township dwellers aligned with the UDF. Inkatha affiliation may have been a response to violence in some cases, rather than a catalyst. Ultimately, no one could afford to remain unaligned in the civil war between Inkatha and the UDF.

Unlike Inkatha, the UDF was fairly loosely organized. It was never a political party. It was a broad front of progressive organizations united primarily, and sometimes only, by common opposition to apartheid. Only an organization with its own constitution, which could thus be identified as distinct from the UDF itself, could affiliate to the UDF. Although people often called themselves UDF members in the 1980s, the organization did not have, or recruit, individual members, nor did it have a membership list or claim any membership figures.

Although UDF organizational patterns were fairly uniform throughout South Africa, the front also adapted to variations in local circumstance. The UDF might rely more heavily on church or civic association networks in particular areas, for example, depending on which organizations were more locally prominent. In some parts of South Africa, such as the Transkei, the UDF was able to work through ethnic political structures and networks. By the time the UDF began to sink roots in Natal, however, Zulu political institutions were already formally embedded in the Inkatha party network. Had the UDF not been denied access to ethnic structures in KwaZulu, it is possible to speculate that the organization might have developed a different regional identity and constituency.

Under the circumstances, however, the UDF reached its constituent base through civic associations, trade unions, youth groups, boycott committees, and other independent local level organizations to which individuals already belonged. Many churches were also linked to the UDF, sometimes through ministers and priests who took up the people's struggle, and sometimes through church-based organizations which became politicized. After the formation of COSATU in 1985, the UDF was also represented and organized through South Africa's largest trade union umbrella group, which itself included four hundred thousand members. In many parts of the country, urban township dwellers received consistent, overlapping, and reinforcing messages from multiple sources of influence: the church, the workplace, and community groups. Although the UDF was for the most part not organized in a formal sense, it permeated African civil society and dominated Black South African politics in the 1980s.

This description of the UDF's organizational base should be qualified in two important ways. The first is that at different points and in different places during the decade, civic and youth organizations may have been very well organized. Whereas the UDF was only marginally involved in African struggles at the outset, focused as it was on Coloured and Indian elections to the Tricameral Parliament, it became more intimately involved in African politics and organization as the decade progressed. Some civics organized entire townships into neighborhood and street cells, which were effective networks for mobilization, information gathering and dissemination, leadership grooming, and fund collection. Depending on the strength of the civic itself and other contextual variables, such organization may have been perceived as more or less connected to the UDF. Organization also came under more or less state repression in different areas after 1986. By systematically culling the top levels of leadership, by banning leaders and prohibiting them from meeting with more than one person at a time, and by infiltrating organizations at all levels, the South African government successfully undercut in the late 1980s even the diffuse and flexible organizational network that supported the UDF.

The second qualification is that in Natal and KwaZulu African politics was different from the rest of the country, and UDF organization was different. The existence of Inkatha, the allegiance of many urban as well as rural dwellers to Inkatha, the party's ethnic base, and the ideological conservatism of Inkatha made African politics, and the parameters of the UDF, more rigid in Natal than elsewhere. Whereas the UDF campaign to make the country "ungovernable" was intended to undermine the White government that upheld the system elsewhere in South Africa, in Natal it was directed primarily against the homeland government and Inkatha. Later in the 1980s, when the two sides engaged in a full-scale civil war, sides were strictly drawn. Some neighborhoods, and even streets within neighborhoods, were UDF-controlled, and some were Inkatha-controlled. People living in either were forced to demonstrate allegiance to, and to fight for, their side, or risk being labeled as traitors, with vicious consequences. UDF affiliation in Natal was not the casual and loose alignment that it may have been for all but the most committed elsewhere in South Africa.

By the time the UDF became engaged in African politics in Natal, after 1984, it was able to take advantage of grassroots organization that had already emerged in response to activism around particular issues. In Durban and Pietermaritzburg, Natal's two largest urban areas, protests and popular mobilization resurged in the early 1980s. The brutal repression of the KwaMashu school boycott in 1980 triggered the first wave of popular sentiment against Inkatha in the townships. Although the Congress of South African Students (COSAS) was generally weak in Natal, the organization picked up support in Durban after the boycott.[58] Probably more important than the boycott itself, which was part of a wave of school boycotts that swept South Africa in 1980, was Inkatha's response to it. Inkatha warrior regiments were first formed to attack KwaMashu school boycotters, angering many students and parents and establishing a precedent for conflict between Inkatha and a more radical, progressive constituency.[59]

Beginning in 1982 a number of local-level organizations began to emerge as community members responded to grievances that town councilors were unwilling or unable to take up. The first major civic struggle in Durban's townships concerned bus fare increases in late 1982. Commuters from most of Durban's townships boycotted buses for months. Each township had a Commuter's Committee under the umbrella of a Joint Commuter's Committee. The committees organized alternative taxi services and in some cases negotiated flexible schedules for employees who had to walk to work.[60] The following year many of these township activists and networks coordinated again to protest planned rent increases. People in these communities thus became organized and mobilized by local activists in 1982 and 1983 around local grievances, against town councilors. Organization arose from consecutive moments of politicization. The Lamontville activist Msizi Dube formed the Joint Rent Action Committee (JORAC) to coordinate rent boycotts in the Durban townships. His assassination later that year, by a town councilor allegedly affiliated with Inkatha, sparked a wave of violence and unrest against councilors and other apparent "collaborators."[61]

By the time the issue of incorporation into KwaZulu was raised, starting in 1984, the Durban townships were already highly politicized with well-developed parallel political organizations in place. Township residents opposed incorporation because they feared they would lose Section 10 rights, which allowed them to live and work in Durban. Housing and services were notoriously even worse in KwaZulu than under South African government administration.[62] Buthelezi favored incorporation because it would extend the territory and influence of the homeland. Simmering hostility over the issue of incorporation first erupted in violence in July 1984 at Msizi Dube's memorial service. A busload of Inkatha supporters attacked the crowd of five thousand people, killing three. Violence continued for the next few months, and the issue of incorporation continued to serve as a basis for mobilization and anti-Inkatha organization throughout the 1980s.[63]

In this period the townships were also organized through youth groups engaged in semipolitical activity. The youth became increasingly involved in overtly political, explicitly anti-Inkatha and anticollaborationist politics as the decade progressed. Some of these youth organizations, however, served in part as recruitment centers for Umkhonto we Sizwe, the armed wing of the ANC, funneling youth out of South Africa and thus weakening activist organization inside the country.[64]

After 1985, in the context of increasing violence, the UDF became intimately connected to the network of community and grassroots organizations that burgeoned in the early 1980s. Until that point, the UDF had been primarily engaged in mobilization in the Indian and Coloured communities, against the Tricameral Parliament system. By the time the UDF turned to township politics, urban political organization in Natal was already dominated by progressive and at least potentially sympathetic community groups with a strong anti-Inkatha stance. Thus there was some ideological and strategic affinity between the national UDF and the anti-Inkatha organizational base it found in place in Natal.

The organizational patterns of the UDF and Inkatha were diametrically opposed. Inkatha was primarily organized through a semitraditional hierarchical system controlled by the chief and his representatives. Inkatha was dominant in rural areas, where such organizational networks retained purchase. Even in urban areas, however, Inkatha controlled whole squatter camps through a local strongman, or warlord, who, though usually not a hereditary chief, assumed a similar role. The strongman could control an area through a combination of fear and patronage, particularly in the context of widespread violence from which he might be able to offer some degree of protection.[65] The UDF, on the other hand, built on an organizational base which had arisen from moments of activism and mobilization and which was, at the outset at least, fiercely democratic.[66] Meetings were common, and open to community members; decisions were voted upon, and participation was highly valued. UDF organization also differed from Inkatha organization in that it was dominated by youth.

Available Ideology

The ANC has dominated Black politics in South Africa for most of this century. The ideology of the ANC underwent many permutations between 1912, when it began as the South African Native National Congress, and 1960, when it was banned and partially eclipsed as the dominant Black opposition. Initially the organization was controlled by a small African elite who hoped to extract concessions, from within the system, for the Black middle class. With some amendment, a fairly conservative strategic and ideological agenda guided the ANC through the 1930s. In the 1940s a new generation of more radical youth entered the ranks of the organization and founded the ANC Youth League in 1945. The Youth League put forth an "Africanist" agenda which involved a move away from working through Whites toward working among Africans. They also advocated the organization and mobilization of a mass base, and ANC involvement in national protest campaigns.

The Africanist strain within the ANC was in tension with competing communist and committed nonracialist strains.[67] By the mid-1950s it appeared that the latter two compatible ideological positions were ascendant within the movement.[68] In 1955 ANC leaders convened a Congress of the People in Kliptown to establish a set of goals and principles. Since 1955 the Freedom Charter has essentially represented the official ideological position of the ANC. Charterism is characterized by a commitment to equality, nonracialism, economic as well as political rights, and opposition to apartheid. It incorporates a commitment to democracy, including full political rights for all people, with elements of African socialism.

Various aspects of ANC strategy in the period before it was banned bear scrutiny in relation to subsequent ideological possibilities. The ANC had a history of working through and with chiefs and other traditional leaders. The organization was in particular firmly embedded among traditional elites in KwaZulu, where the majority of the ANC's rural branches were located in the 1940s.[69] In addition, the ANC had no firm position on the matter of "working within the system." In some places, ANC members and leaders stood for election to government-created bodies. Elsewhere, such activity was taboo, and the difference was mainly a matter of local politics. Finally, although the ANC grew more radical in the 1940s and 1950s, it never went so far as to reconceptualize its racial identity. The ANC was an organization for African South Africans that cooperated with Coloured and Indian opposition organizations, but the distinction among these groups, along lines designated by the apartheid system, was not seriously questioned.

In 1960 the ANC was banned. In 1963 most of its top leadership was accused of treason and sentenced to life in prison. Black South African politics entered a period of dormancy. The top leadership had disappeared, midlevel leaders were banned and intimidated, and followers were disillusioned and frightened. It was in this context that Steve Biko became politicized in the late 1960s. Biko was a member of the National Union of South African Students (NUSAS), a White-dominated student organization that wavered between liberal and radical agendas. At the end of the 1960s NUSAS was really the only oppositional organization operating in South Africa, and many young Black students belonged to it. They remained a minority within the organization, though, for only a minority of Black people were able to garner tertiary education.

Biko soon became frustrated with what he perceived as the subservient position of Africans within the opposition, and he began to develop a separatist ideological position.[70] The South African Students Organization (SASO) was inaugurated in 1969, and Biko was named president. Black Consciousness (BC) evolved as the ideological position of SASO. In Biko's words, Black Consciousness is "the realisation by the Black man of the need to rally together with his brothers around the cause of his operation—the blackness of their skin—and to operate as a group in order to rid themselves of the shackles that bind them to perpetual servitude."[71] It was an oppositional ideology designed to undermine a dominant perception of White superiority and the legitimacy of race classification. It advocated solid Black unity against Whites, with the understanding that Black was a matter of mental attitude, not skin pigmentation.

Black Consciousness was much more radical in its intentions and strategies than the ANC had been. It aimed to change the way people thought, and to undercut basic assumptions about the possibilities of opposition within apartheid. Biko redefined all groups classified as nonwhite by the government, including Coloureds, Indians, and Africans, as Black. Black Consciousness assumed unity among them on the basis of their common oppression. The BCM also condemned collaboration, or working within the system, regardless of ultimate intent.[72] As early as 1970 Biko attacked Buthelezi and Kaiser Matanzima of the Transkei for collaboration with the homeland system.

As a result of government censorship, youth coming of age in the 1960s and 1970s were largely ignorant of the long history of struggle that preceded the BCM. Black Consciousness was the dominant opposition ideology in South Africa throughout the late 1970s. At this point it suffered an eclipse for two reasons. First, Biko was assassinated by the government, the BCM leadership was driven underground, and its publications were banned. Second, young activists became disillusioned with what they perceived as the limits of BCM: its lack of organization or a clear program of action.[73] At the end of the 1970s, then, opposition politics had no clear ideological orientation or direction. The upsurge of mobilization that began in 1980, including the 1980 school boycott and various strikes and protests, was not organized by any national political group and had no obvious ideological commitment beyond opposition to apartheid.

It was not until 1983 that the United Democratic Front emerged to organize and articulate Black political opposition to apartheid. Ideologically, the UDF defined itself as Charterist, but it obviously owed a clear conceptual debt to the BCM. Its decision to organize across racial lines, and to include all nonwhites as Black, was a legacy of BC, not Charterist, commitments. The UDF did not take a stand against working with Whites, though, in that regard following Charterist nonracialism rather than Africanism. The UDF articulated principles of redistribution and economic democracy which had roots in the Freedom Charter, but it also held a principled commitment against collaboration, a BC position.[74]

Within the framework of possibility suggested by the ideological legacy of Black political opposition in South Africa, Inkatha's ability to locate itself was somewhat more tenuous than that of the UDF. In 1975 it also articulated both Charterist and Black Consciousness traditions. Buthelezi differentiated between what he called the "true ANC," the organization before it was banned in 1960, and the Charterist tradition as it evolved within South Africa after 1960. Until 1960 there was room within the ideological parameters of the ANC to work through the system; it was only once Charterism was claimed by the UDF that noncollaboration was defined as a sine qua non of the struggle. The IFP also defined itself in Black Consciousness terms as representing and mobilizing African and Zulu cultural identities, and reinforcing African cultural values and norms. Within the BCM, a return to African roots was perceived as an important step toward the reclamation of Black identity.

At its inception then, Inkatha sought legitimation by dipping into multiple streams of South African opposition ideology. During the 1970s, moreover, it was possible, if in retrospect somewhat conceptually incoherent, to do so. The 1970s were a period of oppositional disorganization and uncertainty. Although BC was ideologically dominant, it failed to extend much beyond students, and it never developed a mass following or organizational base. Such narrow political space as there was was not successfully filled by a nationally dominant opposition organization, and Buthelezi presumed that he and Inkatha could fill that role. Moreover, the divisions among ideological positions within the Black opposition were less pronounced, and none had sparked major conflict or violence. For example,

Albert Luthuli, a prominent Zulu chief and the last ANC president before the organization was banned, accorded the ANC and Inkatha equal political respect, and Buthelezi and Mandela were both frequent visitors in his home.[75]

Until the end of the 1970s Buthelezi maintained ties to the external mission of the ANC. After a meeting between Buthelezi and Tambo in London in 1979, however, the ANC broke definitively and publicly with Inkatha, denouncing its participation in the homeland system. There were other matters the two organizations could not agree on: Inkatha claimed to condemn the use of violence, while the ANC had endorsed "armed struggle" in 1961. The ANC supported uprisings, unrest, and radical opposition to the system; Inkatha supported only peaceful negotiations to end apartheid, opposing any type of unruliness, protest, boycotts, or strikes. After 1979 the ANC made several public statements regarding its opposition to Inkatha, ending a period of confusion for activists in South Africa who opposed Buthelezi's place within the homeland structure but supported his antiapartheid, pro-ANC rhetoric and his aspirations for Black liberation. After the break it became increasingly difficult for Buthelezi to continue to articulate a Charterist ideological position or to claim for Inkatha the ANC tradition.

It did not become impossible, however, until the foundation of the United Democratic Front in 1983. The UDF retrieved a Charterist heritage and developed a strong mass base, organizing through existing civic and other organizations, initially around the issue of the Tricameral Parliament. In Natal after 1985 the UDF represented itself as a clear ideological alternative to Inkatha, where the ideological space that each occupied was partly circumscribed by, and reactive to, the other. The UDF finally robbed Inkatha of its ability to project itself nationally as a Black liberation organization in the Charterist tradition by clearly dominating that space itself, thus narrowing Inkatha's ideological options.

Inkatha was thus partially forced to retreat to an ideological position of ethnic chauvinism by a dominant oppositional culture that rejected the political party of a homeland government. Inkatha had in fact avoided mobilizing an ethnic Zulu identity for political purposes until its power base in Natal was threatened by the UDF after 1983. Inkatha itself, for example, was first named Inkatha yaKwaZulu but was almost immediately renamed the Inkatha National Cultural Liberation Organization, to avoid an exclusive reference to Zulus or to KwaZulu.

After 1983, however, Inkatha used a two-pronged strategy to consolidate its homeland base. First, it mobilized Zulu ethnic identity, partly through allusions to tradition and heritage, to reinforce the legitimacy of the tribal hierarchical structure through which it exercised control. Chiefs were able to wield political control in KwaZulu because people continued to accord them power. And part of the reason people continued to accord them power was that the chiefs and the system within which they operated were successfully legitimated in the dominant discourse. Inkatha's second prong, and a second reason that the people continued to accord power to the chiefs, was that the chiefs provided material benefits. By dispensing patronage through them, Inkatha propped up the chiefs, and the chiefs in turn propped up Inkatha.

Buthelezi also began in the 1980s to forge an alliance with a White elite. In 1980 Buthelezi initiated a commission to study the viability of uniting KwaZulu and Natal into a single economic unit. The Buthelezi Commission involved many prominent academics and White businessmen in Natal. Many of the same protagonists joined forces again to work on the Kwa-Natal Indaba proposals in 1986. The Indaba negotiated a plan to unite KwaZulu and Natal into a single political unit. Natal would be governed by a consociational system in which members of each race would have representatives at provincial level and veto power. Consensus would be the decision-making rule.[76]

Although the Indaba proposals were never implemented, they generated important debate and were fairly influential in White political circles in the 1980s, particularly in Natal. The Buthelezi Commission and the Indaba cemented strong alliances between Natal's White business interests, ostensibly liberal Progressive Federal Party (PFP) politicians, and Inkatha. The Indaba was also perceived as a moderate and potentially viable solution by other liberal White South Africans and international observers in the 1980s. Buthelezi was able to portray himself as a moderate Black alternative to the ANC and UDF. The Indaba talks cast him as reasonable, committed to capitalism, and amenable to entrenching White power long into the future. He was received by President Reagan in the United States and by Prime Minister Thatcher in Great Britain, primarily on the basis of the profile and reputation afforded by the Indaba accords.

Whereas it was possible as late as 1979 to hold allegiance to both Inkatha and the ANC, mainly by adhering to a broadly antiapartheid, Black liberationist ideological position, during the 1980s the UDF denied a place for Inkatha within the Charterist fold. Inkatha's ideological space was partially self-defined, but in some sense the party was also forced to mobilize an oppositional ethnic identity against the more broadly encompassing Black national identity of the UDF. In conventional political terms, Inkatha was conservative and the UDF was radical. The UDF was nonracial, antiethnic, and noncollaborationist. Inkatha was the political party of an ethnic homeland government, paid, and at least partially controlled, by Pretoria. The ideological stance of the two organizations was consolidated and entrenched in the context of competition for dominance in the same political space.

Inkatha portrayed itself as the moderate Black alternative to the radicalism of the UDF in the 1980s. In this way it situated itself within both Black and White political paradigms. Inkatha's position as the government of an ethnic homeland was embedded in apartheid ideology. Its apparent position as a moderate Black political alternative opened the space for dialogue between Inkatha and the White liberal opposition. And finally, its retrieval of certain aspects of dominant opposition ideologies placed it within the circles of Black politics. It was in this latter circle that it was least successful, however, as noncollaboration emerged to dominate the ideology of extraparliamentary opposition.

Resonance

To what extent, and how, did Zulus respond to the multiple forces at work to shape their political identities during the 1980s? Did Zuluness become a politically salient identity for most Zulus? Did Zuluness become a more overtly political identity for Inkatha supporters than it was for non-Inkatha supporters? Did Zulus in general display attitudes and characteristics not displayed by other Africans? Did identities change over time?

In a longitudinal study of intergroup relations conducted between 1972 and 1982, intergroup rankings—how members of one group ranked other groups—remained fairly consistent. Zulus generally displayed a narrower range of difference between in-group evaluations and out-group evaluations than Sothos and Afrikaners. Although all groups evaluated themselves highest, Zulus perceived less difference between themselves and others than did most other groups. Zulus placed English-speaking Whites, who represent the second-largest group in Natal after the Zulus, closest to themselves on a distance scale, and Afrikaners and Coloureds, of which there are few in Natal, furthest away. Sothos and Indians occupied a middle position.[77]

One small survey of women in Nqutu, a rural village in KwaZulu Natal, provides a sense of the political identities of rural women. In 1978, one percent of the respondents said that it was Inkatha's role to help all races, 1.5 percent indicated that it should help all Zulus, and 14 percent said that it should help all Blacks. For this group at least, which might be expected to hold a stronger ethnic identity (because they are permanent inhabitants of an ethnic homeland, have least access to other population groups and education, and are most tied into a "traditional" Zulu way of life), Blackness appeared to be more politically dominant than Zuluness in the late 1970s.[78]

A 1980 survey of Zulu Inkatha supporters in KwaMashu demonstrated a similar lack of Zulu ethnocentrism. Forty-one percent of the respondents claimed

Inkatha membership. Sixty percent of Inkatha supporters believed that the major issue facing Inkatha was enhancement of Black unity. Eighteen percent thought that it was reduction of unemployment, and 11 percent thought that it was abolition of discrimination. In 1980 nearly three-quarters of Inkatha respondents said that it was Inkatha's role to help all races rather than "all Blacks" or "all Zulus."[79] Moreover, opinion polls from the late 1970s and early 1980s indicated substantial support for Inkatha outside KwaZulu Natal, and among non-Zulu speakers.[80] According to a 1977 survey, 23 percent of Xhosas supported Buthelezi, and 25 percent supported the ANC.[81] These strands suggest that Inkatha was not necessarily, and certainly not exclusively, tied to Zulu identity in the minds of many South Africans in the late 1970s and early 1980s.

In this period the attitudes of Zulus and non-Zulus tended to converge more than they diverged. In a question intended to elicit information about levels of dissatisfaction, respondents were asked about their "anger and impatience with life in South Africa today." In 1977 there was no difference between Zulu and non-Zulu responses: 39 percent of both groups were angry and impatient. By 1981, fifty-three percent of Zulu men and 56 percent of all other Black men were angry and impatient. Education was a much better attitudinal indicator for this question: in 1977, forty-five percent of those who were better educated from both groups were angry and impatient, and by 1981 this number had leaped to 68 percent. In 1982, forty-nine percent of (mostly Zulu) urban respondents in Kwa-Zulu Natal and 45 percent of (mostly non-Zulu) Witwatersrand respondents said it was "best for Black South Africans to be careful in politics and not get into trouble." People appeared to be slightly more conservative in rural KwaZulu, generally less so in the Witwatersrand, and least conservative in the urban areas of Natal. For example, 21 percent of rural KwaZulu respondents, 17 percent of Witwatersrand respondents, but only 9 percent of urban Natal respondents said that "Blacks will be too frightened by the army/police to act" if the government did not introduce changes in the coming ten years. The greatest difference was between Zulus living in urban and rural areas, with ethnically undefined Witwatersrand respondents taking a middle road between them.[82]

The same survey roughly measured support for the ANC in 1982, at a time when the organization was banned, by asking, "If the ANC were to come in secretly asking people to help it, what would happen?" Forty-eight percent of respondents in Natal said that most or many would help the ANC. Of those, 46 percent of rural respondents gave answers in those two categories, while 56 percent of urban youth and white-collar workers said most or many would help it.[83]

Other research, and Inkatha membership figures, demonstrate that most of rural KwaZulu supported Inkatha in this period. These results may indicate that approximately half of rural dwellers secretly supported the ANC, and only claimed to support Inkatha, or that they believed that their neighbors secretly supported the ANC. What is more likely, however, is that these results highlight the ambiguity of political identity in this period. In 1982 it was still possible to maintain allegiance to the long-exiled and by then ephemeral ANC, as well as to the more locally dominant and tangible Inkatha. One Inkatha-affiliated analyst similarly concluded that survey data from the late 1970s seemed to suggest that "Inkatha had managed successfully to establish some continuity with the ANC in the minds of ordinary Africans."[84]

As the decade progressed, however, people would be forced to make choices among political affiliations. Support for Inkatha became increasingly incompatible with trade union membership, for example. Buthelezi had relied heavily on a political alliance with business interests to raise his own political profile. He consistently opposed stay-aways and strikes, two strategies favored by both unions and the UDF. Inkatha staked out its opposition to boycotts partly in an effort to assert its authority over urban Zulus. One Inkatha leader stated publicly that a planned boycott would be perceived as a direct challenge to Buthelezi. Inkatha's ultimate inability to undermine union stay-aways in both the Transvaal and Natal in 1985 "signalled a critical weakening of Inkatha influence amongst organized workers. . . . Forced to choose between loyalty for Inkatha and their unions, many supported the stayaway."[85] The implication is that, on this occasion at least, class identity trumped ethnic identity.

As parallel political organizations emerged to contest Inkatha's control of political space, people perceived an increasingly divided political arena. One survey conducted in Lamontville, Klaarwater, and Chesterville in 1983 showed that 84 percent believed that the local civic association, JORAC, was helping the community. Only 20 percent believed that Inkatha helped, and only 18 percent believed that the officially elected, Inkatha-aligned, community council assisted the community. One survey undertaken in three townships under threat of incorporation in 1984 shows that 89 percent, 87 percent, and 79 percent of the residents, respectively, opposed incorporation into KwaZulu.[86]

Surveys suggest that political differences between some Zulus in Natal and Africans in other parts of the country became manifest after 1983. Fifty-four percent of respondents to a 1984 survey in Durban preferred Inkatha or Buthelezi, while 34 percent chose either the UDF, the ANC, or Mandela. In the Witwatersrand and Port Elizabeth, on the other hand, only 14 percent chose Inkatha, while 38 percent chose the liberation triumvirate.[87] Although the extent of support for the UDF is roughly constant, Inkatha was clearly available as a real political alternative only in Natal after 1984. When juxtaposed with the change in Inkatha discourse after 1983, this result suggests that Inkatha began to be more closely identified with an exclusive Zulu identity, and became less readily available to non-Zulus, after 1983. Nevertheless, the reverse was not also true. Inkatha did not manage to gain significant support from Zulus outside of Natal. In the Witwatersrand, 29 percent of Zulus and 27 percent of non-Zulus supported the ANC in 1986.[88]

By 1986 some Zulus in Natal appeared to identify somewhat more ethnically than they had before, and more ethnically than other groups in South Africa. In a survey of African women conducted in four areas—Durban, Pretoria, Soweto, and the Eastern Cape—55 percent of the Durban respondents, who are more than 90 percent Zulu, identified themselves primarily with relation to their ethnic group. Thirty-four percent said they were "first of all" Black, and only 11 percent identified primarily as South African. In Soweto, which is ethnically mixed, only 20 percent identified ethnically, while 46 percent identified as South African. In the Eastern Cape, which is primarily Xhosa, 19 percent identified ethnically and 43 percent identified as Black. In sum, in 1986 most Africans in Soweto claimed a South African identity, most in the Eastern Cape claimed a Black identity, and most in Natal claimed a Zulu identity. When asked, "To which of these regional groups do you feel you belong?" more than a quarter of the Durban respondents gave their homeland as a response and only 16 percent named South Africa.[89]

There are no survey data that address the relation between UDF and Inkatha affiliation and identity explicitly. The same people were not asked, "Do you support Inkatha or the ANC?" and "Would you say you were first of all Black, Zulu, or South African?" Although 34 percent of Zulus supported the UDF, ANC, or Mandela, and 34 percent identified primarily as Black, we do not know the extent to which respondents in these two groups overlapped. Data cannot be used to accurately infer the effect of political affiliation on identity in urban areas in the 1980s. Evidence from rural and urban areas provides better comparative data because we do know that rural dwellers overwhelmingly supported Inkatha. Unfortunately, intervening demographic variables affect the strength of these results. Whether rural dwellers differ from urban dwellers because they are Inkatha members or because they live in rural areas and are thus enmeshed in a separate social, political, and economic cosmology is unclear.

We do know, however, that rural dwellers appear to have changed between the beginning and the end of the 1980s, and that political differences between rural and urban dwellers appear to have grown more pronounced. Rural Zulus were more likely to perceive political identity in terms of their ethnic group in the second half of the 1980s. In a 1987 survey several different groups were asked the question, "If all Black people voted in South Africa, Zulus would be small in number and other groups might have more power in government. Would people like you feel weak and insecure or do you agree that blacks are all one people, it would not matter at all?" Seventy-nine percent of Zulus in Soweto responded that Blacks are all one people. Fifty percent of rural Zulus replied that Zulus would be weak and insecure, and an even greater 64 percent of migrant workers claimed that Zulus would be weak and insecure.[90] This evidence suggests that ethnic identification was correlated not with rural "traditional" versus urban "modern" lifestyle, because urban hostel dwellers were closer to rural inhabitants than to their urban neighbors, but rather with affiliation to Inkatha. By the second half of the 1980s a majority of both rural dwellers and migrant workers supported Inkatha. Survey data show that affiliation with Inkatha or the UDF represented the primary dividing cleavage of Zulu politics in the 1980s, and that this cleavage was partly iterated in ethnic terms.

For both Inkatha and UDF supporters, Zulu identity had political resonance, and a particular political significance, in the 1980s. Political identity was explicitly tied to ethnicity for Inkatha members, and UDF affiliation included the categorical rejection of ethnicity. Initially constrained by the ideological dominance of Charterism and the BCM, Buthelezi placed Inkatha in the mainstream oppositional tradition. In the highly circumscribed realm of ideological possibility defined by Black opposition in South Africa, ethnicity was not available as a source of political identification in the 1970s. Inkatha retreated to an ethnic nationalist base in particular after its exclusion from the liberation movement. The mobilization of ethnic identity seems additionally to have been suggested by the nature of the party's institutional power base, as the government of an ethnic homeland, and by its organizational structure, mainly through the traditional Zulu hierarchy of chiefs and headmen. Inkatha political entrepreneurs settled on the mobilization of ethnic identity in response to incentives and worldviews generated by available ideology and the organizational base of the party, as well as by the referents of political institutions.

Although Inkatha aimed to unite all Zulus behind a common ethnic identity, it was successful only among a stable rural majority and a shifting urban minority. Ethnic political identity resonated primarily among those who continued to be ethnically organized in this manner, namely rural inhabitants of KwaZulu and recent migrants to the city whose primary ties remained to the rural areas and who were rejected by established urban dwellers. Ethnic political identity failed to take root among those mainly permanent urban dwellers who had already absorbed the Charterist tradition, were predisposed against Inkatha because of differences on such issues as incorporation into the homeland and radicalism, and were organized through grassroots networks inspired by popular protest. Ethnic identity was more politically salient among those who retained primary connections to a rural area and social system, were not politicized in the Charterist tradition, and who competed against township dwellers for access to resources. Whether Zulu identity resonated, and among whom, depended on organization, available ideology, and material conditions.

3 Of Kings and Chiefs

The Politics of Zulu Identity After 1990

Almost every factor that might reasonably be expected to play a role in the construction of political identity among Zulus was different at the beginning of the 1990s than it had been a decade earlier. The widespread violence that characterized the political landscape of Natal in the second half of the 1980s had reverberating repercussions for material conditions, social and political organization, and the permeability of the boundaries of identity. The war in Natal also took place within the larger context of dramatic political change and power realignments on the national and regional stages. The political institutions and ideological alignments that bound the parameters of politics in the 1980s were significantly reconfigured by the events and actors that shaped South Africa's democratic transition after 1990. The relative positions and strengths of the parties primarily involved in the mediation of Zulu political identity—the UDF, the ANC, and Inkatha—were capsized.

Political Institutions

In February 1990 the NP government unbanned the ANC, the PAC, and the South African Communist Party (SACP) and released Nelson Mandela from prison, dramatically changing the landscape of South African opposition politics and, concomitantly, the role and fortunes of Inkatha. As a result of explicitly Charterist and pro-ANC UDF activism in the 1980s, the ANC rose to a level of political prominence within South Africa that it had not enjoyed since before it was banned in 1960. As recently as 1980 the historical role and tradition of the ANC was unknown to many Black South Africans, and certainly to a majority of Whites.[1] Had the democratic transition occurred a decade earlier, Inkatha would probably have occupied a much more central negotiating position. By the time the ANC was unbanned in 1990, however, it had moved to center stage, with overwhelming international acclaim and widespread support among Black South Africans.[2]

The sudden rise of the ANC's national and international profile sidelined Inkatha in South African politics after 1990. Most immediately, it appeared to cut the party out of the transition process. During the 1980s Buthelezi and others in Natal had envisioned the KwaNatal Indaba as the conceptual and organizational base of an eventual political transition. First Natal would be jointly governed by Blacks and Whites in a consociational arrangement, and then the system could be adapted for use in the rest of South Africa. Almost as soon as de Klerk came to power in August

1989, however, he began to court the still-imprisoned Mandela. By setting the stage to negotiate a transition from apartheid with representatives of the liberation movement, rather than with the internal, conservative Black leadership represented by Buthelezi, the government severely undercut the previous political prominence of the Indaba, of Inkatha, and of Buthelezi himself.

Negotiations between the ANC and the NP began almost as soon as Mandela was released. On February 16 the ANC sent a delegation from Harare to discuss talks about talks. The ANC established a steering committee to arrange the details of negotiations. In May the two sides held their first full-scale bilateral meeting, emerging with the Groote Schuur Minute, which committed the government to work out the modalities of releasing political prisoners, to ensure normal and free political activity, and to lift the state of emergency that had been in place since 1986. The ANC refused to end the armed struggle but agreed to suspend armed action while negotiations continued. In August the sides met again and concluded the Pretoria Minute, further clarifying the structures of transition. By the end of the year, though, relations between the two sides were strained by the violence that wracked the country. Meetings in December were cold and made little progress.

In June 1991 Inkatha's legitimacy was seriously undermined by revelations that came to be known as Inkathagate. The *Weekly Mail* newspaper revealed that the South African government had funneled money to Inkatha to help the organization pay for two mass rallies held in late 1989 and early 1990. The NP's intention was to demonstrate that Inkatha, a conservative Black party that had condemned sanctions, enjoyed considerable popular support among Black South Africans.[3] The second rally sparked violence that left 50 dead, 150 wounded, and 6,000 homeless in five days. Evidence of IFP collusion with the government, including significant government support for Inkatha in its war with the UDF, undermined Inkatha's claim to independent and oppositional political status. Inkathagate handed the ANC a serious moral and political advantage in terms of its claims to legitimately represent the voice of the people.

Inkathagate also undermined the government as a credible negotiating partner.[4] De Klerk called an emergency meeting to reshuffle his cabinet ministers. In what amounted to a concession to the ANC, the controversial defense minister Magnus Malan and minister of law and order Adriaan Vlok were removed from their positions. In September 1991 the ANC and IFP signed a National Peace Accord to end violence.

It was not until December 1991, almost two years after informal negotiations began, that Inkatha was included in the transition process. The Congress for a

Democratic South Africa (CODESA), which included twenty political parties and homeland governments, met in December for the first time. It was set up to operate on a decision-making rule of "sufficient consensus." In practice, sufficient consensus meant that the ANC and the NP agreed. Many of the issues that were to be discussed at CODESA had already been agreed to in bilateral talks between the government and the ANC.

The apparent prior arrangement between the ANC and NP angered other parties to the talks. The Pan Africanist Congress walked out. The IFP also threatened to boycott unless both the KwaZulu government, represented by the king, and the IFP, represented by Buthelezi, were allowed places at the table. Buthelezi, meanwhile, abandoned his own long-standing claim to represent the Zulu people because the IFP sought to present itself as a national political party on a par with the ANC. At the same time, the IFP demanded that the Zulu people had a right to representation through the Zulu king, at that time a political pawn of Buthelezi himself. It became necessary for Buthelezi to explicitly deny that the IFP represented Zulus in order to claim an independent base that would guarantee separate political roles for him in his dual capacities as IFP leader and traditional adviser to the king.

Multilateral talks were short-lived, ending when CODESA II stalled in May 1992. By then the ANC had grown impatient with the slow pace of change. The NP had won an overwhelming mandate from White voters to continue negotiations in the March 1992 referendum and had achieved some international recognition. This bolstered the government's confidence to move slowly and control the process. The ANC called for mass action in an attempt to force the pace. On the second day of the mass action campaign, in June 1992, two hundred Inkatha supporters rampaged through the ANC-dominated township of Boipatong, near Johannesburg, and killed forty-nine people. Mandela blamed the government for colluding with the IFP and for failing to enforce law and order, and he cut off talks.

Approximately one million people responded to the ANC's call for a nationwide stay-away on August 3. A few days later the ANC staged a march on the Ciskei city of Bisho. The homeland military fired into the crowd, killing twenty-eight and leaving two hundred injured. This disaster, which was ultimately the result of poor judgment and brinksmanship on the part of the ANC, the NP, and the homeland government, drove the NP and ANC back to the negotiating table, this time without other parties.

In September the ANC and NP agreed to a Record of Understanding that would guide the remainder of the transition process. Among other things, the Record banned the use of traditional weapons (used by IFP followers) and provided that hostels (IFP strongholds in the Transvaal) would be fenced. The IFP predictably rejected the terms of the understanding. The NP and ANC continued to meet in working groups throughout that year and had two more major meetings in January and February 1993. In February the two sides converged on an agreement for the transition. On April 1 the Multiparty Negotiating Process (MPNP), this time including twenty-three parties, was convened to broaden the scope of agreement, and in November 1993 the parties concluded a democratization pact.

The IFP responded by entering into an alliance with other groups, such as the Afrikaner nationalist Conservative Party and some homeland leaders, that opposed the moderate center emerging from NP-ANC talks to dominate the transition. The Concerned South Africans Group (COSAG) was united primarily by a common perception that it had been marginalized in the transition process. In October 1993 the loose partnership of COSAG was converted into a formal negotiating coalition called the Freedom Alliance (FA). The FA, along with some other minor parties, pledged to boycott elections, but the NP and ANC, both of which by then had a stake in a successful transition, ultimately managed to involve all major players, including the IFP, in the democratic process.[5]

In an election fraught with irregularities and fraud, the IFP won 50.3 percent of the provincial vote in KwaZulu Natal. The narrow majority gave the party forty-one of the eighty-one seats in the provincial parliament. The ANC came second with 32.2 percent of the vote and twenty-six seats, while the NP won 11.2 percent and nine seats. Nationally, the IFP emerged as the third-strongest party, after the ANC and the NP, with 10.5 percent of the vote and forty-three out of four hundred seats in the National Assembly. Ninety percent of IFP votes came from KwaZulu Natal, however, firmly establishing it as a regionally based party. Both the ANC and the NP, conversely, demonstrated that they enjoyed a national support base. Additionally, the IFP's primary opponent, the ANC, won 62.6 percent of the national vote, trouncing the IFP in the national arena it had tried so long to break into.

The 1993 interim constitution, which was negotiated between the government and the ANC and expired in 1999, was adopted by the all-White South African parliament as its last act in December 1993. The constitution mandated a government of national unity (GNU) in which every party that held twenty seats in the National Assembly was entitled to cabinet portfolios in proportion to the number of seats it held. After the April 1994 election, this translated into a twenty-seven-member cabinet in which there were eighteen ANC members, six from the NP, and three from the IFP. Any party that won at least eighty seats in parliament—or the two largest parties if none reached that benchmark—was also entitled to designate an executive deputy president. This rule, which resulted in the appointment of F. W. de Klerk from the NP and Thabo Mbeki from the ANC, extended the principle of inclusion through the executive branch.

In 1995 the Constitutional Assembly, composed of members of all the parties in proportion to the number of votes they won in election, began to negotiate a permanent constitution. Under the terms of the final constitution, there is no provision for power sharing after 1999, although the ANC has said it would continue to invite other parties to join the cabinet in an effort to promote unity. After it became clear that the NP would no longer have a guaranteed role in government, the party withdrew from the so-called government of national unity to better assume an oppositional role in anticipation of elections in 1999.

Constitutional negotiators replaced the old system of single-member, first-past-the-post constituencies with a lower house based on list-system proportional representation (PR), with half of the four hundred members elected at large and the other half from party lists in each of the nine new provinces. The ninety-member senate has ten members from each region nominated by the parties represented in the provincial legislature and elected on the basis of list-system PR. South Africa's choice of the list system attenuates the representative function of parliament because members of Parliament (MPs) have no constituent base.

South Africa's interim and final constitutions are notable also because they include a rule that any MP who ceases to be a member of his or her party will also lose his or her seat and will be replaced by someone else from the party list. The nondefection clause makes for an extremely strong parliamentary whip system, in which party leaders can essentially guarantee a solid bloc of votes. This feature undermines the capacity of backbenchers to act as an opposition to party leaders and diminishes their leverage in party debates.

The postapartheid political system has a quasi-federal structure. South Africa is divided into nine provinces, each of which has its own provincial government, run by a provincial parliament, and a premier, chosen by the party that wins provincial elections. The first premier of KwaZulu Natal was provincial IFP leader Frank Mdlalose. The interim constitution devolved a still contested number of powers to the provincial level. The ANC pushed for centralization of many of those powers, such as education and the remuneration of chiefs, already established as provincial in the interim constitution, and the IFP, whose power base is located at the provincial level, walked out of the constitutional assembly. The final constitution, ultimately adopted without IFP participation, returned many of the powers previously vested in the provinces to the central government.[6]

The KwaZulu homeland government continued to operate throughout the transition period and to govern the territory of KwaZulu, which ceased to be legally separate from Natal after 1994, into the posttransition era. Legislation passed in 1990 established the Joint Services Boards, including nominated representatives of the South African government and the KwaZulu government, to oversee the provision of services on a regional basis.[7] KwaZulu government headquarters, in three huge and modern office buildings in the remote village of Ulundi, are intact in the postapartheid era, filled with civil servants more or less engaged in the business of running the affairs of rural KwaZulu. These are, for the most part, the same civil servants who ran KwaZulu as a homeland, and very little appears to have changed. The ANC opposition in the provincial parliament has repeatedly lambasted the IFP for dragging its heels, failing to plan and implement development projects, and allowing KwaZulu Natal to lag far behind the other nine provinces in terms of planning development and building infrastructure.[8]

Mobilizing Discourse

The discourse that Inkatha uses to define its own identity and its constituent base has become more ambiguous since the beginning of the transition period. Whereas it retreated to an ethnic platform in the 1980s, partly under UDF attack and partly because of its homeland power base, the transition opened the space for Inkatha to partially reinvent itself.

As the terms of South Africa's postapartheid political system were negotiated, it became clear that if nothing else, the "new South Africa" would not include ethnic homelands. Inkatha's access to institutionalized power would disappear unless it could govern something else. As a party with strong regional support and little chance of national dominance, the IFP is vehemently federalist. Although support for federalism is not a new position for Inkatha—the KwaNatal Indaba proposals were essentially federalist—federalism has become more central to the IFP platform in the postapartheid era. The party's more scientific arguments revolve around the proper exercise of power. IFP member of provincial Parliament (MPP) Farouk Cassim has warned, "If power then is concentrated in the center, and everyone begins to become restless, central government will respond in the only way it knows. To crush. It's a given fact that if you put a big pair of boots onto someone's feet, they'll use that to walk all over you. . . . Power is a corrosive thing and it should never be given to anyone in large measure. . . . As Lord Acton says, power corrupts, absolute power corrupts absolutely. . . . Power must be divided." Cassim's colleague Ziba Jiyane expressed similar sentiments: "After liberation, to ensure that there's freedom, there has to be plurality, and by which we understand different centers of power that check each other but also by which we understand cultural expressions being expressed as diversity that also finds itself in the unity of the state as a whole. But diversity in terms of autonomy for regions."[9]

This line of argument devolves power—and responsibility for power checking—to, the provincial level. Within the structure of a federal system in which the IFP governs the province of KwaZulu Natal, the party has strong incentives to reinforce the place of the province as the primary level of government. Buthelezi has even threatened to withdraw from national politics altogether to focus his energies on governing KwaZulu Natal.[10] The IFP may have done more poorly than expected in local government elections in Gauteng because it urged its supporters to wait and vote in KwaZulu Natal elections held the following year.

The discourse of IFP leaders includes a strong element of provincialism. In their effort to assert such identity, the party is aided by recent historical contingencies. Eight of South Africa's nine provinces have newly drawn boundaries. Only Natal has retained its original territory, though it too has undergone spatial amendment as the KwaZulu homeland was reincorporated after twenty years of separation. As of 1997 KwaZulu Natal was the only province to draw up its own constitution, even though the national constitution allows provinces to do so. Buthelezi has retrieved a legacy of Zulu cooperation with other racial and ethnic groups to create a historical precedent for a single, unifying Kwa-Natal identity:

One of the greatest assets that we as a people possess is our complete lack of racism. King Shaka conquered to incorporate, he did not conquer to subjugate. From the very beginning of Zulu time all races were welcome in KwaZulu. Zulu history has even produced white Zulu amakhosi. We have never debarred any person from our society on the grounds of race, colour or creed. There are amongst us today members of every race group in the country. We are one people here rejoicing in the memory of King Shaka. We are not celebrating the memory of King Shaka as blacks only. The Kingdom of KwaZulu of the future will be a democratic kingdom in which the vote of every person regardless of race, colour or creed will be equal to every other vote. There will be no time in the future of the Kingdom of KwaZulu in which there will be blacks pitted against Whites, Indians, or Coloureds. We achieved our success at the polls not only because of black votes. We drew solid electoral support from Whites, Indians, and Coloureds because they saw the value that there is in our Zuluness as an integral part of the multi-racial society that KwaZulu-Natal in fact is.[11]

Provincial identity is also established through reference to outsiders. The people of KwaZulu Natal are drawn together through the construction of their common victimization. IFP political entrepreneurs weave multiple strands of antipathy into a tenuous unity. Historically, voters in Natal have supported the party that opposed the governing National Party. They understand their alienation from mainstream White South African politics in both ideological and ethnic terms. English and Zulus, who constitute the numerical majority in Natal but the minority elsewhere in South Africa, were united by a common non-Afrikaner identity in an era when central government was dominated by the Afrikaner National Party. Peter Smith, an IFP MP, described the phenomenon:

If you talk to Whites or Blacks you've got your Cinderella province history. We're the Cinderella province. We got screwed because, of the four provinces, we had the fewest number of Whites and the fewest number of NP supporters. So the national budget was allocated on the basis of how many Nationalist-supporting Whites there were in the province. On that basis we got the lowest budget in the country for the last forty or fifty years. So the whole notion of having your budget determined by Pretoria is anathema to everyone in the country—White, Black, or Coloured. Secession ideas all come from that sort of thing. Then you've got the whole history of central government interference in things like education. In fact the whole country had one National Christian Education system. But Natal had its own system and we didn't have anything to do with that. The whole issue of the kingdom. It's the only kingdom. The whole issue of the Indaba and the Buthelezi Commission. The IFP had a particular place here in the seventies and eighties.[12]

According to Arthur Konigkramer, a member of the Provincial Parliament and the publisher of the Inkatha newspaper *Ilanga lase Natal,* "We were punished . . . because we were English speaking [and] we had the Zulus, which were the biggest obstacle to the implementation of apartheid. So we were punished for two reasons. And . . . you can see in fact we were subsidizing, mainly Gauteng. And we still are. We were paying more taxes than we were receiving. So we were actually giving away money. We were not even getting our own taxes. I would suggest to you that that is still the case."

This history, retrieved to tell a story to unite a people, serves a dual purpose when extended into the present day. The IFP has substituted the ANC for the NP. The ANC, as the central government, is accused of playing the role formerly played by the NP; linking the ANC to the apartheid government is a delegitimizing tactic. David Ntombela, a warlord and IFP MPP, has complained: "We believe that we can't go for election if powers weren't given to the province. We want those powers to be on the people. Not the government on top telling the people what they must do. Because if we support that, it shows that it is the government of apartheid. The previous government, they used to tell the people you must carry *dompas,* you must carry a pass book. And also lots of rules were coming from central government, the apartheid government. And we really believe that if freedom is freedom, all those things must be gone."

The ANC, and Mandela himself, have contributed to the perception of victimization that pervades Natal's political elite. In response to a series of challenges and threats from Buthelezi, Mandela publicly stated in September 1995 that the central government could and would cut off Natal without a cent if the provincial leadership did not toe the line.[13] IFP leaders like Cassim repeated Mandela's threat for months, as evidence of the danger posed by central government to the province:

Now already, what the ANC is putting on the table is a clear indication that they want the power. Listening to what Mandela was saying, had this constitution not been in place and there was some other constitution, he would have turned the taps off. But not because this province deserved that treatment, but simply because it was a province that was out of line with the other provinces in not having put the ANC in power. . . . In other words, as fine a man as he is . . . if even he is inclined to think that way, and he's in the virtually unique position amongst African leaders, with his standing, for him to think like that, subliminally indicates that the dangers we have been talking about. . . . What happened here in South Africa happened because the Nats [National Party leaders] were able to lay their hands on the power and once they got the power they went berserk. And now another group gets their hands on the power and they do the same.

After the 1994 election the IFP provincial government renamed Natal the Kingdom of KwaZulu Natal. The naming further distinguishes the territory from other provinces and gives it a kind of organic, natural quality, as well as an apparent root in history and tradition. The actual historical basis for a kingdom is fragmentary and inconclusive. No Zulu kingdom ever governed the entire territory now demarcated as KwaZulu Natal. Nevertheless, the naming is a defiant act meant to suggest the possibility of a regional government that is not subordinate to central government. A kingdom has the possibility of national sovereign status in the way a province or state cannot. Taken along with other measures, such as drafting a provincial constitution, the renaming of the province suggests that the IFP's first commitment is not to a united South Africa. Although the kingdom is clearly tied to, and based in, a history and traditional structure of government that is particularly Zulu, the IFP has tried in part to uncouple the kingdom from any Zulu ethnic claims or attributes. According to Cassim, "If we were to take a referendum tomorrow, my safe bet is that 80 percent of the people would show allegiance to the king, would support the kingdom. And that's a very high percentage on any poll. Across the board. Whites, Indians, Zulus. They would say yes, the king is here, he has a very important role to play, and there's this whole chain and link. So there are all these things here that identify us as being somebody different." Peter Smith adds: "Zulu self-determination is inclusive of everybody who resides within the kingdom. So you can even talk of Zulu self-determination, freely embracing the constituents of the province. Which overlaps with the kind of regional self-determination that I would talk about as a federalist."

Despite some apparent effort to rewrite history to create a single Kwa-Natal identity, to demonize the central government in order to present a credible threat to the province, and to make a kingdom out of an arbitrarily drawn territory, the IFP's power base remains among rurally based Zulus. Appeals to Zulu autonomy and freedom occasionally pepper the more "rational" and "scientific" arguments that dominate the IFP's federalist discourse, and the unit of the Zulu nation sometimes replaces the provincial unit as the relevant vehicle for the devolution of power. It is not always clear whether power is meant to be devolved to the provincial government or to tribal leaders.

At Shaka Day celebrations held in Umlazi in 1995, Buthelezi spoke in one of his many distinct official capacities, as chairman of the KwaZulu Natal House of Traditional Leaders: "The Zulu nation face[s] misery and more suffering in its quest for autonomy. . . . Zulus will have to bear further sacrifices and difficulties to achieve the promised land of our freedom and prosperity. . . . I will never, ever divest myself of the heavy responsibility and often painful duty to lead our nation into the promised land."[14]

In the face of the defection of the king, the IFP claims that the king does not command a political following among the Zulu people, even as it refuses to relinquish a "special relationship" with the monarchy. Senzo Mfayela, an IFP member of Parliament, outlines the paradox: "But you know, for us, this whole war with the king is helping us a lot," Mfayela says. "Because all the time the people have been saying there's no Buthelezi, there's no IFP. They just milk from the king and if you remove the king from them they'll fall apart. Now, it's happened and there's still Buthelezi and there's still the IFP. And we're getting stronger. . . . You see, that's where most people make a serious mistake."[15] But according to Thomas Shabalala, member of the Provincial Parliament and the so-called warlord of Lindelani, "Even if there is that problem, those that believe Dr. Buthelezi, or are followers of Dr. Buthelezi, . . . all of us still respect our king. We are not separated from our king. Even Dr. Buthelezi himself still likes his king. But the ANC is coming in and trying to divide us from the king because we are IFP members. No, we still love our king and nobody will ever separate us from him. That is a fact and a promise."

The IFP argues that the Zulu king was mostly a figurehead who had unique status but was finally bound by the decisions of the chiefs. As Mfayela has said:

We are Zulus today because of King Shaka. And when King Shaka defeated other tribes, he did not destroy the other tribes. He left each tribe intact with its own chief who had all the powers. If Shaka can come today, defeat you with your tribe, he will leave you with all your powers and your people. The only thing that you have to do is to call your-self a Zulu, after that, and secondly, all you have to do is maybe every two years send a few cattle to him and every year you have to send about a hundred men to go and help him fight. That's all that you had to do. Other than that you ran your own area, you made your own laws, you killed people if you wanted to (laugh). So every tribe was left intact and independent. So Shaka did not make the tribes. He found the tribes there and he left them there. Basically because there was no way that Shaka could have been able to sup-press people like Mtetwas, Buthelezi, Mlenje, Ngcobo. He couldn't oppress them. They had to agree to be part of the kingdom in order for him to rule over them. So Shaka never had his own people. He got people through their own chiefs.

Which is of course precisely the way that the IFP "gets people" today. Mfayela describes the relationship between the king and the chiefs in a way that coincides almost perfectly with the current relation between the IFP and the chiefs.

To further strengthen the role of the chiefs, the IFP uses the language of tradi-tion, heritage, and inviolability. The chiefs are inherent to African politics, or-ganic to the Zulu nation. "Because the real mission," according to Arthur Konig-kramer, "is to destroy the amakhosi. And that is not possible. It's got nothing to do with what the IFP believes or doesn't believe in. It is just not possible. You cannot destroy them. That's thousands of years old. It just doesn't go away. And if you think that you can manipulate it by buying the chiefs off, you're making a big mistake. Because again, the chiefs are the people. And if you buy a man off, the people will soon get to know, and the chief will be removed."

Whereas the IFP presumes to "respect" and uniquely understand the age-old institution of chiefs and headmen, Konigkramer retrieves a colonial history of external domination over a traditional order and places the ANC government in a long line of "outsiders" who have tried to manipulate the chieftanship for their own purposes: "You see, the ANC is doing exactly what the Nats did and what all the colonialists did. Exactly the same. They are in fact a new set of colonialists. The first thing you do when you want to manipulate Black people is you want to manipulate the chiefs. The amakhosi. The British did it. The Afrikaners did it. The Nats did it. And now the ANC's doing it."

Nevertheless, it has become increasingly less relevant and more difficult for Buthelezi and the IFP to mobilize ethnic Zulu sentiment for political purposes. It is less relevant because South Africa's political system is no longer organized on an ethnic basis and the IFP, as a provincial government, has a greater incentive to consolidate the entire territory it dominates by reaching beyond its ethnic base. It is more difficult because elections have demonstrated that the ANC commands the allegiance of roughly 50 percent of the Zulus in KwaZulu Natal, and the ANC has effectively challenged the IFP's use of traditional symbols and structures to mobilize an ethnic support base.

Since 1990 the ANC has also begun to engage in Zulu politics, competing with the IFP to represent Zuluness and retrieving its own version of Zulu history and meaning. This represents a decisive shift from UDF discourse in the 1980s, which was antiethnic, and in particular anti-Zulu. It was the UDF position in the 1980s, and not ANC ambiguity in the 1990s, however, that represents the exception in this century. The ANC has a long history of political engagement in Natal, which has often included working with and through traditional leaders and hierarchies.[16] It is this history that the ANC has been at pains to emphasize since 1990.

In 1991 and 1992 one major point of contention between the ANC and the IFP was over the IFP's claim that its members had a right to carry "traditional weapons"—including, paradoxically, clubs, homemade maces, baseball bats, and guns—to political rallies. Because the NP government appeared unwilling to restrict the IFP, ANC provincial leaders finally took matters into their own hands, as ANC MPP Sibusiso Ndebele recalls:

Until about 1992 the issue of traditional weapons was a big issue here, because the government of de Klerk said that Zulus were allowed to carry their traditional weapons. And we were trying to do everything, going to the police, to de Klerk, to Goldstone, whomever, to get them to make it illegal to carry traditional weapons. We were saying, "But we are also Zulus and we are not carrying traditional weapons." Finally I made a decision and it caused quite a stir within the ANC even. I said, "We are also Zulus and so we also have the right to carry our own traditional weapons." And I said that to the people, because, you know, we don't have the right to tell any Zulu not to carry those weapons. . . . It was at Inanda. There were about sixty or seventy thousand people there, and they were carrying anything that could vaguely be called a traditional weapon. They had spears, clubs, everything. It made quite a stir. . . . And we were using the same slogans about Zuluness and about the king, and Shaka. We were using the same slogans.

Other ANC strategies were designed to acknowledge Zuluness and to link it historically to the ANC, Ndebele said, as well as to defuse its politically separatist dimension:

Then we had the Sonke festival. Sonke means "all of us," and the slogan of the festival was many cultures, one people. It was a response to ethnic mobilization. It was in October 1993. Nineteen ninety-three is eighty years from 1913, when King Mtimizwe, the king of the Zulus then and the grandfather of the present king, was made the first honorary president of the ANC. So we used the symbolism of the king, and we also used many other symbolisms. One hundred years since the arrival of Gandhi, fifty years since the start of the ANC Youth League, twenty years after the Durban worker's strikes, which led to the legalization of the trade unions. And we invited all the kings of southern Africa. From the Eastern Cape, the Transkei, the Lesotho king, the Swazi king, from KwaNdebele in the Northern Transvaal.

Soon after the April 1994 election, rumors began to circulate that the relationship between Buthelezi and the Zulu king was souring. King Zwelithini had allegedly invited Mandela to Shaka Day celebrations in September 1994. When Buthelezi found out, he insisted that the invitation be rescinded, and the king then tried, unsuccessfully, to cancel the event. Buthelezi denied rumors of a split, but the rift was fully exposed when he stormed into a studio and attacked the king's spokesman, Sifiso Zulu, with a knife, on national television. This stunning encounter was broadcast repeatedly in South Africa.

The ANC began to make overtures toward the king at least as early as 1992. "And of course we invited the Zulu king" to the Sonke festival, Ndebele said. "He did not attend because he was blocked by Buthelezi. But importantly, two of his daughters attended, demonstrating that the alliance was building even then between the king and the ANC." Newspaper reports alleged that the king was motivated in part to change his political allegiance by a promise of significant remuneration from the ANC. Such allegations are probably true, but because the king's salary and allowance had been controlled by the KwaZulu government and Inkatha, the ANC probably also offered the king greater independence and the opportunity to slip the noose of Buthelezi's control. According to Ndebele, "The IFP had the king. And that's why now in fact they want to risk everything because they have lost the king. And they are not going to have him anymore. With us, it's not going to help us to have the king as a member of the ANC or whatever. . . . The king has been there, the IFP there," next to the king, as he demonstrated with his hands, "and the ANC has been there," far away. "Now the king moves away from you. If he moves away from you, to the center, he is moving toward the ANC, but he is not moving to the ANC. He is moving to the center. And that's what's happening."

It is still unclear, however, what political role the king has to play in KwaZulu Natal. Provincial ANC leaders evidently believe that the king represents an important ethnic asset for them and that the allegiances of those Zulus whose politics are ethnically mediated will be divided by the split between the king and the IFP. "So going all out to these areas now is to show that there is an alternative," Ndebele asserts. "And we are becoming more and more that alternative. The major thing, of course, was the switch of the king. That's why the rally yesterday was so important. Because up to now the king had not called a rally on his own to actually demonstrate who's got support. The IFP had a rally at Umlazi, three thousand people. . . . The king has got a rally there. It's ten to fifteen thousand people. At least the papers say that. And the IFP had another one at Taylor's Halt, and another one on Saturday at Empangeni. The king tops ten thousand, and Buthelezi comes up with something less than three thousand people."

The structure of the Zulu ethnic hierarchy has been torn apart by the IFP and the ANC as they vie for provincial dominance. The king is allied to the ANC, and the chiefs mostly remain loyal to the IFP. The ANC and IFP have begun to articulate conflicting histories of the structure of traditional Zulu government. The IFP focuses on the preeminence of the chiefs as the ultimate repository of ethnic power. The ANC's historical precedent conversely retrieves a strong Zulu king with authority over his chiefs. In May 1995 Prince Sifiso Zulu delivered a speech at the University of Natal entitled "The Role of the Zulu King":

The role of King Shaka was to found the Zulu nation. He formed a strong Zulu Army, became Commander in Chief thereof, and fought to incorporate all peoples into one single army and state. King Shaka developed the Zulu nation from a clan into a strong political grouping whose composition, according to Professor Mazisi Kunene, was inter-family and international. . . . In effect Shaka put an end to the existence of mini-kingdoms and formed one strong kingdom where equality was the cornerstone of social order. Supreme political authority rested with the King. Supreme judicial authority rested with the King. The King had authority to recognise and depose the Chiefs of the nation through whom he exercised authority over the nation. Though the Zulu Kingdom was not an authoritarian state, the Zulu King was not a constitutional monarch.[17]

The ANC combines elevation of the king with the delegitimation of the chiefs. Whereas IFP leaders focus on the organic qualities of the chiefs, ANC leaders stress the transient and tenuous history of the institution of chiefs, arguing that the chiefs who today govern rural Natal are not hereditary leaders but are rather descended of chiefs installed by the illegitimate colonial and apartheid systems. The ANC portrays the current set of chiefs as the product of recent political maneuvering, not timeless lines of heredity. Ndebele observes:

Then you strengthen the chiefs. The thing was becoming moribund here. The chiefs were not getting any salary, they were getting some allowance, twenty rand a case or something like that. In the seventies or eighties the chiefs was a dying institution. Then the bantustan system revived those chiefs upward. Now the whole system of rulership of blacks was to be based on that. Therefore they got more power over their subjects for one thing, the magistrate would only listen to them, the police would only listen to them. So then they would then start with the KZP [KwaZulu Police], and they were strengthened by . . . automatic weapons. So then they became tyrants over their own people. They were given so much power. And they weren't paid very much. But they were given a lot of power to raise funds from their tribe or whatever.

Adds Jacob Zuma, provincial leader of the ANC and a Zulu, "Now in some areas the chiefs were actually removed from the areas they occupied. Totally removed and occupied by other people. And in some areas they were killed. The process of that fight, because they understood that the chiefs were critical, they were actually installing other chiefs, people who were never chiefs before, in order to ensure that they had a chief who was under the control of the authorities then."[18]

The ANC is also establishing its Zulu credentials by highlighting those aspects of its own history which are particularly Zulu. During the 1980s Inkatha made much of the supposedly Xhosa character of the ANC. The theme of traditional enmity between Xhosa and Zulu people is common in South Africa, although it has almost no basis in historical reality. In a move apparently designed to undercut the image of the ANC as an "outsider" party, the ANC stacked its provincial government and party hierarchy with Zulu elites in the transition period. These leaders retrieve an ANC lineage intimately connected to Zulu kings, chiefs, and politics in KwaZulu Natal. Zuma introduced his secretary to me as a Zulu princess, "a member of the Zulu royal family," he claimed proudly. He went on to explain the long history of the ANC and the Zulu ethnic hierarchy:

Well, then the Union of South Africa was established, you had already modern people, people who had received education, helped in the main by churches, some of them were actually ministers, who then thought now we have to fight things the modern way. And in order to fight the modern way, they'd seen things politically, and they thought they needed to establish an organization. And you needed an organization that would take the character of a national organization. That's when and why the ANC was formed. Because of the role [the chiefs] played in the struggle against colonization, they were then recognized as an important stratum in society and formed part of the new political leadership. They were talked to, some of them, before. That's why in the very first officials of the ANC some of the chiefs participated from as far as Lesotho and Swaziland. But the then Zulu king was an honorary president of the ANC. King Dinuzulu. The father of Solomon. Once that happened, that the chiefs were seen as part of a new organized political force in the country, by the ANC, and they were therefore—because the talk then was we were defeated because we fought separately—in different areas, because we were not united. The ANC sought to unite everybody. Every other African tribe into one kind of nation. With amakhosi occupying what was called the House of Chiefs within the ANC structure.

Since 1990 both the ANC and the IFP have manipulated the symbols of Zuluness for political purposes. They retrieve separate and conflicting stories regarding what counts as truly Zulu—how the Zulu hierarchy operates, and what types of ideological and organizational patterns are organic to the Zulu nation—in order to construct a version of Zulu identity that is compatible with their respective political agendas and alliances. The political role of Zuluness appears fluid in the immediate postapartheid era, as its boundaries and possibilities are renegotiated and contested.

Material Conditions

International economic sanctions, drought, falling commodity prices, strikes, and unrest sent the South African economy into a tailspin in the second half of the 1980s. The economy entered a recession in 1989 from which it did not begin to recover until late 1993. South Africa received practically no direct foreign investment. Unemployment soared as manufacturing slowed and many companies were forced to close. Hundreds of thousands of Africans fled to the cities as drought forced them off the land and influx control and pass laws were relaxed to allow greater freedom of movement. Urban areas throughout South Africa were overwhelmed by the sudden population explosion, and informal settlements of mostly unemployed people sprung up around cities all over the country.

In KwaZulu Natal, unemployment doubled from 12 percent to 25 percent between 1980 and 1991. Natal had the highest unemployment levels in the country in 1991, at a time when the national average was 19 percent.[19] Three years later, 61 percent of the population of the KwaZulu homeland was labeled "poor." The African population of Durban jumped from an already unmanageable, or at least unmanaged, 1.7 million in 1985 to 2.1 million in 1990, then to 2.6 million in 1995. In 1995 as many people were living in informal settlements as in formal housing, including townships and traditionally White and Indian areas.[20]

Migration and socioeconomic differentiation patterns were uneven in KwaZulu Natal and different from other areas for two reasons. First, apartheid restrictions had essentially been lifted a decade earlier, and Durban had already seen its most massive influx in the early 1980s. Second, movement and settlement patterns in Durban were affected by a decade of violence between Inkatha and UDF supporters, who had established strongholds in certain areas and decimated others.

Although African settlements around Durban continued to grow, a declining proportion of the growth was due to immigration from rural areas. About one-third of the approximately 2.1 million Africans who lived in informal settlements around Durban in 1990 had moved directly from a rural area. The remaining two-thirds, 1.4 million people, had moved within the urban area from a township or another informal settlement.[21] Much of this intraurban movement was related to insecurity regarding land, tenancy, and violence. People moved to gain a more secure or advantageous foothold in the urban area—from one squatter area to another, for example, or because they were fleeing violence. Extreme dislocation undermined the stability of the townships and established networks of interdependence. Many people who were longtime urban residents in established townships in the 1980s lived in informal settlements on the periphery of the urban area in the 1990s.

The combination of the earlier economic transition to manufacturing, which led to a more stable but smaller workforce, and the upheaval of the 1980s, continued to exacerbate class differentiation among Africans in Durban. In the apartheid era, townships included a wide range of socioeconomic groups, ranging from the very wealthy to the very poor, were held together by legislation that prohibited mobility. As restrictions were lifted, socioeconomic differences have been spatially reflected: wealthier residents have moved off to newly constructed housing developments, and the poor or socially marginal have moved to shack areas.[22]

Class differentiation has thus emerged as the defining feature of the organization of living space in Durban in the 1990s. It is the salient marker of difference. In the 1980s, conversely, the relevant urban cleavage was between urban residents, regardless of socioeconomic status, and rural immigrants. Township residents differed from shack dwellers along multiple indexes. Rural immigrants, who placed a tangible burden on the townships, retained primary attachments in the rural areas and were associated with "backwardness" and "traditional practices." There was, as a result, more room for the ethnicization of the dominant urban cleavage in the 1980s than in the 1990s, when Zulus were stratified along new and different lines that include class and region more prominently than ethnicity.

Organization

Whereas squatter areas and townships were divided between Inkatha and the UDF in the 1980s, clear lines of physical demarcation started to blur after 1993. Beginning in the second half of the 1980s, both Inkatha and the ANC began to consolidate territorial control over urban areas as a way of extending and solidifying their power bases. Townships, and areas within townships, were controlled by either the UDF or Inkatha into the 1990s. Violence was most deadly in pockets where neither side had consolidated control. Boundaries and tight spatial organization began to break down as violence abated and as internecine violence between opposing factions of the same political group became a more common feature of the conflict in the 1990s.[23]

Squatter areas are likely to be more vulnerable to domination by a faction or individual with control over resources, because access to necessary goods like land, security, and services is not regularized through official channels. Many squatter areas were run by "warlords," who controlled access to land and other resources. In shantytowns, unlike in townships, "he who controls land controls access to residential space, and the right, given by *de facto* control over land and resources, to extract surpluses through rent, levies, taxes, etc."[24] In many cases, warlords or strongmen emerged from local power struggles under circumstances of social upheaval, economic dislocation, and government withdrawal from the provision of goods and services and the control of movement. Many were not initially affiliated to either the ANC or Inkatha. In the context of political violence in the 1980s, however, all local leaders claimed some allegiance to one side or another and consolidated support for "their party" in "their area." To the extent that they were able to offer protection, under circumstances of widespread and often random violence, they were likely to enjoy some legitimacy.

Strongholds controlled by warlords affiliated to either the ANC or Inkatha were organized similarly. Thomas Shabalala explained how he gained control over Lindelani, how he exercises power, and how his power translates into support for the IFP: "I can say that I joined politics in 1976. I was just a normal person, not knowing politics. . . . I began to like the IFP and like the leader, Dr. Buthelezi, and I joined in 1976. . . . I carried on, attending the meetings, learning the constitution, learning about the IFP, and people started listening to me when I was recruiting members to join the IFP and I became a very strong leader, or people started following me in when I was preaching the bible of the IFP."

In fact, Shabalala has almost certainly reinvented the origins of his relationship to Inkatha. Although a large minority of young male residents of KwaMashu, where Shabalala lived, were Inkatha members in 1980, and he may well have affiliated to Inkatha at that time, he was not an Inkatha leader. For most members in the late 1970s and early 1980s, Inkatha membership was latent; it was not a salient form of self-identification. Thus the tale of his own commitment is probably retrieved for the purposes of devising an ideological party-political lineage to sustain his Inkatha credentials.

Shabalala's rise to power in Lindelani appears related to primogeniture: "There came a time in 1983 where we came to this area which is called Lindelani. . . . It was just the bush when we came here. So I started building my own house. . . . And then people in that area as they were coming in 1983, they wanted a leader in this area. We decided, residents in this area, when we were approached by government officials that what we were doing was wrong, to build these shacks, you know. And there were very few shacks at that time, so this became a very fast-growing area. . . . Less than three months we had over four thousand shacks in the area."

It appears from his own account that Shabalala's position in Lindelani derived from the fact that he was one of the earliest settlers there. As such, he had some prior rights which new immigrants were bound to respect. Newcomers, arriving singly or in small family units, were in the position of having to request permission to build. So long as Shabalala could control access to land, an ability that derived primarily from his established leadership position among the first settlers, he could continue to reproduce a power dynamic through subsequent waves of newcomers:

Then it happened in 1985 that I was elected by the people. There were about twelve candidates. I didn't stand as a candidate. . . . But out of the crowd where I was standing the people started looking for me and they elected me the leader of the area, with another who was called Mrs. Dlamini. We were two leaders in this area at that time. And that was how I became a leader. I carried on with my work. To help the people. I made them join the IFP, the organization that I believe in, the leadership, and nearly half a million members came out of this valley. And we carried on getting assistance from the government. I learned where to go if there's anything that the community wants or requires. I began to know the correct channels and which departments I must go to at Ulundi [the former capital of the KwaZulu homeland], until I got to the stage where we are now.

Shabalala emphasizes the organic quality of his leadership by highlighting the manner of his nomination. ("The people started looking for me . . .") The implication is that he was their natural leader. Although he is not a chief, nor of chiefly lineage, he plays an equivalent role in Lindelani. By inserting himself into a traditional political structure that has prior resonance in KwaZulu Natal, Shabalala was further able to increase his own legitimacy. In addition, his ability to extract resources from the government, which are then channeled through him to the community, makes his position as leader appear less arbitrary. If the community derives benefit from his leadership, there is more reason to support him than to support someone else.

In fact, for an informal settlement, Lindelani has a large number of resources: a day-care facility, access to transport, garbage pick-up, a training center which offers some technical classes, and partial electricity. Moreover, Shabalala closely guards the resources that are available: his office, the public telephones, the post office, and the day-care center are all in the training center which is the only concrete structure in Lindelani. He owns the only liquor store, and he runs the taxi service which is Lindelani's only public transport system. "Lindelani was a trust land at that time," he recalls. "We were fighting very hard that we would be incorporated into KwaZulu so we could be headed by Ulundi like other townships. So at the end it happened that we were handed over to Ulundi and we came under KwaZulu government. That was in 1986. . . . [The training center] is being funded by the same people who were funding it at the time of the old government, which is the Department of Manpower. They are still funding it, although they've cut the funds."

During the 1980s and early 1990s much of Shabalala's legitimacy derived from his ability to protect people who lived in his area. He boasted that there was no violence in Lindelani, and this claim was apparently true.[25] He maintains order, and protection, through a group of young men apparently employed by him in a number of capacities, including driver and bodyguard. Many, however, have no apparent official capacity, and mostly hang around, well-armed. They claim to work for Shabalala. Although there may be no violence within Lindelani, Shabalala and his men have been steeped in the IFP-ANC conflict, and ANC sympathizers refuse to enter the area.

Shabalala is sensitive to rumors of strong-arm tactics:

Say, about half a million [people live in Lindelani]. From 350,000 and more. It is hard to give a correct figure because I'm having refugees flocking to my area every day from where there's violence in their areas. They're always flocking here. I'm overcrowded now, but I can't say to them, go away. Nobody will come and kill you in my area, because there's unity in this area. If one person shouts or cries, we all come out to assist. That's how it works here. So they are living in our area. . . . No, there's no violence at all. There's unity here. . . . But if you hear people that are against my leadership, especially the ANC, they even give me a name in the past, calling me a warlord when I didn't even know what is a warlord! Because it is a new name in South Africa. . . . Because I am strong for my party, the IFP, they are calling me a warlord. But from the ANC side there is nobody who is being called a warlord. I wonder why? . . .

If you are an ANC don't come here. If you are a UDF, don't come here. We learned from the UDF, which was a structure of the ANC. And then in 1990, when they were unbanned, they came out clearly to have these un-go, no-go areas, strongholds, and we followed them. We matched them on that. There they have areas where they are strong where the IFP cannot put their foot in. In the past they used to necklace you.[26] Now it's not so strong, but in the past they believed in that, that if you are an opposition party, we must necklace you. I come from an area which was a stronghold of the ANC, long ago in KwaMashu. But some were forced to [join the ANC] because if you live in this area you must join our party. This is a stronghold of our party. Like in my area. Some believe in the ANC but they have to keep cool because they know it is a stronghold of the IFP. Some of them had to leave the area because they don't believe the policies of the IFP, which it is its stronghold. So in KwaMashu it's the same. Some people are forced in, some went in because they thought if I don't join, I will be necklaced, I will be killed, my house will be attacked. So to protect my property I must join the ANC. It is like that.

The background of violence or potential violence affects the parameters of organization. If violence becomes a feature of the expression of identity, it diminishes the possibility of dual or ambiguous allegiance. Identity may become a matter of survival. Once ethnic and political identities were mobilized in a violent way in KwaZulu Natal, local leaders were able to capitalize on fear to reorganize their political landscape. Inkatha-aligned "warlords" and ANC-aligned youth and civic organizations obtained levies from residents for protection and sought to underpin their power by securing their communities.

Under violent conditions local leaders have a unique opportunity to mediate identity. Political parties depend on local power brokers to reach communities and to mobilize such political actions as stay-aways, boycotts, and political rallies. In the context of endemic political violence, local leaders can guarantee that everyone in their territory will attend a rally, respect a boycott, or vote for a particular political party.

Violence creates an atmosphere that binds people to potentially coercive and corrupt leaders whose village or patronage area they dare not leave because they fear retaliation or labeling as traitors or spies. The end of violence is likely to undercut much of the leaders' power base as most parties to violence are reinforced, if not originally created, by the violence itself: violence ensures allegiance as group membership affords some sort of protection. In the early 1990s Pietermaritzburg, Durban, and the suburban corridor between them were starkly divided, in the manner described by Shabalala, between Inkatha and UDF "areas." Although ANC power brokers were rarely called warlords, as Shabalala wryly noted, they performed the same functions.

Since 1994, however, violence in Natal has dropped significantly.[27] If it is true that violence can reinforce and solidify networks of organization, then we might expect such ties to grow less binding and networks to become more fluid as violence decreases. In fact, Durban has ceased to be divided between restricted IFP and ANC areas, and Shabalala made the point that by 1995 Inkatha members could move more freely in former ANC strongholds. For him this was an indication that the ANC was growing weaker, though election results do not bear out his analysis. In Durban the ANC trounced the IFP in local government elections in 1996. It is more likely that parties are no longer able to "control" entire areas as they were under conditions of generalized conflict between political groups.

Starting in 1990 the IFP tried to extend its organizational network beyond KwaZulu, to Zulus working as migrant laborers in the Witwatersrand. It did this, in part, by exporting violence to those areas, which had remained fairly peaceful in the previous decade.

The apartheid migrant labor system had forced men to live in single-sex hostels organized by ethnic group. Zulu men would occupy one hostel, which might house upward of one thousand men, and another hostel would house primarily Sothos. Most of the hostels in the Witwatersrand area are occupied by Zulus—about one-third of all Sowetans are Zulu. Inkatha used the hostels to extend its influence in the Witwatersrand.

There is some history of low-level conflict between hostel-dwellers and township residents, along similar lines as the conflict between squatters and township residents in Durban, over resources. Before 1990, though, this conflict was not politicized in a way that linked either side to a political party. After 1990 the hostels became Inkatha strongholds. By organizing through the hostels, Inkatha was able to extend its influence beyond a regional base to challenge the ANC for national dominance. Non-Inkatha members were evicted from the hostels or killed, and hostel-dwellers began to attack township residents. The conflict between the IFP and the ANC on the Rand was ethnicized into a feud between Zulus and Xhosas. Inkatha used Zulu lines of affect to organize outside KwaZulu. It recruited support in the hostels among people who were already alienated from mainstream township life. Zulu ethnic identity may have had more resonance in an environment where people were physically and socially isolated, economically stressed, and predisposed to see themselves as different from those around them. It was among this socioeconomic sector, for example, that Zulu identity resonated in Durban in the 1980s. There is no evidence that Zulu township dwellers, who might have occupied an ambiguous political space with contending loyalties at a time when Zulu identity was gaining political salience among hostel dwellers, moved toward the IFP in the transition period.[28] Nevertheless, violence on the Witwatersrand was articulated in ethnic terms as a conflict between Xhosas and Zulus, in which the ANC was linked to a Xhosa ethnic identity, even though the party has not claimed ethnic status.

Interviews with hostel dwellers provide some insight into how identities may be constructed, on the basis of prior organizational networks, under conditions of violence. Although participation in violence was motivated by ideology or political commitments for some, many participants explained their involvement in terms of survival. Five out of thirteen hostel dwellers involved in violence near Johannesburg claimed that they had joined Inkatha after 1990 because of the

"Transvaal war." In other words, the violence itself precipitated their subsequent political affiliation. Three joined because all Zulus were "clubbed together": others assumed that because they were Zulu, they were members of Inkatha, and treated them accordingly. Some informants said that they supported the UDF in the 1980s but joined Inkatha after 1990 because "ANC supporters are killing anyone who speaks Zulu, regardless of whether he is pro-ANC or not."[29] In fact, this was more likely to be true of hostel dwellers than of Zulus in general, as the violence was not characterized by conflict within township neighborhoods, though Zulus live side by side with members of other ethnic groups in areas like Soweto. In a short time the hostels were purged of non-Zulus and of those who refused to affiliate to Inkatha, thus reinforcing the ethnic and political homogeneity of living space.

Inkatha also tightened control over rural areas through the chiefs after 1990. As in the rest of South Africa, the ANC had enjoyed significant legitimacy and support in rural Natal in the 1950s and 1960s. The UDF had emerged in the 1980s as a mainly urban, youth-dominated, and antitraditional front which many of the chiefs were practically opposed to, if not least because it threatened to undermine and delegitimate their personal power bases. Inkatha leaders probably feared, however, that the chiefs might support the newly unbanned ANC, to which they may have held a prior political allegiance. Some chiefs, such as Chief Maphumulo, Chief Mlaba, and Chief Xolo, did in fact emerge in support of the ANC, and violence flared in some rural areas as Inkatha attacked politically dissident chiefs and their followers. Maphumulo was killed in 1991, and Chief Xolo survived two attempts on his life before he fled to Durban. His cousin, an Inkatha supporter, has been installed as chief in his place.[30]

Inkatha support in KwaZulu Natal is overwhelmingly rural, and the rural vote is mediated by the chiefs. A chief is in a position to practically guarantee that everyone in his area will vote for a given party—in part because many people continue to believe in the authority of the chief, and in part because the chief has sanctions available to force the people to do his bidding. Many people in the rural areas do not believe that their vote is secret—with good reason—and they are not likely to risk their lives or their livelihood to exercise political choice. One ardent urban ANC supporter told me that his mother, who is apolitical, regularly attends IFP rallies, traveling at some personal risk in buses provided by Inkatha, because she fears that the chief, an Inkatha supporter, will take away their family land.[31]

The IFP's access to chiefs allows it to exercise strong centralized control, and the party is able to translate decisions taken at the highest levels into action at the grassroots level in a short period of time. Inkosi Ngubane, the provincial minister for environmental and traditional affairs, bragged, for example, that only his office could contact all of the chiefs in KwaZulu Natal and have them in Ulundi the next day.[32] He mentioned this in the context of Mandela's efforts to meet with the chiefs to discuss the issue of remuneration, and he was making the point that most chiefs lack telephones or fax machines and can be contacted only through an elaborate personal network available to the IFP alone.

Even as the IFP solidified its ethnic base, it tried to expand beyond its ethnic boundaries. After the Prohibition of Political Interference Act was abolished in 1990 and it became legal for different races to join the same party, Inkatha changed its name to the Inkatha Freedom Party and opened its doors to all races.

The IFP's first priority appeared to be strengthening its regional base. It recruited prominent members of White political parties in Natal, such as Mike Tarr of the Democratic Party and Jurie Mentz and Peter Miller of the National Party, and publicly eschewed its Zulu and even Black identities. Mfayela explained:

Basically we thought, as a party in 1990, after de Klerk's speech and the release of Mandela, politics had changed dramatically in S.A. It was no more a case of fight against apartheid. That was gone. So we entered a new phase of politics where we had an open political market and we were now moving away from protest politics to the politics of building one S.A. that includes everybody. . . . And there was a big exodus of Whites into the IFP. And they played a very crucial role, getting the IFP to understand . . . how Whites in this country think politically. And they are an important constituency in this country, so any party that wants to be taken seriously has to address White concerns. That's why you see so many Whites in the IFP hierarchical system. And you see a lot of Indians as well.

Ntombela emphasized the inclusiveness of the renamed party: "After that, when apartheid died, the national council of the IFP, we called it Inkatha Freedom Party to show that it was free to any nation that they can freely join the IFP. . . . It's not true that Inkatha is for Zulu nation. No, no, no. It is also for Sotho nation."

Since the election the IFP has also begun to organize a Coloured constituent base. IFP leaders contend that as a federally organized party it could represent the interests of Coloureds and others in the Western Cape as well as those of Zulus and others in KwaZulu Natal. IFP MP Peter Smith explained his party's strategy to expand into the Western Cape and to capitalize on what he perceives as a preexisting provincial identity. He makes explicit the constraints that political elites operate within when they choose which identities to mobilize, and where:

[The Western Cape is] a good province from a federal perspective . . . because if you take the nine new provinces that we have, this one and the Free State are the only two which are essentially unaltered. And although the Western Cape is only a subcategory of what was once the Cape Province, it is probably true to say that people in what is now the

Western Cape strongly identify with an area that they call the Western Cape. Whereas what is Northwest? It takes a while to become a Northwesterner, or Northeasterner, or whatever you're going to be. Western Cape has a bit of a regional identity to start with. . . . We've formed quite a few branches there recently. In Mitchell's Plain, Athlone, all over. Three of the guys we've actually got are young Coloured activists. We should have, in the total metro area, something like twenty branches, I should think. I mean the young Coloured guys in particular are very determined.

For its part, the ANC was able to capitalize on the dominant position of the UDF in urban Natal. Whereas the UDF was severely weakened in most of South Africa by state repression and the state of emergency after 1986, the situation in KwaZulu Natal was different. Aside from funneling money and equipment to Inkatha, the South African government was less active in Natal politics in the 1980s and largely allowed violence to continue unchecked. Thus the UDF came under less pressure there than elsewhere. Toward the end of the decade, in fact, the UDF began to gain ground in the war against Inkatha. After 1990 the strategic position of the ANC was reinforced by its ability to organize and recruit openly and legally for the first time in thirty years. By 1994 the ANC dominated the townships in Durban and Pietermaritzburg and controlled most of the informal settlements around Durban as well. Inkatha was forced to retreat to urban strongholds in Lindelani, Mshayazafa, and parts of Malukazi.[33]

Although the UDF in Natal was not crushed by state repression, neither did the movement retain a strong organizational network at the end of the 1980s. The front dominated most of the urban area around Durban and Pietermaritzburg, but its control was consolidated in the context of war rather than politics, and it did not possess branches, or any other type of political organization. Moreover, civic associations, which had initially provided an organizational grassroots network for the UDF in 1984 and 1985, had ceased for the most part to operate or to engage politically during the second half of the decade.

What the presence of the UDF in Natal did afford the ANC, however, was a clear place in the polarized political landscape of the province. Those areas that were controlled by the UDF became "ANC areas." Even as late as 1996, when local government elections were held in KwaZulu Natal, the ANC could boast very few branches in the greater Durban area. Nevertheless, it won a massive victory in urban areas, essentially shutting out the IFP, and increasing its majority over the results of national elections in 1994. The ANC has gained almost complete control of Natal's urban areas in the postapartheid era, despite its apparent organizational vacuum.[34]

Before the ANC can begin to make significant inroads into rural KwaZulu, however, it believes that it needs to sever links between the IFP and the chiefs. Whereas the UDF tried during the 1980s to sideline the chiefs altogether, the ANC is now trying to undermine the relationship between the IFP and the chiefs by proposing that chiefs be paid by central, not provincial, government. Because the national government is controlled by the ANC, the ANC and not the IFP would be in charge of the remuneration of chiefs under the terms of the ANC proposal. Mandela has even suggested that chiefs should be paid as much as members of parliament, a proposal which is almost certain to woo some chiefs, many of whom make under R500 (less than $100.00) per year. Chiefs' salaries are officially based on their education levels, but IFP stalwarts have been able to expect additional benefits, including cars and houses, regardless of their education. ANC officials claim that their purpose is not to bring chiefs under the ANC sphere of influence but to remove them from IFP control to allow for true democracy and freedom of association in rural areas. Skeptics doubt the ANC's intentions. Territories ruled by chiefs sympathetic to the ANC, such as that of Chief Mlaba, who is a Member of the Provincial Parliament for the ANC, voted solidly ANC in both 1994 and 1996.

The ANC has also tried to include traditional leaders from KwaZulu and elsewhere in South Africa in governing and decision making through an organization called the Congress of Traditional Leaders of South Africa (CONTRALESA). CONTRALESA has essentially acted as an advisory board in the transition and posttransition period, and the ANC is making further efforts to involve traditional elites in an official capacity in South African government. An official place for traditional leaders has been enshrined in the final constitution. The politics of inclusiveness coincide nicely with the ANC's retrieval of Zulu identity and its efforts to reach constituencies it perceives as ethnically embedded through preexisting sociopolitical networks.

Available Ideology

The ideology and strategy of Black politics in South Africa was structured by its relation to the White minority government even before, and certainly through, the apartheid era. Although Black politics was influenced by a wide variety of ideas, partly inspired by the writings of Frantz Fanon and the Black Power Movement in the United States, for example, what emerged as politically salient depended also on local perceptions of political cleavage issues.

In 1990 the apartheid government began to negotiate the terms of its own demise. In 1994 it gave up the last vestiges of domination. The ANC became the senior partner in a power-sharing system in which the IFP was also represented. The opposition had become the government.

A government has both more and less leeway to outline its own ideological position. It is less constrained because it has power over political institutions. It has greater ability to organize a political system compatible with and supportive of its own ideology. In South Africa, for example, the ANC negotiated a democratic system that does not include mandatory racial classification, racially separate parliamentary chambers, the prohibition of political participation and action, and homelands. All of these circumscribed political possibility in the apartheid era. On the other hand, the government may have less ideological scope because it is constrained to govern. It must have a positive political agenda; it cannot limit its ideological platform to mud slinging and criticism of the government.

The positive political agenda of the ANC has included forging unity and common purpose among South Africans. Mandela in particular seems committed to this goal and has put his own significant moral weight behind the effort. This has made for an interesting evolution of the relationship between the UDF/ANC and Inkatha/IFP. Although political and ideological battles between the ANC and IFP did not disappear, their substance changed in the transition period. The ANC has retreated sharply from broad condemnation of Zulu culture and traditions, engaged in by the UDF in the 1980s, to include room for all South Africans. The ANC has gone some way toward uncoupling Zuluness from the IFP in the popular perception, so that rejection of the IFP does not presuppose the rejection of Zulu identity. ANC ideology on the matter of identity has reverted to what it was in the 1950s and 1960s and has emerged as more multiracial than nonracial in the postapartheid era.

The ANC was long an umbrella organization united primarily by opposition to apartheid. By 1997 it described itself as the senior partner of an alliance of the ANC, the Congress of South African Trade Unions (COSATU), and the South African Communist Party (SACP). Despite this claim, communism was largely unavailable to the ANC as an ideological position in South Africa in the 1990s. The fall of the Soviet Union, communism in Eastern Europe, and the Berlin Wall, as well as the ostensible democratic transitions begun in those countries in the early 1990s, helped to transform the discourse of change in South Africa from one of communist revolution to democratic transition. In the postapartheid era, the agenda of communism has been displaced by the agendas of governance, economic growth, rationalization of the economy, and democratic consolidation.

What is left is unclear, and it is probably fair to say that the ANC does not articulate a single ideological position today. On the South African political spectrum, the ANC lies to the left of the DP, NP, and IFP, but closer to the center than the left. The ANC is to the right of the PAC on redistribution questions but to the left of the PAC's endorsement of an African nationalist position. The ANC is committed to redistribution, but as a government responsible for governing, it has been advised that at some level redistribution may be incompatible with growth, that the country may not be able to afford the type and extent of redistribution it needs, and that talk of redistribution alienates those from whom resources will be extracted, as well as international investors. As a result, its economic policy moved from a reconstruction and development program (RDP) to a growth, employment, and redistribution strategy (GEAR), a fiscally conservative program focused on growth. The ruling party has moved with caution to try to avoid alienating any of its multiple constituencies. Some observers predict that the ANC will not long be able to walk this tightrope and that it will break into its constituent units toward the beginning of the new century.[35]

The fact that the ANC has dropped many of its pregoverning commitments may affect its popularity among the significant sector of the population that expected more from the end of apartheid. The "youth," led by dissident ANC leaders Peter Mokaba and Winnie Mandela, emerged as a powerful voice of opposition within the ANC during the transition period. This group, which was not constituted as a separate political unit until the transition, objected to the cognitive dissonance between the ANC's stated ideological position during the struggle and its willingness to negotiate with, and make concessions to, the government. The ANC did not have perfect freedom to reinvent itself ideologically, in light of its own prior commitment to a more radical political agenda, as well as the ideological and material expectations that many constituents brought to the postapartheid era.

The ideological positions that guided the path of the IFP in the 1980s were a combination of free-market economics, federalism, moderation, cooperation with White liberals, and Zulu nationalism. This curious mixture resulted at least in part from the plethora of distinct political arenas the IFP negotiated in the last decade of the apartheid era. Its positions were the complex product of distinct relations with separate interlocutors.

Among other consequences, the democratic transition in South Africa created a single common political arena. No longer was it true that Black politics took place in a different space, over different issues, than White politics, which were also separate from Coloured and Indian politics. Political parties could organize across racial lines, and they contested the same issues. They were engaged with, and at least partly defined by, each other. This is exemplified in part by the fact that South Africa's political parties can now be arrayed along common political continua, even if there are many such continua and parties may shift position depending on the issues that define them.

Because of Inkatha's previous engagement in multiple arenas, the transformation of South Africa's political space may have had a particular effect on the party. No longer does it interact separately with multiple partners. Its provincial party leaders include people who think of themselves primarily as Zulu nationalists, committed federalists, free-market liberals, admirers of Buthelezi, religious zealots, and English speakers with provincial allegiance.[36] These individuals are now all in the same party, engaged in the same debates. As a result, there is little ideological coherence in the postapartheid IFP, and there has been a series of splits within the leadership: between so-called hard-liners (who wish to withdraw from government) and soft-liners (who advocate negotiation), between provincial MPS and national party leaders, between Indians and Africans, between Africans and some Whites, and between Johannesburg leaders, Natal leaders, and national leaders.[37]

In the political space created by democratic transition in South Africa, the ANC and NP occupied the large moderate center of the political spectrum and largely excluded other parties. The most unlikely effect of this transformation was that it became strategically sound—but more important, ideologically possible—for the IFP to enter an alliance with the Afrikaner nationalist "White right" on the common ground of ethnic nationalism. Nationalists united to object to the moderate, nonracial, politically liberal center emerging to dominate politics. Moreover, as the number of White right-wingers who voted for the IFP attests, this alliance made sense to constituents.[38]

The IFP's own prior mobilization of Zulu identity for political purposes, and the fact that its stronghold is in rural KwaZulu, is likely to lock it into some type of political engagement with Zuluness in the medium term. Although the party began to downplay its own Zulu credentials as early as 1990, it relies overwhelmingly on the rural Zulu vote. The IFP will have to continue to legitimate Zulu lines of affect and hierarchies so long as it depends on Zulu chiefs and headmen to "get out the vote" in their areas.

What is ideologically available in the 1990s in Natal is at least partly constrained by the violence and parameters of politics in the 1980s. The dominant political cleavage among Black South Africans in Natal is still drawn around local-level power issues that are often articulated in terms of the ANC-IFP divide.[39] The cleavage may have lost some of its ideological content, however, as the two parties have moved closer together on matters of identity. Particularly in the wake of local government elections, in which the ANC swept the cities and the IFP retained almost solid control of rural areas, KwaZulu Natal's dominant political cleavage appears to be less ideologically or ethnically and more demographically mediated.

Resonance

The results of national elections in 1994 and 1999, as well as local government elections in between, offer some insight into the way people appear to identify politically.[40] Public opinion polls provide further insight into political identities in KwaZulu Natal, and into the ways in which these might have changed in the context of broader transformations in the socioeconomic and political arenas. Qualitative research, including focus groups and extensive interviews, adds depth to the correlations found in survey data and is likely to provide better answers regarding why people make the political choices they do.

Unfortunately for this purpose, election results in KwaZulu Natal were the least reliable in the country. The 1994 election was tainted by corruption, fraud, intimidation, and mismanagement. The IFP's last-minute decision to participate in the election was a logistical nightmare for election organizers, who had not even been able to set up polling stations in KwaZulu. Nevertheless, there is reason to believe that the pattern of results is broadly accurate. Where the IFP had a strong presence, it was able to increase its margin of an already-likely victory. At the worst, fraud probably helped the party win more handily in areas that it would have won anyway.

In 1994 the IFP won 77 percent of the vote north of the Tugela River, in the region which encompasses the traditional territory of Zululand. In the Empangeni region, which includes the KwaZulu homeland capital of Ulundi, the IFP won 89.7 percent (with recorded participation of more than 100 percent!). The ANC made more inroads in the Newcastle region, where the IFP won only 60 percent. South of the Tugela, which includes the urban areas of Durban and Pietermaritzburg, the ANC was the largest party with 43 percent, compared to the IFP's 34 percent. In many of the townships of Pietermaritzburg, the ANC won more than 90 percent of the vote. Although most of the people who voted for the ANC and the IFP were Africans, analysts estimate that about 31 percent of Whites voted IFP on the regional ballot, with most of these splitting their ticket and voting NP on the national ballot.[41]

Because almost all of the voters in KwaZulu Natal are Zulu, and the IFP won only slightly more than 50 percent of the vote, ethnicity does not appear to be a very strong predictor of party preference. The relevant cleavage, rather, appears to be along urban/rural lines: most urban Zulus vote ANC and most rural Zulus vote IFP. In local government elections in 1996, for example, the IFP was virtually shut out of Durban and Pietermaritzburg. Still, the rural vote appears to be primarily mediated by chiefs. In rural areas where the chief was an ANC supporter, such as in KwaXimba, the area of ANC MPP Chief Mlaba, most people voted for the ANC.

The ANC also won one district in the south of KwaZulu Natal, which is predominantly Xhosa-speaking. Election results there indicate, however, that ethnicity continued to be a poor predictor of voting patterns. In Mount Currie, which is 50 percent Xhosa-speaking, the ANC won 84 percent of the vote to the IFP's 2 percent. In adjacent Alfred, which is also 50 percent Xhosa, the ANC won 34 percent and the IFP 59 percent.[42]

Moreover, party preferences do not appear consistent. Considering in particular the recent, and in some areas ongoing, history of violence in KwaZulu, electoral politics exhibit a surprising degree of fluidity. The IFP won 51 percent of the vote in 1994 but only 42 percent in 1999. The ANC gained roughly 7 percent, coming in very close to the IFP with 40 percent. The United Democratic Movement gained 1 percent, though it is not clear whether its voters moved predominantly from the IFP or from the ANC. Other opposition parties moved around significantly as well. Support for the DP increased by 6 percent, and support for the NNP fell by 8 percent. The Minority Front, a newly formed Indian nationalist party, won 3 percent of the vote. In the run-up to the 1999 elections, KwaZulu Natal had the highest number of undecided voters in South Africa, and voters in KwaZulu exhibited comparatively low levels of party identification, the very cleavage that organized a decade of bloody violence that had not begun to taper off until 1994.

Opinion polls indicate that many South Africans continue to identify the IFP with Zuluness. Forty-three percent of South Africans believe that the IFP looks out for the interests of Zulus. More than 50 percent think that it looks out for the interests of one group, potentially identified in regional or racial terms. Blacks and Whites perceived the IFP as exclusive, rather than inclusive, to almost the same degree: 55 percent and 56 percent, respectively.[43]

Among Zulus themselves, the perception of exclusiveness was weaker. Only 41 percent of Zulus agreed that the IFP represents only one group.[44] Nevertheless, one Zulu woman in Durban interviewed in a focus group said, "I identify [the Zulu nation] with Buthelezi and Inkatha, but from school I used to think it meant just the Zulus." In other words, as she was growing up, Zuluness did not have the specific political content it now does. The IFP now dominates the symbols of Zuluness. Another Zulu ANC-supporter said "The Zulus to [Buthelezi] are IFP members only." This respondent perceives an even more exclusive IFP that denies Zulu identity to non-IFP supporters.[45]

IFP supporters, however, appear to perceive their own party differently. Less than 10 percent of IFP supporters agreed that their party was exclusive in 1994. This contrasts with almost 50 percent of FF voters and 40 percent of PAC voters who said that their respective parties were exclusive, and less than 1 percent of ANC supporters who thought that the ANC represented only one group. Whereas racial or ethnic exclusiveness appears to be a positive attribute for FF and PAC supporters, it is not, seemingly, for IFP voters. This may indicate that most IFP voters are not motivated by Zulu nationalism or by a potentially conflictual ethnic chauvinism. Twice as many IFP members hoped their children would *not* think of themselves in communal terms as hoped they would.[46] These results also do not coincide perfectly with the identity that IFP leaders appear to be trying to mobilize in the postapartheid era, which is at least partially exclusive in both ethnic and regional terms. Such identity may not resonate in the aftermath of violence.

The relation between political identity and ethnicity among Zulus appears relatively murky in the postapartheid era. Fifty-five percent of Zulus surveyed believe that they belong to a distinctive community. Of those, 46 percent perceive the relevant community in ethnic terms. Zulus, however, are the least likely of all South African ethnic groups to identify their language and culture as very important to them. People in KwaZulu Natal are also much less likely to claim that they belong to a distinctive community than people in the Eastern Cape, an ANC stronghold, though their level of identification was moderate compared to most other provinces.[47] One survey indicated that 72 percent of those who would vote for the IFP identify primarily as Zulu.[48] Presumably, then, almost 30 percent do not. Among respondents who identify primarily as Zulu, 41 percent supported the ANC and 37 percent supported the IFP.[49] Moreover, ANC members interviewed in a focus group setting in 1993 did not distance themselves from Zulu identity. Asked how he felt when addressed as a Zulu, one ANC supporter responded, "It's like someone trying to hit me because I'm deaf. You cannot take it away from me." Another said, "The Zulu nation is big and respected, but people are now misusing the whole nation for their personal benefit."[50] He appears to identify with "the Zulu nation" while condemning its manipulation for political purposes.

On the basis of hundreds of interviews and informal discussions conducted over the decade ending in 1994, two Natal researchers have reached a series of conclusions regarding the salience of Zuluness in the political arena. They find that most Africans in KwaZulu Natal describe themselves as Black or as Zulu. Relatively few think of themselves primarily as South African. People who identify as Zulu mainly explain their identity with reference to the language they speak at home or to their customs. Occasionally they identify as Zulu because they live in Kwa-Zulu. Their experience of Zuluness appears primarily private, contextualized by the home, although some perceive Zulu identity with relation to the state. None of these identities is exclusive, though, and people tend to identify differently under different circumstances, alternately as Black, or Zulu, or South African. Zulu and de Haas confirm that many of their respondents who identify primarily as Zulu in the 1990s do not support the IFP.[51]

The occasion of Prince Sifiso's speech at the University of Natal demonstrates the fluidity of political identity and the changing place of Zuluness in politics. A decade before, the University of Natal campus was dominated by the UDF. Any spokesman of the then-IFP-aligned king would have faced serious opposition and derision if he had dared to speak on campus. The prince's speech was eagerly anticipated, however, and the venue had to be changed at the last minute to accommodate the thousands of people who went to hear him. He was greeted by the solidly ANC-supporting students with traditional Zulu cheers and songs. Furthermore, his entire speech was on the subject of Zulu traditional hierarchies, the role of chiefs, and the king. The crowd was enthusiastic and clearly responsive to his message. The speech focused on the supremacy of the king over the chiefs, clearly understood as an allegory for the supremacy of the ANC over the IFP in the complex symbolism of postapartheid Zulu politics. In 1986 the UDF-aligned predecessors of Prince Sifiso's audience would have attacked any spokesman of the king and scorned reference to Zulu history and tradition. But by the mid-1990s the symbols of Zuluness had been prised from their IFP hinges and had become, for the moment anyway, more acceptable, and possibly even more relevant to the ANC members who had rejected them for so long.

An extensive quotation from a man who works in Durban but returns to his rural home every weekend provides insight into the complexity of a Zulu perception of Zulu identity and of the way at least one person perceives political identity and meaning in flux:

In my area my chief is not political. No politics. He is not for ANC, not for IFP. In 1983 my chief was killed. There were people coming from townships, and they said he was IFP and they killed him. But he was not IFP. He was killed for nothing. And so then there is a new chief, that one's son is chief. And he is not IFP. He doesn't talk about politics. In my area the police don't come, it is my chief's place. If there is a problem I don't go to the police, to Pietermaritzburg, to Durban. I go to my chief. In my area the chief is a good thing. He is the biggest power in my area, you must always go to your chief for a problem. Then if there is a problem, then you go to local government. But first you go to the chief.

All people from the farms like their chief. The chief is a good thing, very important. Anything, any problem, the chief will help you. Not like the political people, they are just getting money for themselves.

The chiefs don't support the IFP. What happened was the chiefs were paid by KwaZulu government. The IFP is under the KwaZulu government. It is like a son to the KwaZulu government. The chiefs did not say, "I support the IFP, I want the IFP to pay me." It was in the constitution, when we were in the Zulu government, that all chiefs must support the IFP because it was under the Zulu government, and we must all be together. That's why they say the chiefs support the IFP. But they don't, they just get paid from them.

The IFP used to be for the Zulus when it was under the KwaZulu government, and it had the king, and it was for all Zulus. But now I don't know, it's all mixed up now. The king went away from Inkatha, maybe moves to the ANC, now the IFP is not so much for Zulus. Because the ANC is also for Zulus. We are all Zulus. Not ANC or IFP only. But ANC, IFP, political people, they are all telling lies. Playing like a ball, nothing for the people like me, small to the ground.

[The IFP] used to be, some years ago, maybe [for the chiefs more than the ANC]. I don't know how long. When it was KwaZulu government, Inkatha was for the chiefs. Now I don't know so much because everything is changing, the chiefs are confused. They are saying everything is happening in Pretoria. What is this about who is going to pay us? Now it is the ANC, IFP, NP, all the parties, and there is violence. Before there was only Inkatha, for the Zulus, but now there is violence. Everything mixed up now.

This man is a fairly traditional Zulu who retains a primary attachment to his rural home even though he works in the city. He is fairly clear about his perception of the nature of Zulu identity, and he connects Zuluness to both chiefs and the king. Whether he mentioned these particular attributes of Zulu identity, as opposed to language, for example, because his experience of Zuluness is mainly public or because we were discussing politics is unclear. Nevertheless, he appears to have internalized much of what the IFP has designated as Zulu, or definitive of Zuluness.

At the same time, his sense of both the IFP and the ANC is as epiphenomena. Both parties are "playing games" and have nothing for people like him. He scorns the idea that either represents or protects Zulus, or that there is any organic relation between either party and Zulu identity. He states repeatedly that the chiefs appear to support Inkatha because they are paid by Inkatha. He insists that the relation is economic, not natural, and suggests that the chiefs would have allegiance to the ANC if they were paid by them. To him, neither party appears salient to Zulu identity, nor does party affiliation appear to define a relevant cleavage in 1995.

The cleavage that does appear salient to this interviewee is between township dwellers and rural people. He blames "people coming from the township" for killing his chief. But he dismisses the apparent party-political motivation of the assassination ("they said he was IFP") by denying that the chief had any affiliation. He pushes the debate back into the realm of clashes between urban and rural Zulus. At other times he says: "The people in the townships always have a gun," which he contends is not the Zulu way, and that they "don't like the chiefs." He resists attribution of the division between urban and rural Zulus to party or ideological divisions but does perceive that township dwellers reject Zulu identity. For him, it is at this level that Zuluness intersects with the relevant cleavages of politics in KwaZulu Natal in the postapartheid era.

Between the 1980s and 1990s, the political institutions that partly described the parameters of politics in Natal shifted in important ways. The KwaZulu homeland was dissolved and integrated into the province of KwaZulu Natal. The Black majority, previously allowed to participate politically only in KwaZulu, voted in national and provincial elections. The ANC and IFP competed openly for political supremacy, and the IFP won control of the provincial parliament with a bare majority of votes.

Shifts at the level of political institutions appeared to affect the mobilizing strategies employed by IFP political elites after 1990. As the IFP faced the certain prospect of losing its institutional power base—the homeland—it began to expand the boundaries of its identity to include a broader regional constituency. It reached out in particular to politically moderate White English speakers in the province with whom the party had already developed political ties in the 1980s.

Although ANC discourse in the 1990s differed substantially from UDF discourse in the 1980s, mainly in that it tried to appropriate, rather than reject, a Zulu identity, this shift is related only tangentially to change at the institutional level. It is partly the result of the ideological predisposition of those ANC leaders who had been in prison or exile since the 1960s and emerged to dominate the party in the 1990s. Exiles and political prisoners were mostly unaffected by the impact of the BCM in the 1970s and its ideological and strategic legacy for the UDF in the 1980s. They returned from prison or abroad with practically the same ideological commitments they had held in the 1960s, which included an ambivalent and sometimes close relation to ethnic hierarchies. The anti-Zulu identity of the UDF was also constituted in the context of a war against a party that identified itself as Zulu nationalist; it changed as that party began to transform its own identity. The organizational base of the ANC is also broader than that of the UDF, and less dependent on the organizational networks of trade unions and civic associations with antiethnic predispositions. Some ANC leaders also doubtless calculated that in the context of elections and open party competition for votes, its interests would be better served by creating an all-Zulu provincial party hierarchy, and by highlighting its own ties to Zuluness. It is not obviously true that this assessment was correct, but in so doing the ANC partially undercut the ability of the IFP to paint the ANC as an anti-Zulu party.

What is possible in the new political arena still depends in part on the rules and incentives of the old political arena. Neither set of political elites had perfect freedom to reinvent itself in the transition from apartheid. The fact that the IFP and ANC were the relevant political players at all was contingent on politics in the 1980s and the arrangement of provincial power at the moment of transition. Each was further constrained by its own constituent and organizational base, as well as by its relative strength. The ANC was reinforced by political power outside the province, while the IFP was buttressed by a reservoir of rural voters whose support was essentially guaranteed.

Moreover, what resonates, and the extent to which Zulus respond to the changing discourse of political elites, is limited not by the imaginations of the leaders but by the lived experience of the followers, delineated by organization, material conditions, and available ideology. In Natal people in rural areas were organized through ethnic hierarchical structures; people in urban areas were divided between relative newcomers organized by Inkatha in a semitraditional way and those organized through civic and trade associations later affiliated to the UDF. As violence escalated over the course of the 1980s and increased suddenly after 1990, these prior networks grew increasingly tight and spatially bounded. Conflict reinforced the power of local elites to control whole neighborhoods by constructing and maintaining tight organization in the context of violence, for both defensive and offensive purposes. Thus violence also enhanced the power of local elites to suggest and reinforce political identity. As violence diminished, for reasons largely external to the conflict itself, the power of warlords also diminished, and organizational patterns became more fluid.

Material conditions also affect the resonance of political identities. As class began to overtake primogeniture as the relevant cleavage of urban life, as people moved into neighborhoods defined by income rather than by length of stay, ethnicity appears to have grown less politically salient. Recent migrants to urban areas, who maintained rural attachments and strained resources allotted to long-time urban dwellers, were ethnicized by township residents as a backward, tribal group in the 1980s. The conflict was initially based partly in a struggle over material resources, which plays some role in explaining how the ethnic division of Zulus could gain political salience. Changing material conditions, which over the course of a decade shifted the socioeconomic composition of the urban areas, also played a role in undermining the polarization of Zulus along ethnic lines.

Politics has divided Zulu identity into private and public aspects in the 1980s and 1990s. Inkatha appropriation of Zulu symbols in the 1980s overwhelmed the meaning of Zulu identity and crowded out its private expression. To identify as

Zulu in the 1980s was a practical statement of Inkatha affiliation. By 1995 Zulu identity had shed much of that political baggage and become newly available as a social or cultural identity with no overdetermined political innuendo. IFP and ANC supporters alike came to recognize that Zuluness is used by both parties for political purposes. It is widely acknowledged that the ANC controls the king and the IFP controls the chiefs. What is imagined as the traditional Zulu political and social hierarchy has thus been sublimated to the overtly political arena of provincial party politics. As the internal coherence of the Zulu cosmology is upset by apparently external influence, the salience of Zuluness as a political identity may wane even for those rural dwellers who continue to receive reinforcing and overlapping messages regarding their political identities. The diminished political resonance of Zulu identity may affect its private expression but should not be expected to render Zulu identity any less socially or culturally salient.

Despite the fact that KwaZulu Natal was wracked by civil war for the decade between 1984 and 1994, no special political institutions were designed to overcome the problems of that divided society. The sole concession made to the conflict was to stipulate IFP victories in Provincial Parliament elections that seemed clearly fraudulent to a majority of observers. Nevertheless, the interaction of political institutions, mobilizing discourse, available ideology, organizational networks and material conditions has undermined the political salience of Zulu identity in the immediate postapartheid era. Whether Zulu identity will regain political salience, for whom, and whether it can again frame a bloody civil war, are open questions.

In 1999 the ANC and IFP were still engaged in a strange rite of reconciliation. Although peace talks between the two parties to end the war in KwaZulu faltered as both sides walked out repeatedly amid unreasonable demands, the parties simultaneously engaged in discussion about forming a coalition government in KwaZulu. Since neither of the two front-runners won more than 50 percent of the vote, a government could be formed only in coalition. In less than a decade the ANC and IFP have moved from violent and bloody civil war to voluntary power sharing in a government of national unity. Many of the same people who killed over party affiliation a decade ago now "cannot decide" which party to vote for. Even though violence may interact with organizational patterns and ideology to make political identity more stark in certain periods, the effects of violence also appear to be potentially transient. Even in the context of violence or its memory, political identities mediated by ethnicity and ideology can take fluid form.

4 In Defense of Whiteness

The Politics of Afrikaner Identity, 1978–1990

In the past century, Afrikaner identity has at times appeared so politically salient as to determine the possibilities of politics in South Africa. At other times, it has been virtually invisible, unmobilized and seemingly unmobilizable. Afrikaner political identity went through one such sea change, from political dormancy to limited salience, between 1980 and 1995. The political reincarnation of ethnicity has been limited to a minority of Afrikaners, however, thus further splitting an ethnic group already divided by socioeconomic, cultural, and regional differences.

Afrikaner identity was not politically salient as recently as 1989. It was not mobilized by political elites, the Afrikaner "nation" was not articulated as a separate and relevant political group by any mainstream political voice, and most people did not behave politically on the basis of an Afrikaner identity. For White Afrikaans-speaking South Africans—those people who have been called Afrikaners in the past century—race and class, not ethnicity or language, were the relevant markers of political identity in the 1980s.

The group that split away from the National Party (NP) to form the Conservative Party (CP) in 1982 initially characterized itself in purely ideological terms—as conservative. The conservatives resisted political reform and advocated a return to old-style apartheid. Their constituency was rooted in region and class and consisted mainly in urban workers and farmers from the Transvaal whose organizational and ideological networks remained available to the right wing. It was not until after 1990, and in particular after 1992, that the White right adopted an Afrikaner identity, eventually making reactionary conservatism concomitant with the political expression of Afrikanerdom.

Historical Precedent, 1933–1978

The term *Afrikaner* was first used in the early 1700s to distinguish between those colonizers of Dutch descent who made their homes in Africa—who cleared land to farm and settled with families—and those who passed through under the auspices of the Dutch East India Company. *Afrikaner* meant African, and denoted a claim, and no less a commitment, to the continent. As farmers with permanent intentions in South Africa, Afrikaners had interests and needs that often clashed with those of the Dutch East India Company, on which they occasionally depended for support and trade.

Afrikaner identity became more tangible and salient during and after the Great

Trek, in which scores of families moved north from the Cape, partly to escape British rule and partly in protest against the British abolition of slavery in 1833. The history and mythology of the Great Trek have been used throughout the twentieth century as a unifying and mobilizing tool for the politicization of Afrikanerdom. Afrikaner identity was further engaged with the founding of the Boer Republics of the Transvaal and the Orange Free State in the 1860s. Repeated clashes with British imperialism in the second half of the nineteenth century probably played the most consistent role in mobilizing a more coherent Afrikaner ethnic identity, however. In the 1870s the British annexed the Afrikaner-controlled diamond fields and the Transvaal Republic. At the turn of the century, the Anglo-Boer War, fought over control of the Boer Republics, played a critical role in strengthening Afrikaner nationalism.[1]

In this period, however, divisions among Afrikaners remained practically as prominent as divisions between Afrikaners, English speakers, and Blacks. Moreover, although on the one hand Afrikaner identity was expressed publicly, the Afrikaans language was gaining currency and legitimacy, and Afrikaner organizations began to emerge, on the other hand Afrikaner identity was not politically dominant, nor was it actively mobilized by mainstream political elites. The mobilization of Afrikanerdom as a discrete political unit did not begin until the 1930s. Until then, White political affiliations tended to divide primarily along class and regional, but not ethnic, lines.

The Broederbond was started in 1918 by a frustrated Afrikaner urban petit bourgeoisie with little chance for upward mobility in the English-speaking world of trade and business. The Bond was initially a cultural movement dominated by teachers and academics that focused on linguistic and kinship ties to empower Afrikaners. In 1929 the Broederbond established the Federasie van Afrikaanse Kultuurvereenigings (FAK) to coordinate and invigorate Afrikaner cultural groups.

The leader of the National Party, Albert Hertzog, began to use the term Afrikaner for political purposes in the 1920s. Hertzog described the boundaries of Afrikanerdom in subjective terms. All White South Africans with primary allegiance to South Africa were Afrikaners.[2] Afrikaners were distinguished from non-Afrikaners by loyalties, not blood ties. "France, Holland, Germany, and England each had a share in the origin of this *volk* and thus the name Afrikaner includes them all, both Hollander and Englishman, who have learned to unite their concerns with those of the land which they have made their home." Moreover, Hertzog believed it was possible for people to become Afrikaners: "I was right when I said Sir Thomas Smartt *is not yet* a true Afrikaner."[3]

The United Party, an amalgam of Hertzog's National Party and the South

Africa Party, was elected to power in 1933. With the backing and organizational support of the Broederbond, Malan then split from Hertzog to create the Herenigde (purified) National Party (HNP). It was in this period that the Broederbond and the HNP embarked on a project to politicize an exclusively Afrikaner *volk,* divinely ordained, determined by descent, and united by language, kinship, tradition, and values. Afrikaner identity was bound as a politically imperative ethnic affiliation, no longer as a matter of choice and loyalty.

The purpose of the political project was to unite the Afrikaner petit bourgeoisie, farmers, and urban workers in a coalition with nascent Afrikaner capitalists, against English capitalists who were perceived to dominate politics.[4] The task of replacing class with ethnicity as the salient cleavage of South African politics was made easier by a coincidence between the two: Afrikaners generally occupied a lower socioeconomic position than English-speaking South Africans. Through the Broederbond, the FAK, and the Dutch Reformed Church, the HNP was able to penetrate Afrikaner civil society to create a strong link between the party and cultural and religious identities.

In this era, Afrikaners were politically mobilized primarily against "Hoggenheimer," the caricature of the fat and domineering English capitalist. English capitalism was constructed as the single dominant threat to Afrikaner economic advancement, as well as to the Afrikaans language, culture, and traditions. Political and cultural entrepreneurs argued that only through ethnic solidarity could Afrikaners hope to compete with the English to improve their material position and to stop English language and culture from eventually eradicating Afrikaans.[5] Although apartheid and the control of African labor and mobility to protect Afrikaners' economic position was part of the HNP political platform in the 1940s, Afrikaners were mobilized as a distinct ethnic unit against the English, not against Africans.

An HNP—Afrikaner Party (AP) alliance won the 1948 election by a bare margin of five parliamentary seats, with a minority of total votes cast.[6] Approximately 30 percent of Afrikaans speakers voted for the HNP-AP alliance, which later united as the National Party. The coalition won every rural constituency in the Transvaal and made important gains among white laborers.[7] After this initial victory, Afrikaner support for the National Party grew steadily for decades, increasingly less bound by class and regional differences.

By the 1960s the National Party had consolidated Afrikaner support behind it.[8] NP control of the government had considerably improved the economic position of Afrikaners compared to other groups. The gap in per capita income between

Afrikaners and English narrowed from a ratio of 100:211 in 1946 to 100:156 in 1960. In 1946, thirty percent of Afrikaners were farmers, 40 percent were manual laborers, and 29 percent occupied white-collar jobs, mostly as teachers and clerics. By 1960 these figures had shifted to 16 percent, 40 percent, and 43 percent, respectively, and by 1970 to 9 percent, 32 percent, and 57 percent.[9] Afrikaners advanced most rapidly in the public sector, but they made some inroads into the private sector, where their aggregate share of the economy, excluding agriculture, nearly doubled, from 9.6 percent in 1948 to 18 percent in 1963.[10] As a group, Afrikaners were clearly upwardly mobile.

The economic and political progress of Afrikaners probably reached its apogee during the 1960s. In 1961 South Africa gained independence from Britain to become a republic, long a dream of Afrikaner nationalists. Although Afrikaners never achieved parity with English speakers in the business world, the civil service was staffed almost exclusively by Afrikaners, and by the 1960s all of the public sector companies, such as Sanlam, Armscor, and Telkom, were run by Afrikaners, creating enormous opportunities for almost full and expanding Afrikaner employment.

In addition, apartheid was in its ideological heyday in the 1960s. Hendrik Verwoerd strengthened the ideological tenets and at least the internal legitimacy of apartheid by going beyond plain racism to "separate development" as a justification for the political system. Separate development, bolstered by "grand apartheid" legislation, supposedly guaranteed political and cultural self-determination for each ethnic group within its own territory. Each group was to have ultimate responsibility for its own affairs. Many of the so-called pillars of apartheid were built or reinforced during the sixties.[11]

Finally, South Africa was a wealthy and relatively stable country in the 1960s. It had seemingly endless mineral wealth, much of which was considered strategically important to the West. The country's vigorous growth rate, which continued through the mid-1970s, made many White South Africans rich and propelled most of the remainder at least into the middle classes. Agricultural subsidies and high market prices created large food surpluses, which South Africa usually exported at a loss. Internal Black challenges to the state, such as the nationwide 1960 pass book campaign and the increased radicalization of the African liberation movements, seemed to be under control after the Rivonia Trial, which sent Nelson Mandela and many other ANC leaders to prison in 1963. Harsh government repression created a lull in Black activism, fostering an impression among Whites of relative quiescence, which lasted until the mid-1970s.

In this period the government relaxed the successful Afrikaner mobilization project. The NP continued to be organized through an extensive cultural and religious network, and its constituent base remained Afrikanerdom. But the extreme mobilization of Afrikaner identity in opposition to English speakers, an effort that had attended and secured the National Party's rise to power in the 1940s, was no longer in evidence. The party sat on its ethnic laurels, secure with the Afrikaner vote, and embarked on a national project to foster a White South African identity and to make inroads into the opposition United Party's English-speaking support base. After 1960 the NP began to focus on the interests of Afrikaners as members of a White race, rather than as a distinct ethnic unit.

In the late 1970s South Africa's economic, strategic, and ideological strength began to wane. The government embarked on a far-reaching reform effort to try to shore up state legitimacy, broaden its support base, strengthen a flagging economy, and secure White interests. The NP had abandoned the politics of Afrikaner ethnic mobilization in the 1960s in an attempt to broaden its support to include White English speakers. In the 1980s it tried again, with limited success, to reinvent the parameters of South African politics to create the possibility for a broader polity to include middle-class non-Whites. This strategic reform effort precipitated a conservative breakaway from the NP in 1982. Although the Conservative Party gained momentum and credibility as the decade progressed, by 1990 most Whites appeared to fear the continuation of apartheid more than its end.

Political Institutions

The National Party was federally organized by province and anchored by two regional power bases that competed for supremacy within the party structure—the Cape and the Transvaal. In 1978 Prime Minister Vorster, of the Transvaal, was implicated in a scheme in which money was secretly funneled overseas to finance propaganda to promote South Africa's image. Corne Mulder, who was the leader of the NP in the Transvaal and tabbed to succeed Vorster, was also the head of the Department of Information, which was responsible for the scheme. Both men resigned in the wake of the Information Scandal. When Vorster relinquished his position as prime minister, Cape leader P. W. Botha was elected to succeed him in an intraparty vote. Although the rivalry between the two wings had long been a feature of National Party politics, it was exacerbated by the sudden disgrace of the north and the unexpected power-grab by the south.

North and south were roughly divided along ideological lines as well. The party in the Cape was considered to be more *verlig,* or enlightened, whereas the Transvaal faction was more *verkramp,* narrow. Corne Mulder in particular was a leader of the right-wing faction, and his anticipated leadership would have taken the party and the country in a conservative direction. When Botha came to power, however, he began immediately to make reforms that significantly undermined apartheid ideology and the political structure of the previous era.

Under the leadership of Botha and the ascendance of the Cape faction, the National Party first began in the late 1970s to plan for a Tricameral parliament that would include Coloureds and Indians. In order to broaden the state's power base and legitimacy, the reformers also began to make plans to incorporate Africans into the system, though without central government representation. The verkramp faction, headed by the new Transvaal leader Andries Treurnicht, opposed these reforms from the outset because they directly undermined the separate development shibboleths of apartheid. When the NP formally committed itself to a tricameral parliamentary system, Treurnicht and seventeen other members of Parliament, all from the Transvaal, left the party. In March 1982 they formed the Conservative Party.

Unlike its ideological predecessor the Herstigte National Party, which left the NP in 1969 to pursue a conservative agenda but never won a parliamentary seat, the CP enjoyed immediate credibility and support. Treurnicht, a former minister and president of the Broederbond, had all the trappings and stature of a respectable Afrikaner leader. When his Waterberg seat was challenged in 1983, he won it back easily, and CP candidates started to win by-elections throughout rural Transvaal almost immediately.

The party remained regional and class-based, however. In 1987 it contested national elections for the first time and became the official opposition, winning more seats than the liberal Progressive Federal Party, all in the Transvaal. It was not until the 1989 election that the party moved out of its regional enclave to gain a national following, although its support was still concentrated in the north. Most of its support also came from people in the lower socioeconomic groups. The CP made inroads into lower-middle-class working areas around Johannesburg, such as Boksburg, Germiston, and Carletonville, dominating local-level politics in these cities by the late 1980s.[12]

The institutional structure devised by NP leaders at the end of the 1970s confined it to very narrow parameters of reform. The 1983 constitution provided for the Tricameral Parliament, but the terms of incorporation were ultimately unacceptable to the majority of both Indians and Coloureds. The addition of separate parliamentary chambers for each racial group was a reform that remained within the confines of the apartheid structure, based on separate group representation. In this system Whites retained control because the ratio of representation was White 4, Coloured 2, and Indian 1; even a united non-White front could not trump the

White vote. This ratio was justified as a reflection of population: there were more Whites than Coloureds and more Coloureds than Indians—which was true as far as it went. But it also problematized any future incorporation of Africans into the system, because there were more Africans than all three of the other groups put together. If Africans were incorporated as a racial unit under the same formula— the only way they could be accommodated within the apartheid structure—they would easily dominate all other groups.

Thus the institutional structure that the NP devised to broaden its support base also limited its room to maneuver and defend its constituency. Within the narrow confines of White South African politics, the formation of the Conservative Party redefined the NP as a moderate party, cleaving a narrow line between the more liberal PFP and the more conservative CP. In the 1987 election the NP lost support to both sides. The party had started an era of reform, thus alienating conservatives, but stopped short of real change and reversed itself in mid-decade, clamping down harder than ever on Black civil society and thus alienating liberals. The party had nowhere to go.

The reformation of South Africa's political institutions to accommodate a broader segment of the population was driven by the Cape provincial party leadership. Regional divisions within the NP were exacerbated by radical changes unilaterally implemented by the increasingly insular and bureaucratically driven ascendant faction from the south. Divisions between north and south, which had long affected intraparty cleavages but had remained latent, grew more pronounced and finally split the NP in 1982. Institutional reforms appear to have played a role in dividing Afrikaners politically for the first time since 1948.

Mobilizing Discourse

The National Party performed a delicate discursive ballet in the 1980s, trying simultaneously, and often unsuccessfully, to appeal to its multiple constituencies, to reform and rationalize apartheid, and to shore up the economy. The NP maneuvered under conflicting imperatives to maintain the considerable White privilege it had built and sustained for four decades. When the reactionary wing of the NP left to form the Conservative Party in 1982, it had the choice of making an appeal to class, ethnic, ideological, or racial identities. It chose the latter two. The split was not perceived in ethnic terms but rather reflected ideological differences over how to secure White interests. The relevant group was White, the relevant policy issues were ideological.

Although the National Party's support base remained among Afrikaners throughout the 1980s (only 25 percent of its support came from English speakers), this was more of a historical artifact than a function of the political climate of that decade. The NP had mostly ceased after the 1960s to mobilize Afrikaner identity or to make ethnic appeals to shore up its base of support. It had more recently engaged in the business of (White) nation building, rather, attempting to foster a common sense of nation among English and Afrikaans-speaking South Africans. The party tried, with some initial success, to move beyond its ethnic base in part to undercut the strength of the British-dominated opposition party.

The changing parameters of South African politics made Whiteness a salient and coherent political identity for the NP to mobilize in the 1980s. Botha, in the 1985 speech in which he declared that South Africa had "crossed the Rubicon," promised "balance of thinking and devotion in the National Party—the only political party which is representative of the vast majority of White South Africa."[13] The South African economy nosedived in the late 1970s, promoting economic imperatives to the top of the government's agenda. Botha needed desperately to bring big business, most of which was English-dominated, into partnership with the government. Whereas state and capital had competed uneasily, and even contentiously, in South Africa for most of the twentieth century, the nation's failing economy and international isolation forced Botha to turn to the business sector for help. To create common responsibility for the nation's future, Botha had to open the ethnic *laager,* close ranks with the English, and forge a common White national identity: "But of course, we shall need the closest cooperation with the private sector. I hope they will stand up and be counted as they did in the past when I called on them for their cooperation. When I was Minister of Defence and the world started an arms boycott against South Africa, I called upon the private sector to support the government in providing our own arms, which they did successfully. I now appeal to them again to stand together for South Africa, not for any other interests."[14]

In the late 1970s and early 1980s, apartheid ideology was gradually supplanted with capitalism as the driving legitimation of policy. The shifting grounds of justification were accompanied by NP demonization of communism, anticapitalist and foreign, as the greatest threat to the state. The ANC was represented as the embodiment and tangible manifestation of the actual danger that communism represented to South Africa. The ANC was dangerous not because it demanded an end to apartheid but because it sought to replace the country's "democratic" capitalist system with communism. Communism would involve property confiscation and massive redistribution—and destroy the White South African way of life. Botha said: "We can ill afford the irresponsibilities and destructive actions of barbaric Communist agitators and even murderers who perpetrate the most cruel deeds against fellow South Africans because they are on the payroll of their masters far from this lovely land of ours."[15] As the 1980s progressed, Blackness and communism became entwined in both official and popular discourse. If the ANC came to power, the government predicted that South Africa would become a communist country "like the rest of Africa"; standards of living would plummet, Whites would be robbed of everything they owned, and the nation would fall apart. White South Africans had only to look to their borders—to newly independent countries such as Mozambique, Angola, and Zimbabwe—to construct the evidence that the future would be grim. Only the market, by reducing unemployment and giving potential communists (Africans), a stake in the system, could stave off a communist takeover. As Botha put it, "The danger must be avoided that unemployment, particularly in white areas, creates a breeding ground for communism. The small top layer of whites at the pinnacle of the labor pyramid is continually getting smaller as against the base with a broad Black foundation."[16]

The rallying cry that captured the communist threat to the South African state was "total onslaught." The nation (defined as White, but beginning to include Coloureds and Indians by 1980) was under siege, attacked by communists on its borders and by communists (Blacks) within its borders. White South Africa was under a "total onslaught," and its survival required desperate measures. In another era survival may have meant standing one's ground and resisting change. In the 1980s, however, survival was redefined to include reform and strategic flexibility, discarding what was superfluous to retain what was crucial to the maintenance of White privilege. The response to the danger of "total onslaught" was "adapt or die," as Botha said famously in a 1980 speech.[17] In this vein, NP member of Parliament Jurie Mentz criticized Treurnicht and the CP: "He and his party (the CP) are running away from the realities of South Africa. That is what they are running away from. They are clinging to the integrity of Dr. Verwoerd as if things are still the same now as they were in his time. We face up to the problems of the time as the situation develops."[18]

Part of the project of institutional reform involved the depoliticization of ethnic and racial identities. Whereas the National Party had tried to demobilize class divisions in the 1930s and 1940s in order to forge a unified Afrikaner political identity, in the 1980s it tried to reassert class cleavages in its effort to reinvent the possibilities for incorporation. Botha hoped to undermine Black opposition to the regime by forging a common identity among the middle classes of all racial groups. Incorporating Coloureds and Indians into the Tricameral Parliament was one prong of this strategy. Improving African education, providing permanent residence rights for long-term, consistently employed, urban Africans, and allowing Africans to move into more skilled, better-paying positions, was another. "We hope to create a middle class among the nations of South Africa," Botha declared. "Because if a man had possessions and is able to build his family life around these possessions, then one has already laid the foundations for resisting Communism. If anyone has something to protect, to keep as his own, then he fights Communism more readily."[19]

Ultimately, however, the NP's attempt to cross-cut racial divisions with class-based interests was undermined by its inability to discard the apartheid paradigm. The structure it created to reform the system—the 1983 constitution, which provided for a Tricameral Parliament and Black Local Authorities for Africans in "White South Africa"—continued to operate on the basis of group identities. Coloureds were represented by Coloureds in a separate Coloured house, and so on. Whiteness remained politically salient in a parliamentary system that juxtaposed White representation with Coloured and Indian representation in separate houses. Political entrepreneurs lacked incentives to mobilize inclusive class identities that crossed racial boundaries within an institutional structure that continued to divide political representation and participation along racial lines. MP J. J. Vilonel of the NP demonstrated the extent to which Whites, and not Afrikaners, were the group to protect: "The CP now rejects this logical legislation which the Whites say they want. We must not forget that we held a referendum and the Whites said they wanted it. The Whites said that they were prepared to reflect on their own affairs, but that they were similarly prepared to accept that there should be a Tricameral Parliament. The Whites accepted the system in its entirety" (6/18/84, vol. 115, col. 9145).

Throughout most of its forty-six years in power, the NP had been sufficiently dominant to structure the possibilities of White politics. The party controlled important segments of the press and television and was able to control almost completely the dissemination of information and disinformation among South Africans. It largely determined the agenda of politics and debate. Further, the identities of other White political parties were at least partly constituted by their relationship to the dominant party. They engaged on terms established by the NP. The Conservative Party was thus not entirely free to control its own identity or place on the political spectrum.

The MPs who walked out of the National Party caucus in 1982 to form the Conservative Party represented constituencies that were alienated by NP reforms— particularly Transvaal farmers and the urban working class. Treurnicht tried as early as 1979 to generate a labor constituency by uniting White workers against the first wave of labor reforms.[20] His effort to politicize a White worker identity was unsuccessful at that time, however, in the absence of a class-based cleavage structure. Workers may have failed to identify in predominantly class terms, in part because the political world was organized in racial terms. The CP subsequently ignored advice to mobilize a class identity later in the 1980s, denying that its constituency was class-based and continuing to appeal to Whites on the basis of racial and ideological, not class, identities.[21]

Neither did the right wing attempt to politicize an ethnic Afrikaner constituency in this period.[22] A review of CP speeches and parliamentary debates from the 1980s suggests that Afrikanerdom was actually not politically mobilized in that period, or articulated by political elites as a relevant political identity. In hundreds of pages of parliamentary debates between 1983 and 1985, CP MPs mentioned the word *Afrikaner* only four times, and never to describe the CP constituency.[23]

The CP did present itself as the "true NP," but by 1982 the identity of the unreformed NP was White, not Afrikaner. The structure of the political system, widespread upward mobility, Black opposition, and shifting patterns of political organization made Whiteness more salient than Afrikanerdom. In some sense however, it is difficult to disentangle Afrikaner and White identities. By the 1980s Whiteness had become the most salient feature of Afrikaner identity. It was in no way contradictory to say "I will protect Whites" and "I will protect Afrikaners." The CP could say one and mean both. What the party did in fact say most often, however, was that it was concerned with the interests and protection of Whites. Conservative Party member of Parliament F. J. LeRoux, for example, declared: "Let me tell the Speaker and the Hon. member for Innesdal that we shall be opposing this new dispensation until justice is done in regard to White sovereignty, and White hegemony over our own affairs in our own territory has again come into its own" (6/18/84, vol. 115, col. 9120). A colleague, Ferdi Hartzenberg, sounded a similar note: "I say to the Hon. the Minister that it is true. Those public amenities of the Whites are congested and the Whites are being crowded out in their own fatherland. The Hon. the Minister is no longer fighting for a fatherland for the Whites. . . . The CP is championing the cause that the fatherland of the Whites is restored to them, and we shall not rest before we have accomplished that" (5/2/84, vol. 116, col. 32).

The language of betrayal formed part of CP discourse from the outset. The CP claimed NP leaders misled voters, and its own members of Parliament, about its intentions to reform. Conservative members from the NP would have abandoned the party long before if they had been made aware of its liberalizing course. The

NP's putative betrayal was not interpreted in ethnic terms, however. The NP was not branded a traitor to Afrikanerdom, as would later be charged; rather, it had betrayed the conservative, antireform wing of its own party. As Hartzenberg put it, "When the voters asked us if we were going to bring in the Black people and the Coloureds, we said that we were not going to do so because the government had promised us that that was not going to happen" (5/2/84, vol. 116, col. 33).

In the 1980s the CP did not demand a separate ethnic dispensation or territory for Afrikaners. It sought, rather, a return to Verwoerdian apartheid, which included separate homeland representation for each African ethnic group, as well as for Coloureds and Indians. The majority of South Africa would be retained for Whites, without distinction of language or heritage. "That is what the CP stands for," F. A. H. Van Staden told Parliament, "each population group having its own electoral act for its own elections for its own people, on its own territory for its own Parliament" (5/3/84, vol. 116, col. 9169). Le Roux called partition "the policy that has always applied in South Africa and also in those countries where deeply divided communities must co-exist. The eventual solution was partition. Partition has been NP policy over the years" (5/3/84, vol. 116, col. 9124). As late as 1990, CP member of Parliament Corne Mulder published a statement titled "The Soul of the White: Negotiables and Non-Negotiables."[24]

Material Conditions
In the twentieth century, manufacturing gradually overtook mining and agriculture as the backbone of South African industry. The rapid growth in manufacturing in the 1960s and 1970s raised the value of South Africa's imports, in machinery and equipment, above the value of its exports, leading to a severe balance-of-payment deficit by the mid-1970s. GDP, which had grown continuously for two decades, began to fluctuate wildly in the mid-1970s, and the 1976 Soweto uprising led to a massive outflow of foreign investment and capital. In combination with work stoppages and other disruptions, this caused the GDP to contract in the late 1970s. Production subsequently collapsed and unemployment soared to 30 percent by 1980. When the price of gold dropped sharply in 1981, the South African government was forced to turn to the IMF.[25]

During the 1980s the relative economic position of Whites began to decline. The growth of manufacturing made South African capitalists increasingly dependent on a stable skilled and semiskilled Black workforce. Whites represented a comparatively small and declining sector of the labor pool, with dwindling influence. In response to demands from business, the government relaxed, or failed to enforce, many of the restrictions on Black employment in skilled positions or in posts previously occupied by Whites.[26] Thus White labor felt its race-based privileges eroded by Black upward mobility. Whites' real-wage levels also dropped during the 1980s as businesses concentrated salary increases among the lowest-paid (Black) employees.[27] White registered unemployment jumped from six thousand in 1981 to thirty-two thousand in 1986.[28] Although these figures still represent virtually full employment, this was nevertheless a sudden and unprecedented fivefold leap in unemployment, with psychic repercussions on Whites' sense of economic security.

The changing structure of the South African economy led to a disjunction between the interests of different sectors of an increasingly diversified Afrikanerdom.[29] The interests of Afrikaner capitalists and large-scale commercial farmers (mainly fruit and wine exporters in the Cape) clashed with those of small-scale farmers, concentrated primarily in the Transvaal and Orange Free State, and White workers. Capitalists required a freer, more stable urban labor pool; small-scale farmers relied on restrictions on labor mobility to ensure a supply of cheap labor in rural areas. Artificially high producer prices, which kept farmers happy, were untenable for workers when inflation started to outstrip wages. Business owners sought cheaper labor; White workers demanded wage increases.

The NP, previously identified as the party of workers and farmers, tried to rationalize and jump-start the economy by favoring business over worker demands. The first indication of the party's realignment came soon after Botha entered office, when the government sided with management against the White Mine Worker's Union strike to defend racial job reservation in 1979.[30] As the NP turned away from its traditional support base, the party began to court business. Business was still dominated by English speakers, and the NP's decision to court the business sector was significant for the class and ethnic realignment it signaled. At a 1979 conference of the nation's business elite Botha said, "We may have our differences, but we are creating reciprocal channels to plan national strategy in South Africa as a team."[31] The NP successfully organized two such unprecedented conferences to bring business and government together in a working relationship.[32] In an effort to stave off economic ruin, the NP chose to abandon some segments of its traditional support base.

In sum, the economy, which had benefited all Whites for almost forty years, went into decline in the 1980s. When it did, the government was forced to make strategic decisions to shore up growth. Those decisions cut some segments of its traditional constituency out of the economic pie. It set the stage for division among Whites, and more specifically Afrikaners, who had previously been united behind a common political and economic project. Business, which grew to include a much larger portion of Afrikaners in the apartheid era, was pitted against the interests of Afrikaner agriculture and labor, and the state sided with the former.

Organization

Even before the NP came to power in 1948, it relied on an extensive network of cultural, religious, and economic associations in Afrikaner civil society to mobilize support and establish a connection between Afrikaner cultural identity, political identity, and the party. The leadership of the National Party was entwined with the leadership of the Broederbond, the FAK, the Dutch Reformed Church, trade unions, and universities. At least until 1980 NP ideology permeated most levels and spheres of discourse, reinforced through the organizations and networks that continued to dominate and structure life for a particular segment of Afrikaners.

Under the leadership of Botha, however, the party began to move away from its populist tradition and grassroots organization. There was a growing perception on the ground that party elites were acting autonomously. Whereas ordinary party members had been able to express their views and criticisms freely within the party structure before the 1980s, Botha centralized decision making, bureaucratized the civil service, and militarized civil society.[33] The branches and districts that made up the party structure were largely bypassed in the search for new policies. The reformed National Party relied on technical expertise, commissions of experts to investigate particular policy issues, and research bodies such as the Human Sciences Research Council. Many intellectuals—law professors and political scientists, for example—held influential government positions in the Botha administration, from which they were often able to circumvent bureaucratic and party structures to enact reforms.[34]

The National Party's withdrawal from Afrikaner civil society left a vacuum that the CP was able to occupy relatively easily after 1992. Almost one-fourth of the Transvaal district and branch committee members defected to the CP soon after it split from the NP, leaving the NP's local-level organization in chaos. The National Maize Producers' Association, a farmers union based in the Transvaal, became a leading right-wing voice, and its cooperative network also grew into an organizational base for conservative opposition to the NP. After the split, both the FAK and the Afrikaans Student Bond fell under CP control.[35]

Carel Boshoff, a leading right-wing ideologue, was the president of the Broederbond in 1982. The CP split created deep rifts within the Broederbond as the CP and NP struggled for ideological control of the organization. The NP was finally victorious and forced the resignation of Boshoff in 1983, but many right-wingers then left the organization to form the Afrikaner Volkswag (AV).[36]

The political split also precipitated divisions among the three Calvinist "sister churches"—the Nederduitse Gereformeerde Kerk (NGK), the Hervormde Kerk, and the Gereformeerde Kerk. Whereas these churches had long supported and justified apartheid ideology through their own theological doctrines and reading of the Bible, the split forced them to reevaluate their position. The largest and most influential of the churches, the NGK, issued a document rejecting apartheid and refuting its biblical foundations in 1986.[37] The Gerevormeerde Kerk was still wracked with internal contradiction as late as 1990 but remained relatively conservative. The Hervormde Kerk opted to follow the conservative line and maintain racial exclusivity. The Afrikaans Protestante Kerk split from the NGK after its 1986 decision and is the most decidedly right-wing and politically active of all the churches.[38] The church splits clearly reflected party divisions—a 1982 survey showed that only 22 percent of NGK members preferred the CP or the HNP, whereas 40 percent of HK members supported the right-wing parties.[39]

The organizational base developed by the CP over the course of the 1980s was thus explicitly rooted in Afrikaner culture and religion, even though the party mostly avoided the mobilization of support on the basis of Afrikaner identity. Ethnic networks were available to conservative leaders because they already belonged to these organizations and groups, and because they had extensive experience with politics and mobilization in this context. Where the CP was unable to hijack the ideology of an organization, as in the case of the Broederbond, it formed a parallel organization (the AV). The CP moved into the organizational space relinquished by the NP. The fact that this organizational network was ethnically based lay the groundwork for the repoliticization of Afrikanerdom in the next decade.

Extraparliamentary right-wing groups began to proliferate and gain strength in the 1980s. Although the CP differed from most of them in that it did not endorse violence against the state, and therefore did not formally ally with these organizations, they cooperated to strengthen and broaden conservative antigovernment sentiment. Many had an explicitly Afrikaner or Boer identity and had been "out in the political wilderness," as Robert van Tonder of the Boerestaat Party put it, for many years.[40] Memberships in most of these organizations overlapped, and the CP relied in part on this network to get out the vote in a particular stronghold such as Ventersdorp, for example.[41] Such cooperation and elite interpenetration reinforced the potential for the CP to develop an ethnic character.

Political identity was affected in two distinct ways by the organizational base usurped by the Conservative Party in the 1980s. First, the CP's cultural and religious network led it to become more closely linked to Afrikaner identity and an ethnic mobilization project as the decade progressed. Second, Afrikaner identity became increasingly identified with conservative ideology, in part because of the organizational symbiosis between right-wing and Afrikaner cultural groups. They occupied the structural space that had been abandoned by the more moderate NP.

The type of organization developed by the CP over the course of the 1980s lent ethnic content to a split which was precipitated in part by changing material conditions and political institutions. Afrikaans speakers were divided into different groups by a worsening economic situation which drove competition between different sectors, and by reforms which prompted political infighting between different regions. The split was originally articulated, and apparently understood, as an ideological, regional division. It was only later that the more conservative, northern, poorer group began to identify politically in ethnic terms as Afrikaners. The ethnicization of this split appears to have been at least partly a function of the organizational base that was available to the ruling party's conservative opposition.

Available Ideology

By the 1980s the Afrikaner nationalist ideology that brought the NP to power in the 1940s, and which saw it through its political and economic apogee in the 1960s, had been almost fully replaced by what can primarily be described as political pragmatism. The apartheid ideology that sustained White supremacy came under increasing pressure in the 1970s and 1980s, both as it grew economically and socially untenable and as it came under internal and external ideological siege. Internally, apartheid was assailed by those ideologues who believed that the apparent problems with the system lay in the unwillingness of the government to implement it fully. According to these ideologues, groups should be kept further apart, laws governing African movement and rights should be more effectively enforced, and White interests should be supported at the cost of all other groups.[42] Rejecting that stance were the verligs, who believed that apartheid could survive only if reformed, that it must become less onerous by incorporating more groups on limited terms. Externally, apartheid came under increasing pressure from Black Consciousness, nonracialism, and even liberalism. From abroad, antiapartheid sentiment gained a toehold in the Civil Rights Movement in the United States and in concomitant demands all over the world for equality and freedom. Most African colonies gained their independence in the 1960s. Mozambique and Angola, on the South African borders, became independent in 1975. The ideological legitimacy of White supremacy was contested on almost every front in the 1960s and 1970s—a refracted image of what had essentially been taken for granted in the 1930s and 1940s.

The 1978 Information Scandal undermined the faith of many Whites in their elected leaders and may have been one signal of the end of ideology as a basis of government or policy. Political elites forfeited the presumption of a moral basis when seeking to justify a particular action. Because apartheid ideologues relied to an unusual extent (for modern political leaders) on biblical and moral justifications and appeals to propriety and decency, the exposure of corruption at the top levels of leadership was more destructive to the apartheid state than it might have been to another government. The substance of the scandal—namely the effort by the ruling party to "sell" their government to skeptical audiences overseas—further suggested to South Africans that there was something wrong, and in fact unjustifiable, about the system. If apartheid was to continue, it would have to be on the basis of necessity, not of "rightness." Leaders and people both retreated from ideological justifications to "rational" and "technical" language, commissions of experts, and the free market.[43]

The ideology of the market, in fact, largely replaced separate development as the language of justification for government policies in the 1980s.[44] Beyond its apparent ideological bankruptcy, apartheid had also grown economically untenable by the late 1970s. Part of the rationale for encouraging the market was to remove the government from the economic sphere in which many of its policies, such as job reservation and influx control, brought it into conflict with Black labor, capital, internal opposition, and international opinion. The NP may have hoped that by scrapping laws governing employment it would place responsibility for the "efficient allocation of labor" into the hands of the market, thus narrowing the sphere of the political and removing the state as the site of conflict.[45] For most White South Africans, economic security had long since replaced normative commitments to group-based political participation as the legitimating foundation of apartheid. Although the shift did not happen overnight, by the early 1980s the ideological justification of apartheid had moved from the fortification of Afrikanerdom to the maintenance of stability, aversion of revolution, and fortification of the economy.

The group that emerged as the right wing of South African politics after 1982 was defined in part by its refusal to relinquish the traditional justifications of apartheid. It was ideologically conservative in the sense that it advocated a return to the status quo ante. It was reactionary to the extent that it was driven largely by response to government reforms and what it perceived as ideological chicanery. The right wing continued to believe that apartheid was morally justifiable and that Verwoerdian apartheid had been betrayed not by progress and "enlightenment" but by weak political leaders who lacked commitment and stamina.

These political elites appealed in the main to people who had verkrampte ideological commitments. Afrikaner NP supporters had by the 1980s been split ideologically for twenty years between the northern verkramp and southern verlig factions. Three arguments are commonly marshaled to explain long-standing ideological differences among Afrikaners. The first is historical—Cape Afrikaners stayed behind when their compatriots embarked on the Great Trek, were not involved in the foundation of the Boer Republics, and either (*a*) are thus genetically different from Boere Afrikaners or (*b*) have a distinct cultural and social history from northern Afrikaners, with different commitments.[46] The second explanation is material: Cape Afrikaners are wealthier, benefit disproportionately from government policies that favor exporters, and are less vulnerable to the loss of race-based privilege.[47] The third explanation is racial: because only a minority of the population of the Cape is African, Cape Afrikaners do not fear swartgevaar, "black danger," which is part of the motivating drive that "closes" political ideology in the north.[48] Irrespective of the merit of these arguments, regionally divided Afrikaners held more or less distinct ideological commitments in the 1980s, and ideological commitments appear to correlate with the cleavage that developed between NP and CP constituents in the 1980s. Until 1989 the CP did not have one parliamentary seat outside of the Transvaal. It never made significant inroads into the Cape.

Resonance

Election results and polling data suggest two things about political identity among Whites in the 1980s. First, political identities were extremely fluid. This is evident from party affiliation and voting patterns, as well as from attitudes toward apartheid, reforms, and African participation in government. Second, ethnicity, which was the primary cleavage of White politics through most of the apartheid era, was not salient in the 1980s and was subsumed by demographic and ideological differences which became more relevant markers of political identity.

During the 1980s the political identities of White South Africans were characterized more by flexibility than by stability. Government liberalization, reformist speeches, and the information scandal precipitated a 40 percent swing to the right in traditional NP farming and mining areas in 1979 by-elections.[49] Surveys show that Afrikaner support for the NP dropped from 82 percent in 1976 to 56 percent in October 1982. Thirty percent of Afrikaners preferred the CP or the HNP to the NP in an October 1982 poll.[50] Although NP and CP support came mostly from Afrikaans speakers, and Progressive Federalist Party and later Democratic Party supporters were mostly English speakers, both constituencies lacked commitment to their parties and no longer appeared to vote for ethnic reasons. In the 1987 election, almost 50 percent of Afrikaners deserted the National Party. Thirty percent switched to the Conservative Party, but about 18 percent moved to the more liberal PFP.[51] The NP's loss of Afrikaner support was balanced by a dramatic increase in support among English speakers. In 1989 an unusually large bloc of voters remained uncommitted throughout the campaign, and support for each party fluctuated wildly between one opinion poll and the next as well as between opinion polls and the election.[52] A small but prominent group of Afrikaners left the NP to contest the 1989 election as independents, garnering enough support to stake a claim as a third political voice within Afrikanerdom.

Among Afrikaners, attitudes toward apartheid and exclusionary race-based politics changed significantly during the 1980s. In 1985, seventy-eight percent of Whites believed that the future under a White government would be good; only 11 percent thought that it would be bad. By 1990 only 41 percent thought that such a future would be good, hardly more than the 36 percent who expected it to be bad. The future under a government consisting of Whites, Coloureds, and Indians—consistent with the Tricameral Parliament status quo in the 1980s—was considered good by 49 percent of Whites and bad by 21 percent in 1985. By 1990, twenty-nine believed it to be good and 37 percent thought that it would be bad. Sixty-three percent of White South Africans agreed in 1990 that Africans should be included in government.[53] In one longitudinal survey of Afrikaner university students, the perception that separate development was unfeasible and impractical doubled to 52.6 percent between 1985 and 1988. This shift appears particularly decisive when one considers that it took place in only three years.[54]

Although almost all Whites feared the end of White minority rule, many nevertheless conceded that apartheid had become untenable. In response to a question about the sources of internal threats to South African security, 34 percent of elite Afrikaners said that apartheid represented a serious threat. A further 47 percent believed that it represented some threat. By 1988, then, more than 80 percent of elite Afrikaners believed that apartheid, a political system devised to secure White interests, threatened White security. Eighty-three percent of prominent Afrikaners also considered Afrikaner-dominated political parties and movements to the right of the government either a serious threat or some threat.[55]

What emerges most notably in surveys of White South Africans in the 1980s is a convergence of perceptions and fears, regardless of class, regional, and ideological differences that appear to affect how they voted in the decade. Two sets of surveys of Afrikaners that fit a conservative profile were conducted in 1979 and 1984.[56] Two hundred of those interviewed in 1979 lived in the Waterberg area, which prides itself on being the most conservative district in the country.[57] Interviewees were asked about their expectations for the future of South Africa and of their own place within it. Despite the NP/CP split which occurred between the first and second surveys, which might have been anticipated to affect political expectations, the results are remarkably similar. About 80 percent of respondents believed that their physical safety would be threatened and that their economic position would decline under majority rule.

These results are similar to those of a 1987 survey based on a national sample of Afrikaners and English speakers, despite the different demographic, socioeconomic, and ethnic profile of the respondents. In the 1987 survey Afrikaner respondents were more or less sanguine on different questions, depending most likely on the immediate salience of particular issues. On average (adding the percentage who thought things would be worse on each question and dividing it by the number of questions asked), 84.2 percent of (conservative) 1984 respondents and 86.2 percent of (nationally representative Afrikaner) 1987 respondents believed that things would be much worse under majority rule.[58] Afrikaners and English speakers from the 1987 survey substantially agreed that life for Whites would not carry on as before, that the physical safety of Whites would be threatened, and that the income and living standards of Whites would suffer.[59]

Why, if almost all Whites believed that they would be seriously threatened under a majority rule system, did some go along with the NP and acquiesce to a democratic transition that would lead to majority rule, while others resisted such a move by supporting the CP or resorting to extraparliamentary politics? Survey evidence does not support the hypothesis that middle- and upper-class urbanized Afrikaners feared a transition less than poorer, rural Afrikaners, or that the latter took a reactionary political stance because they perceived a greater threat from the end of apartheid and majority rule. All Whites, including English speakers, felt extremely threatened in the last decade of the apartheid era.

The difference among them lay in their perception of the solution. During the 1980s, and increasingly as the decade progressed, Whites were divided politically by ideology. In 1984, seventy-nine percent of Whites agreed that separate representation should be retained; only 10 percent believed that it should be abolished. By April 1990 Whites were much more divided: 45 percent believed that separate representation should be retained, while 27 percent thought that it should be abolished.[60] Whereas 60 percent of White South Africans supported a nonpolitical strategy, such as economic development or security action, to deal with South Africa's political problems in 1988, only 20 percent thought that a nonpolitical solution was viable by 1990. By 1990, forty-four percent of Whites favored a liberal solution, as opposed to 24 percent who advocated a conservative solution.

The schism between English- and Afrikaans-speaking South Africans, which was highly politicized between the 1940s and the 1960s, had largely been subsumed by the 1980s. Although the dominant cleavage of White politics in the apartheid era appeared to lay along ethnic and linguistic lines, these divisions were overlaid with demographic and ideological cleavages. Afrikaners were traditionally poorer and more conservative, and English speakers were wealthier and supposedly more liberal. As a result, it is difficult to unpack which was the dominant and dividing cleavage, notwithstanding the mobilization of ethnicity by the ruling party against the opposition. Once ethnicity ceased to be mobilized for political ends, after the 1960s, class and ideology grew increasingly dominant as indicators of political affiliation. Surveys indicate that ideological differences between Afrikaners of different socioeconomic status were much greater than differences between Afrikaans and English speakers of the same socioeconomic and demographic background. School integration was favored by 76 percent of upper-middle-class English speakers and 73 percent of Afrikaans speakers from the same socioeconomic group, but by only 8 percent of the poorest Afrikaners. Sixty-seven percent of wealthy Afrikaners and 62 percent of wealthy English speakers favored the integration of public transport; only 12 percent of poor Afrikaners supported integration.[61]

The reorganization of parliamentary representation to accommodate Coloureds and Indians along with Whites in three separate chambers probably played a role in reinforcing the political relevance of Whiteness. The resurgence of Black activism, the radicalism of the United Democratic Front, and NP reforms that eased restrictions on Black movement and employment opportunities contributed to a general perception of threat from "terrorists" and "communists," both of which groups were defined as Black. The perception of the threatening Other as Black also bolstered White identity.

At the same time, the organization of the White right through Afrikaner cultural and religious institutions lay the groundwork for the resurgence of Afrikaner political identity in the 1990s. Such institutions as churches, trades unions, and student and cultural groups were repoliticized as they became the site of struggle for political dominance between the NP and the CP.

During the 1980s, however, Afrikaner identity was not politically mobilized by CP or NP leaders. The CP consistently referred to its constituent base as White and championed the interests of the farmer and the working man against the interests of the urban business elite. Polls show, moreover, that Afrikaner farmers and laborers held substantially the same views as Afrikaner elites and English speakers regarding problems in South Africa and their fear for the future. Whites of almost all socioeconomic, ethnic, and ideological backgrounds and commitments felt a roughly equal threat from the prospect of an end to apartheid. Middle- and upper-class Afrikaans and English speakers were ideologically closer than Afrikaners of different socioeconomic groups. Ethnic lines failed to mark clear ideological cleavages among Whites in the 1980s.

Survey results demonstrate that Whites' political identities were neither stable nor ethnically based in the 1980s. Both Afrikaans and English speakers switched political parties with unprecedented frequency, Afrikaners were divided along ideological and demographic lines, and attitudes toward the major tenets of apartheid shifted substantially and quickly.

Quick shifts in political identity are not surprising under conditions of considerable flux among the factors that interact to construct identity. The 1984 constitution, with provision for a Tricameral Parliament that included non-Whites, polarized the electorate. Material conditions were worsening, with differential impacts on different segments of the White population. Government alignment politicized a widening class cleavage. Organizational patterns changed in some areas as the right wing took over many of the grassroots networks that had sustained NP populism for over thirty years. And available ideology was in flux as the political spectrum expanded to accommodate a third party on the right, and as all three parties were forced to reposition themselves with regard to each other. The fluidity of the factors that affect political identity combined to ensure that political identity would itself shift significantly in the decade that preceded the end of apartheid.

5 Jelly Bag Bones

The Politics of Afrikaner Identity After 1990

The political identities of most Afrikaners in the 1990s continued to be mediated not by ethnicity but primarily by class, ideology, race, or demography. Moreover, the political party supported by most voters of Afrikaner descent does not articulate an ethnic Afrikaner identity. The focus of this chapter is therefore those parties that are demonstrably driven by ethnic imperatives, and that subsection of Afrikaners whose political identity is tied to ethnicity. After 1990, as the National Party abandoned the apartheid political project, the collection of parties and extraparliamentary groups to the right of the NP embraced Afrikanerdom and engaged in the mobilization of ethnicity, forging a symbiotic connection between Afrikaner identity and a conservative political agenda. Political elites attempting to mobilize Afrikaner nationalism for political purposes have had only limited success, however, and Afrikaner identity appears for the most part to lack resonance in the nascent politics of postapartheid South Africa.

Political Institutions

President Botha began to lose control of the National Party and of the government after suffering a stroke in early 1989. By August of that year, the inner circle of the NP had ousted Botha and replaced him with F. W. de Klerk, leader of the NP in the Transvaal and decidedly not Botha's choice for successor. Although de Klerk was widely considered to be a party man with few innovative ideas or reform goals, he surprised even those close to him by immediately beginning to lay the ground for negotiations. In October the government released seven remaining Rivonia trialists—all except for Nelson Mandela—and in November it opened beaches to all races and announced that it would repeal the Separate Amenities Act. In December, de Klerk officially received the still-imprisoned Mandela at his residence.[1]

On February 2, 1990, de Klerk shocked South Africa and the world by abrogating the ban against the ANC, SACP, PAC, and other liberation movements in his first Opening of Parliament speech. One week later he released Mandela without the precondition that he renounce violence, the prerequisite for release in the Botha era. In the next few months the government met officially with the ANC and announced its intention to repeal the "pillars of apartheid"—the Group Areas Act and the Population Registration Act. In June 1990 de Klerk himself first described his reforms as irreversible.[2] The era of White politics was over.[3]

The structure of the political system itself remained fairly stable during the transition period. The remaining apartheid laws were abolished and some transitional councils, where local government was shared between statutory (existing White) and nonstatutory (Black) representatives, were instituted. The Prohibition of Political Interference Act was abolished, and most political parties opened their membership to all races. This probably had the greatest effect on the National Party, to which many Coloured and Indian members of Parliament from the Houses of Representatives and Delegates defected during the transition period. By the end of 1993 the NP controlled all three houses of Parliament. For the most part, however, the institutions of White domination remained the same: the 1983 constitution remained in force until 1994, and the Tricameral Parliament continued to govern.

During the transition, however, it appeared that de Klerk could rely on much less institutional support than Botha had had in the previous decade. Botha had been minister of defense before he came to power. He relied heavily on the military and security forces, whose leaders played important decision-making roles among his personal advisers. During the 1980s the state and civil society became highly militarized. The military, in turn, was loyal to Botha. De Klerk, on the other hand, had been minister of education, and he had no particularly strong bureaucratic constituency within the state. In fact, his ouster of Botha and the fast pace of his reforms made many in the military openly hostile to him. Neither de Klerk, nor the ANC, nor outside observers could be sure that the military would back him. In the end, the apparent threat of military recalcitrance never amounted to anything—the military remained quiescent, if not loyal, throughout the transition and into the postapartheid era. Nevertheless, the possibility of military revolt or defection to the right bolstered the CP and partially undercut the negotiating strength of the NP.

Almost immediately after de Klerk took power, the NP started to lose electoral support. The party lost votes to the left and the right in the 1989 general election, winning its lowest number of seats since 1953. With the loss of twenty-nine seats, the NP retained an overall majority in parliament, though it received only a plurality of the popular vote. In November 1989 the Cape NP seats of Vasco and Ceres went to the polls in by-elections. Although the NP retained both seats, the vote swung to the right by 13 percent and 5 percent, respectively. In Umlazi, an NP stronghold in Natal that was 80 percent English speaking, the CP more than doubled its support to 43.6 percent in a 1990 by-election. This pattern of rightward swings continued through February 1992 in Randburg (10.9 percent), Maitland (27 percent), Ladybrand (7.8 percent), Virginia (15.8 percent), and Potchefstroom (11.2 percent).[4]

The apparently decisive gains of the right ended abruptly, however, with the March 1992 Whites-only referendum on negotiations. The CP campaigned for a No vote, against further negotiations. With 85 percent turnout, the highest ever in South African electoral history, 68.6 percent of Whites voted to continue negotiations.[5]

Although the institutional structure of politics was not significantly different in the transition period, the norms and expectations of political possibility shifted as everyone anticipated the dawning of a new constitutional era. In 1994 everything changed. The interim constitution, adopted in 1994 and destined to last for five years, was based on equality and universal rights and suffrage. List-system proportional representation was adopted as the electoral rule, and the country was federally constituted into nine new provinces. Provincially elected governments were granted power over such constitutionally designated areas as parks, traditional leaders, and some development and fund allocation.

National and provincial elections were held in April 1994. South Africans (and many resident foreigners) voted once for national and once for provincial government, and had the option of splitting the ballot, voting for different parties for provincial and national government. Before the election, each party published a list of the people who would be appointed, in order, in proportion to the percentage of votes the party won. If a party received 10 percent of the vote, for example, the top ten candidates on its list might be appointed to Parliament. Under this system, voters choose parties, not individual representatives, and members of Parliament are not responsible to particular constituencies. All voters are in a common voting pool and can vote for any party. There is no race-based electoral rule that might require Whites to vote for a White party and Blacks to vote for a Black party.

In an electoral compromise negotiated between the ANC and the NP during the transition, however, local government elections were organized differently. In order to safeguard the interests of White minorities in rural Transvaal and Free State towns, where Africans have a clear majority in every district, the NP insisted that Whites have a reserved set of seats that would guarantee them continued representation, as a group, at the local level. In the north, where Africans are the majority, this electoral rule works to overrepresent Whites. In an ironic twist the NP may not have foreseen (but may also have decided to live with), in the Cape, where Africans are the minority and Coloureds (and Whites) are the majority, Africans are overrepresented.

The legacy of apartheid is that racial groups remain spatially segregated. Within a town, it is relatively easy to draw districts that are racially homogeneous. In local government elections, most White districts were contested by CP, FF, and NP candidates, while most African areas were contested by the ANC, and maybe the IFP and PAC. Coloured areas were often hotly contested by both the ANC and the NP.[6] Only in major cities like Johannesburg and Pretoria, where districts are more heterogeneous and the political stakes are higher, was one likely to see parties contesting elections across those ethnic divides. Most parties announced their intentions to contest elections in all constituencies in the 1999 elections, when they planned to be better organized.[7]

In homogeneous districts, where White politics are separated from Black politics, political dynamics may be different from those in an open election. With "White seats" guaranteed, there may be no incentive for "White parties" to form a coalition in an attempt to pool, rather than dilute, the White vote, as would be strategic in a PR system with some sort of threshhold. Such a pooling incentive may have motivated some conservative voters to moderate their national vote in the 1994 elections, for example.[8] It may also have affected the calculations of traditional CP voters in Pretoria (where districts were contested by all parties), who voted overwhelmingly for the NP in 1995 local government elections.[9]

Neither do racially segregated districts create incentives for traditionally White parties to attract Black voters, as they otherwise might if Whites, constituted as a group, were perceived as a "permanent minority" in a plurality system. A party that represents "White interests" could win only by also representing the interests of at least some Blacks. Local government elections had built-in incentives for even small and radical parties, such as the CP, to contest elections, and for people to vote for them. In short, local government elections were organized in such a way that they satisfy the electoral criteria of consociational systems and are subject to many of the same criticisms regarding the potential for reinforcing identities in more, rather than less, conflictual ways. Because these electoral rules were intended to govern only the single transitional election, they are in fact not likely to have any long-term effect. Other things being equal, the manner in which districts are drawn should be expected to be more important.

Mobilizing Discourse

In the postapartheid era, the right wing is engaged in the project of repoliticizing an Afrikaner political identity that had not formed part of the dominant discourse of politics for more than twenty years. The right controls the articulation of Afrikaner nationalism, making it synonymous with conservative, sometimes racist ideology. The majority of Afrikaners are not part of this political project. Although they may feel strongly about their language, culture, and heritage, their identity as Afrikaners is not politicized. For many, Afrikanerdom retains important cultural and linguistic meaning and symbolism, but they do not perceive the group as a primary unit of political affiliation. They seek in part to decouple Afrikanerdom from the reactionary political ideology that now defines it.[10] This group appears to represent the majority of ethnic Afrikaners, but because their ethnic identity is not politicized, they are introduced only to demonstrate the depth of ideological division among ethnic Afrikaners. Because the most moderate group engaged in Afrikaner politics is the Freedom Front, there is no politically salient "liberal" voice of Afrikanerdom.

Afrikanerdom has been reinvented and remobilized to accommodate, in ethnic terms, the ideological split between "moderates" and conservatives that took place in the 1980s and was exacerbated in the transition period. The meaning, goals, and boundaries of politicized Afrikanerdom have become highly contested as different groups on the right attempt to co-opt the cultural symbols and meaning of Afrikanerdom for their own political purposes. Although the CP was largely responsible for re-creating a politicized Afrikaner identity, and dominated the discourse of Afrikaner nationalism through most of the transition period, the Freedom Front has emerged as the primary political vehicle of Afrikaner nationalism in the postapartheid era.

Afrikaner history has been checkered with subjugation and dominance. For forty-six years, however, from 1948 to 1994, Afrikaners dominated politics and discourse through the National Party. Although Afrikaners never managed to overtake their English-speaking counterparts economically, they controlled politics and government, the military, the civil service, and the patronage that these generated. Perhaps most important, Afrikaners dominated the discourse that bounded the realm of political possibility, albeit with significant challenges from an increasingly vocal and powerful opposition.

The apex of Afrikaner political power in South Africa was in the 1960s. Afrikaners were almost all united behind the NP, Verwoerd was president, the economy was booming, internal opposition was under control, external opposition was still muted, and Afrikaners were moving quickly up the economic ladder. Apartheid ideology, the discourse that legitimated Afrikaner power, was dominant enough to determine the parameters of even opposition politics, and the security forces were powerful enough to mute the Black opposition discourse that challenged apartheid ideology.[11]

The NP's virtual monopoly on South Africa's political discourse started to wane as the foundations of Afrikaner power began to erode. At what point the discourse of apartheid began to crack is an arguable question; that it had cracked irrevocably by February 1990 is certainly true. On April 27, 1994, Afrikaners lost the remaining symbols of privilege and power that supported their hegemony.

The move from dominance to opposition is surprising in that it was accompanied by very little resistance from the people it most negatively affected. It is likely that the terms of the debate had already shifted so dramatically by 1994 that most Afrikaners, and Whites more generally, had come to accept that a transition from apartheid was inevitable. Many even supported a transition to democracy, despite its attendant loss of privilege, as a way of averting potential disaster.

Others, however, rejected compromise. They appropriated the prior discourse and legitimation of the state, portraying themselves in part as the inheritors of the Afrikaner project abandoned by the NP. But they also elaborated a discourse more ethnically pure and nationalistically zealous than ever was embraced by the NP, even in the heyday of ethnic mobilization. A segment of this group (the CP, the Afrikaner Weerstandsbeweging (AWB), the Boerestaat Party, and others) refused to participate in what it considered its own demise; those who did participate, namely the Freedom Front, struggled to find their niche.

The move from dominance to marginalized opposition is not only one of position. Being in opposition is not just like being in power but having less access to state resources. Opposition involves different framing techniques, a different manner of conceptualizing both movement and self, different goals, and different mobilization strategies.

Perhaps the most salient transition-period debate in the right wing revolved around participation. The National Party was a populist organization that controlled and mobilized support through trades unions, cultural organizations, churches, universities, and youth groups. During the apartheid era, there was a high level of political participation among Afrikaners. Voting was seen as a civic, even a Christian, obligation.[12] Participation, moreover, followed preapproved patterns; it was within the system. Noncollaboration, therefore, did not form part of the repertoire of Afrikaner political expression for at least sixty years, and more likely not since the aftermath of the Anglo-Boer War at the turn of the century.

Although the Afrikaner Volksfront (AVF) right-wing umbrella group officially endorsed an election boycott, a substantial segment under the leadership of Constand Viljoen reversed that decision at the eleventh hour, registered a party, and fielded candidates in the April election. They framed their decision in scientific terms, claiming that entering the elections was the only rational way to achieve Afrikaner self-determination. Joseph Chiole, chief whip of the Freedom Front, outlined the electoral philosophy: "We looked at the possibility of, you know, the election taking place in April, and we did a full SWOT analysis . . . strengths, weaknesses, opportunities, threats. And after we'd done that, unemotionally, absolutely in an unemotional manner, the answer came out that we had to take part in that. There was no choice. If you couldn't stop or prevent the election, or get a full Afrikaner state before the election, then you had to take part." Those who opposed them, and boycotted elections, argued that conservatives could better advance their agenda if they remained an outside threat to the new government. For them, participating in elections was tantamount to legitimating a system which was unacceptable on moral grounds. But Conservative Party leader Ferdi Hartzenberg gave a different perspective: "Well, the major reason [the Conservative Party boycotted elections] was to make our point. That we are not accommodated. The aspirations of the Afrikaner people have not been met. . . . And for that reason we realized that if you participate in the election then you are part of the system and then they will play games with you. They will not give you anything, but if you stay outside, you will put them in the position where it is necessary for them to satisfy you. That is the reason why we stayed out of the elections." Tienie Loots, AWB commandant in the town of Ellisras, took an even firmer stance: "No, we will never participate in elections in South Africa ever again. . . . I see it that way that if I did go and vote I am including myself in the system of what will be the outcome of it. And then I must accept it. I say I don't accept the outcome and I don't accept the election. So if there is the revolution coming on, then I have the right to go and fight."[13]

For those who did not participate, it was important to delegitimize the elections. Boycotters focused heavily on irregularities and corruption in the electoral process and claimed to have inside knowledge that the outcome of the election was negotiated, the results determined before a single ballot was cast. The alleged fraudulence of the electoral process is meant to legitimize their decision not to participate. Wouter Hoffman, Transvaal organizing secretary of the CP, pursued that line: "Just one note about this election. Do you know that this election, the result was not a factual result, it was a negotiated result? . . . In the negotiation process before the election it was decided there should be, there must be, a government of national unity. . . . By saying this I'm trying to give you the reasons that we think the National Party knew they were just handing over power to a Black communist-dominated majority."[14] Loots agreed: "Look, the outcome of the election in April was decided on before the elections. Let me tell you there was not one ballot paper that came into account for the result. The result was put out before the election."

The individual who defies the system and refuses to participate has ceased to be a citizen acting out his or her civic duty. The move outside the system requires a new conception of the self and of the broader movement. Political participation is redefined as corrupt because the system is illegitimate. On the other hand, political action outside the system, in opposition to it, is defiant; its focus is the higher ideal of freedom and, in this case, self-determination for the group. Nationalist Afrikaners assert that the move from apartheid to democracy robbed them of their freedom. They are now a "subjugated ethnic minority" ruled by a potentially ruthless majority; an "indigenous people" whose culture and language are threatened by a hostile majority that holds most of the power. Afrikaner nationalists identify themselves as an indigenous people to align themselves with other minorities around the world, to deracialize the meaning of their chosen identity, and to claim membership in a group sanctioned by the United Nations, long the symbol of South Africa's exclusion from the outside world."Take a look at this document" on the rights of indigenous people, Hoffman urged. "We had two representatives at the recent meeting [Indigenous People's Conference] in Geneva. And we are the only White nation among all the other coloured nations represented there. They say that the group of suppressed indigenal people in the world represents something like 350 million people." Koos de la Rey, chairman of the North Rand constituency of the CP, added: "And then the United Nations has a committee on minorities. . . . The CP sent two representatives and they went there with the hope of being allowed to address the meeting. Their hopes were fulfilled. Both of them received an opportunity to address them, and they were well received. Present at that meeting were representatives from about 150 different minority groups all over the world who feel they want their own autonomy."[15]

The Afrikaner nationalist movement has also appropriated the language and discourse of the liberation struggle. In search of a historical precedent that will legitimize their own extraparliamentary status and tactics, Afrikaner nationalists have turned, strangely enough, to the history of the ANC and PAC in the period of their disfranchisement. They use that precedent to bolster their own confidence that working outside the system can be effective, and to appropriate the moral high ground occupied by the ANC. The mobilizers of Afrikaner nationalism describe themselves as freedom fighters and the movement as a freedom struggle, terminology that has a very specific and loaded meaning in the South African context. Ferdi Hartzenberg outlined the strategy: "Previously, before the election, they said a freedom struggle is 80 percent psychological and 20 percent military. I think in the case of the ANC it was less than 1 percent. It was a psychological warfare. I think we must now take up that attitude that it is a psychological warfare. The discrimination that is now done in reverse. Taking place against us. And therefore we start with the soft option, negotiations." Louw Hartzenberg, branch chairman of the North Rand constituency of the CP, pointed to the ANC's example: "Think of the ANC. What did they achieve when they were not even in government? When they were not even a political party? So you can't say that if you're not in the cabinet you're completely isolated." Daan van der Merwe, meanwhile, straightforwardly co-opted the idiom of the antiapartheid struggle. The former Conservative Party MP said, "I spent my whole career in the struggle for my people. I am a freedom fighter. I'm not a politician, I'm a freedom fighter."[16] The leader of the Boerestaat Party, Robert van Tonder, suggested a logic for the stance: "Because the people who established freedom in Africa are the Boer people, not the Africans. We were the first freedom fighters on the whole continent of Africa. We fought the British already in 1848 at the Battle of Boomplaas in the Free State in order to establish our freedom. So that is 106 years before the first African state achieved freedom, that was Ghana in 1956. So you see now, it's so ironic that the ANC comes and they want to break down our monuments. I said "Good Lord, are you freedom fighters or aren't you?' "

The Volkstaat has emerged as the focal issue of postapartheid Afrikaner politics. The idea of a Volkstaat reaches back to the 1960s, but Afrikaner nationalists admit it had little support until recently. Early apartheid ideologues believed that a Volkstaat was the natural culmination of Verwoerd's ideal of grand apartheid. Each of South Africa's ethnic groups would be granted sovereign independence in order that they might govern themselves and thus avoid violent conflict. Afrikaners, as an ethnic group, would also eventually have an Afrikaner homeland. What happened in fact was that White South Africans retained control of 87 percent of the territory of South Africa, and so long as this control was not threatened, proponents of an Afrikaner Volkstaat were ideologically sidelined.

It was only after the right wing realized that a return to apartheid had become strategically impossible that Afrikaner nationalists embraced the concept of an ethnic homeland. The Volkstaat serves three purposes for Afrikaner nationalism. First, it is a tangible goal that represents a seemingly viable alternative to apartheid. Second, it can be legitimated through comparison to other internationally recognized struggles for ethnic self-determination. Israel is the most commonly used comparative example. Third, it presumes a volk, which provides a natural group-based ideology and an ethnically coherent constituency with preexisting lines of affect. In 1987, Louw Hartzenberg observes, Afrikaners "didn't much know about the Volkstaat and they did not really think that we were going this way that we are going now. So I think they were not much bothered at that stage. They know that people is talking here and there about the Volkstaat but they think, oh well, it will come right. . . . I think on that stage we were still on the ladder, climbing up. Maybe we can stop this whole process at this stage." According to Hoffman, "What we want eventually is our own territory where we can have our own country and are governed by our own people, and we can have our own education system, our own tax system, our own police, army if that be necessary. Economically, there must be interaction because you can't have your own separate economy in a small country." And AWB spokesman Fred Rundle invokes the example of Israel:

Where did the Israelis get their state, the state of Israel? You know where they got it? Where the people were prepared to fight for it. They were also against odds greater than what we're fighting. They were against odds of maybe thirty to one. And yet they created their own state out of nothing. If they didn't, they would have been like all those other states. No values for their children in their own religion, Judaism. And I mean you can see all over the world, even in Russia, where they were subjected to communism for seventy years. Today they are fighting on an ethnic basis. Same in Yugoslavia. In Britain, religious. So unless you draw boundaries in this country now, history will draw boundaries for us. Because these people are deluding themselves thinking we can be one nation. I mean I wouldn't allow myself to be ruled by a black man. Not that I think he's incapable. It's just that with my own people I can trust them. They are from me. But a black man is going to look after his own people. And he has a different culture. Different values.[17]

Although the leadership of the White right is now partially united behind the goal of a Volkstaat, there is little consensus over where the homeland should be or who should be allowed to live in it. Some people envision an Afrikaner state in a presently underpopulated area to which nationalists would be able to move. Carel Boshoff IV of the Volkstaat Council describes an example:

Orania was an empty town. It was a totally empty town, for sale, and the people bought it and they started to move in. So there was no economic basis or problem of intertwined interests with other people. So you could really start de novo in that situation. Which is of course a little superficial, but it shows that something of the kind could really work. It was started by people who did not accept the solution of being in these northern parts of the country. Just because it was overpopulated. And from that point of view they said the whole initiative should concentrate on this sparsely populated area. There did emerge something of a change in the rhetoric. The Oraniawerkers was still very much in the rhetoric of White homeland, white people stand together, something like that. And the Freedom Foundation language was more sensitive to the idea of not being racially based but with a cultural way of explaining yourself.

Others, like van Tonder, demand the entire territory of the Boer republics of the last century: "The Boer nation is a small state and it is located within the Transvaal and the Free State because those were our independent, internationally recognized states. And I am the leader of the party that says we want that state back. Not a Volkstaat, as they call it. I mean, I always ask those people the question 'Who is your volk and where is your staat?' But I say the Boer state is the Transvaal and the Orange Free State. We just want it back. We're not trying to get majorities in the new South Africa." Still others, like Chiole, hope that a Volkstaat would emerge from "growth points," in areas where most Afrikaners currently live which might eventually connect to form a contiguous territory: "The terminology being used is *Volkstaat*. I personally prefer Afrikaner Volksrepubliek. Our strongest support is in Gauteng, the PWV [Pretoria-Witwatersrand-Vereeniging area]. But then we also had very strong support in certain areas. Now the Volkstaat Council, which came into being as part of the agreement, are working on those results. And they will most probably be making their report on which areas are very strong Afrikaner bastions within the next six weeks or two months. So we actually envisage not one particular area, but perhaps a few areas which we hope to couple up by means of a canton system."[18] For some in the White right, the existence of a Volkstaat is the sine qua non of participation in the system.[19] For others it is an eventual goal which needs only to remain on the table, not necessarily to be implemented.[20]

The strategic move from the goal of apartheid to the goal of a Volkstaat has required a redefinition of the volk, and the many conceptions of the Volkstaat are based on at least as many definitions of the volk. Although in theory apartheid divided people on the basis of ethnic group, practical divisions fell along racial lines: English and Afrikaners were allowed to marry and have children, Whites and Coloureds were not. For this reason and because in posttransition South Africa, under majority rule, Africans are the most relevant racial Other, Whiteness remains an important feature of Afrikaner nationalism. For most Afrikaner nationalists, Afrikaners do not include Coloureds, even though they also speak Afrikaans and share a common ancestry.

Nevertheless, that part of the political spectrum which was defined as the White right as recently as 1989 has been redefined by the protagonists themselves in ethnic terms, as Afrikaner nationalist, since 1992. Whiteness has become secondary to ethnic nationalism. The Volkstaat is for Afrikaners, not Whites, and Afrikaner nationalist parties (the CP and the FF) mobilize around language, separate education, religious freedom, the retention of Afrikaner holidays and monuments, and other cultural and symbolic issues relevant to an Afrikaner ethnic, not White racial, identity. According to Hoffman, "Our policy is based on ethnicity, cultural differences. Our main striving is to keep people of similar cultures together as far as possible."

Strategically, Afrikaner nationalist leaders have probably recognized that "Whites" do not constitute a category of "indigenous people" that is likely to receive much international sympathy or legitimacy in its efforts to achieve a homeland and some measure of self-determination. Carel Boshoff emphasizes, "The Freedom Foundation language was more sensitive to the idea of not being racially based but with a cultural way of explaining yourself. And that's important."[21] Furthermore, in the 1980s the White right still expected to make major inroads into the NP support base which drew from English as well as Afrikaans-speaking Whites.[22] Once the boundaries of their support were delimited by the referendum and elections, the right reconsidered its strategy and its appeal.[23] It no longer pretends to represent, or tries to mobilize, all White people.

Some influential thinkers have struggled nevertheless to establish a historical precedent for incorporating other "Europeans" into the Afrikaner nation on ethnic terms. Van der Merwe observes that "Afrikaners are from mainly the middle class, sort of the lower to middle class of Europeans, so I have more Netherlands in my background but also German and French. So the Afrikaners, as a people, there's not a very good word in English for volk, but we are bred in southern Africa of French, Netherlands and German origin." According to Ferdi Hartzenberg,

If you take the Afrikaner nation, there are English-speaking people now of whom you can say they are truly English-speaking South Africans. But their grandchildren will be Afrikaans. My ancestors were German. They arrived from Germany, they couldn't speak Afrikaans. But now I'm an Afrikaner. I cannot speak German. The natural language of South Africa is Afrikaans because there were people coming from Germany, from the Netherlands, from Britain, from France. And in South Africa, as a result of the environment, a new language and a new nation developed. But it was formed out of the existing nations of Europe. But when the first man said I am an Afrikaner, he was the first Afrikaner. Since then they multiply. So there are people living in South Africa now who are speaking other languages and ultimately . . . their offspring will become Afrikaners. But in the meantime we say that we respect that they are not Afrikaans-speaking, but they are South Africans. But we realize that it is a long process because nation building is not a thing that happens overnight. It is a long process that is taking place. What is the definition of a nation? In place of every nation you have the nucleus, and more than the nucleus you have the nation with the same characteristics. But at the periphery you also have the people who are becoming part of the nation, and they are already part of the nation. So to me it is not a matter of speaking Afrikaans. It is a matter of what are your values, what are your aims? Are you in favor of self-determination or are you in favor of a unitary state? Because that is a very important thing in South Africa. And if you share the idea of self determination and cooperation with all the nations, then already you associate with that values and that aims. And then it is not important what language you speak.

Hartzenberg conflates Afrikaner identity with a particular set of values and aims—non-Afrikaans speakers can become Afrikaners if they endorse the CP's ideological stance. On the other hand, the FF has identified itself as a distinctly Afrikaner nationalist party, closed to other groups of ethnic nationalists. Unlike some other groups on the right, it does not anticipate attracting a Coloured nationalist constituency, for example.[24] The FF does, however, envision forging electoral alliances with other ethnic nationalist political groups against the "unitary state" ideals of both the ANC and NP, which now occupy the dominant center of South African politics. Chiole describes the political spectrum:

You see that now in December the old [Coloured] Labour Party has decided to carry on. But now they are only going to work for the Coloured people in South Africa because they see that the Coloureds are being ignored and it's felt that . . . their interests [are not being looked after]. That action, to my way of thinking, is the birth of the Coloured people as a people in South Africa. And I think there will be very strong ties between the Freedom Front, which is the parliamentary voice of Afrikaner nationalism, . . . [and] Coloured people that believe in Coloured nationalism. There's actually very strong ties between us and Inkatha, which is actually a Zulu nationalist, although they haven't defined it in those real terms yet, but they believe in a sovereign Zulu kingdom and so on, which is nothing less than Zulu nationalism.

Robert van Tonder is the leader of the Boerestaat Party, a small political organization that has never contested elections. Van Tonder is nonetheless an important and long-standing conservative ideologue with close connections to other political leaders. His definition of Afrikanerdom and group boundaries may in the end turn out to be influential, and he is at least one competing voice of politicized Afrikanerdom. Van Tonder's effort to redefine and constrict the boundaries of Afrikanerdom received significant attention in the postapartheid era:

Cape Town is a little foreign even to us. We very seldom go to Cape Town. You see, because there is actually a difference. It's not actually a part, well, it's not a part of the Boer nation. It's not part of Transvaal and Free State which used to be the Boer Republics. Our people moved away from Cape Town more than 150 years ago because it was British dominated and foreign and they suppressed the language and everything, and so we had the Great Trek and we established our own republics. So there's a big difference which I always make between a Boer and an Afrikaner. An Afrikaner is anyone who speaks Afrikaans. That includes the Coloured people and the Cape Dutch people, as we call them; you know, they speak Afrikaans but they're not Boer. . . . They have a different sentiment. Because they never shared our history. Because the people who established freedom in Africa are the Boer people, not the Afrikaners.

The boundaries of the group are being narrowed in other ways. Ideologically "unsound" Afrikaners are being defined out of the group. Afrikaners no longer include liberal "traitors," even if they share common ancestry. The renegotiation of Afrikanerdom is accompanied by historical references to supposedly inherent and genetic differences among Afrikaans-speaking Whites which serve to "ethnicize," and establish a precedent for, this split. This language is peppered with allegations of treachery, individuals named as traitors, and the notion of the *volksverraier,* the traitor to the nation. Modern day traitors (NP leaders, mostly) are called *hensoppers,* the name given to Afrikaners who fought on the side of the English in the Anglo-Boer War. Some people have begun to call themselves Boere-Afrikaners, to differentiate themselves from liberal Afrikaners. Boere-Afrikaners are hard-line nationalists (not liberals), they are working men and farmers (not doctors and lawyers), and they live north of the Orange River (not in the Cape). Van de Merwe explained bluntly, "I will speak against F. W. de Klerk because he is a traitor to the nation." Hoffman points to another traitor, or at least a potential one: "We also have very serious reservations about General Viljoen, the position he played in the whole process. There are very serious question marks about his loyalty to the Afrikaner people." Van der Merwe provides a quasi-biblical rationale:

And within the Afrikaner line, well, one of the subjects that I studied before I went into parliament was anthropology, and the Afrikaner, you will find it's like—I don't know whether you know the Bible, the Cain and Abel. You've got the two, I think there were two peoples born in southern Africa. You've got the Cain and you've got the Abel because . . . I cannot understand, I've analyzed the difference between me and F. W. de Klerk. Although we come from the same mother and father, Africa and Europe, and we are a twin, a twin. But he is the Cain Afrikaner because from the beginning he sides with the enemies of the Abel Afrikaners to kill us, to wipe us out.

Louw Hartzenberg further elaborates the distinction between rural and urban Afrikaners:

Because there you will get the real people that are concerned. . . . You know, the people in the country they're very much concerned with where the country's going. In a big town like Jo'burg, Cape Town, Durban, they're so busy making money they can't be bothered. They don't care a damn. . . . They won't attend any meeting, while in the country and the smaller towns when there's a meeting, no matter what your political affiliation is, when there's a meeting they'll go there, and they'll listen and decide. That is really true, you know. But in town . . . the people that's going to meetings here is so few, they can't be bothered. They're so busy with their things, making money, doctors or lawyers, or whatever.

De la Rey concurs: "I think that in urban areas people are chasing money and they don't really care about the future. As long as they have a house and a nice car, and a huge fence around their property, they don't really care." Van der Merwe is explicit that all Afrikaners are not welcome in the Volkstaat: "When we have our homeland, our nation, I would like these [liberal] Afrikaners to stay [in South Africa]. They can go to Azania, they can stay with the English and the Jews and the Blacks and what have you. I would like to get rid of them. I would like them to mix with other people so you can see from the outside that they are not part of me."

And finally, Loots provides a searing indictment of the National Party and of the unitary state ideology: "The NP got no culture. They are nothing; they reckon they're humans, but they are bastards according to me, if you know what I mean. They are Coloureds and Blacks and Whites, they're a lot of bloody mongrels, that's what they are. They got no pride in themselves. They're a whole lot of jelly bag bones."

Afrikaner nationalists have justified internal divisions within Afrikanerdom by retrieving select segments of history. In particular, many harken back to the Great Trek. Today, the Great Trek has been retrieved and reinterpreted to stand as the marker between those who submitted to alien rule and those who, through great personal sacrifice and hardship, stood up for what they believed in and set off to find a territory of their own where they could govern themselves. Today's Afrikaner nationalists claim to be descended from, and genetically linked to, those who embarked on the Great Trek. At the least, they are their ideological progeny. Reformers and "liberals" are of the stock of Afrikaners who remained in the Cape. As van der Merwe says: "You have the Afrikaners like F. W. de Klerk, you go back 100 or 150 years ago and he would have sided with the British government. He would never have been a member of the trek moving north."

Willie Lewies of the Transvaal Agricultural Union (TAU) elaborates: "This part of the country [is] very politically active. It's the former Waterberg constituency, [and] from the beginning of the century we're conservative. I myself am descended from the Voortrekkers, my great grandfather [was] Piet Retief, who was killed by the Zulus, and my other grandfather [was] Andries Pretorius, who was the leader of the people. . . . He was the person in charge at Blood River. . . . So we are from that type of people. We never wanted to be governed by other people, and we still don't want to be governed by other people; we want to be governed by ourselves, and we will be, eventually, I'm quite sure about that, whatever happens."

Political splits among Afrikaners are essentialized as an intrinsic trait of the Afrikaner character. Afrikaners are characterized as stubborn people who do not necessarily follow their leaders or each other. They are independent thinkers who may often find themselves in conflict with other people with whom they should naturally be allied. The split is called a *broedertwis*, a fight between brothers, which crops up as a consistent feature of Afrikaner history. Thus there is nothing new or worrisome, or threatening to the Afrikaner nation, about the current broedertwis. In fact, it is simply the most recent link in a long chain of similar intra-Afrikaner conflicts which themselves partially define the meaning of Afrikanerdom. According to Lewies, a Hollander once told him, "This is the history of your people. In Europe you fought with everyone, and you couldn't get on, and your forebears said okay, let's go across the sea; and on the trip some ships sank, and the sharks ate them and then they get to the south coast of Africa and we fought the Dutch government and then the British government, and eventually we couldn't live with them and we went north, and then we got here and we started fighting with each other. And that's the history of our people. Genetically we're like that."

Material Conditions

The economic downturn that started in the late 1970s worsened in the 1980s. International economic sanctions after 1986 led to a serious foreign-exchange deficit that undercut economic growth. A 1993 IMF survey of twenty-four developing countries ranked South Africa second to last, with an average annual rate of growth of 0.5 percent in GDP between 1983 and 1992. The economy went into the longest and deepest recession of its history in March 1989; it contracted for four years, with real economic growth rate as measured by gross domestic product hovering between -0.4 percent and -2.1 percent between 1989 and 1993. Real GDP per capita declined by 4.3 percent in 1992. Analysts blamed the recession on drought, transitional uncertainty, increasing violence, and the slow growth of the major industrial countries.[25] The recession ended in 1994 and the economy has continued to grow since then: in 1995 GDP grew at 3.3 percent, its highest level in seven years.[26]

The South African Reserve Bank announced in June 1993 that except for the depression in the 1930s, the recession had had more serious repercussions for living standards and employment than any other economic downswing this century. Because of the drought and the introduction of a value added tax (VAT) on basic foods, food price inflation soared to 19.6 percent in 1991 and 25.3 percent in 1992. Liquidations increased by 28 percent to 2,408 between 1991 and 1992. Total employment in the nonagricultural sectors began to decline in 1989. It dropped by 0.5 percent in 1990 and by 2 percent in 1991 and again in 1992. About 288,000 jobs were lost between 1989 and 1992. Private-sector employment decreased by 0.7 percent, 3.4 percent, and 2.9 percent in 1990, 1991, and 1992, respectively. Public-sector employment was mostly stable in the same period.[27]

Although this recession was long and widespread enough that it affected all South Africans, some sectors were particularly hard hit. White employment in construction and manufacturing decreased by 3.9 percent and 2.4 percent, respectively, between 1991 and 1992. Whites fared better in the public sector, except in public corporations, where employment decreased by 12.5 percent, and agricultural marketing boards, where it decreased by 6.7 percent between 1991 and 1992. In 1992 between five hundred and six hundred farmers gave up farming because of drought, and it was estimated that more than one thousand farmers would have to be "phased out" of agriculture because of drought in 1993. Between 1990 and 1992, more than one hundred thousand jobs were lost in agriculture. Between 1988 and 1992 the contribution of agriculture to GDP fell from 6.4 percent to 4 percent. Hardest hit were (predominantly Afrikaner) food producers in the Transvaal and Orange Free State, which is in any case the driest and least obviously arable part of the country. Real production in the agricultural sector fell by 24 percent in 1992, although it began to recover in the first half of 1993. Better weather conditions reduced the number of liquidations in the agricultural sector by 10.7 percent in 1993.[28]

Both the ANC and the NP began to float ideas about affirmative action during the transition period. At a conference in 1991 the ANC suggested that a "programme of education and training of public servants in preparation for the dispensing of services to accommodate the historically disadvantaged be implemented in an affirmative action program." The NP minister of justice said in 1993 that "the government supported affirmative action to address underdevelopment and past discrimination." By 1993 the state-owned companies, or parastatals, Telkom, SABC, Transnet, Eskom, South African Airways, and the Small Business Development Corporation had all begun to implement affirmative action programs. The goal of many of these programs was not to employ more Africans but to move them up the corporate ladder into managerial and executive positions. A survey of seventy-one companies in 1989 indicated that 99.3 percent of senior managers were White. Affirmative action goals projected that only 90.2 percent would be White by 1995. In the same period, the percentage of White middle managers was expected to drop from 97.2 percent to 88.9 percent, and of professionals from 86 percent to 72.9 percent.[29]

The wage gap between Whites and other races also narrowed in the 1990s. In the construction sector, the ratio of White to African earnings dropped from

4.7:1 in 1991 to 4.3:1 in 1992, while the ratio between the two in the manufacturing sector decreased from 3.6:1 to 3.4:1. Excluding agriculture and mining, the average real annual increase in earnings between 1991 and 1992 was −0.3 percent for Whites, 0.2 percent for Africans, 0.9 percent for Indians, and 2 percent for Coloureds. The average household income for Africans increased by 17 percent between 1987 and 1992, whereas Whites' household income increased by only 10 percent. The Central Statistical Service reported that White households' share of total personal income in South Africa decreased from 62 percent in 1978 to 54 percent in 1988.[30]

By 1994, then, most Whites were worse off economically than they had been ten years before, and in a deteriorating position, both absolutely and comparatively. The groups that were hardest hit remained, as in the 1980s, farmers and laborers, particularly in construction and manufacturing, where many White workers are concentrated. Public corporations, which were controlled and almost exclusively staffed by Afrikaners during the apartheid years, also contracted during the 1990s and retrenched thousands of employees. In 1996 the government began to privatize many parastatals, a course of action that promised to result in extensive additional layoffs in the future.

Although the economic slump of the transition period was largely the result of trends begun in the 1980s, Whites tended to blame it on the transition itself and on South Africa's apparent instability. Those who were hardest hit by the recession most resisted transition from the apartheid system, which had long secured their race-based privilege. Economic vulnerability played a role in strengthening bonds of reciprocity and mutual assistance among them, and may prompt those in lower socioeconomic groups to close ranks. Most often, Afrikaners continue to make up the bulk of White lower-middle-income groups, suggesting that worsening economic conditions may have played a role in creating an environment in which the mobilization of ethnic identity for political purposes might resonate.

Organization

Until 1994 the Conservative Party was the dominant political voice of a right-wing network "characterised by cross cutting and coinciding membership and interlocking elites."[31] The CP's dependence on this organizational base propelled it into an increasingly Afrikaner identity during and after the democratic transition. Except in Natal, where sugar cane farmers are mostly English speaking, Afrikaners continue to dominate agriculture as they did during the NP Afrikaner politicization project of the 1930s and 1940s. The urban working class is also mainly Afrikaans speaking, and isolated on the periphery of cities like Johannesburg. In many northern Transvaal towns, people speak English poorly. The right-wing constituency was organized through Afrikaner cultural and religious groups that continue to structure social and spiritual life in the small farming communities, rural towns, and urban working-class areas of northern South Africa.

In small towns, where people are isolated and rely on each other for support and help in times of crisis, where everyone seems to be related to everyone else, and they have all grown up together, there is a very tight sense of community. Going into town on a Saturday morning is a full-blown social affair, as people slow down to greet each other at intersections, exchange gossip over the counter at the bottle store, and gather over cups of coffee, and later in the day brandy and coke, at the agricultural cooperative (where they can buy seeds, fertilizer, tractors, and all other manner of farm equipment) to exchange news about the weather, crops, labor, and, increasingly, attacks against farms.

In this atmosphere, community mobilization can be highly effective. Multiple pressures from church, unions, school and local government boards, friends, relatives, and local political elites send reinforcing messages. The majority of the organizations that continue to govern the daily spiritual, social, and occupational life of rural Afrikaners are hooked into the right-wing network dominated by the Conservative Party and the Freedom Front. Moreover, populist mobilization through grassroots organization was part of an Afrikaner political tradition begun by the NP. The political organization of civil society was familiar to rural Afrikaners, and familiarity itself probably reinforced the legitimacy of the organizational network at a time of extreme flux.

After de Klerk's liberalizing announcements of 1990, the strategy of the right wing was to question the legitimacy of the government, to claim that it had no mandate from the White electorate for negotiating away its power, to demand another Whites-only election, and to insist on a return to Verwoerdian apartheid—a plan they called "partition." The party focused its energies on winning by-elections, extending its organizational network, raising its political profile, and mobilizing opposition to government reforms. The CP's success in by-elections gave the party leaders confidence that they could continue to operate within the system to reverse reforms and turn back the clock. Between them the opposition parties held seventy-two seats in parliament.[32] The NP had only ninety-three. If the CP could gain enough support within Parliament, or mobilize popular demand for a new election, the government would be morally, if not constitutionally, obligated to test its mandate in another election.

The most important aspect of CP strategy in the period between 1990 and 1992 was that it remained within the system and, by extension, continued to organize as a political party. Although Treurnicht began to make speeches incorporating scriptural justification for revolt and organized mass action against reforms, the party and most of the rest of the right wing continued to play by the rules of politics devised by the NP.[33] Because the CP probably failed to realize how far the government would go, and how far the electorate would go with it, the party believed that it still had incentives to operate, and to organize its constituency, within the parameters of White politics.

These incentives changed after 1992. The March 1992 referendum decidedly undercut and virtually immobilized the right wing. CP leaders had believed the party could win another Whites-only election and gain a mandate to reverse the reform process.[34] The government, in fact, took a significant gamble by calling a referendum on the future of negotiations in order to shore up support for the process. Whether a majority of Whites supported the negotiations was decidedly unclear until March 1992. The CP wavered for some time over whether to contest the referendum or to call for a boycott in order to delegitimize the process and force an election.[35] In the end, it launched a campaign for a No vote.

Against most expectations, only about one-third of the electorate sided with the right wing against the government. The government undercut CP strategy by calling a referendum rather than an election, and even further hamstrung the right by winning it in a landslide. The referendum essentially invalidated CP demands for another election because it had tested electoral support for reforms, the very issue on which the right wing based its demands for a new election. The referendum also delimited the support base of the CP at a minority of 30 percent of the White population. It consolidated the NP's support base, marginalized the White opposition, and put the government in a stronger negotiating position. Opposition to reforms seemed to have peaked, and it appeared that 70 percent of Whites would follow de Klerk through the transition. The NP apparently reasoned that this was a sufficient support base.

The referendum took the place of another Whites-only election, and the government unilaterally suspended by-elections after 1992. For the CP this marked the end of White politics. The sudden change in the context and meaning of politics prompted a reevaluation of the ideology, organization, and strategy of the right wing. As Chiole put it, "After the 1992 referendum, it became more and more clear to those that couldn't see it before that we were going to be controlled by the ANC in a unitary state. The Afrikaner lost his political sovereignty where he was the ruler over nearly half of South Africa. . . . You cannot get everything out that you've lost, and that is where the philosophy changed. Fine, we've lost that, but now we must get something out."

Although the right wing was divided along multiple fault lines throughout the 1980s and 1990s, it was largely anchored politically by the CP until 1992. After 1992 the CP itself split and the party appeared to lose direction. The right wing fractured, mainly along strategic lines, with organizational repercussions.

Long before the referendum, the CP secretly harbored an internal split between "hard-liners," led by Ferdi Hartzenberg, and "pragmatists," led by Andries Beyers. The hard-line party executive voted to boycott the referendum and to call on its supporters not to participate in the vote, hoping that a low turnout would delegitimize the exercise. The pragmatist wing threatened a walkout and open confrontation if the party boycotted the referendum, forcing party leaders to overturn their decision at the last minute to avoid the appearance of dissension within the party.[36] Because this decision was later perceived to have been a strategic blunder, it exacerbated differences between the two wings of the party.

The referendum pulled the rug out from under the CP, and party leaders later agreed that it was such a severe blow that the party floated adrift for many months.[37] Although the right wing and the party machinery still controlled many Transvaal local governments, splits in the party undermined its organizational base as groups realigned themselves. The pragmatists lost ground within the party after the referendum debacle for which they were blamed. Hard-liners gained ascendancy, particularly after Treurnicht died in 1993 and Hartzenberg became the leader of the CP.

Party factions hijacked their own organizational bases; some unions and local governments, for example, aligned themselves with pragmatists, and others joined with hard-liners.[38] Thus in the second half of the democratic transition, the membership and organization of the CP was split along ideological and strategic lines. The ascendant faction moved outside the institutional system of South African politics, refusing to participate in negotiations, aligning itself more closely with extraparliamentary and even paramilitary organizations on the right, and eventually refusing to contest the 1994 elections. The organizational base of the CP, which had consisted mainly in branch networks and party offices, took on a paramilitary hue. Many local-level CP leaders organized commando units designed to protect farms in rural areas.[39] Many CP members who had previously shunned radical organizations like the AWB joined the paramilitary group in the transition period.[40] Although their commitment did not last and most had lapsed again by 1995, the paramilitary option was popular during the transition and was linked to the CP organizational base.

In August 1992, five "pragmatist" CP members of Parliament left the party to form the Afrikaner Volksunie (AVU) under the leadership of Andries Beyers. The

AVU differed strategically from the CP in that it was determined to participate in negotiations, which the CP continued to boycott, to secure an "autonomous region" within a federally structured South Africa. The AVU never really differed ideologically from the CP, or at any rate its ideological position remained ill-defined. It is still unclear, for example, whether it intended to include Coloureds, as Afrikaans speakers, in its autonomous region.[41]

In September 1992 the CP founded the Concerned South Africans Group, a nonracial right-wing alliance including the AVU, Vekom, and three conservative Black homeland leaders: Buthelezi, Mangope of Bophuthatswana, and Gqozo of the Ciskei.[42] COSAG opposed bilateral negotiations between the ANC and NP and advocated a confederal system, with substantial devolution of power to ethnic groups.

In May 1993 the entire right wing was drawn together under the umbrella of the Afrikaner Volksfront, led by General Constand Viljoen. The AVF aimed to unite the fractious conservative factions behind the goal of an ethnic homeland for Afrikaners. Aside from Viljoen, who was not connected to any political party, most of the executive council of the AVF was drawn from the CP and continued to boycott political participation.

In March 1994 Viljoen defied the recalcitrant AVF executive and broke away to form a political party to contest the April 1994 elections. Although Viljoen and his party, the Freedom Front, had the support of "the generals" (an influential group of five former South African Defense Force commanders who had joined the right wing) and other Volksfront pragmatists, the CP and most of the AVF alliance continued to insist on boycotting elections. Once again the right wing was organizationally and strategically fractured, and Viljoen won only 2 percent of the national vote. Moreover, FF supporters made more use of the split ballot than any other group. Although the party won more than 600,000 votes in provincial elections it received only 400,000 votes nationally. This was a significant drop from the 1992 referendum, in which the right wing won 875,000 votes. Many right-wingers may have heeded the CP's call to boycott elections, but many more had probably become disillusioned with the infighting and machinations of the political leadership and withdrawn from politics altogether. Still others may have returned to "traditional" political homes in the NP.[43]

By and large, however, the right wing managed to retain the support of roughly the same number of voters as it had in 1989. Although the conservative pole of White politics was riven with internal disagreement, it was well organized in the sense that its network permeated all levels of civil society in areas where its constituency was based. The CP itself was severely weakened by the defection of the pragmatists, and the Freedom Front gained the support of many who voted for the CP in the 1980s, but the right wing as a whole neither gained nor lost significant support between 1989 and 1994.

The fact that it was organized in part through cultural and religious groups almost certainly played a role in ethnicizing a split that had largely been perceived as ideological and regional in the 1980s. It was not until 1992, however, when the strategy of the right wing changed from "partition"—a return to Verwoerdian apartheid—to self-determination and the demand for an Afrikaner Volkstaat, that Afrikaner ethnic identity became the central, dominant, and publicly articulated feature of the right-wing political project.

Available Ideology

Afrikaner identity is available for political mobilization in the postapartheid era in part because it is embedded in prior ideological legitimation. As a political identity, Afrikanerdom draws heavily on the Great Trek and the two Boer Wars, which themselves derive political content and salience from prior mobilization during the preapartheid and apartheid eras. The political and public articulation of Afrikanerdom was mediated by an extensive cultural and religious network that built and maintained the ideology sustaining apartheid, group-based politics, White supremacy, and ethnic nationalism. The network that occupied Afrikaner civil society and spiritual life reinforced the political party that traditionally occupied political life—the NP.

It is, in fact, through the multiple interlocking organizations of Afrikaner civil and political society that a coherent voice of Afrikanerdom was created. Afrikaner identity can be private, in the sense that people speak Afrikaans at home, occasionally eat "traditional Afrikaner" dishes, and hold character traits that they label as Afrikaans. Nevertheless, it is primarily in public expression—in church, at meetings, on commemorative holidays—that Afrikaners practice traditions, play music, articulate views, and wear costumes that mark them as members of a distinct group, and through which a group identity has been constructed. In the absence of such organizations and public ideological reinforcement, Afrikaner identity would probably be atomized, private, and irrelevant to politics in South Africa.

As it is, Afrikaner political identity has been linked, historically and ideologically, to apartheid. When the NP government came to power on an apartheid campaign platform in 1948, it rode a tide of nascent Afrikaner ethnic nationalism. Apartheid was the ideological and institutional structure that supported the Afrikaner political project. It may be argued that Afrikaner identity was embedded in a political ideological history that both sustained and constrained it. When the NP started to move away from its cultural base and ceased to mobilize political support through this network in the 1970s and 1980s, Afrikaner political identity was partially demobilized. The demise of apartheid in the 1980s was accompanied and spurred by an endogenous critique that set many Afrikaners ideologically and politically adrift.[44]

The ideology that justified apartheid and drove Afrikaner nationalism in this century rested heavily on biblical justification and Calvinism. In 1986 the largest Afrikaner church, the Dutch Reformed Church (DRC), publicly denounced and apologized for apartheid. This was a crucial event for two reasons. First, it was in part the Dutch Reformed Church, through its interpretation of the Bible, that had provided the moral justification for apartheid ideologies of separate development, group rights, and race-based exclusion. The political ideologies of many Afrikaners rested on the teachings of the church. Its renunciation of apartheid sparked a crisis of ideological dissonance for many ordinary people.[45] Apartheid and the church both comprehended beliefs that Afrikaners had long held to be self-evident, as well as institutional foundations of group identity; the church's disavowal of apartheid forced a choice between value systems.

Second, by contesting the ideology of apartheid, the foundation of the Afrikaner political project, the Church forced the matter of ideology into the arena of political identity and into Afrikanerdom. From the mid-1940s through the late 1970s, the apartheid political project and the Afrikaner identity it supported were internally coherent and faced no serious challenges from within the laager. People processed political information in a way that made sense to them, in light of their own experience and of the multiple reinforcing messages they received from political, religious, cultural, and economic platforms.[46] When the messages received began to contradict each other, the question of ideology was flushed from a latent, taken-for-granted place, and thrust into the foreground of contention. Both the matter of ideology and its substance grew more contested after the church, which played a dominant role in the reproduction and dissemination of Afrikaner political ideology in civil society, renounced apartheid. People and organizations were forced to review their ideological commitments in light of the fracture among the producers of political ideology. Once ideology was contested, it grew more salient.

Some people left the DRC to join one of the sister churches that had either declined to take a stand (thereby ostensibly endorsing the status quo) or explicitly taken a proapartheid stance. One dissenting sect formed the Afrikaanse Protestante Kerk (APK), which was overtly political in that it differed from the established churches only on the matter of political ideology and support for apartheid. The APK is an explicitly right-wing organization. Most people, however, muddled along in the Dutch Reformed Church, trying to reconcile their religious and political ideological commitments.

It was in the context of this ideological crisis that the NP began to negotiate the end of apartheid in 1990. It was also in this context that the right wing struggled to redefine itself in the transition period. Although a return to Verwoerdian apartheid no doubt held practical and personal appeal for many White South Africans, the grounds of its ideological justification had imploded by 1990. At the same time, ethnic self-determination became an international, and internationally sanctioned, phenomenon at the end of the Cold War. Countries all over the world appeared to be dividing along ethnic lines, and such divisions reverberated with at least one aspect of apartheid ideology—ethnic nationalism.

For many Afrikaners, ethnic self-determination is a natural extension of apartheid without the burden of discrimination. In this ideological climate, a Volkstaat in which Afrikaners can govern themselves without governing others cleaves the narrow line between the competing ideological imperatives of apartheid and democracy. A Volkstaat in which the majority is Afrikaner can be governed by straightforward majority rule, without any elaborate electoral mechanisms or conditions of franchise to safeguard group rights. It can be organized both institutionally and ideologically as a small, homogeneous nation-state. Because the Volkstaat relies on ethnic, not racial, self-determination, it draws the relevant boundary around Afrikaners, not Whites. Whether or not people continue to perceive Whiteness as the single-most relevant feature of Afrikanerdom, ideological coherence demands that political boundaries be drawn around the Afrikaner ethnic group, not the White racial group.

The ideological dissonance that accompanied the end of the apartheid era for many Afrikaners has been replaced by two competing ideological paradigms that make sense to most White South Africans. These paradigms make sense in part because they draw on broader and older traditions. The first, which has incorporated many Afrikaners but does not include an Afrikaner political identity nor Afrikaners as a political unit, is capitalist democracy. Within the confines of White South Africa, capitalist democracy has been the ostensible engine of politics and economics since the 1960s, at least. The postapartheid era is represented as an expansion of the franchise under circumstances in which capitalism can be expected to continue to safeguard the interests of those who have accumulated assets.[47] The second ideological paradigm, which dominates the right wing, is based on group rather than individual rights. It explicitly incorporates Afrikaners as an ethnic group and lays claim not to apartheid—now accepted as at least unfeasible, if not morally bankrupt, by the bulk of the reactionary right—but to ethnic self-determination in a sovereign territory.

Resonance

In the immediate postapartheid era, efforts to mobilize reactionary Afrikaner nationalism for political purposes and in conflictual ways have met with limited success. Contrary to almost all predictions that Whites would never give up power or that the threat of Black majority rule would trigger a violent Afrikaner back-lash, the majority of Afrikaners followed the NP through the transition into a postapartheid South Africa without even a protest, let alone serious violence.[48] Although Afrikaner identity enjoyed a political resurgence among a minority of Afrikaners in the transition and immediate posttransition periods, by the second national election in 1999 it appeared mostly dormant again, with the parties of Afrikaner nationalism losing significant numbers of voters to the left.

In South Africa's first two democratic elections, most Afrikaners did not vote for the party that claims to be the political torchbearer of Afrikaner nationalism. Although ethnic support bases are impossible to calculate from 1994 election returns, we can surmise that all of the support for the FF came from Whites. One hundred percent of those who supported the FF claimed to have voted. Among CP supporters, who would also have voted FF because the CP boycotted elections, only 74 percent claimed to have voted.[49] Because we do not know how many CP supporters remained in 1994, however, we have no basis from which to deduce how many Afrikaners boycotted elections. Polls indicate that 83 percent of FF support came from Afrikaners and 17 percent from English-speakers.[50] The FF's 2.2 percent of the total national vote equaled roughly 425,000 votes. This is something less than half of the approximately 900,000 votes the CP received in 1989 elections—representing 30 percent of the White vote and 50 percent of Afrikaners. We may deduce, then, that roughly 25 percent of Afrikaners voted for the FF in national elections in 1994. If 10 percent boycotted the elections and another 10 percent voted for the DP or the IFP, then some 55 percent of Afrikaners voted NP in 1994 (as opposed to probably about 40 percent in 1989). Increasing Afrikaner support for the NP is corroborated by polling data that show support dropping for the right wing (CP, AWB, Volksfront) and support concomitantly rising for the NP between July 1993 and February 1994.[51] Roughly 60 percent of Afrikaner voters voted for the NP in local government elections in 1995 and 1996.[52] By 1999, however, polls indicated that almost 30 percent of Afrikaners voted for the DP.[53]

In 1994 National Party voters' second choice of parties was spread evenly among the DP, the IFP, and the CP, with the ANC a slightly less frequent alternative.[54] It is thus clear that the NP plays the role of a catch-all party in South African politics, representing a range of different ideological and political perspectives. Among those NP voters whose second choice was the CP, race almost certainly remained a highly politicized identity. These voters probably chose the NP over the CP for strategic reasons, because it was larger and likely to be more powerful against the ANC. Most of those who voted for the NP, however, claimed to be driven by performance-related reasons. In a national survey, only 0.6 percent of those who voted for the NP (of which 30 percent were Coloured) said that they were attracted to de Klerk because of his race. None of the respondents claimed they were attracted to de Klerk because of his ethnicity. Sixty-six percent of NP voters preferred de Klerk because of expectations of future performance, integrity and trust, and ability and competence.[55]

As a result of ticket-splitting, the FF received greater support in 1994 provincial elections than it did in national elections. Due apparently to strategic voting, the FF received roughly one-third more regional than national votes. During the campaign FF party leaders stressed that the tally of the provincial vote would be used to ascertain the feasibility and location of a Volkstaat. In provincial elections the DP, FF, and NP won almost the same number of votes in 1994 as they received in 1989 parliamentary elections. The DP and FF share of the vote dropped substantially in 1994 national elections, however, with the NP winning approximately 65 percent of the White vote, compared with 48 percent in 1989.[56] Although the NP did not explicitly mobilize racial or ethnic identity among Whites in the run-up to the 1994 election, it is likely that the party continued to be perceived by many on the right as a protector of "White" interests. In the immediate postapartheid period the NP was able to capitalize on an oppositional identity as the largest party next to the ANC. Between 1994 and 1999, however, the renamed New National Party lost the bulk of its support, in particular outside the Cape, and fell into fourth place, with less than 7 percent of the vote.

Significant demographic and socioeconomic cleavages exist among conservative and moderate White voters. The highest levels of support for the FF came from the poorest group of voters, with monthly household incomes below R599 ($100). Read another way, among the poorest group of White voters, support for the FF was close to support for the NP. Among all other economic groups, support for the NP ranged from three to ten times as high as support for the FF. About 13 percent of rural White voters and 14 percent of urban Whites supported the FF in 1994. The rural White vote was more or less tied up by the FF and the NP, whereas urban Whites were more likely to vote for the DP, IFP, or ANC.[57] FF fortunes also varied significantly by region. More than 40 percent of the FF's total vote came from the Gauteng province, which includes Johannesburg and Pretoria. The party also did significantly better in the northern parts of the country—Northern and Eastern Transvaal, North-West province and the Orange Free State—that were dominated by the CP in the 1980s.

Polls indicate that performance, leadership, and race appeared to drive most FF supporters. In one September 1994 survey, respondents were asked why they were attracted to their candidate. Among FF supporters, 25 percent said that integrity and trust drew them to Viljoen, 24 percent said that they were attracted to him because of race, and 15 percent cited his ability and competence. Reliability drew 10.5 percent, ideology 8.5 percent, charisma 8.2 percent, and 3 percent claimed that ethnicity attracted them to Viljoen. Fully half of those who supported Viljoen in elections cited performance-related reasons such as integrity, trust, ability, competence, and reliability. Another one in six were attracted by Viljoen's ideology and charisma.[58]

The strength of these data rests on people's second choice of parties. If people are deciding, for example, between de Klerk and Viljoen, who are both White, it is hardly relevant to cite race as a criterion of choice. Yet this does not necessarily mean that race or ethnicity are irrelevant to these voters. They may take for granted that the choice is among White candidates. The dominant second choices of Freedom Front supporters were the IFP and the CP.[59] For those who have narrowed their electoral options to the Afrikaner nationalist or the Zulu nationalist party, it seems clear that ideology—a belief in a group's right to ethnic self-determination—and not race, drives politics. CP supporters favored the AWB slightly over the IFP and the NP. Here it seems that race did trump ideology for the majority, especially because the AWB has little to recommend it (in the way of strong leadership or a well-honed political platform) beyond a firm commitment to White hegemony.

Even though race was chosen by only half as many FF voters as those who cited all the performance-related reasons combined, it was the second—most commonly cited reason that FF supporters gave for supporting Viljoen. One in four people who voted for the FF liked Viljoen either because he was White or because they believed he would protect the privileges of Whiteness, depending on how one interprets the question. Either way, the preference points strongly to the continued politicization of color among FF voters. At the same time, only 3 percent cited ethnicity as their reason for supporting Viljoen. Although these responses appear to demonstrate that Whiteness is still more salient to conservative voters than Afrikanerdom, the results may be more semantic than actual. Ethnicity is a word that is not traditionally used to refer to Afrikaners. In South Africa ethnic groups are African, not White. Ethnicity has been used to denote difference among Africans and to divide them into separate homelands. Afrikaners call themselves a race or a nation, following a now-obsolete usage of *race,* as in "the German race." Thus it is impossible to determine from these data whether respondents supported Viljoen on the basis of political identities mediated by Afrikaner ethnic, or White racial, identity.

Other data indicate, however, that Afrikaner ethnic identity experienced a brief political resurgence for a minority of Afrikaners in the postapartheid era. Although the FF won only 2.2 percent of the total vote in the April 1994 election, the fact that the party was formed only four weeks before the election makes such a showing reasonably respectable. That it won one-third more in regional elections, in which voters were urged to register support for a Volkstaat, suggests that at least a subsection of votes for the FF were ethnically driven. Forty-three percent of Whites claimed that their major reason for supporting a party was that it "protects my language and culture."[60] An idiom of exclusion and incorporation survives, but it is articulated via language and culture representing ethnic, and not racial, concerns. In local government elections in 1995 and 1996, the FF and CP together won 4 percent of the vote, almost doubling their support base.

In addition, it is possible to deduce from speaking to Afrikaners, from reading editorials and published letters in newspapers, and from observing politics in the mostly Afrikaner towns of the northern provinces, that Afrikaner identity was more politically salient among right-wingers in 1994 and 1995 than it had been in the 1980s. The Afrikaans language, for example, was a nonissue throughout the half-century of NP rule, when it was one of two official languages, the primary language of government and the civil service, and a requirement in all schools. Since 1994 Afrikaans has emerged as a major political issue for the right wing. The future of Afrikaans is allegedly threatened because it is not privileged over the other ten official languages. This issue is obviously particular to Afrikaans speakers, not all Whites, and has become central to right-wing discourse. Many hundreds of newspaper letters have defended the continued right of Afrikaans to linguistic preeminence and have decried the loss to Afrikaners of their linguistic heritage.

In particular in 1995 and 1996, right-wingers also discovered renewed interest in such Afrikaner cultural and historical celebrations as Day of the Vow ceremonies. Attendance at these events increased somewhat but included new content as it came to signal a particular political identity. Celebrations were organized exclusively by right-wing groups and political parties and were rarely, if ever, attended by "moderate" or "liberal" Afrikaners. Afrikaner cultural celebrations became the province of the political right wing. Conservatives were drawn to such events by political, ethnic, and perhaps even moral imperatives. One man explained, "Ja, nee. I didn't used to come at all, but now it's important, hey? We have to work for the party, be active. We have to stick together, Afrikaners. It's our heritage, our ancestors."[61] The main speakers at the numerous events I attended were always CP or FF party leaders.

Many Afrikaners became politicized only in the postapartheid era. In some towns, women in particular began to organize and mobilize around the issue of schooling. The problems they articulated involved a threat to standards of education, language, and culture. The latter two issues have specific Afrikaner content, and this type of local-level political action dovetails with the broader politicization of Afrikanerdom. Women collecting signatures on petitions for Afrikaans-medium schooling could be found at Afrikaner cultural festivals organized by right-wing political parties.

By 1999 Afrikaner identity appeared to have lost some of its political salience, even among the minority with which it previously resonated. The Freedom Front lost roughly three hundred thousand votes, winning less than 1 percent of the vote in 1999. The CP did not contest elections in 1999. Part of the FF's support may have gone to the newly formed Afrikaner Eenheidsbeweging, which won 0.3 percent of the vote, or to Louis Luyt's Freedom Alliance, which won 0.5 percent. A prominent minority of conservative right-wingers from the AWB, FF, and NNP have left Afrikaner nationalism for the liberal DP, however.[62] Among Afrikaners, political identity appears extremely fluid in the decade surrounding the nation's democratic transition.

Afrikaner identity appears to have been partially eclipsed by the politics of postapartheid democracy. Many people who feel a strong connection to an Afrikaner identity have nevertheless chosen to vote strategically for a larger party that may be better able to protect their economic and security interests. This imperative was partly operative as FF voters split their vote in 1994 and appeared to dominate voters' thinking by 1999. Even Afrikaners who supported the FF or the CP did not for the most part embrace the concept of a Volkstaat. Only 18 percent of Afrikaners interviewed in a 1993 survey said that they would be prepared to move to a Volkstaat, demands for which anchored the FF's party platform. Only 6 percent were prepared to move if their standard of living fell.[63] The right wing long threatened violence and a massive uprising if the transition proceeded, or if the NP gave away too much power, or if the ANC took over. Ultimately, most

Afrikaners preferred to watch and wait rather than take up arms, even as time marched past the many lines they had drawn in the sand.

The political salience of Afrikaner identity can be measured in two ways. First, do political elites attempt to mobilize ethnic identity for political purposes? Do they define their constituent base in ethnic terms, and do they use ethnic appeals to attract a support base? Second, do people themselves make political decisions based on their ethnic identities? Do the opinions, interests, and perceptions of members of one ethnic group differ noticeably from those of members of other ethnic groups? When we use this two-pronged approach to the problem of measuring political identity, it appears that Afrikaner identity was politically dormant in the 1980s, that it was politically mobilized and salient for a minority of Afrikaners after 1992, and that it receded again after 1994.

How Afrikaner identity came to be repoliticized, for something less than one-third of all Afrikaners, is a complicated matter. The process appears to have evolved in three parts: Afrikaners were first divided, then forged into separate political groups, and finally defined in more or less ethnic terms. The effects of conditioning and proximate factors in determining the relative salience of Afrikaner political identity varied over time and across space.

After 1990 and the beginning of the end of the apartheid era, Afrikaner identity began to reenter the political arena. When de Klerk lifted the thirty-year ban on the liberation movements in February 1990, the White right's perception of its political options began to change. In particular after 1992, once government actions precluded the possibility of a return to apartheid and it became clear that the CP could not marshal sufficient support to achieve its goals democratically, the right wing was reduced to two options. It could go outside the political arena and try to achieve its goals by nondemocratic means, or it could change its goals. In a way, it did both. Thus it is clear that the transition from apartheid affected the incentives that drove political elites to mobilize some, but not other, political identities.

Nevertheless, it was not inevitable that the right wing would turn to ethnic mobilization in search of a constituent base. The CP might have avoided characterizing itself in ethnic terms if it had not adopted the ideal of a Volkstaat as its central mobilizing issue after the 1992 referendum. In the absence of the referendum on the future of negotiations, which forced the right wing to redefine itself and to reinvent its political space, the CP might have continued to muddle along at the right pole of the South African political spectrum without necessarily delineating a clear ethnic identity. Once it became clear that the political arena would be opened to include Africans, and that the exclusive ideological position of the CP would reduce it to a permanent minority status, the right wing set to work to redefine the boundaries of citizenship in ethnic terms.

The efforts of conservative White politicians to mobilize Afrikaner ethnic identity for political purposes have met with only limited success, however. There are roughly three million Afrikaners in South Africa; at its height, ethnic identity may have been politically salient for a maximum of about one-third, or one million, of them. This is true for material, organizational, and ideological reasons.

Afrikaner identity appeared to resonate politically among those who believed they were isolated and ignored by the NP government in the twilight of its reign. As economic recession and drought worsened in the early 1990s, forcing many farmers into bankruptcy and workers into unemployment, and the state continued to ignore the demands and pleas of an increasingly desperate subsector of Afrikaners, isolated communities were forced to turn inward. They relied on a local network of friends, family, and civic organizations to weather South Africa's worst recession in over fifty years. Economic hardship may thus have played a role in strengthening ties of reciprocity and a sense of community in many of the hardest hit areas of South Africa.

In addition, Afrikanerdom is politically salient to those whose lives are structured by the civil network that forms the organizational base of the right wing. Freedom Front and CP voters differ from NP voters along an organizational axis. The former are more likely to attend church regularly, to belong to Afrikaner cultural organizations, to send their children to Voortrekker Camp (the Afrikaner equivalent of Boy Scouts) and to attend such Afrikaner national celebrations as the commemoration of the Day of the Vow. In the postapartheid era, the right wing lacks organizational access to the majority of Afrikaners who have moved out of the traditional Afrikaner cultural and religious civil society network, while rural farmers and the urban working classes retain ties through ethnic organizational networks.

The political appeal of ethnic affiliation may also be limited because the Afrikaner political project has been harnessed to a radically conservative ideological position which does not fit the lived experience and ideological framework of the majority of middle- and upper-class Afrikaners. Most Afrikaners are intellectually and ideologically linked more closely to a Western liberal ideological tradition mediated by their interaction with English-speaking elites, and by their participation in the Western-dominated world market, than to Afrikaner nationalist ideals. The majority of Afrikaners accepted that apartheid was untenable before de Klerk entered office in 1989. Whites by and large supported and embraced new national symbols, such as the flag and the national anthem. The drama and trauma of the democratic transition itself may have played a role in generating a common South African identity.[64] Most Afrikaners have rejected as unfeasible the demands for an Afrikaner Volkstaat that anchor the political position of the right wing. Most Afrikaners appear, for the moment, ideologically moderate, and prefer to try to negotiate a common future with other South Africans than to retreat to an ethnic laager.

So long as the Afrikaner political project continues to be tied to a particular, extreme, ideological position, it is not likely to appeal to the majority of its potential (ethnic) constituency. Whereas the Afrikaner politicization project of the 1940s served to unite Afrikaners behind one common political cause and party, the NP, the mobilization of Afrikanerdom in the 1990s has further divided Afrikaners in a way that could ultimately cause a redefinition of the ethnic group.

That Afrikaner identity has only limited political appeal in the immediate postapartheid era does not mean that it could not gain salience in the future. If indeed South Africa's relevant political cleavages were to develop along ethnic lines, Afrikaners might organize along Afrikaner lines, if only in response to the prior mobilization of other ethnic groups. If the NP, for reasons now unforeseeable, decided to mobilize an Afrikaner identity for political purposes, its extensive organizational network and resources would afford it greater access to, and probably success among, currently depoliticized Afrikaners. If the Afrikaner political project was decoupled from conservative ideology, it might appeal to moderate Afrikaners. If middle- and upper-class Afrikaners began to feel the ill effects of affirmative action on their employment possibilities or upward mobility, they could develop a common ethnic sentiment in response to a perceived threat. If local elections continue to be contested under power-sharing rules, they may produce incentives for the mobilization of Afrikaner nationalist sentiment which could in the end be self-reinforcing.

The political salience, meanings, and boundaries of Afrikaner identity remain indeterminate and fluid. Although the political institutions of South African democracy have been established in what we may assume is a permanent way, the other factors that interact to shape political identity continue to shift. The parties that once combined to attract the bulk of Afrikaner support, the NP, the FF, and the CP, persistently renegotiated a political space in the context of shifting variables. By 1999 the CP had disappeared, and the New National Party and Freedom Front fared much worse in the second democratic election than they had in 1994. Although much of its potential support was probably lost to nonvoters rather than to other parties, the abysmal showing of the Freedom Front is probably a fair indication that Afrikaner identity surged and again declined in the decade after the end of apartheid. The second election results suggest that the political identities of many White South Africans remain in flux, and the political meaning and boundaries of Afrikaner identity in particular are highly indeterminate. It is impossible to predict whether Afrikaner identity will be repoliticized as South Africa attempts democratic consolidation, although it is unlikely to soon attract more than the minority it garnered in transition.

6 Then I Was Black

The Politics of Coloured Identity, 1982–1990

The label *Coloured* was imposed on South Africans of mixed, Khoisan, or Malay descent by the apartheid government. A Coloured person was officially defined as "a person who is not a White or a Black person."[1] In a political and social system that depended upon the classification of all individuals into racial groups, which in turn determined their economic, social, and political possibilities, Coloureds, by their very existence, inhabited an oppositional space. They existed at the intersections of multiple racial classifications, occupying a residual, clearly *non*-racial category. Coloureds defied racialization. Under apartheid, those "outside" racial stereotypes were redefined in racial terms, to support the ideological proposition that the world was naturally divided into separate races that belonged apart. South Africa's minority Indian population was similarly reclassified as an Asian race, for example, whereas Japanese were "honorary Whites."

As a result of its self-conscious construction by the White minority government for overt political and social purposes, the politics of Coloured identity was fraught with tension and ambiguity throughout the apartheid era. Many Coloureds resisted calling themselves Coloured, using instead the term "so-called Coloured," and by the 1980s both of the major political groups that dominated "Coloured politics" articulated an oppositional Black, not Coloured, political identity. *Black,* used in its political sense, was an inclusive non-White identity that encompassed Indians, Africans, and Coloureds.[2] Moreover, Blackness was not conceived as a racial category; it was an antiapartheid oppositional identity of political and ideological, not social or cultural, significance. Blacks were bound by common oppression, not pigmentation. As a statement of opposition against the White apartheid government, Black identity had more or less resonance among different segments of the population in the 1980s, depending on interlocking and interrelated material conditions, organizational patterns, and available ideology.

Historical Precedent, 1902–1982

Although the term *Coloured* was used to describe people in South Africa long before the apartheid era, its meaning was more fluid in the nineteenth century: it referred generally to all non-Europeans and was a category people were able to transcend. The term was first used to describe political organizations—The Afrikaner League (coloured) and the Coloured People's Association—after 1880.[3] Both of these organizations were short-lived and only marginally important, but they mark the beginning of a conception of Coloured as a category with potential political content.

The first important political organization rooted in Coloured identity was the African People's Organization (APO), started at the end of the Boer War in 1902. The establishment of a Coloured political organization was preceded by two events which may have served as partial catalysts of a sense of explicitly Coloured opposition. The British government of the Cape colony made the extension of Coloured rights into the Boer Republics part of its war propaganda, presenting discrimination against Coloureds as a justification for involvement in the Boer War. Coloureds therefore threw their support behind the British war effort. The British in fact reneged on their wartime promise to extend the franchise, and the Treaty of Vereeniging, which ended the war, left open the question of non-European political rights.[4] Coloureds began to fear that discrimination in the interior would extend to the Cape, rather than the other way around.[5]

In the same period, an outbreak of cholera among Africans at the Cape sparked White demands for the segregation of non-Whites. Coloured elites demanded that Coloureds be exempted from residential segregation imposed on Africans. They subsequently formed the APO as "a permanent organization to protect the liberties of the Coloured people." The APO was, from the outset, an elite and conservative organization that demanded that "civilised Coloureds" be allowed to take their place alongside Whites as "civilised men."[6] At the same time, however, it aimed "to promote unity between the coloured races," by which it meant non-Whites. This ambiguous phraseology foreshadowed the persistent tension of Coloured politics in the twentieth century: the commitment to work with other non-Europeans while defending the rights of Coloureds and trying to assimilate into, and acquire the privileges of, Whiteness. Nevertheless, by 1904 *Coloured* had come to denote the relatively narrower group of people that it continues to describe today, and Colouredness began to include political content.

Although Coloured political, economic, and social rights were gradually eroded from the turn of the century on, Coloureds enjoyed higher political and social status than Africans, and they remained on the common voter's roll in the Cape until 1956. Many Cape districts included a significant number of Coloured voters, and White parties depended on Coloured votes to win close elections. The APO used the Coloured vote as a weapon to extract promises from White political party leaders. Parties had incentives to promise the Coloured electorate a share in White privilege and preferential treatment over Africans. In 1923, for example, the National Party proclaimed a "New Deal" for Coloureds, offering them a Civilised

Labor Policy which promised advantages over Africans, although it continued to reserve greater advantages for Whites.

Abdullah Abdurahman, who led the APO from 1905 until his death in 1940, consistently aligned the organization with the British-dominated South Africa and United parties over the Afrikaner-dominated National Party. He tried to influence politics by enticing British parties to support Coloured causes in return for a guarantee of Coloured electoral support, and by sending delegations to request exemptions or plead special status for Coloureds to sympathetic party and government leaders.[7] His politics were characterized mainly by reaction to specific legislation or threats to Coloured privileges. At the same time, Abdurahman tried consistently, but ultimately without success, to align the APO with other non-European organizations. He refused to accept *Coloured* as a separate racial or political category and tried to advance the cause of Coloureds within a broader alliance.

Nevertheless, the APO retained a distinctly Coloured identity. It was in part the strategy of the organization that forced it into Colouredness. Its principal political figures were fairly conservative. They had no interest in revolutionary tactics or in overthrowing the system; rather, they wanted a place within it. And so they worked through the established system to petition for such a place. But the system defined and responded to them as Coloureds, thereby forcing them to accept Coloured identity as a basis of political articulation. Although Abdurahman ideologically resisted "Coloured politics," the APO was forced into race-based organization, mobilization, and identity because it chose to operate inside the system. As a result, the APO itself unwittingly reinforced Colouredness as a politically relevant category.

The APO faced a challenge from more radical organizations within the Coloured community starting in the 1930s. As the government eliminated Coloured privileges and a new generation of political activists assumed the mantle of political leadership, Coloured politics grew less moderate.[8] Groups such as the National Liberation League (NLL) and the Non-European Unity Movement (NEUM) rejected a narrow Coloured identity in favor of an inclusive Black identity, a working-class alliance, and a mass-action strategy. In 1936 the NLL coordinated the All African Convention, including representatives of the African, Indian, and Coloured groups, and in 1939 it organized a day of protest against the Servitude Bill, drawing ten thousand African and Coloured demonstrators to Cape Town.

By 1948, when the NP came to power, successive legislation had significantly eroded the position of Coloureds relative to Whites. The 1909 Act of Union barred non-Whites from sitting in Parliament. In 1930 the franchise was extended to White, and not Coloured, women, and in 1931 further qualifications for White voters over twenty-one were abolished. These measures diluted the strength of the Coloured vote by increasing the number of White voters. At the same time, the NP took advantage of new laws that made it easier to challenge the right of individual Coloureds' to vote. They barred thousands of people from registering to vote, as only those with the money and time to defend their position in court succeeded in overturning challenges. Even the Civilised Labour Policy, which ostensibly protected Coloureds' economic status, undercut their position by providing incentives for employers to hire Whites over Coloureds, barring Coloureds from holding certain positions, and prohibiting non-Whites from supervising Whites.

When the National Party government came to power in 1948, it further fixed divisions between Whites and Coloureds. The NP won office on an apartheid platform that officially designated Coloureds as a distinct and separate racial group, with racially designated rights, status, and access to resources. The NP proposed the segregation of Coloureds and Whites in every sphere of life. Over the next twenty years, the government legislated its ideological vision to entrench private and public racial separation and White racial superiority.

The 1950 Population Registration and Group Areas Acts spatially segregated Coloureds, Whites, Africans, and Asians by registering all South Africans according to racial group and forcing members of different races to live in separate areas. The Separate Amenities, Immorality, and Mixed Marriages Acts barred people of different "racial groups" from public interaction, as well as from private social, sexual, and marital relationships.

Social separation between Whites and Coloureds was intended to reinforce divisions in the political sphere. The NP removed Coloureds from the common voters' roll with the 1956 Separate Representation of Voters Act. The move was intended in part to undercut what the NP perceived as the opposition Liberal Party's support base. The National Party considered Coloureds a political threat because they had supported the British in the Boer War and in the two World Wars, because they were thought to identify closely with the British, and because they had historically supported British over Afrikaner-dominated parties.[9] The 1956 act barred Coloureds from membership in White political parties, permitting them instead to elect four White members of Parliament. Coloured voters consistently chose English-speaking members of dominantly British parties to represent them. In 1968 even this representation was withdrawn, and in 1971 Coloureds were restricted from municipal politics.

In the meantime, the government established a series of separate political institutions for "Coloured politics." The Coloured Advisory Council (CAC) lasted from 1943 until 1950, when all but four of its members resigned in frustration over the NP's nonnegotiable apartheid policy. In 1959 the Union Council of Coloured Affairs (UCCA), an appointed, unrepresentative, and ineffectual body, was established as part of the Separate Representation of Voters Act to advise the government on matters of "Coloured concern." It was replaced in 1968 by the only slightly more representative Coloured Persons' Representative Council (CPRC).

Up to a point, some Coloured people cooperated with the government to represent the interests of Coloureds, forming Coloured political organizations that operated within the system. The government-appointed Coloured Advisory Council focused primarily on the socioeconomic needs of Coloureds, requesting more funds for housing and education, for example. It was the CAC which first recommended that a Coloured Labour Preference Area be established to safeguard the economic interests of Coloureds against Africans. Some CAC members also founded the Coloured People's National Union, based on "sound Christian principles," which sought to advance the interests of Coloureds in cooperation with Whites.[10] In 1964 the Federal Coloured People's Party (FCPP), which endorsed Christianity, apartheid, and a separate Coloured identity, was established by the former chairman of the UCCA, Tom Swartz.

Fearful lest the FCPP dominate the arena of reformist Coloured politics, Richard van der Ross and others founded the Labour Party of South Africa in 1966. The LP rejected apartheid and called for a nonracial, democratic, and noncommunist South Africa. It identified itself as a worker's party. Although its charter explicitly committed the party to the promotion of Coloured interests, it was increasingly influenced by the Black Consciousness Movement after 1972; the party dropped all reference to Coloureds from its constitution in the late 1970s.

The Non-European Unity Movement dominated Coloured extraparliamentary politics throughout this period. The NEUM was mainly an elite intellectual organization controlled by teachers. It advocated noncollaboration and nonracialism. The NEUM's strict ideological positions and fiery rhetoric prevented it from cooperating with other non-White political organizations, such as the African National Congress and the South African Indian Congress, which were more strategically flexible and refused to abide by the NEUM's strict nonracial and noncollaborationist charter. The NEUM's principled position essentially restricted it from any political activity, which was in effect all its members, mostly government-employed teachers, could afford to do safely. Other oppositional Coloured political organizations, such as the Franchise Action Committee (FRAC) and the South African Coloured People's Organization, did, on the other hand, participate in broader ANC campaigns and played an important role in creating an organizational, not just rhetorical, common ground between Africans and Coloureds against apartheid. The FRAC, for example, participated in the Defiance Campaign and the Congress Alliance in the 1950s.

In the twentieth century Coloured identity was more or less politically salient for differently positioned members of the Coloured community at different times. Groups like the NEUM that explicitly shunned identification with Colouredness had differential access to, and resonance among, different segments of the population. Nonracialism appealed to younger, better-educated Coloureds and was most powerful among teachers, where it developed a strong organizational base. But the NEUM existed alongside a conservative political agenda that also drew popular support from Coloureds. Parties like the UCCA and FCPP embraced an explicitly Coloured identity and operated comfortably within a segregated apartheid political hierarchy, drawing support from a conservative, religious, middle class. Multiple political traditions have long coexisted within the supposed racial boundaries of Colouredness.

In the late 1970s and early 1980s government reforms and political opposition to them widened the parameters of political possibility—including expression, identification and action—for Coloureds. Institutional reforms allowed Coloureds access to central government representation for the first time in almost thirty years. Simultaneously, the response of opposition leaders to state attempts to co-opt Coloureds and fracture opposition gave political substance to Black identity. Changes in the structure of the South African economy widened the gap between skilled and unskilled Coloured workers in the 1970s and 1980s, while changes in laws governing unions and the abolition of the Coloured Labour Preference Policy opened the space for economic and political organization across racial lines. The political, social, economic, ideological, and organizational fluidity of the 1980s engendered significant shifts in political identity.

Political Institutions

From 1969 until 1980 Coloureds were represented in government through the Coloured Person's Representative Council. The CPRC consisted of forty elected members and twenty members appointed by the National Party government. Even though Coloureds were required by law to vote, only 36 percent voted in the 1969 CPRC election, and this figure dropped to 25 percent by the next election in 1974. The Labour Party won twenty-six of forty seats in the 1969 elections, but the government appointed an additional twenty apartheid-supporting Federal Party members, making the LP the minority party. The power of the CPRC to make laws and policies affecting Coloured people was curtailed by the fact that Coloureds also fell under the jurisdiction of central government and of local and provincial authorities. The Council passed only three laws between 1969 and 1976, none of which was significant or original.[11]

Although the CPRC was reportedly effective as a forum for the public articulation of Coloured interests and demands, the majority of Coloureds rejected the system and continued to insist on central government representation and the abolition of apartheid. Field studies conducted in 1974 indicated that only 27 percent of urban Coloureds supported the CPRC. Seventy-nine percent of Coloured leaders rejected the CPRC and separate Coloured representation as ineffectual.[12] The Labour Party, which consistently trounced the Federal Party in CPRC elections, subsequently boycotted the forum to delegitimate it. The government finally abolished the CPRC in 1980 after continuous LP boycotts made it not only impotent but a symbol of government illegitimacy and a space for political opposition.

By 1980 the government had also decided to make some concessions to Coloured demands for more effective and direct representation in an effort to induce some degree of cooperation with the system. As part of a larger reform effort aimed at stemming the rising tide of internal opposition and external censure, the NP amended the constitution to allow for a Tricameral Parliament to represent Whites, Coloureds, and Indians in separate chambers. The 1983 constitution continued to exclude Africans from representation at central government level. Members of all three parliaments were to be elected by the race groups they were meant to represent, and none were appointed. Whites would vote for the House of Assembly, Coloureds for the House of Representatives, and Indians for the House of Delegates. All three Houses were represented at the ministerial level, in proportion to their share of the population. By this equation, racial groups were represented in accordance with their proportion of the total population, a 4:2:1 ratio for Whites, Coloureds, and Indians, respectively. Even if Coloureds and Indians cooperated on specific legislation, Whites still controlled the government with a majority on the President's Council. The Tricameral Parliament operated from 1984 until it was dissolved in December 1993 in anticipation of South Africa's first national democratic elections in April 1994.

Despite the structural inequality inherent in the Tricameral system, representation at central government level had certain benefits for Coloureds and Indians during the 1980s. Until 1984 local government in Indian and Coloured areas was carried out by management committees (MCs), which were partly elected and partly nominated. Management committees were under the jurisdiction of White local authorities, and although local authorities were required to consult MCs, they were under no obligation to accept their recommendations. MCs therefore had no real authority and always lacked legitimacy because they were rejected by the major parties in both Indian and Coloured politics.

As a result of demands by the Houses of Delegates and Representatives, Management Committees were granted certain final decision-making powers after 1984. These included "the allocation of business licenses, the allocation of houses and eviction of tenants, the approval and planning of new housing schemes, and the final say in the leasing and utilization of immovable property." The existence of political allies at central government level gave the MCs much greater access and clout: the matter of management committees' power was at one time taken up at cabinet level, for example.[13] Additionally, in 1986 a law was passed allowing the Cape administrator to remove (White) councils that failed to cooperate with MCs.

The House of Representatives had control over other important resources, such as housing, after 1984. Moreover, it had more money available for housing development than the previously responsible White controlled Department of Community Development had had. In 1986 and 1987 the House of Representatives allocated R7 million to upgrade low-income housing in the Cape flats.[14] In hindsight, it does appear that the Tricameral system did provide some occasionally substantial socioeconomic benefits to Coloureds and Indians in the 1980s. Although the system never gained the legitimacy necessary to be sustainable, it represented a tangible material improvement over the previous system for those it included.

Mobilizing Discourse

In the 1980s "Coloured politics" was dominated by two organizations: the Labour Party and the United Democratic Front. The LP was a reformist Coloured political party which had participated in the CPRC with the strategic goal of changing the system from within. After much soul-searching and some defections, the LP leadership decided to participate in the Tricameral Parliament and to stand for elections. The UDF was organized in 1983 for the sole purpose of opposing, and mobilizing support against, parliamentary reforms perceived as co-optive. Coloured politics had a long history of division between "rebels" and "realists," between people who opposed any type of engagement with an unjust system and those who believed that there was some benefit to be derived from cooperation. The greatest political cleavage within the Coloured community was between those who sought to overthrow the system and those who chose to work within it. In the 1980s the UDF and the LP anchored the opposite extremes of this spectrum.

Nevertheless, by the 1980s the ideological terrain of Coloured politics had narrowed sufficiently that both organizations generally articulated an inclusive Black identity defined by a common experience of oppression. Both Labour Party and UDF leaders explicitly stated that they represented Africans as well as Coloureds. That portion of the Coloured political spectrum that had historically articulated a Coloured political identity and had sought a place for Coloureds next to Whites, and separate from Africans, appears to have been almost totally eclipsed in the political climate of the 1980s. Although the LP was demonized by its UDF opponents as collaborationist, it actually claimed an identity not too far from that of the UDF itself, as Black. The party's minister of budget clearly identified himself as Black when he proclaimed during a House of Representatives debate in 1985: "Is there, then, a difference between the digestive tracts of a White and a Black man? Do the privileged people really believe that the years of neglect have caused the Black man's stomach to shrink so much that 30 cents worth of bread is enough to satisfy his hunger, while the White man's stomach need 60 cents worth? Do the people really believe that our elderly people do not get cold?"[15] Labour Party MP J. Douw made the point more explicitly: "When it comes to Blacks there are more subdivisions. I want to tell White South Africa that I am unconditionally Black in the South African context. I am a Black man since I use the same entrance as he does. I suffer under the same oppressive measures as that Black man. When I speak, I speak for that man and I include myself" (3/11/85, p. 1007). A 1987 UDF pamphlet entitled "We Remember Comrade Biko" explained the meaning of Black identity: "Black Consciousness philosophy gave expression to self-definition which meant a rejection of white stereotypes of Blacks and negative references such as non-white. The place of these negatives were taken by positive epithets such as Blacks to refer to all so-called non-white South Africans. The Black Consciousness Movement strove to break down the artificial barriers that were set up by the state to divide the oppressed into Africans, Indians, and Coloureds."

The absence of a parliamentary chamber for Africans robbed this majority constituency of representation in Parliament. No political party represented Africans at the level of central government. The LP therefore claimed this group as its own constituency. For example, Labour Party MPs entered into debates in the racially segregated House of Representatives on the abolition of pass and other laws that affected Africans but not Coloureds. The LP consistently refused to restrict its membership to Coloureds even though the party was legally required to do so. Thus it was in part the structure of the political system, which excluded African representatives, that allowed the LP to expand the boundaries of its constituency beyond Coloureds even as the political structure simultaneously restricted its official power base to Coloureds only. The LP did not, for instance, extend the parameters of its constituency to include Indians, who had their own house in Parliament and thus, in theory anyway, their own representatives.

Labour Party MP T. Abrahams demanded support from a National Party colleague on behalf of Africans: "He told us that he was doing everything possible to make the necessary changes in legislation affecting the African people of this country. We are in full sympathy with him in this regard, but what I am calling for here is for this whole issue to be expedited. . . . We want action, we want movement" (3/12/85, pp. 1085–1086). P. S. Jacobs linked the plights of Blacks and Coloureds: "I represent these Blacks and am very grateful for these concessions. . . . The so-called urban Coloureds are treated as badly as the urban Blacks. Like the Blacks, the Coloureds are also often driven away from various places. There are those who imagine that the Coloureds live happily here in South Africa, that we enjoy the same privileges as our White counterparts. That is untrue, we are also cooped up in our apartheid cage, in our townships. We have as many and as few rights as Blacks in their neighborhoods" (1/30/85, p. 166). F. E. Peters outlined the philosophy of inclusion: "This party informed the Government in 1978 that we rejected in toto the Government's decision to preserve the Western Cape and any other area as a Coloured labour preference area. We saw this as another device to bar Black South Africa to live and work in the area of its choice" (3/4/85, p. 825).

For the UDF the decision to mobilize a broad-based racially inclusive constituency, to include Africans and Coloureds as well as all other racial groups, was driven by ideology as well as strategy. Charterists believe in nonracialism, which denies the importance and sometimes even the existence of race, and UDF politics was characterized by mass action, which required the broadest possible participation. A UDF pamphlet calling for a Youth Day stay-away in June 1986 described participation in both Coloured and African townships: "People fought battles with the police in the streets of Langa, Elsies River, Manenberg, Bonteheuwel, Guguletu, Retreat, and elsewhere in Cape Town." The Mowbray and Gardens Youth Congress made a point of being religiously and linguistically inclusive, issuing pamphlets in English, Xhosa, and Afrikaans and saying, "When Botha sjambokked [whipped] parents, priests, and Imams, did he have no choice?" UDF leader Allan Boesak confirmed: "And we want all of South Africa's people to have their rights. Not just a selected few, not just 'coloured' or 'Indian' after they have been made honorary Whites."[16]

In an explicit effort to be inclusive, the UDF purposely identifies both African

(Langa and Guguletu) and Coloured (Bonteheuwel, Manenberg) townships as sites of violent confrontation between the government and civil society. Pamphlets were often translated into three languages, and in the instance cited above included reference to both priests and imams, a nod to the substantial Muslim minority of Coloureds.

One step in denying the boundaries that created a group called Coloured, separated it from other groups, and gave it substance, was calling the group "so-called Coloured." In Charterist circles in the 1980s it was not possible to say "Coloured" without the preceding "so-called."[17] The point that Coloureds and others were trying to make was that they had not named themselves, that they had been named by a government they considered illegitimate, for reasons they considered illegitimate, and that the name itself had negative connotations, defined as a group that was neither White nor Black.[18] By calling themselves "so-called Coloureds" people inscribed their identities in opposition to, and rejection of, the state.

That the Labour Party, a group whose position in government depended on the representation of Coloureds and whose acceptance of a role in a Coloured house of Parliament suggested recognition of race as a relevant organizing principle, resorted to the use of the modifier "so-called" illustrates the extent of its usage and penetration even into political discourse within the system in the 1980s. A speech by Peters illustrates the principle:

Mr. Chairman, the Labour Party does not speak for the so-called Coloureds only. We negotiate for all South Africans. It is through our request, having had discussions with the government, that the State President decided to halt the forced removal of Blacks to Khayelitsha, that the influx control has been lifted, including bringing about improved living conditions and amenities in the present Black townships of Langa, Guguletu and Nyanga. Our aim is to see that the Blacks are also elected to this government. The Labour Party, in a short space of time, have achieved more than any other so-called Coloured political organization. Ours is a long record of achievements. (1/30/85, p. 159)

Both Labour and the UDF sublimated narrower racially based identities to a pan–South African identity. In so doing, they legitimized the territory of the state and tried to build on nationalistic sentiment. This grew partially out of the claim of each group to represent all people who lived in South Africa. It also indicated acceptance of the boundaries of the state and of an identity which derived from a territory defined and consolidated first by White colonial rule and then by apartheid. The UDF minister of budget said, for example, "The Labour Party is committed to promoting and advancing the dignity and rights, as well as the socioeconomic and cultural well-being, of all South Africans irrespective of race, colour, or creed because we respect and care for all God's creatures, including Whites" (1/30/85, p. 161). Despite radical rhetoric, the UDF's claims were thus also, broadly, within parameters limited by the state. A 1989 Gardens Youth Congress pamphlet explained the role of the UDF: "We provide a home for youth who want to contribute toward building a united, non-racial, democratic South Africa. We form part of the broad National Democratic Movement and as such our members are able to sustain links with youth from other group areas. These links are essential in building non-racialism in practice and in bridging the gaps that apartheid has imposed on us. . . . The principle of non-racialism is that the importance attached to the colour of one's skin should be the same as, say, the importance attached to the colour of one's eyes, i.e. none at all."

Although they embraced an apparently inclusive national identity, both the Labour Party and the UDF constructed an identity in opposition to "Whites." Whites were attacked in their role as government, as ethnic Afrikaners, as apparent sympathizers, and as "big business." The common thread, though, the connection among all of these groups, was their Whiteness. Ultimately it was skin color, not political affiliation, ideology, or exploitative capacity, that identified the relevant enemy. Labour Party MP Allan Hendrickse warned, "I want to say to those people on the outside, and in particular to the Afrikaner people who own the power in this country—any culture or any group that requires the statutes of law to protect their identity, culture, or group, has nothing of value within that culture" (1/31/85, p. 204). Douw complained:

The Honourable Member for Mamre said that he understands the problems of the Afrikaner. We have had too much understanding and patience for too long. The other day an event of major historical importance took place in the Skilpad Hall in Pretoria. The Afrikaner Volkswag was formed there, and of course the AV are the people whose forebears referred to my forebears, who fought for S.A. when many of our present leaders were locked up in concentration camps, as "pandours." . . . Since the upsurge of Afrikaner nationalism in the 30s, the National Party continuously, blatantly, unscrupulously and shamelessly used certain Afrikaner cultural organizations to keep us behind. The AV is just a continuation of this. (3/11/85, p. 1010)

The UDF-aligned Fattis and Monis strike support committee similarly highlighted its opposition to Whites in a 1980 pamphlet: "The bosses tried to break the strike by attempting to divide the workers. They offered to take back the 23 Coloured workers. But the workers were united. They refused to go back to work without their fellow African workers. They stood up for each other because, as one said 'we were all there for the same purpose.'" This pamphlet is illustrated with a cartoon of a fat White boss trying to separate Coloured and African workers holding hands over his head.

The most salient difference between the LP and the UDF was strategy. Both organizations were committed to ending apartheid, both had been influenced by the Black Consciousness Movement, both undercut the political relevance of Colouredness, and both perceived Whites as the Other. But they had very different ideas about how best to effect change in South Africa and were thus aligned along a more or less standard left-right political continuum. The more conservative Labour Party was ostensibly anticommunist, although the party's own economic platform was fairly unclear. It condemned violence of any sort, as well as unrest, school stay-aways, and civil disobedience. The LP continued to believe in the value of the rule of law and in the legitimacy of official government channels for political expression. It sought negotiation. As Labour Party MP D. Lockey explained: "The time has arrived for all moderate South Africans to realize that there is only one policy for this country, and that is the middle-of-the-road policy. The Labour Party has pledged itself irrevocably to this policy of peaceful negotiations. The Labour Party will serve as the catalyst. We shall show the Black man that there is no more time to feel frustrated. There is a place for all of us here in South Africa" (1/30/85, p. 148). Hendrickse fully outlined the LP position on participation:

In the opinion of some people, participation in the system of separate racial representation in any shape or form, and irrespective of any reasons advanced for doing so, is impermissible in principle and harmful in practice. . . . The basic error in this argument lies in the fact that it regards the boycott not as a tactical weapon to be employed if and when objective conditions permit, but as an inflexible principle which must under no circumstances be varied. . . . And this is where we have our differences with so many people in terms of the boycott movement. The boycott has now become a firm principle and not a tactic to the employer. We boycotted, but we boycotted when we needed to boycott. (1/31/85, p. 194)

The UDF, on the other hand, shunned negotiation. The UDF intended to make the country ungovernable, to topple the system. It believed that unrest and mass uprising were the only principled responses to the inherent injustice of apartheid. A pamphlet issued by the UDF-affiliated Cape Youth Congress (CAYCO) Steenberg branch outlined the position: "Consumer boycott continues as a weapon against continued oppression and exploitation. We must continue not to buy at white shops to show that we have not been scared by police brutality and SADF [South African Defense Force] presence in our areas. Our people's continued refusal to buy at white shops has cost big business the loss of thousands of rands. We salute those people who have helped to crash the profits of the exploiters. Support the consumer boycott. Amandla Nguwetu [power to the people]." This flier is illustrated with a photo a Coloured man being harassed by a white policeman.

The strategic differences between the LP and the UDF were important for three reasons. First, they partially dictated the latitude of each organization to construct ideology and identity. Second, by suggesting alliances among political groups, they reconfigured the landscape of South African politics. Third, they were sufficient to create more animosity and mutual demonization, including occasional violence and intimidation, between the UDF and the LP than between either group and any other group in the Western Cape in the 1980s.

Despite its use of the phrase "so-called Coloured" and inclusive understanding of the term *Black,* the Labour Party was to an extent constrained, by its participation in the Coloured House of Representatives, to see the world in terms of officially designated groups and rules applying to separate groups. Thus there was a tension within the Labour Party between its stated ideological position and structural-strategic imperatives. J. D. Johnson, a Labour Party MP, claimed a Coloured constituency even as most of his colleagues identified a broader base: "Like the late D. F. Malan, who made his mark as far as the Afrikaner was concerned, the leader of the Labour Party has done the same for his people. Today the Labour Party is the mouthpiece of the Coloured community of South Africa" (1/30/85, p. 170). Another LP member of Parliament, A. Williams, also made explicit reference to Coloureds: "According to the 1983–84 financial year, of the total amount allocated to the various departments of education, 52.8 percent was allocated to White education, 29.9 percent to African education, while 11.5 percent of the entire budget went to so-called Coloured education and 5.8 percent to Indian education" (3/11/85, p. 1003).

In the context of oppositional politics in the 1980s, LP strategy coincided most closely with that of Inkatha. Inkatha also condemned violence, communism, and unrest, and its position also derived from the structures and institutions of the apartheid government. Both groups also rejected economic sanctions. Such alliances further served to identify the relevant cleavages in South African politics along a liberal-conservative dimension. Hendrickse suggested the latent empathy between the two groups: "Your difference with Chief Buthelezi in terms of this rationale is that he certainly thinks in terms of his strategies. As a matter of fact, at this particular junction, I think South Africa owes much to Chief Buthelezi because he has come out against the question of violence. Compare this to other so-called leaders—I have not heard Bishop Desmond Tutu condemn violence and neither have I heard Dr. Allan Boesak condemn violence" (1/31/85, p. 201). Peters also registered support for Inkatha: "I say that timeous negotiation with credible leaders, not only Nelson Mandela but also men with measurable support like Chief Gatsha Buthelezi, is necessary. This man has done more than most other leaders to denounce disinvestment, both in South Africa and abroad. I would willingly offer my own seat to the Chief and I know that my electorate would support such an offer" (3/4/85, p. 823).

The animosity, political wrangling and public recriminations between the UDF and the LP further reinforce the importance of strategy as an organizing principle of politics. Hendrickse attacked UDF strategy: "Through his actions, Dr. Boesak is polarising people within Black boundaries. Never before have we had such a polarisation between Coloureds and Africans, and he must examine whether he is not perhaps the cause of this polarisation. I believe there is a meeting going to be held in Mitchell's Plain to uphold his integrity. I do not need a mass meeting to uphold my integrity, or my sense of morality" (1/31/85, p. 190). Sass echoed Hendrickse's condemnation: "I should like to give attention to the destructive work which radical organizations in this country are doing, for example the burning down of shops. . . . We had an example in the Transvaal where these radicals told a person to close his shop the next morning otherwise they would burn it down. He closed his shop and they burnt it down anyway. Is that the constructive work they are doing? . . . I cannot understand how some members of the house support Sacos and have ties with the UDF" (1/30/85, p. 146).

The UDF in turn attacked the Labour Party as collaborationist. As one CAYCO pamphlet, "Unite Against a Gutter Education," described the difference: "The Labour Party wanted to prove to us that they are the authorities and are determined to do the will of their masters. We want to say again that the vast majority of oppressed South Africans do not recognize or accept them as leaders, spokespersons, or even as persons. Some people ask 'How can they do this to their own people?' The answer is simple. They are not our people. They are Botha's people, and they are our enemies. Our people are all those South Africans who love and fight for justice, freedom, and a non-racial democratic South Africa." The UDF News stated bluntly: "The Labour Party rides with apartheid. The LP is riding the apartheid train, and for this they are paid R43,000 per year."[19]

Although not directly involved in Coloured politics, the National Party dominated South African politics and political discourse throughout its hegemony from 1948 until 1994. Morever, the ruling party was attempting to play a role in the construction of Coloured identity in the 1980s. When the Cape faction of the NP rose to power in 1979, it began to implement a strategy of rapprochement with

Coloureds. By then, the National Party's Cape ideologues had begun to argue that Coloureds needed to be "drawn back into the laager," from which they had been systematically excluded since 1948, in order to strengthen the White power base in South Africa and to undermine what they feared might be an emerging Black Power Movement. An editorial in the state-run newspaper *The Citizen* made just that point:

The government must act, as a matter of some priority, to bring the Coloured people back into the special relationship they had vis a vis the Whites. We stress: the alienation of the Coloured must not be allowed to continue unchecked. Coloured people have become more radical. Far too many Coloured people have thrown in their lot with Black militants, instead of regarding Whites as friends and natural allies, as people with whom they can join hands to ensure a peaceful and prosperous future for all. The fact that there is a new militancy among Coloured students, a linking up of Coloured youth and Black school radicals, is warning enough that we risk losing the support not only of the older but of the younger generation of Coloureds as well.[20]

One NP adviser warned in an internal memorandum: "The future of black identity amongst the Coloureds depends on the measures through which the aspirations of the population group are befriended by the government. If it is not greatly defended, a withdrawal to Black identity can be expected as a means to achieve greater political and social rights."[21]

The LP and the UDF both mobilized oppositional identities more or less connected to an inclusive Black political identity in line with Black Consciousness discourse. As an explicitly political oppositional identity, rather than as a racial identity, Blackness dominated the discourse of Coloured opposition politics in the 1980s. The UDF and the LP were divided primarily by their respective relations to the system they both opposed, and by different strategies for coping with their political space. Although their differences, and subsequent antagonism in this regard, are significant, they apparently did not affect the identities the two groups sought to articulate.

Material Conditions

The drop in real growth rates that South Africa experienced in the 1970s continued and even worsened in the 1980s. GDP growth averaged only 1.4 percent per year in 1980–1990, and negative real growth rates were recorded in 1982, 1983, 1985, and 1990. Income per capita also fell, as the population grew at an annual average rate of 2.6 percent. South Africa's low growth was fueled by unfavorable commodity prices in international markets, especially gold, by drought in 1983 and 1984, by political instability, which caused a net outflow of capital, and by low overall investment in the late 1980s and early 1990s as a result of sanctions. The prolonged economic downswing of the 1980s had an uneven effect on different race groups in South Africa.

Between 1975 and 1991 the mean income of the poorest three-fifths of African households decreased by almost 40 percent. In the same period, the poorest two-fifths of Coloured households decreased only slightly, while the rest grew strongly. In 1969 Whites earned eleven times more than Coloureds, who in turn earned 20 percent more than Africans. By 1988 Whites earned only three times as much as Coloureds, who then earned twice as much as Africans.[22]

The Coloured Labour Preference Policy (CLPP) was first advanced as apartheid policy and implemented in 1954. The Western Cape, the territory south of the Orange River and west of a line running from Gordonia to Knysna, was designated as an area reserved for Coloureds. The CLPP aimed at the "ultimate elimination of all Natives from the region of the Western Cape." By 1957 magistrates in the peninsula were already able to report a decline in the African population. In 1962 the area of the CLPP was expanded significantly, and in 1964 the Bantu Labour Act, which provided the statutory provisions for enforcement of the CLPP, was established. Specific regulations stipulated that employers in the Western Cape were required, in the absence of special authorization, to employ Coloureds in preference to Africans. Employers were required to apply for Coloured labor, and only if the magistrate was satisfied that no Coloured labor was available would permission be granted to the employer to apply to the "Bantu labor officer." African labor from the homelands was allowed on a single-contract basis. In 1966 the African complement in all industrial and commercial enterprises was frozen, and the government announced that it would seek a 5 percent annual reduction in future years.[23]

At the same time that the preferential status of Coloureds relative to Africans was entrenched by the CLPP and other laws, their subaltern status with respect to Whites was reinforced. Coloureds' upward mobility was restricted by such laws as the 1956 Industrial Conciliation Act and the 1965 Shops and Offices Act, which reserved many jobs for Whites and prohibited non-Whites from supervising Whites. The fact that Coloureds were prohibited from advancing beyond certain positions and that Africans were in turn prevented from holding skilled jobs created more or less serious problems for Cape employers in need of better-skilled employees. Throughout the 1960s and 1970s, employers had an uneven record of compliance, sometimes upholding, sometimes subverting many of the labor laws that underpinned apartheid.

Despite the CLPP, by the 1970s the economic position of most Coloureds had deteriorated dramatically. The remuneration of Coloured employees relative to Whites dropped from 41 percent in 1945 to 24 percent by 1970.[24] The 1970 census indicated that half of all Coloured males and 75 percent of all Coloured females earned less than R500 per year, well below the official poverty level of R130 per month.[25] Coloured unemployment and underemployment rose rapidly between 1961 and 1976.[26] During the 1970s alone, the Coloured unemployment rate rose from 13 percent to 27 percent.[27] In 1976, the year of the Soweto uprising, the Theron Commission reported that there were no permanent and continuous employment opportunities for at least the bottom 30 percent of the Coloured workforce.[28]

Coloured wages in the skilled and semiskilled sectors began to increase after 1970.[29] The share of Coloured labor in manufacturing in the Western Cape went from 50 percent in 1960 to 60 percent in 1970. This in turn reflected the upward mobility of the Coloured working class. The proportion of Coloured men and women classified as unskilled fell from 52 and 62 percent, respectively, to 42 and 45 percent between 1960 and 1973. Although these improvements translated into better opportunities for skilled workers in the 1970s and 1980s, most Coloureds were still either unemployed or working as unskilled laborers.[30] After 1970 some of the strictest labor laws were relaxed, and skilled Coloured workers were increasingly engaged in jobs that had previously been the preserve of White workers. This combination of forces had two effects: the widening wage gap between skilled and other Coloureds exacerbated class cleavages within the Coloured community, and the upward mobility of Coloureds in the manufacturing sector increased tension between White and Coloured workers.[31]

Part of the reason for the displacement of unskilled Coloured laborers was a sudden influx of Africans into the Western Cape to perform unskilled jobs for lower wages in the late 1970s. In this regard the government tacitly collaborated with employers to allow them to hire cheaper, albeit ostensibly "illegal," labor.[32] The African population in the Cape Peninsula increased from approximately 75,000 in 1960 to nearly 250,000 by 1975.[33] By 1981 Africans accounted for 54 percent of the unskilled workforce in the Western Cape.[34]

The Botha government came to power in 1979 and tried, as part of a strategy to undermine increasing Black radicalism and potential solidarity between Africans and Coloureds, to create, and co-opt, middle classes of Coloureds and Africans that would "have a stake in the system." Beside safeguarding the relative privilege of Coloureds, the CLPP created advantages for the few Africans resident in Cape Town with Section 10 permanent residence status. They too were protected from the much poorer contract labor from the Transkei and Ciskei homelands. The NP remained committed to the Coloured Labour Preference Policy until 1984, when the policy was finally scrapped in line with wider reform efforts.

Like many of the government reforms in the 1980s, however, the abolition of the CLPP had an uneven practical effect. The CLPP was abolished only after new, stricter, nationwide legislation made it redundant. The government enforced influx control more strictly in the 1980s than it had in the previous two decades, particularly in the Western Cape, where police arrested thousands of African men and women for pass violations and other minor legal infractions.[35] The abolition of the CLPP did not have the effect, for example, of integrating the workforce. Nevertheless, employers were much more willing to hire "illegal" Africans in the 1980s than they had been previously, when the rules were stable and enforced. Thousands of Africans came to Cape Town in search of employment, even if they lacked papers. The huge squatter area of Crossroads went up in the 1980s, for example, and was continuously rebuilt and expanded, even though many parts of it were repeatedly bulldozed and burned by police and Army forces trying to erase "Black spots."

Thus in the second half of the 1980s unskilled workers who still made up the largest portion of the Coloured labor force began to feel pressure from a large pool of unemployed Africans moving into the Western Cape. Prejudices against Coloured workers, who were perceived by employers as less reliable than Africans and were in any case more expensive, may have also privileged Africans over Coloureds where members of the two groups applied for the same jobs.[36] Skilled, clerical, and professional workers were not similarly threatened because very few Africans in the Western Cape had the education and training necessary to compete for their jobs. The disparity between skilled and unskilled or unemployed Coloureds grew wider. Although Coloureds have always been heterogeneous along class as well as linguistic, religious, and cultural lines, economic conditions at the end of the 1980s further stratified the community and polarized interests that, while not exactly competing, did not coincide either.

Organization

As the preeminent political organizations vying for the support of the Coloured community in the 1980s, both the Labour Party and the United Democratic Front were fairly well embedded, both ideologically and organizationally, in the Coloured areas of Cape Town. The UDF was organized primarily through existing local-level civic, youth, church, women's, and other organizations, which provided it with access to the grass roots while eliminating the need to build a network from the ground up. The LP was a functioning political party with branches throughout the Cape, and constituencies to which its elected representatives were responsible.

UDF leaders were initially drawn primarily from the Coloured and Indian communities. As the decade progressed, the UDF had roughly equal numbers of Coloureds and Africans among its leadership both in the Cape province and at national level. The leadership of the UDF was, moreover, fully integrated. This was true at the highest echelons, as well as at local levels, where UDF leaders of different race groups planned, organized, and socialized together. Activists from this era agree that the UDF leadership was nonracial and that there was a strong sense of unity and commonality among comrades from all racial and ethnic groups. Among even local activists, there was a very high level of awareness of a common Black oppositional identity, and references to racial or ethnic differences were rare and considered ideologically unacceptable.[37]

The UDF was organized through the affiliation of preexisting progressive groups with established networks and local level legitimacy. Although the UDF itself had no individual members, it had affiliates, which in turn had members. Civic associations, youth groups, religious organizations, trade unions, women's associations, and groups mobilized around such issues as housing, utility rates, or pensions were drawn into the net the UDF cast across Black civil society in the 1980s. The affiliation of religious leaders and church groups provided the UDF with a ready-made organizational network, as well as a local-level speaking platform already imbued with moral authority. UDF leaders recruited religious figures, such as Allan Boesak, who would lend the legitimacy of their stature and role in the community to the liberation struggle.[38]

In the Western Cape, the most important community-based organizations, each with their own branches, were the Cape Areas Housing Action Committee (CAHAC), the Cape Youth Congress, the Western Cape Civic Association (WCCA), and the United Women's Organization (UWO). Civic organizations, called simply civics, were also established to oppose the "collaborationist" management councils officially tasked with governing non-White local affairs. These were for the most part organizations that grew out of local grievances and activist demonstrations against such grievances. To the extent that they were able to address the needs and concerns of people, the civics were able to make the benefits of membership and activism tangible. UDF-affiliated groups organized rent and bus boycotts to bring down utility rates and fares, for example. As a result, many of them had a kind of organic quality. Most were at least firmly embedded in their communities.

Once the UDF was launched, however, it also played a role in forming civic and other organizations. By the second half of the decade, almost all of the Coloured and African townships in the country had civic associations, which, in many cases, acted as the government at the local level. Part of the UDF's strategy "to make the country ungovernable" was to withdraw from government, by refusing to pay rent, utilities, and so on, and to make civil society impenetrable by setting up parallel structures of governance within civil society. The civics, which often enjoyed considerable power at the local level, were a key element of this strategy. Nevertheless, the civics were not universally perceived as legitimate. Leaders sometimes resorted to intimidation and violence to enforce boycotts and strikes, for example. The groups had variable levels of support in different areas at different times.

Despite racial integration at the level of leadership, and a firm commitment to nonracialism, the organizational base of the UDF remained segregated. There were "few formal organizational links between coloured and African areas."[39] That Coloureds, Indians, and Africans did not organize in common was in large part a function of the spatial history of racial segregation and separate development. Under apartheid, people of different racial groups did not live, go to school, go to church, or work in the same areas. Almost by definition, grassroots organizations whose purpose was to address local needs had to be racially segregated. The needs and interests of Coloured people differed from those of Africans to the extent that the groups were socially, economically, and geographically stratified. Even when they had the same needs, they were in different places. Thus the nonracial ideology of the UDF was undermined by its organizational strategy. In a racially determined society like apartheid South Africa, only a group that lacked a program of action, such as the Black Consciousness Movement or the NEUM, could remain ideologically pure.

Trade unions, which were a significant organizational base for the UDF, were sometimes able in the 1980s to play a role in integrating Coloured and African workers on the factory floor, in a way that may have resonated politically. Throughout most of the century, unions in the Western Cape were essentially reserved for Coloureds alone. The 1924 Industrial Conciliation Act excluded the majority of Africans from the definition of the term *employee,* thus precluding their unionization. The 1956 Amended Industrial Conciliation Act prohibited the registration of unions including more than one racial group. Most unions adhered to these restrictions, thus entrenching the racial division of labor. In the Western Cape, only the South African Congress of Trade Unions (SACTU)–affiliated Food and Canning Workers Union (FCWU) rejected the legislation and continued to organize an unregistered African union. The FCWU claims to "have always been working as though there is no separation between the two—we are one union and the workers see it that way—we have a strictly non-racial policy which we carry out at all levels."[40]

In the early 1980s the prohibition against organizing across racial lines was lifted, and nonracial unions, such as those affiliated to the Congress of South African Trade Unions, began to dominate labor organization after 1985. On the factory floor, then, Coloureds and Africans tended increasingly, though still not predominantly, to be organized together in the second half of the 1980s. Union organizers believed that this had an effect on relations between Africans and Coloureds.[41] The secretary of the long-integrated FCWU said: "The factories with a long experience of unionization are definitely less racially divided. . . . The extent of Coloured/African divisions depends to a great extent on the history of unionization in the factory concerned."[42]

For the most part, organization in the unions tended to mirror and reinforce segregated organization elsewhere in the Western Cape. It also appears, however, that integrated labor organization became increasingly common (though still not the norm) over the course of the 1980s, and that it may have had an effect in breaking down racial barriers.

Although organizational links between Coloured and African townships in the day-to-day operation of the UDF were weak, UDF campaigns and mass actions were coordinated at the level of the multiracial leadership and included all race groups. UDF-style politics were characterized by huge meetings, nationwide stayaways, and widespread civil disobedience, all designed to cross racial boundaries and to increase the cost of apartheid to the government. Most UDF campaigns in the Western Cape involved Africans and Coloureds equally. Joint action was possible in part because the Western Cape had a political history of interracial unity and cooperation in mobilization. Unrest and political activism, in both African and Coloured communities, reached unusual peaks in the late 1970s and early 1980s. The 1980 Fattis and Monis strike, for example, in which African and Coloured workers went on strike in support of African workers who had been fired, represented an important moment of worker solidarity across ethnic lines and was a political landmark in the Western Cape. Other events, such as the 1980 school boycotts that started among Coloured students in the Western Cape, gained momentum and spread to African and Coloured schools nationwide. Although the organizational base of the UDF was racially segregated, the history of joint protest and the integration of the leadership facilitated the organization of campaigns, including boycotts and protests, across racial lines.

Unlike the UDF, the Labour Party was established only in Coloured areas. The party was organized at the local level through hundreds of party branches in Coloured townships. In the 1980s these branches appear to have been attached more closely to LP politicians, as respected members of their communities, than to the party itself. Members of Parliament were elected by constituencies, and they retained the sense that they were working for those constituencies when they went to parliament.[43]

Labour Party MPs were in many cases respected members of the local community with fairly long histories of community involvement.[44] Some LP activists and MPs were active in civic associations, although most of these were forced out once the civics became more politicized and partisan, under the influence of the UDF. In many cases, the MPs drew consistent support as individuals even as the fortunes of the organizations to which they affiliated, such as the LP, waxed and waned. Most LP members of Parliament, for example, were members of the CPRC and carried a constituent base through to the Tricameral Parliament.[45]

The LP also had close relations with the management committees charged with local government in Coloured areas. Most MCs were dominated by the Labour Party, whose policy it was "to keep a tight grip on Management Committees to derive maximum political benefit for the party."[46] The management committees represented the political power base of the party, and many MPs were former MC members. Allan Hendrickse, the chairman of the Minister's Council in the House of Representatives and the leader of the Labour Party, was simultaneously a member of the Management Committee for Uitenhage.[47] Through both MCs and party branches, the LP was able to distribute patronage and thus expand its base of support, even as the party's close relation to politics at the local level enabled it to respond to local needs.

For most of the 1980s both the LP and the UDF had firm organizational networks in the Coloured townships of the Western Cape. The organizational base of the UDF, however, was undermined after 1986, when the government imposed a nationwide state of emergency that prohibited political meetings and mass funerals, banned many political publications, and allowed detention without trial. Many UDF leaders were detained or went underground in the late 1980s, thus undermining the organizational network the movement had built up. As successive layers of leadership were culled from the ranks of the group, the UDF grew increasingly disorganized and unable to effectively marshal support in a sustained and controllable way. The LP, on the other hand, was subject to none of these constraints, and the party was able to strengthen and reinforce its organizational base as the decade progressed and the UDF lost power at the local level.

Available Ideology

The inclusive potential of Blackness was not new to Coloured politics in the 1970s. Political groups in the Coloured community had rejected a narrowly based Coloured identity in favor of a broader Black identity as early as the 1930s. In 1938, for example, Johnny La Guma of the National Liberation League "urged Coloureds to support black unity." The NEUM, which long dominated the space of radical opposition to apartheid in Coloured politics, began in 1943 to "forge a Black united front against all segregatory measures."[48] Although Whites were not generally included, a heavy Trotskyite influence in Coloured opposition politics drew the line around workers of all races.[49] When the anti-CAD held its first national conference in Cape Town in 1943, Ben Kies argued for the inclusion of White workers "since they were equally oppressed by the system."[50]

The 1961 banning of the ANC, PAC, and SACP left an ideological vacuum in South African opposition politics which was not filled until the Black Consciousness Movement began to gather momentum in the early 1970s. The BCM redefined Coloureds, Indians, and Africans as Black. Because it rejected apartheid designations of racially based group identity, an inclusive Black political identity was inherently oppositional. Black identity derived from common oppression by Whites, not from skin color. It was always conceived as a political, not racial, identity.[51] Black Consciousness strove to overturn conceptions of Black as inferior and to encourage Blacks to embrace their Blackness and Black Power. Black Consciousness was hegemonic in opposition circles in the 1970s, and it was the official ideology of the South African Students Organization, which dominated student politics at Coloured as well as African schools in the 1970s. In 1972, for example, eight of the eleven candidates elected to student government at the University of the Western Cape, an officially designated Coloured university, were SASO members.[52]

There are at least two reasons that Black Consciousness had ideological resonance for a significant subsector of Coloureds at the beginning of the 1980s. First, many of those in the younger generation who were politically active in the 1980s had developed political consciousness and been politicized through the BC prism in the 1970s.[53] The BCM had no organizational network or political structure of its own. Therefore, students with SASO affiliations went on to join a wide spectrum of political groups, including the UDF, as well as the LP and Inkatha. Because Black Consciousness had no strategic or organizational agenda of its own, adherents carried it into diverse political organizations that were subsequently influenced by the doctrine. Second, participation in government-sanctioned bodies had been thoroughly delegitimized, in part by the Labour Party itself, by the end of the decade. The LP was at pains to distance itself from a collaborationist ideological position, and from more conservative counterparts to its right (such as the Federal Party), even as it made a strategic decision to work within the system.

Black Consciousness began to lose salience by the end of the 1970s for three reasons. First, Steve Biko, the ideological soul and founder of the movement, was arrested and murdered, and most of the rest of the leadership was banned, driven underground, or arrested. Second, Black Consciousness faced a challenge from Charterists returning from jail in the late 1970s.[54] Many either were, or had been influenced by, ANC leaders imprisoned in the 1960s.[55] Third, people grew disillusioned with the inherent weakness of the movement—its exclusive focus on raising political consciousness at the expense of developing an organizational network and program. It remained an elite, conceptually and ideologically driven movement which lacked organizational underpinnings and tangible goals. Black Consciousness was important in creating the parameters of possibility for organization and mobilization but was not itself capable of moving beyond rhetoric into action. Although the organizations that emerged to contest oppositional space in the 1980s had ideological debts to the BCM, none fully endorsed Black Consciousness, and some, like the UDF, even grew partly out of a sense of frustration with, and rejection of, the failure of the BCM to engage politically.

Thus, although both the UDF and the LP included fairly dominant BC strains, neither was primarily a Black Consciousness organization. The LP espoused commitments to federalism, nonviolence, nonracialism, anticommunism, and a negotiated end to apartheid. The party was, by 1984, almost twenty years old, and it had occupied a series of positions along the ideological spectrum of Coloured politics. It began as the moderate opposition to the conservative FCPP but seemed to grow more radical over the course of the 1970s as it turned increasingly to the boycott as a political strategy. Ultimately, though, the LP took up the conservative end of Coloured politics in the 1980s, when its own more conservative flanks were marginalized, and when the UDF seized a dominant position to its left. Throughout its career, the LP has mostly failed to define its own political space and has been defined, in the main, reactively, by comparison to other parties.

The UDF, on the other hand, was officially a Charterist movement. It placed itself firmly in the ideological space of the banned ANC, used ANC colors, and invoked ANC leaders. Unlike the ANC, however, the UDF was launched to protest Coloured and Indian elections to the Tricameral Parliament and was primarily involved, at the outset, in the Coloured and Indian communities, among those who would vote in the new constitutional dispensation. In the beginning, the leadership of the UDF was dominated by Coloureds and Indians, whereas the ANC had always been primarily led by Africans. Unlike the ANC, for which cooperation with the system had been a matter of tactical expediency, the UDF maintained a principled commitment to noncollaboration. This commitment placed it firmly within the space of Coloured politics, where noncollaboration had a long and venerable tradition. In South African opposition politics, it was only the predominantly Coloured NEUM that had ardently maintained noncollaboration as a principle, not only a strategy, of opposition.

In 1983 the LP was an established mediator of Coloured politics. Its own ideological position had evolved significantly in fifteen years, and it had been influenced by the BCM in the 1970s. Although part of its ideological stance was worked out in the context of participation in the Tricameral Parliament and was thus responsive to the politics of the 1980s, the LP was simultaneously embedded in its own prior ideological space. The UDF was, conversely, brand new in 1983, with no apparent prior ideological commitments. The founders of the UDF, though, were mainly Coloureds and Indians with prior commitments that worked themselves out in the new political space afforded by the government's decision to reform. The combination of the Tricameral Parliament, which created the possibility for entrance into the system as well as the spark for oppositional mobilization against the system, and a relatively more open political space, played a role in affecting ideological salience.

Resonance

Polling data, elections results and turnout, and records of UDF support and participation in boycotts, school stay-aways, and rallies, as well as interviews and impressionistic evidence, reveal how Coloureds reacted to the discourses that dominated their political world and how they perceived their own identities in relation to objective structural conditions and elite political mobilization and organization.

One survey of Coloureds conducted in 1969, just before the first election for the Coloured Person's Representative Council, found that Coloureds identified little more with their own group than they did with other groups. Coloureds appeared to have a low level of group identification. As they moved up the socioeconomic ladder, Coloureds felt closer to both Whites and Blacks. They felt least close to Afrikaans-speaking Whites, and closer to Africans than to Whites generally. Coloureds of high and middle socioeconomic status were closer to Africans than to any other group. At the time, analysts speculated that "Coloureds might be ripe for a general non-White power movement, should one arise," although "they are not likely to support a Coloured power movement."[56]

As it happened, a "non-White power movement" did arise, in the form of the Black Consciousness Movement in the early 1970s. The balance of evidence suggests that Black Consciousness resonated at least among Coloured students and activists in the 1970s. The BC South African Students Organization dominated student politics, even at the University of the Western Cape, an officially designated "Coloured university."[57] Allan Boesak was loudly cheered at the 1976 Labour Party conference when he declared that Black Consciousness had had a decisive impact on black youth.[58]

The popular influence of the Black Consciousness movement became apparent during the 1976 Soweto uprising. On June 16, 1976, African students in Soweto protested against Afrikaans-medium instruction in school. The government responded violently, which in turn served to radicalize more students and to extend sympathy for the protesting students into the wider communities from which they sprang. Boycott-related violence spread throughout South Africa, sweeping through the Western Cape as African and Coloured students boycotted schools, rioted, and defied police orders. Coloured students appear to have been equally inspired by, and equally dedicated to, boycott and confrontation against authority as were their African counterparts, as sadly evidenced by the death toll. In the Western Cape, fifty-four Africans and fifty-three Coloureds were killed by the police in the aftermath of the Soweto uprising.[59]

Student leaders of the protest argued that Afrikaans was the "language of the oppressor" and insisted on English-medium instruction. Whereas very few Africans speak Afrikaans as their home language, it is the first language of 85 percent of Coloured people. The widespread participation of Coloured students in the protest indicates that they pointedly chose a Black political identity over an Afrikaans language identity in this instance.

The extent to which Coloureds generally internalized an inclusive oppositional political identity, in which they perceived common cause with Africans against Whites, is a difficult question. Thirty-seven percent of Coloured respondents in 1982 agreed that "forming a united front with Blacks against the incumbent government is an effective way of achieving equal political rights."[60] This question simultaneously addresses strategy and identity. More than one-third of Coloureds identified with Africans against Whites for political purposes. Although the question clearly addresses the matter of common identity, it includes strategic issues. If Coloureds perceived Africans to be as weak as or weaker than they were, they might not believe that forming a united front with that group would be tactically effective, regardless of identification.

Other polling data indicate, in fact, that most Coloureds, as well as most

Africans, did not advocate forming a front against the government at all, with any group. Eighty percent of Coloureds favored negotiations as the best way to effect change, according to a 1986 poll. This evidence has been used as an indicator that Coloureds are more conservative than Africans and less inclined to engage in protest. These figures, however, do not prove that. One 1985 poll shows that more than 80 percent of Africans also favored negotiations with the government, more than twice as many as condoned any sort of violence.[61]

In 1982, forty-eight percent of Coloureds agreed that "if the Tricameral Parliament was implemented, Blacks would think Coloureds were stabbing them in the back."[62] Such a response may be a clearer indicator of alliances and closeness to a particular group. The idiom "stab in the back" connotes a relationship between the stabber and the person who is stabbed. People stab friends in the back by consorting with, or defecting to, the enemy. Thus, by agreeing that Africans would think they were being stabbed in the back, respondents tacitly acknowledged that they identified with Africans and would consider participation in the Tricameral Parliament a form of betrayal.

Coloured support for the UDF may be another measure of political identity and of the extent of political solidarity between Africans and Coloureds in the 1980s. The national launch of the UDF took place in Cape Town in August 1983. The launch itself was considered a spectacular success, drawing between six thousand and fifteen thousand people, according to different estimates. The UDF's first campaign, against management committee elections in Coloured areas, was also effective. Voter turnout varied from 2 percent to 12 percent in the Cape Peninsula. In early 1984 the national UDF launched the Million Signatures Campaign to raise the profile of the UDF and to demonstrate broad rejection of the Tricameral Parliament. Although the campaign was abandoned long before one million signatures were gathered, eighty-seven thousand signatures were collected in the Western Cape. This was double the number collected anywhere else in the country, and almost all signatures were collected in Coloured areas.[63] In 1984 the UDF started its campaign against the Tricameral elections, focusing mainly on disrupting Labour Party meetings (with so much success that the party stopped holding them), and distributing media door to door. Elections were widely boycotted—the average poll in the Cape Peninsula was about 5–6 percent of eligible voters (11 percent of those registered, which was about half of those eligible). In the rural areas, about 15 percent of eligible voters voted, which may indicate that the UDF had a stronger urban support base, or at least that it was better able to prevent urban residents from voting.

The UDF became increasingly involved in confrontation and protest in 1985, and the Western Cape had one of the highest sustained levels of unrest in the country in the mid-1980s. The UDF encouraged student protesters at the University of the Western Cape and at Coloured high schools to boycott school as part of a nationwide "challenge against the state." The Western Cape UDF called a consumer boycott, which was launched at four meetings with a combined attendance of ten thousand people in August 1985.[64] A police ban of a UDF march in September of that year provoked widespread clashes between demonstrators and police in Coloured and African townships. Twenty-eight people were killed in three days. Five hundred Coloured schools and colleges were closed by the government in September 1985.

Joint activism and mobilization between 1984 and 1986 may have affected the political identities of some Coloureds. Indiscriminate policing in response to the 1985 consumer boycott, for example, appeared to intensify resistance and strengthen commitment to the boycott.[65] One poll showed that Coloured support for P. W. Botha dropped by 12 percent between 1984 and 1986. In 1984, thirty-five percent of Coloureds surveyed expressed dissatisfaction with the political situation. In 1986, fifty-three percent were dissatisfied. Between 1984 and 1986 Coloured support fell for every political leader except Allan Boesak, the head of the UDF in the Western Cape. An increasing number of respondents believed that the unrest had caused greater unity than division between Coloureds and Africans. Between 1980 and 1986 more Coloured people felt that they had grown closer to Africans than to Whites.[66]

There is a point, however, at which people may begin to feel that the cost of violence is too high. At this point, if it is possible, they may withdraw from the arena of violence, often also the arena of politics, and distance themselves from those who are engaged in violence. By mid-1986 state repression had frightened many people away from action. As one activist explained, "The emergency gives that fear of mass detention. In 1985, people thought that speakers and leaders at meetings would be detained. Now they realize that just going to a meeting they can be detained, even in church services."[67] Thirty-five percent of Coloureds surveyed supported the declaration of a state of emergency in 1986.[68]

Participation in UDF campaigns in the Western Cape, among both Coloureds and Africans, dropped off after 1986. The consumer boycott almost dissolved under the state of emergency and was finally called off in January 1987. Participation was higher in the 1988 management committee elections and in the 1989 Tricameral Parliament elections than it had been in 1983 and 1984, respectively, although it still failed to approximate levels that would suggest actual legitimacy.[69] When asked to rate the performance of the House of Representatives, 60 percent of respondents gave the House an overall negative rating, and 32 percent were neutral.[70]

The mobilization of an oppositional political identity that embraced an inclusive sense of Blackness defined in political and not racial terms was without doubt a salient feature of "Coloured politics" in the 1980s. In the context of a political structure dominated by a White minority government that excluded most South Africans from meaningful political participation on the basis of race, opposition to the system essentially marked the only possibility for Coloured politics in that decade.[71] Both the "radical" UDF and the "moderate" LP were influenced by the Black Consciousness Movement and placed themselves in an oppositional space defined at least in part as "Black." Blackness delineated a political, not a racial, space.

Black political identity in the 1980s may be measured by support for the formation of a united front with Africans, by the extent of belief that entering the Tricameral Parliament would constitute a betrayal of Africans, and by support for the UDF. Coloured participation equaled African participation in an opposition alliance explicitly defined as Black. Black identity resonated primarily among Coloureds who were socialized through the BCM and later the UDF in school, and who were organized through civics, trade unions, and churches that affiliated to the UDF and reinforced this message.

It may nevertheless be true that the concept of Blackness was never fully prised from its racial hinges and remained a controversial identity for many Coloureds to embrace. To the extent that Blackness was perceived as a denial of Colouredness, many people may have had difficulty discarding an identity that had such a large practical effect on their life chances and social, economic, and political standing. As an exclusively political identity lacking in any broader social or cultural ramifications, however, Black identity was in fact easily compatible with Coloured identity, and evidence shows that many people held both comfortably. A Black political identity was practically universal among politically mobilized non-Whites on the left.

7 Now I Would Say I'm a Coloured

The Politics of Coloured Identity After 1990

Black political identity appears to have lost much of its salience for Coloureds—both at the elite and at the mass levels—in the postapartheid era. The transition from White minority rule to multiparty democracy, and the changes it has generated at the material, organizational, and ideological levels, has shifted the parameters of possibility for Coloured political identity. As the context of politics has changed from antiapartheid opposition to participation in a nonracial democracy, an inclusive Black oppositional identity has grown increasingly obsolete.

Although many of those who identified as Black in the 1980s called themselves Coloured in 1995, Coloured identity still does not appear to be politically salient for most Coloureds. The limited political resonance of Colouredness is constituted primarily by opposition, formerly to the White minority government and now to an "African majority government." If Colouredness has political content, it is constituted by exclusion. Many Coloureds perceive that they are as marginalized by the (African) ANC government as they were by the (White) NP government.

Although Colouredness may play a role in defining political, as well as social and economic, space, it is not a good indicator of political preference. For Coloureds, political identity is mediated primarily by ideological commitments, socioeconomic position, and location in particular organizational networks, not by attachment to ethnic or racial categories. Coloureds demonstrate a degree of political heterogeneity that belies the relevance of conceiving Coloured as a political category.

Political Institutions

South Africa's political structure, and the place of Coloureds within the structure, shifted dramatically between January 1990 and the end of 1994. After de Klerk replaced the aging and ailing P. W. Botha as president in September 1989, it became immediately apparent that he had in mind a more robust reform program. Nevertheless, nobody was prepared for the announcement, in his first Opening of Parliament address, on February 2, 1990, that the ANC, PAC, and SACP were no longer banned. Nelson Mandela was released from prison the following Sunday. South Africans were either jubilant or outraged, but everyone was overwhelmed and shocked.

For Black South Africans the most immediate and tangible benefits of this new era of reform was the repeal of most major apartheid legislation. During the 1991 parliamentary session the government revoked the 1913 Black Land Act, the 1936 Development Trust and Land Act, the 1950 Population Registration Act, the 1966 Group Areas Act, and the 1984 Black Communities Development Act. The Population Registration Act, which officially registered every individual according to racial group, and the Group Areas Act, which was responsible for tens of thousands of forced removals, including the famous removal of the Coloured community from District Six in Cape Town, were the most onerous, emotionally charged, and immediate pieces of apartheid legislation for most Coloureds.

Although the 1984 constitution and the Tricameral Parliament remained in place throughout the transition period, Tricameral politics changed significantly after 1990. In 1990 the National Party opened its membership to all races. In March 1991 the NP launched its first nonracial party branch in the Coloured community of Eersterus, near Pretoria. In May five Labour Party MPs indicated that they would join the NP, and Peter Marais, a Coloured member of the President's Council, said that "the National Party without its apartheid policy is the natural home for the majority of the Coloured community." By October 1991 nearly one-quarter of the delegates at the NP's Cape congress were Coloured.[1]

By June 1993 the Labour Party had lost its majority position in the House of Representatives. There had been no elections, but many Labour Party MPs had crossed the floor to join other parties. Most defected to the NP, although some, including LP leader Allan Hendrickse, joined the ANC. The LP had problems with corruption and had amassed a debt it had little hope of settling.[2] With only twenty-seven members left, the traditional "Coloured party" was reduced to the status of official opposition in the branch of government reserved for Coloured politics and representation, the House of Representatives. The party officially dissolved itself in 1993. By that time, the National Party in fact controlled all three houses of Parliament, with forty-six members in the House of Representatives and twenty-one in the (Indian) House of Delegates.[3]

After the ban was lifted against the ANC in 1990, there was intense debate within ANC and UDF ranks about the fate of the UDF. Most people felt that the two organizations occupied the same ideological space and that the UDF leadership, and support base, should collapse into the ranks of the ANC. Others feared sacrificing the UDF's still-strong organizational base and internal legitimacy and hoped that the ANC could incorporate the UDF as an organization into its ranks, as the ANC later did with the SACP and COSATU.[4] In the end, the UDF was disbanded in 1991. Many UDF leaders and activists moved easily into ANC positions, although others, among them a seemingly substantial number of Coloureds, left politics altogether or felt sidelined in the new organization.[5] Thus by the end of the transition period, both of the organizations that had shaped and mediated Coloured politics in the 1980s had disappeared.

The political institutions, rules, and electoral laws negotiated between the NP and the ANC in the transition period may have affected the parameters of Coloured politics in different ways. In the initial stage, the two sides agreed to a power sharing arrangement in which all parties who won more than twenty seats in Parliament would receive cabinet positions in proportion to the number of seats they won. Consensus was to be the decision-making rule at cabinet level. Additionally, the two largest parties would hold vice presidential positions, thus extending the principle of power sharing through to the executive branch of government.

Despite these concessions to "nation building" and "minority rights," and the fact that proportional representation was chosen as the country's electoral system, the postapartheid institutional structure was perceived by many who feared it as a majority rule system. Critics reasoned that the party with the largest share of the vote would appoint a president and would be represented in proportion to its (large) share of the vote. This appeared majoritarian relative to the type of strict consociational system that the NP had initially demanded, in which parties representing separate racial segments of the population would share equally in governance. This principle was the basis of the 1987 KwaNatal Indaba proposal, which had been touted as a model for a postapartheid political dispensation. A political structure based on the principles of the Tricameral Parliament, including a fourth branch for Africans, was probably the standard by which many measured those institutions that were ultimately agreed upon, and by which they may have judged those institutions to be basically majoritarian. Coloureds were returned to the common voting roll, but so were Africans, which severely diluted the strength of the Coloured vote.

In the interim, a final constitution was negotiated by all parties in a constitutional assembly and passed by a two-thirds majority. It came into effect in February 1997. Under the terms of the final constitution, the provision for power sharing in a government of national unity was abandoned. After 1999 the party that won the election would govern the country. Although the ruling party may include members of other parties in the cabinet in the interest of generating national unity, such a gesture would be entirely voluntary. Moreover, nonruling parties may reject such overtures for fear of being co-opted. Once it became clear that the provision for power sharing would be dropped from the final constitution, the NP withdrew from the GNU, for example, in order to strengthen its place in opposition and to distance itself from government policy.

At the local-government level, two types of electoral system were negotiated. In urban areas, people vote for individual representatives who form a multiparty local government council. The mayor is elected separately and is not simply chosen by the majority party. In rural areas a more consociational electoral arrangement was agreed upon. The NP insisted that a particular number of seats be set aside for each racial group. This provision was designed to safeguard the interests of White farmers in rural Transvaal towns and districts, who would be vastly outnumbered by Africans in an open electoral system. Where Whites were the minority, such a system was to their advantage. In the Western Cape however, Coloureds are the majority and Africans are a minority. The electoral clout of Africans relative to Coloureds was thus strengthened in the Western Cape by electoral rules insisted upon by the NP. The legacy of apartheid, which separated people by race into different areas, makes it easy to draw local-government district boundaries around racially distinct areas. In 1995 local government elections in rural areas, most parties contested only those wards in which they expected to win. The ANC contested mostly African wards, and the NP largely restricted itself to White areas. Except in Coloured areas, which were generally contested by both parties, the two major parties did not even compete for the same constituent base in most rural areas.

The new constitution divides South Africa's four provinces into nine and includes a quasi-federal structure. All of the provinces except the Free State and KwaZulu Natal have new boundaries. The old province of the Cape was divided into three provinces: the Eastern Cape, the Western Cape, and the Northern Cape. The Western Cape includes essentially the territory demarcated as a Coloured Labour Preference Area in the apartheid era. In the 1994 national election voters chose candidates in national as well as provincial government. Parties contesting the elections made up separate national and provincial lists of candidates, and candidates won in proportion to the number of votes the party received. Voters were able thus to split their ticket and to choose a different party for national and provincial government. The leader of the province is the provincial premier, chosen by the party that wins a majority of the votes at provincial level. A number of powers rested at the provincial level, and the provinces have a fair amount of leeway to act independent of the national government. The only two provinces in which the ANC did not win a majority either in 1994 or in 1999, and which it consequently did not control, are KwaZulu Natal, which is governed by the Inkatha Freedom Party, and the Western Cape, which was won initially by the National Party and in 1999 by a coalition that included the New National Party.

Since 1999 the NP and the IFP have continued to demand both a stronger form of federalism and greater devolution of power to the provincial level. In the final constitution, which was negotiated without the input of the IFP because it boycotted the constitutional assembly, the extent of provincial powers was one of the most hotly contested issues. Ultimately, provinces are vested with fewer powers in the final constitution than they were granted in the interim constitution. The power to determine remuneration and allowances payable to provincial premiers and members of the executive council, as well as to traditional leaders, was removed from provincial purview and vested in the president, for example.[6] Provincial powers are important to the NP because party leaders believe that if they can retain jurisdiction over such policy matters as language and education, and if they can control their own tax base, they can foster an oppositional identity for the Western Cape and solidify their base of support.[7]

Mobilizing Discourse

Three main contenders struggle to define the political meaning of Coloured identity in the postapartheid era: the National Party, the African National Congress, and emergent Coloured nationalist groups. The National Party probably had the most organized and straightforward vision of the meaning of politics for the Coloured community in 1994. The NP framed the country's first democratic elections as the beginning of the end. It was a time for Coloured people to take stock and to unite to protect the last vestiges of privilege accorded to them under the apartheid system. The NP focused on the advantages Coloureds had enjoyed, relative to Africans, under NP rule and warned that politics would thenceforth be about maintaining a place for minorities in a majority-dominated government.

The NP distributed a comic strip called *The Winds of Change* during its electoral campaign in the Western Cape. In one scene a Coloured son asks his father, "What has the NP done for us?" The father responds, "You are at university, we have a roof over our heads, and I have a reasonable income. What more do you want?" In contrast, the comic is filled with images of apparently unemployed African people sitting beside decrepit shacks in abject poverty. The subtext of this widely disseminated message was that the NP had taken care of Coloured people and treated them well compared with Africans. The Coloureds' relative advantage was suddenly threatened by the end of apartheid and imminent "African rule."

The centerpiece of this worldview was the NP's interpretation of the ANC's affirmative action program. The ANC planned, and has since instituted, an affirmative action policy that privileges the "formerly oppressed" in applications for jobs, schools, bursaries, grants, and so on. Throughout most of South Africa, the term *formerly oppressed* refers to African people. In the Western Cape, where the majority is Coloured and Africans are a growing minority, it is unclear which group this policy is intended to help. Although Coloureds were oppressed, they also received preferential hiring treatment in the Western Cape, and they were never as oppressed as Africans.

The ambiguity of this issue made it ripe for exploitation by the NP. It translated easily into the notion that African people were going to get jobs held by Coloured people, which seemed a tangible threat. Many Coloured leaders expressed the fear. Abe Williams, NP provincial minister for welfare in the Western Cape, explained: "But you see what is happening to Coloured people is that they are feeling the hurt of affirmative action against them. When they fought apartheid they were considered part of the struggle against apartheid. But now that apartheid is out of the way, they are not getting the benefit of the new system because they are again being seen as 'you're not Black.' And that is very heartbreaking." Stan Fisher, an NP member of Parliament who is also Coloured, blamed the ANC: "But what made this happen was the affirmative action policy of the ANC. The ANC now seems not to have noticed the fact that the Coloured people has also been the disadvantaged. They are becoming a very, very racist party. To the extent that a lot of people who have been with them in the struggle [are] also losing their job."

The issue of affirmative action also corresponded neatly with the National Party's campaign to define the boundaries of the group they were mobilizing by identifying the Other. The NP identifies Coloureds as *not* Black. The NP denied the inclusive political possibilities of Blackness and tried to make the choice of a Black identity concomitant with, or even contingent upon, the denial of a Coloured identity. The NP racialized Blackness. By calling Africans Black, the party grounds the name in racial terms, makes it inherently non-inclusive, and denies the possibility of a common political bond between Coloureds and Africans as Blacks. Moreover, they project the ANC's use of the term Black as a denial of a separate Coloured identity. Fisher described his perception of the racial position of Coloured people: "As I said, there was enough commonality between the Whites and the Coloureds, as opposed to the Coloureds and the Black. Because in South Africa, unfortunately, the commonality in some areas between the Whites and the Blacks is even more than between the Coloureds and the Blacks in that same area." At another point he added:

Because . . . when they talk of South Africa, they just talk about Black and White. And yet we are a group on our own in this country. . . . Now, where do we identify us? Because this is our country. So why must we be disregarded because we are Coloured. . . . In the past they called us so-called Coloureds, which we rejected, and now why must we now be identified as a Black? . . . How can you be a so-called Coloured person, or so? It makes me sick. Because you're either White, Coloured, or Black. Why should you steer away from what you are? Because we are not Coloured because we are sinners. And that is why we hate that term of "so-called Coloured."

Gerald Morkel, NP member of Parliament echoed Fisher's claim: Whites and Coloureds "share more than perhaps with other groupings. And when I say other groupings I mean specifically Black groupings."[8]

Naming the out-group partially constitutes the in-group. The out-group is now Black. But what does it mean to be Black? What is it that "we" are not? The *Winds of Change* comic went far to define Blackness. One portion of the strip depicts a fourteen-year-old African boy who smokes cigarettes and carries an AK-47. He has just been given the vote. "Thank you, Mandela," he says. "Now I've got the vote, you had better walk carefully, old man." The character stops old Coloured women in the street. He asks them where they are going. If they are on their way to church, he tells them "You won't go to church anymore. Your God is dead. Now the government is God!"

The "Black" identity constructed by the NP included an entire package of traits that would be perceived negatively by socially conservative, middle-class, middle-aged, churchgoing Coloureds. First, Black people are depicted as young, with all of the putative lawlessness and irresponsibility of the youth culture. They are violent, and they have access to dangerous weapons because they are associated with Umkhonto we Sizwe, the ANC military wing which used Soviet-supplied AK-47s during the struggle. In the run-up to elections, Mandela argued that the voting age should be lowered to sixteen to take advantage of the ANC's significant youth base. In the comic, the NP falsely suggests that this proposal had become law. And even though people may think that Mandela can be trusted to run the country, he will not be able to "govern properly," according to the NP scenario, because he will be held hostage to the interests of the "irresponsible voters" that supported him in the election. He will have to "walk carefully" to cater to a radical constituency.

The NP also made much of the communist links of the ANC. Such links were important not so much because Coloureds feared the apparent economic repercussions of communism but rather because communism is associated with atheism. For the NP in the Western Cape, communism doesn't mean anticapitalist, it means antichurch and anti-God. NP organizer Lawrence Solomon explained the association between religion and politics: "The Coloured communities are basically a very religious group of people, so they fear communism. I would say that some of them, they fear the oppression of religion and the repression, that aspect of communism, not so much the economic policy, and what that does to the mind."[9]

Black people were continually depicted as violent, undisciplined, ungodly, and incapable of governing. Abe Williams of the NP focused on some of these issues: "The Coloured people were also very concerned about the discipline in the country, the economy of the country, and what can be achieved. And then they are also very much aware of the escalation of the violence in the rest of South Africa, violence between Black and Black, and so on. And they were also concerned about the deterioration, the collapse, of democracy in Africa. Those things affected the Coloured people too."

One of the issues that gave some credibility to the NP's depiction of African people was the invasion of houses earmarked for Coloured people. Just before the April elections, African squatters took over a block of newly constructed homes that the government had already allocated to specific Coloured families in Delft, a Coloured suburb of Cape Town. It was rumored that the NP orchestrated the event to bring home the main points of its campaign. At any rate, the NP immediately condemned the squatters and took decisive steps to evict them. The ANC, on the other hand, did nothing for two or three days. The party was somewhat unwieldy and unable to react quickly to events. But the ANC was also hampered by indecision over what to do when one segment of its constituency clashed with what it perceived as another segment. The NP capitalized on ANC paralysis to link the party to "Black lawlessness," suggesting that in fact the ANC had condoned the act and that, with an ANC government, Coloured people could look forward to more "Black invasions" into their houses, their jobs, their space, and their rights.

Part of forging a common political identity involves a definition of who "we" are not. The NP has been somewhat less decisive in defining who "we" are. In the postapartheid era, there seem to be multiple threads weaving a Coloured political identity that will support the New National Party's vision of South Africa and its place in it. Some NNP leaders have tried to undermine a racially based political identity in order to build a more inclusive linguistic base. They have tried to forge an Afrikaans-language identity, binding Afrikaans-speaking South Africans, regardless of race. Shahiem Ismael, NP local government councilor from Newclare, described the potential basis of such an identity: "Coloured people are quite scared of the eleven languages. Well, of ten of them. They are eager to protect their culture. Afrikaans is part of their culture. We are born Afrikaans, and I think that is also the main reason why people vote for the NP. Protecting their culture."[10] NP organizer Solomon also picked up on this theme: "But it's a beautiful language and there's a lot of people in this country who love that language. A very sensitive issue. Most Coloureds speak Afrikaans. . . . Afrikaans people did vote NP. A lot of English-speaking people voted for us as well, but not as many as voted for the ANC.

Ja, you see, . . . as they say in Afrikaans, there's that *vasbarheid,* that likeness, which is untouchable. . . . What I've discovered is that with the English-speaking there's that difference, that distance as well. And the language barrier's there. But with the Afrikaner, because they speak the same language, there's that bond." Fisher described the Afrikaans-language usage: "In the family we are bilingual, but sometimes I'm just being obstinate in using Afrikaans because the ANC wants to get rid of Afrikaans. And yet they will have the strongest objection from their own region in the Free State because the language spoken there by the Blacks is Afrikaans. And the Western Cape, the Coloureds speak Afrikaans."

Solomon even refers to something called Afrikaans people: a people whose group identity derives from a common language. Language, of course, is not an unusual basis on which to construct a sense of collective identity. After all, perception, one's sense of reality, is mediated through language. People united by language are often united by other characteristics or are constituted politically. In South Africa, however, the use of Afrikaans as a political unifying device has had an inconsistent history. This is not the first time that the language has been used to link Coloured and White racial groups against Africans, but race has more consistently been used to divide Coloureds and White Afrikaners, to keep them apart to try to maintain the purity of the White race.[11] A language-based identity could theoretically extend to include African Afrikaans speakers, a possibility to which Stan Fisher alludes, although in reality very few African South Africans speak Afrikaans as their first language.

A second strain within the NP focuses less on undermining the importance of race, or substituting language as the key element of identity, than on suggesting that Coloureds and Whites are basically the same race. In this construction, race retains its primary importance as a unit of political identity, but Colouredness is redefined as a subcategory of Whiteness. Coloureds are, in effect, an extension of the White race. Such an argument rests on the denial of a separate identifiable Coloured identity. White Afrikaners and Coloureds share the same culture, the same history, the same humor, and in many cases the same ancestry. There is a "natural" affinity, or understanding, between the two groups. NP organizer Jan Kruger described the relationship: "I think that the Coloured, if you look at the culture system and the culture framework within the Western Cape as such—but not even here, other areas as well—they are people sharing most of, or all of, the norms and value system and mores and whatever you want to call it. You know most of them speak Afrikaans. . . . Just sharing the same values and norms and stuff [with Whites], and then the NP said, everybody's welcome."[12] Fisher agreed: "The Coloureds in the Western Cape has had a very, very long tradition of commonality between the Whites and not the Blacks. Unfortunately. And that is one of the reasons . . . why I said apartheid in the Western Cape was never effective. They could just never divide those two groups," Whites and Coloureds. Williams addressed similar points: "The Coloured people feel a cultural bondage [*sic*] not with the NP but with the Afrikaner. The language, the culture itself, with their morals, the things that concern them about family life and discipline and structures and those things. And then the Coloured people, in the Cape for instance, the Coloured people stems largely from the White community, not from the Black community. So you have that bondage, you see. You have the Coloured family having family in the White community. You see that kind of thing. So there's a long tradition of bondage."

There is a third trend within the National Party that can probably be best described as Coloured nationalist. This articulation of Coloured political identity represents Coloureds as a racially distinct group with its own interests, own rights, accorded on a group basis, and potentially even its own territory. This view of Coloured identity finds a home in the National Party when the party defines itself as the vanguard of minority representation, against the party of the majority, the ANC. Thus the NP can accommodate many different "racial minorities," such as Whites (Afrikaans- and English-speaking), Indians, and Coloureds. Coloured nationalists within the NP embrace the notion of a separate Coloured identity, which includes political content, while rejecting the possibility that such an identity should be articulated through a Coloured nationalist political party. Williams articulated the nationalist line: "Because the Coloured people always felt that the Western Cape belongs to them, that they should be in charge. . . . The Western Cape is our *Volkstaat*." Ismael highlights the resonance of an explicitly Coloured political identity:

[We need] to make ourselves heard by the government as the Coloured community. We are also part of South Africa; we are sick and tired of being caught in the middle between Black and White. . . . Most of our people also voted, also lost from the apartheid system, most of us also went through the same tortures and so on. So the reason for that march was to highlight our complaint and to air our grievances on a priority basis. To say our people is also existing. The Coloured nation is sick and tired of being caught in the middle of apartheid barriers between Black and White. . . . Where do Coloureds stand? Do they regard the Coloured as being South Africans or being Black or White or what? And under the terms of this new constitution, are we also part of this country?

A strong commitment to federalism, in which the Western Cape would gain greater autonomy under the leadership of the NP, was one element of the construction of a separate Coloured identity specifically linked to, and articulated by, the NP. The argument for a federal system in South Africa is embedded in party competition. Demands for a stronger form of federalism mask the efforts of dominant regional parties to strengthen their own institutional power base with respect to the ANC central government, and to construct regionally, and by extension sometimes ethnically, situated oppositional identities. In postapartheid South Africa, the apparently federal demand for the devolution of power to the "local level" often masquerades as democratic jargon for the apartheid-era demand for the retention of control over "own affairs."

Morkel described the power struggle between local and national levels of government:

Because the ANC has got that big majority, they are taking certain decisions. Number one: one thing they are not doing is devolving powers to the provinces as is written in the constitution. . . . In the Western Cape we've got a strong political base, and obviously as a political party we try to strengthen that base all the time. . . . That's what politics is all about. . . . So much so that, as the interim constitution allows, we are also thinking of writing our own constitution for the Western Cape, with the input of all the role players and parties and so on. Because we feel that that's what we want to do, instead of hanging onto what comes out of central government all the time. Where the people in this part of the province will be governed by their constitution, which must be and will be part of the national constitution. I mean there's things like your flag and your crests and many other things that reside under Schedule Six in the constitution [powers vested in the provinces] that we would like to handle here.

In some cases, the same party elites, who are prominent "Coloured politicians" and play more or less influential roles in disseminating ideas about who Coloureds are and what political place they occupy in South Africa, may draw on all three threads of Coloured political identity at once. Abe Williams, probably the most prominent Coloured politician in the National Party, tabbed to be the next premier of the Western Cape before his sudden fall from grace in a corruption scandal in 1996, said both "We are Afrikaners" and "We are not Afrikaners" in the same campaign speech in Laingsburg, Western Cape, in 1995.[13] This suggests at least three possibilities. The first is that there is a sense in which the three strands are perceived as potentially complementary in the National Party's bid to harness Coloured support in postapartheid South Africa. The second is that there is no clear idea, even within the NP, of what Coloured political identity should be. The third is that there is no clear idea of what an Afrikaner is.

The ANC was ultimately unable to compete with the National Party to articulate a dominant framework of Coloured political identity in the run-up to South Africa's first national democratic election. For the ANC, the election was about freedom—from oppression, from exclusion, and from White minority rule. It was a liberation election. The ANC coupled this theme with that of responsible government. It portrayed itself as a party with a moderate, reasonable plan and the expertise to govern and to deliver "A Better Life for All," as its main campaign slogan promised.

What it failed to do, however, was to include Coloureds effectively in their vision of "All." Whereas the UDF had constructed a precarious sense of common destiny between Coloureds and Africans in the struggle against apartheid in the 1980s, the ANC lacked a vision of common oppression in 1994. There are three likely reasons for the party's failure to capture a majority of Coloured votes.

The first is that the formidable enemy apartheid, which was probably partially responsible for generating an alliance among groups constructed as separate, had disappeared. As apartheid waned and the National Party began to reform and to negotiate its own political demise, it became increasingly difficult to construct a credible and threatening vision of the White oppressor as the relevant Other. This example, in fact, highlights the role of an out-group in constituting a common bond, and of imbuing the enemy with an identity against which the content of "our" identity may be contrasted. This is not to say, though, that the construction of difference requires a legitimate enemy or threat. The Other may be constructed from whole cloth. It is simply that the ANC failed to do so effectively. It was not only, of course, that the ANC failed to construct a credible Other of its own but also that the NP did such a successful job of building on a history of racial division and separateness between Africans and Coloureds, and of using affirmative action as a mobilizing issue. The party portrayed an overpowering danger, which it named "Black," and which appeared tangible and threatening in a moment of transition and instability. Eugene Paramoer, a former UDF activist, described the genesis of a Black political identity: "What you had then [in the 1980s] was a people united against the enemy and that was apartheid colonialism in its various manifestations. So that all people suffered, all people fought, and all people, Coloureds, Indians and Africans, lived in abject poverty. I mean Black people." Logan Wort, another former UDF activist, also described an identity driven mainly by opposition: "You joined the UDF because of broad agreement against apartheid. But you don't like apartheid because you want socialism, and some people go against apartheid because they believe it is against their religion, against Islam. So there are people who join for their own specific reasons, and that is what made the UDF such a broad front. And that is what made it possible for us to have such a broad range of people on our side."

Secondly, the ANC partially ceded the ground of Coloured politics to the NP.

According to some Coloured former UDF activists, Africanist sentiment—an assertion of the Africanism of the ANC and a denial of the Blackness of Coloureds—
became manifest in the transition period.[14] Western Cape campaign managers
were split over whether to concentrate resources in the African areas of almost
certain support or in the Coloured areas, where support was much less secure.
Although it may have been through disorganization rather than by design, the
ANC did end up expending more resources among African voters than it did
among Coloured voters, even though Coloureds are the majority in the Western
Cape and represented the ANC's only hope for victory in the province.[15] Thus
although many activists worked tirelessly in campaigning for the ANC in Coloured
areas, ANC leaders, who orchestrated the campaign from national headquarters in
Johannesburg, largely failed to engage in "Coloured politics."

The ANC may also have avoided Coloured politics because of its commitment to
nonracialism, declining any express engagement with people designated as Coloured on terms separate from those employed with African or other groups.
Nonracialism denies race a central political role and, at least in the form that was
dominant in the UDF era of the 1980s, rejects race-based representation in which
Coloured leaders are presumed to uniquely understand and represent the needs of
Coloured constituents. Whether the ANC should "stoop" to that level of politics
was hotly debated in the transition period, and its ultimately lackluster and uneven
campaign among Coloureds probably reflects the internal ideological struggle,
and opposition by many would-be implementers. Joey Marks, former UDF activist,
described the confusion and infighting that accompanied the return of the ANC:

> Within the ANC, . . . because people came from exile, . . . they said we all are Africans,
> or we all are Black. But the ANC, when I went to the first council, . . . I put up my hand
> because people were talking about the Coloured problem. And I said but it's not a Col-
> oured problem, it's an organizational problem. The ANC's not doing its work properly in
> Coloured communities and now you put the weakness of its membership in Coloured
> communities as being a Coloured problem, and I told them that the many problems . . .
> among the different branches . . . should be resolved first, especially in the Coloured
> communities, and only then will the branches be able to implement work which will
> make the ANC visible and acceptable to the broader community. But, of course, you
> know, I was said no, . . . and when I objected to the word *Coloured* being used they told
> me, no, but you are Coloured! And that was the first time in a decade that I'm being told
> by another African that I am a Coloured person, and I perceive myself not as being a Col-
> oured but as being indigenous to South Africa.

Johnny Issel, former UDF activist and ANC member of the Provincial Parliament,
also alluded to the uneasy relationship between the ANC and the politics of eth-

nicity: "A strong . . . Africanist position developed within the ANC. And I personally feel that it's a kind of opportunistic, power-hungry position. How do certain people who seek certain positions within the ANC actually get that? And one way that some did that is by appealing to African people within the movement, purely on the basis that they are African, or that they speak Xhosa." Wort echoed some of Issel's sentiments: "The Africanists are at the present very dominant within the ANC. And people with my perspective, people who believe that we must assert the balance of what the ANC represents more strongly, we are not very strong within the ANC at the moment. Africanists are extremely strong because it is a period for them to ride high, it is postrevolution."

Although Africanism became ideologically ascendant in parts of the ANC after 1994, it appeared to be spearheaded by a small cabal in the Western Cape motivated by an internal struggle for power rather than by any ideological or external political considerations.[16] There is no evidence that the ANC as a party considers itself to be an African organization or that it seeks to alienate Coloureds. Some Africans within the organization have begun to question the validity of prioritizing "Africans in particular" over other ethnic groups.[17] Many within the party flatly deny allegations of racial exclusivity, claiming instead that those who make them are personally disaffected because they did not receive positions in the government or the ANC.[18]

Controversy over how to mobilize Coloured support has generated some ideological fuzziness within the ANC in the Western Cape and could eventually spark an ideological split. There are clearly those in the party who believe that it is necessary to address Coloureds as a constituency with particular interests and needs based on Colouredness. They recognize such a thing as a Coloured political identity with particular features that differentiate it from other ethnically based (African, for example) political identities. On the other hand, there are those who oppose this approach, arguing that it negates nonracialism. Although they recognize the importance of drawing support from people who are called Coloured, they refuse to attach political significance to the fact of their Colouredness. They contend, rather, that other identities that cross ethnic lines, like class or worker identity, should be harnessed to the ANC. Neither position is as yet well defined, and there are individuals who themselves articulate both possibilities.

The first faction is trying to recognize the political expression of Colouredness and to respect the historically generated particularities of the Coloured community while trying to find expression and representation for that identity within the ANC rather than in a Coloured separatist party. In ideological terms, they believe that it is time to swap nonracialism for multiracialism. Some ANC leaders have begun to address Coloureds as Coloureds. The ANC organized its electoral campaign, for example, by breaking it down into African, Coloured, and White organizational units. As early as 1991 there was talk of establishing a Coloured congress within the ANC. Similar discussions about retaining the UDF, which was perceived as a political organization with roots and legitimacy in the Coloured community, took place during the transition period. They were abandoned for the same ideological reasons then, but those who favor a separate place for Coloureds within the party gained momentum in the 1990s. Issel recalled early debates: "There was a strong discussion of starting a Coloured movement, within the ANC, but not formally within the ANC. I would say members of the ANC, you know, but not within the ANC structures."

Although there is an ideological precedent within the ANC for thinking of Coloureds as a separate political unit, the recent history of opposition politics is strictly nonracial. Partly as a legacy of the ideological influence of the BCM in the opposition, Coloureds did not exist as a category with political content in the 1980s. The UDF did not recognize Coloureds as a distinct group in the decade of its oppositional hegemony. Nevertheless, in the ANC in the 1990s, there was at least the possibility of Colouredness. For some, this was disorienting. Paramoer, of the Community Youth Movement (CYM), described the changing parameters of Coloured identity: "We were disgusted with the label *Coloured* and we would say, in disgust—as a way of saying this is not how it is or how it is supposed to be—we would say 'so-called Coloured people.' 'So-called' meaning we didn't call ourselves Coloured people. It was others calling us that. It was the name given us by our oppressors, the colonialists, and the Afrikaner nationalists. And people didn't see themselves, I didn't see myself, as Coloured. Then I was Black. I saw myself as a Black person fighting for the interests of the Black people. . . . [Now] I would say I'm a Coloured. I would say I'm a Coloured. And I wouldn't have said that ten years ago."

Nelson Mandela himself apparently has some commitment to race-based representation. As early as 1991 he argued that "the ordinary man, no matter to what population group he belongs, must look to our structures and see that I, as a Coloured man, am represented. 'I have got Allan Boesak there whom I trust.' And an Indian must be able to say, 'There is Kathrada—I am represented.'"[19] At the national ANC conference in 1994 Mandela proposed that the ANC Executive Committee should reflect the racial composition of South Africa. The suggestion was rejected, even condemned, as destructive to the fundamental tenets of nonracialism, but the fact that it was made at all, and by the president of the ANC, may be a portent of future trends. Mandela is not a lone voice. Chris Nissen, the Coloured

Lutheran minister elected in 1994 to lead the ANC in the Western Cape, has consistently reassured Coloureds that the party's affirmative action policy includes them and does not favor Africans over Coloureds. The government's policy, which was finally spelled out during the campaign for local government elections in 1995, is that all people of color are considered for the eleven thousand affirmative action positions advertised by the Department of Public Administration and Service. The government has gone further to plead with private business not to discriminate in favor of Africans. Chris Nissen, Western Cape ANC leader, made clear the ANC position: "I cannot tell business how to word their advertisements for employment, but I am appealing to them not to discriminate on a race basis because this causes real tension and is divisive. I want to send this early warning signal to businesses which refuse to employ applicants because they are not African that such companies are flaming racial tension in the Western Cape."[20]

Whether nonracialism trumps privileging a supposedly innately "Coloured" set of interests and identity has become an open question. The issue has been hotly debated within ANC circles in the Western Cape. Historical realities and inherited structural positions preclude treating all groups equally with equal results. But treating some race groups differently from others is not nonracial. It is at best multiracial. As an unnamed source in a newspaper story put it, "There is an informal Coloured caucus in the region. People are opposed to the idea of a congress—if we define the ANC as non-racial, how do we justify a movement within it defined racially?"[21]

A policy paper circulating within the ANC in early 1995 argued that catering to Coloureds as an ethnic group would inflame racial tensions between Africans and Coloureds in the Western Cape, dividing the two communities and making it impossible for the ANC to try to represent both. The paper argued that the party should focus instead on such particular constituencies as trade unionists affiliated to COSATU. The argument is based on the assumption that workers' interests, as workers, will crosscut racial boundaries. The ANC also hopes to tap teachers and other middle-class professionals who supported the UDF in the 1980s.[22]

Johnny Issel argues fervently that the ANC must make a commitment to addressing the needs of *people,* not of Coloureds per se:

I was charged by the ANC to go and work in the fishing industry. I would say 80 percent of the fishermen [in the Cape, who are Coloured] voted for the ANC. For three years I've been working amongst fishermen, and the approach that I used, which is of course not original, it is the same approach which we had used for a large chunk of our struggle, was to really get involved in these people's problems and to fight alongside them against the people who were causing their problems. And in that process, to increase their political understanding. I have not signed up a single fisherman to the ANC, but I can take you to a lot of these communities and I can show you how crazy these people are about the ANC. And I have not signed up a single one of them. I have never carried membership cards and all that. And I really feel that the answer is that. To really get involved in people's day-to-day problems.

Willie Hofmeyr, another prominent ANC member of the Provincial Parliament in the Western Cape, also argues against engaging in politics within an ethnic framework. He refuses to compete with the National Party to define Coloureds or to construct a meaning of Colouredness that would find a political home in the ANC: "It would be difficult to out-Coloured the Coloured—I mean, the National Party. They sort of very much tried to articulate the fears, and play on the fears, of the Coloured community."

The coexistence of ideological stances in the post apartheid era makes it unclear who is and who is not a Black comrade. Most people in the ANC continue to use *Black* to refer to the broadly defined group of non-Whites in South Africa and *African* to describe the narrower segment who are neither Coloured nor Indian. Even this convention is being abandoned, though, as Chris Nissen demonstrated by denouncing an ANC promise to write off debt arrears for Blacks but not for Coloureds or Indians: "The RDP is for the benefit of all people, black, white, coloured, and Indian."[23] It is a signal that the ANC in the Western Cape has begun to reject its own apartheid-era terminology, its own "struggle" discourse. In the process, it has ceded the right to name, and to define groups, to the NP.

Ambiguity over the meaning of the word *Black* has sown confusion among former UDF activists in the Coloured community. As Wort put it,

Terminology counted for a lot. Because everything about what the leaders are saying says nothing about Coloured people. Mandela speaks to the nation and he speaks about White fears and how the Black people have suffered and the White this and the Black that. That is how the Coloureds see it. And they were listening, waiting, when are they going to talk about us? And they didn't. And amongst us activists, we were beginning to say, we know they mean everybody, but maybe they should begin to say that, because it's difficult for us because we get to the house and they say but Mandela said nothing about us yet. De Klerk is saying about us. You want us to vote for the ANC, but they never say nothing about us. And . . . the ANC leadership seemed not to have understood this. And it was a difficult thing to fight. Because as a nonracial people, how do you justify coming to speak to the Coloured people? When you're supposed to be nonracial? And we had that moral dilemma among ourselves. And maybe after the election we should have been bold enough to say look, this isn't what it's about. We're actually representing Coloured people here too.

Controversy within the party over whom to represent and how to represent them has led at least one group to split from the ANC for reasons related to race. In February 1995 Coloured delegates from ten interim branches of the ANC Youth League walked out of the annual meeting. They objected to the fact that they were unable to vote because they had not managed to sign up one hundred members in their branches. They subsequently launched the Community Youth Movement, which is ideologically nonracial but which exists only in Coloured areas. The fact that the CYM continues to believe in and support the principles of the ANC creates a dilemma for the party over whether or not to recognize and work with the organization. Paramoer, the leader of the breakaway group, explained his dilemma: "The Community Youth Movement is also a result of that kind of frustration, of having been marginalized *within* the liberation movement, of having been silenced *within* the liberation movement. . . . We don't belong to the ANC or to any other political party. But we share quite a number of the principles that the ANC has. For example we are looking quite favorably at a document like the Freedom Charter because it embodies to us what eventually we would like to see our country turning into. It's our vision, it's our charter. We believe in it. We look at it quite strongly as our freedom charter."

In the medium term, it is likely that both trends will coexist uneasily within the ANC and will continue to hinder the party's ability to define itself and its constituency in the Western Cape. The ANC appears to have renewed its commitment, since the April 1994 elections, to engage in politics in the Coloured community. It is not yet clear whether it will engage in "Coloured politics" in order to do so.

There is a third stance contributing to the cacophony of voices vying to redefine Coloured political identity in the postapartheid era. Various Coloured nationalist parties or groups have emerged since mid-1994. Although they have little or no constituency, they have a voice, and they contribute to the public articulation of Coloured identity. The new Labour Party and the *Kleurling Weerstandsbeweging* (KWB) emerged in 1994 and 1995 as the most voluble explicitly Coloured political voices, but there are other groups and individuals articulating an explicitly Coloured political identity.[24]

The Labour Party all but disbanded after most of its members crossed the floor to join the NP in 1991 and 1992. That part of the party structure which remained entered into an official electoral alliance with the ANC. The party was finally officially dissolved in September, 1994. One week later, it was reconstituted by two members of the old party, Dougie Joseph and Ken Lategan. The new Labour Party defines itself as an ethnically based party representing Coloureds. Joseph described the niche he believed the LP would fill:

The LP was always the mouthpiece for the Coloured community, and that is why we decided to continue. And we must contest the next elections in the name of the LP so that we can stand for the Coloured community. . . . Well, we are an open party, but in the past we [were] always the mouthpiece for the Coloured community, and that is why we are still prepared to do it. Because all of the other political parties, whether they are prepared to say it or not, but they are all ethnic. The ANC are still for the Xhosa. The IFP is for the Zulu people. The NP is for the Afrikaner, the DP for the English-speaking and the liberals. And we as the LP said we are standing for the Coloured people.[25]

The Coloured nationalist groups have been most explicit in defining who the Coloureds are and in fashioning a politicized history, culture, common ancestry, and common space or territory for the group. Joseph added: "The Coloured community, they are homemade. They have no other homeland. You have the Indian people who are coming from Bombay. Our Blacks, they are coming from North Africa. Your Whites, they are coming from Europe, and Coloureds, they are born and bred in South Africa. They have no other homeland. And that is why we feel that on this homeland the settlers have all the power, in our homeland of South Africa. Everybody in South Africa are settlers, except the Coloured community. We are homemade. We are born and bred in South Africa. Nine months after the sixth of April 1692, Coloured has their heritage." Lategan explained their stance in a less colorful, more strictly political vein: "Basically we have to look at the whole question of people who are experiencing being marginalized within the greater sphere. We've got to look at minority rights. Defending the position of people like the Coloured group, for example."

The *Kleurling Weerstandsbeweging,* which means Coloured resistance movement but for which there is no officially sanctioned English name, has not defined itself as a political party, but it plays a role in the political sphere by contributing to the articulation of Colouredness. The KWB asserts that Coloureds are being used and misled by both Whites and Blacks, represented by the NP and the ANC, respectively. KWB leader Mervyn Ross has demanded that the Western Cape be reserved as a Volkstaat for Coloured people. Much of his discourse calls up a threat to the Afrikaans language and to Coloured culture. The KWB has also called for Coloureds to boycott local government elections, using the argument that a vote for either the ANC or the NP would constitute a betrayal of the Coloured people. In a new twist on the old conundrum of what to call Coloureds, Ross has said, "We are not blacks, we are Africans," by which he means people born in Africa.[26]

In a move that reflects the emergence of a new political spectrum in South Africa, both the new LP and the KWB have been approached by other political organizations who consider themselves to be the political representatives of ethnic minorities. The Freedom Front met secretly with LP leaders in February 1995 to discuss a potential pact or alliance between the two groups.[27] IFP minister Sipho Mzimela told a KWB conference that the IFP "stood side-by-side with the KWB against the monster of domination by the ANC." The IFP supports KWB demands for self-determination, drawing a parallel with what he called "the Zulu struggle for self determination in KwaZulu Natal."[28] Basil Douglas, the leader of the Southwest Joint Coloured Association (SOWEJOCA), another Coloured political group in Johannesburg, ran as an IFP candidate for local government elections in 1995, and won.

Material Conditions

Between 1989 and 1993 real GDP fell by 4 percent, creating South Africa's longest recession of the twentieth century. This was a product of such causes as repercussions from the international recession, severe drought, and political volatility. Between 1982 and 1985 investment averaged 24 percent of GDP. In 1992 it was only 15 percent of GDP, undermining the economy's potential to generate growth and absorb work seekers. Between 1990 and 1995 the mining sector lost more than one hundred thousand jobs, and manufacturing lost sixty thousand.[29]

The Western Cape, where 60 percent of all Coloureds live, was spared much of the volatility and economic hardship experienced by the rest of the country.[30] The population of the Western Cape is just over four million, representing approximately 10 percent of the country's population. Fifty-four percent of the population is Coloured, 24 percent is African, and 22 percent is White. Seventy-eight percent of Coloureds live in urban areas. The Western Cape was better equipped than the rest of the country to take advantage of South Africa's new manufacturing growth phase in the 1970s and 1980s. The province does not depend on one major sector or industry and is dominated by economic sectors with strong forward and backward linkages, which encourage regional growth. It also exceeds other areas of the country in the concentration of small, medium, and micro enterprises, which are better for job creation and growth than major industries have proven to be. In most expenditure categories, the Western Cape share of national spending is higher than its 10 percent population share, and in several categories it exceeds the 14.2 percent gross regional product share of gross domestic product.[31]

The Western Cape has a relatively high per capita income level and better scores on most social development indicators than the rest of South Africa. It has the highest provincial Human Development Index (.76).[32] Its unemployment rate was only 12 percent in 1994, and Coloured unemployment dropped from 11 percent in 1986 to 8.6 percent in 1991.[33] The official unemployment rate for South Africa rose from 18.5 percent in 1991 to 29 percent in 1993.[34] Actual unemployment for Africans is probably more than 40 percent.

Despite relative wealth in the Western Cape, there may be a perception among Coloureds that the pie is shrinking and that their share of it is shrinking fast. The African population in the Western Cape quadrupled to 1.2 million between 1980 and 1995. This massive influx of overwhelmingly poor and unskilled workers and their families has created huge shortages of housing, and scarcity of other resources such as electricity, water, and transport, as well as social services such as health care. In the postapartheid era, the Western Cape's relative affluence will probably put the region at a disadvantage with respect to claims toward national resource allocations for social development.[35] If this proves to be the case, it could in turn create the impression that central government is discriminating against the Western Cape.

Additionally, the ANC's affirmative action program has been controversial in the Western Cape. The program, which has quotas for public sector employment and recommendations for private-sector employment, stipulates that the "formerly oppressed" be given preferential hiring treatment. As we have seen, however, because the "formerly oppressed" initially was insufficiently defined, affirmative action has emerged as a political flashpoint in interracial relations in the Western Cape. Affirmative action could in fact threaten the economic chances of employed middle- and lower-income Coloureds, if it is implemented in such a way as to favor Africans over Coloureds. Although the ANC has now stated firmly that it does not intend it to discriminate against Coloureds, affirmative action continues to be used by the NP to mobilize the specter of an economic threat from the ANC, and from Africans.[36]

Organization

As the ANC and NP vied for dominance among Coloured voters in the Western Cape, each had access to very different types and extents of organizational bases. The ANC failed to rebuild the decimated network of grassroots social movements that had sustained the UDF during the 1980s. The NP managed to capitalize on the extensive party branch organizational structure of the Labour Party, most of whose MPs defected to the NP before 1994. Organization was an important component of the ability of the NP to penetrate Coloured areas and to gain the support of a majority of Coloured voters.

One institutional component that contributed significantly to the strength of the UDF in the 1980s, relative to the BCM in the 1970s and even relative to the ANC before it was banned, was an extensive organizational network at the grassroots level. Building on the momentum of the 1976 Soweto uprising and the 1979 legalization of African trade unions, many youth, civic, and women's organizations, as well as African and some nonracial trade unions, were formed in the early 1980s. Most of these grew out of specific issues of local concern and were thus in a sense organic to the communities in which they were embedded. In 1983, when the UDF was formed, many of these organizations affiliated to the broader front, thus entrenching themselves as the link between national and regional UDF leaders on the one hand, and the people on the other. Although nationwide UDF mass action campaigns often revolved around larger political and ideological matters not always of primary importance to the people, popular support was derived through local organizations that addressed local concerns.

In the second half of the 1980s this organizational base and the UDF's connection to it were severely attenuated for three reasons. First, the UDF was effectively banned, and successive levels of leadership were imprisoned or banned after 1986. Second, the UDF began to focus much more attention on national campaigns to end apartheid than on local campaigns to, for example, lower rent. Third, effective local leaders were drawn gradually into the higher ranks, where they spent more time dealing with national issues at the expense of local-level concerns.

Most civic associations affiliated to the UDF in the 1980s merged into an umbrella South African National Civics Organization (SANCO) after 1991. SANCO is not officially attached to the ANC, and it does not operate as an extension of the ANC's organizational network (the way the UDF worked through the civics in the 1980s). Nevertheless, SANCO has endorsed the ANC in elections, and as early as 1997 it announced that it would support the ANC candidate in 1999. In the Western Cape, however, CAHAC, the parent body of civic associations in Coloured areas and an organizational precursor to the UDF, remained outside of SANCO and eventually joined an opposing umbrella organization called Western Cape Community Organization (WECCO). Joe Marks, a former vice president of the UDF, headed WECCO and eventually left the ANC for the DP over the ANC's alleged mistreatment of CAHAC when it failed to join SANCO.[37]

The organizational structure that was (partly) lost to the UDF in the 1980s was not recovered by the ANC in the 1990s. Not only was the relation between the UDF and many of the grassroots organizations undercut by a coincidence of attenuating circumstances at the end of the decade, but many of the civic and youth organizations themselves also disappeared or were severely weakened. The Young Christian Workers and Young Christian Students (YCW/YCS) organizations, for example, which initially took the lead in organizing schools and mobilizing students in the early 1980s, and in which many Coloured activists have their political roots, are essentially defunct in the Western Cape today. The Cape Youth Congress, which was a key link between the UDF and the schools in the 1980s, was absorbed into the South Africa Youth Congress, thus robbing its local branches of resources and initiative. After the ANC was unbanned, the ANC Youth League reemerged, and youth groups affiliated to the ANC were additionally required to work through the Youth League's national bureaucracy. An increasing number of bureaucratic structures were superimposed upon the branches, multiplying the number of meetings that activists were expected to attend, and reducing their direct input and control.[38]

The ANC made a number of decisions that contributed to its organizational withdrawal from Coloured areas. After the ban against the ANC was lifted in 1990, the party was primarily concerned with negotiations to end apartheid, fund raising, promotion of its international profile, and bolstering its negotiating position. Organization was not its primary concern. In August 1991 UDF and ANC leaders decided to abolish the UDF altogether and to collapse the structure and leadership of the UDF, which had a prominent place in Coloured politics, into the ANC, which did not. Allan Boesak noted in 1991, for example, that "for many [Coloureds] the UDF was an organisation that they had built. In the beginning, the ANC was perceived as an organisation that had come back from exile."[39]

The ANC, moreover, did not organize as the UDF had. It did not attempt to harness civic and other local-level groups with prior legitimacy and community attachment to its political agenda, as the UDF had done. It largely ignored many UDF structures that had mediated local politics during the 1980s. Instead, the ANC established party branches. It opened seven in Mitchell's Plain, a large, mostly Coloured suburb of Cape Town, in 1991.[40] By mid-1993, the ANC claimed to have formed 125 branches in the province and to be in the process of opening another 65.[41]

The balance of evidence suggests that the ANC did not have much success organizing this way in Coloured areas, however. In November 1993 one regional strategist admitted that the party was considering suspending the establishment of more branches and replacing them with "working groups" that would have "a presence."[42] Membership in ANC branches failed to extend beyond the activist party elite. All ANC branches were required to have one hundred paid-up members to qualify as full branches. Without the requisite number of members, ANC Youth League branches, for example, are denied voting rights in regional and national Youth League forums. Until then, they are considered "interim branches," and have the right to engage in discussion, but not to participate fully. In February

1995 representatives of sixteen out of nineteen interim branches walked out of the ANCYL provincial conference in the Western Cape. They objected to the fact that they were denied voting rights because they could not muster the necessary membership figures. All of those who walked out were Coloured representatives of Coloured areas, and the subsequent split within the Youth League assumed a distinctly racial flavor. Although some branches in African areas have "interim" status, these are mostly new, and interim status was initially intended to be a transitional stage. Coloured activists contend that because branches remain small in Coloured areas, the practice is racist and renders impotent Coloured activists within the Youth League.[43]

The ANC and some of its leaders who returned from exile or jail also alienated many activists who had been involved in the struggle inside the country. Exiles and prisoners were often more prominent and generally garnered higher leadership positions than internal activists. Exiles took charge of the election campaign in the Western Cape, for example, and failed to involve many of the activists who had been instrumental in organizing for the UDF in the 1980s. Those who had been active in the 1980s had some prior legitimacy, knew more about organization and planning, and were more familiar with the needs and characters of the communities they lived and worked in. Many of the youth leaders who were instrumental in the mobilization and politicization of Coloureds in the early 1980s were sidelined by the ANC and were disillusioned with the reality of post-apartheid politicking.[44]

Unlike the ANC, the National Party was able to use much of an existing branch network in Coloured areas in the Western Cape. It is rumored that many of the Labour Party MPs who crossed the floor to join the NP in the transition period were lured by bribes, perquisites, and salary hikes. By 1994 well over half of LP members of Parliament had joined the NP. The LP was organized on a constitu ency basis, with representatives elected from districts. Each district had one or more branches. Because many of the MPs had been involved simultaneously in management committees, through which some government monies were allocated, LP branches and MCs were fairly well intertwined, both in fact and in the public perception. In many cases the MCs and party branches represented the personal power base of a local leader, and they stood at the center of elaborate patronage networks in the Tricameral era. When asked about their political affiliations in 1994, many Coloureds mentioned food parcels or public sector jobs distributed by Labour Party MPs in the 1980s.[45] Former LP members of Parliament claim that most MPs were able to take their branches with them when they defected to the NP.[46] The importance of the organizational network of the LP branches is highlighted by the fact that the ANC did well in areas where it was able to harness former LP branches.[47]

Although the LP was never as extensively organized as the UDF, in that it did not work through organizations embedded in civil society such as churches, youth groups, and civic organizations, many of its branches were well established and had some longevity in the community. In some cases, LP branches were the only political structures that remained intact in Coloured areas through the transition period. That they had become NP branches was perhaps less pertinent than that they were still there at all, and still attached to the same political elites. Many former LP politicians were additionally long-standing local leaders with extensive and interlocking ties in their own communities. Before moving into the arena of formal politics, many were involved in other public domains, serving on school boards and sports committees, and even in civic associations, in the days when civics focused on addressing local concerns, and before they were politicized and subsumed under the UDF. Many Labour Party MPs had been involved in Coloured politics since the era of the Coloured Persons Representative Council in the 1960s. At a time when politics was suddenly very different and people may have been confused about their new political status and space, these leaders appear to have emerged with renewed legitimacy as "traditional" local elites.[48]

Beyond the ability of the NP to capitalize on the prior existence of LP branches, the party began in the early 1990s to open its own branches in Coloured areas. By mid-1991 the NP claimed to have opened eight branches in Mitchell's Plain, each with more members than the single LP branch in that area. In July 1993 the party claimed to have more than one thousand branches in the Western Cape, and in 1994 Cape NP leader Dawie de Villiers estimated that 45 percent of the NP's regional party membership was Coloured.[49]

Among Coloured voters who voted for the ANC, political meetings and community organizations were cited as the most prominent sources of political information.[50] It may be that ANC supporters were socialized and politicized through community organizations in the 1980s and were more likely to cite such associations as politically important regardless of their relative strength in the posttransition era. It may also be, however, that where local associations remained well organized, embedded in the community, and ideologically attached to the ANC, people tended to vote for the ANC. Leaders involved with unions claim, for example, that they were able to generate widespread support for the ANC among union members.[51] Among those who voted for the NP, family, friends, and respected people in the community were the three most common and trusted sources of political information. It thus seems likely that the ability of the NP to attract a large number of locally prominent and historically legitimate Coloured candidates, who were familiar to the communities in which they campaigned and stood for election, played a role in grounding, and perhaps "naturalizing," the NP.

Available Ideology

What was ideologically available in the 1990s to parties contesting Coloured politics, and to Coloured voters, was partly circumscribed by ideological positions carved out in the previous decade. In the 1980s all mainstream Coloured politics, whether apparently radical or moderate, was oppositional. The exceptions, parties such as Swartz's FCPP, had disappeared by 1981. The space of Coloured political discourse was dominated by the UDF and the LP. Although these two groups struggled to carve out separate ideological and strategic locations, they in fact occupied positions very near each other on the dominant axis of politics.

When the broader political framework that had governed the existence of the UDF and the LP began to disappear after 1990, both parties disintegrated. Although it would be facile to argue that either organization was dissolved because of the sudden evaporation of its oppositional function—after all, other previously op-positional groups have thrived in the postapartheid era—both were casualties of the transition, subsumed by larger political forces.

The ideologies that governed the political possibilities of Coloured identity in the 1980s for the most part disappeared after 1990. More than most people in South Africa, Coloureds appear to have negotiated the transition in an ideological vacuum. Opposition, as previously constituted, was unavailable. And while the ANC and NP, and later the New National Party, vied to redefine the ideological possibilities of politics for Coloureds, these parties appear to have floundered.

Although the UDF in the 1980s and the ANC in the 1990s both espoused non-racialism, the principles appear substantively different, for two reasons. First, the ANC's commitment to nonracialism was always more strategic than foundational. The ANC was an African liberation movement that only latterly admitted members of other racial groups. The ANC had formal ties to, and typically collaborated with, organizations representing the interests of other "oppressed" racial groups, but each had a separate constituent base. Thus the strict nonracialism of the UDF in the 1980s, which was substantially influenced by the BCM and as a result actually denied a place to race altogether, represented a qualitative departure from that of the ANC. In the 1990s both strains of nonracialism coexist, sometimes uneasily, within the ranks of the ANC.

The second reason is that the same ideology had different referents and poten-tially different implications in the 1990s than it had in the previous decade. In opposition to an illegitimate, brutally oppressive regime organized on the premise of racial segregation and discrimination, nonracialism is irreproachably on the side of goodness and light. It attaches to an unassailable moral high ground. As the ideological position of the ruling party, however, nonracialism may be vulnerable to the same criticisms that have been leveled against liberalism—namely, that it is a laissez-faire doctrine that privileges the status quo and those who make up the majority because it refuses to recognize demands for minority rights. To the extent that nonracialism denies the political relevance of race, it cannot accord special status or protection to groups that claim a distinct racial identity.

A commitment to nonracialism, then, may be, or may be perceived as, a commitment to those people who make up the majority in a nation. In South Africa, Africans make up roughly 80 percent of the population. When Mandela, for example, proposed that the ANC leadership reflect the racial composition of South Africa, he was trying to make the party more racially representative. Although he may have been opposed by those in the ANC who believe the party should be distinctly "African," the primary opposition came from those who argued that his position undermined the nonracial commitments of the party. The proposal was rejected for such apparently sympathetic ideological reasons, but the net effect was that the party hierarchy has continued to be dominated by Africans. For people inclined to see political representation in racial terms, as are many South Africans, due in large part to the legacy of apartheid, such willful disregard for racial composition may be translated as disregard for racially defined groups of people, and, in particular, for minorities. Whether the ANC intends this outcome is unclear, although leaders consistently deny that the party is anything but fully inclusive.[52] In 1997 the ANC announced its intention to move from nonracialism to multiracialism. Whereas nonracialism is the refusal to recognize individuals as members of racially constituted groups, multiracialism is the explicit recognition of all race groups equally. Thabo Mbeki heralded the move as an important step forward for the ANC, but it remains to be seen what sort of tangible effect it will have on party policy.

In the postapartheid era the NP has attempted to define itself partially in opposition to the hegemonic majoritarian possibilities of the nonracialism of the ANC. It emerged in the first democratic elections as the self-styled guardian of minority rights. The minorities it allegedly defends are defined in racial terms: Coloureds, Whites, and Indians. The NP also defends Afrikaans speakers but not Afrikaners, and apparently not Zulus, although they could presumably count as an ethnic if not racial minority. The postapartheid ideological stance of the NP is dictated in part by its oppositional status, within parameters partly limited by its own historical ideological position. The NP persists in the belief that political identities are racially determined. But it is also true that the same ideological stance has acquired a different sense and implication, now that it is espoused by a party in opposition, in the context of majoritarian democracy in a multiracial society.

The protection of minority rights, the expression of the rights of groups (as essential, and essentially political, units), and demands for cultural and linguistic protections, as well as some ethnic and cultural autonomy, now anchor opposition to the ANC government. The ideological spectrum that appears most salient to the organization of cleavages in South African politics runs from an apparently liberal commitment to the protection of individual rights to demands for the protection of group rights. The opposition to majority rule is anchored in the status of minority rights.

It appears to be the case, then, that what is ideologically salient in postapartheid South Africa, what organizes politics and political space, is at least partly scripted by those cleavages that were constructed as politically salient in the apartheid era. Although race itself does not emerge as the organizing principle of politics, the place of race in politics continues to dominate ideological debate.

Resonance

In the transition and postapartheid eras, dating from 1990, political elites from the NP, ANC, and various "Coloured nationalist" groups have hotly contested the political meaning of Coloured identity. At least five possibilities have been articulated: Coloureds form a subset of the White racial group; Coloureds form a subset of the Black political group; Coloureds are an indigenous African group with their own claims to a distinct identity; Coloureds are a subset of an Afrikaans-language group; and "Coloured" is not a politically relevant identity. Not all of the potential political meanings of Colouredness are mutually exclusive. The NP articulates both Afrikaans-language and White/Coloured racial identities, for example. The ANC tries to foster South African and nonracial identities.

To what extent do people formerly classified as Coloured internalize the identities that political elites try to make salient in the postapartheid era? Election and survey results suggest that each of these identities has some limited resonance among different individuals. It is not clear, though, that most people readily identify "Coloured" as a social or cultural identity, with one of the particular political identities listed above. *Coloured* was more readily available as a form of self-identification after 1994 than it was in the last decade of the apartheid era, but it has not yet developed a distinct political voice, and does not appear to resonate politically, or to include specific political content, for most Coloureds.

In the Western Cape, where 60 percent of Coloureds live and almost 60 percent of the electorate is Coloured, approximately 69 percent of Coloureds voted for the NP and 25 percent voted for the ANC in the country's first national democratic election in 1994.[53] These results immediately suggested to many political pundits that most Coloureds were racist and anti-African. The vote was an expression of Coloured identity as defined by common sentiment against Africans. "It is rather a feeling that there is not enough which is common between brown and black people. Although they share certain things there exists a great gap when it comes to culture, religion, language, and attitudes toward family life."[54] For others, election results demonstrated that Coloured political identity was mediated by strong historical, ancestral, and cultural ties with Whites, and particularly Afrikaners. The vote was interpreted as an expression of Coloured identity as an extension of White identity.[55]

Although this may have been true for some people, survey results do not necessarily support these conclusions. In mid-1993 fewer than one in four Coloured voters in the Western Cape considered themselves supporters of any party. They identified closely with neither the NP nor the ANC, although the extent of identification varied by party. Whereas 90 percent of Coloureds who would vote for the ANC claimed to identify with that party, only 45 percent of those who planned to vote NP claimed that they identified with the party.[56] Coloureds remained the least committed voters throughout the campaign period; and they were *least* committed to the party for which they voted the most. This undermines the proposition that a vote for the NP was an expression of a primordial Coloured racial affinity, or that the NP stood as the natural expression of a Coloured political identity.

Second, a vote for the NP did not automatically express White, White-oriented, or anti-African identity. In one survey conducted in March 1994, fifty-two percent of respondents said that they felt closer to Whites and 48 percent felt closer to Blacks. Of those who felt closer to Whites, 5 percent supported the ANC and 95 percent supported the NP. Thus there appears to be a connection between Whiteness and the NP. Sixty percent of those who said they felt closer to Blacks, however, also supported the NP.[57] There may be a few reasons for this apparently anomalous result. Perhaps closeness to Blacks was not politicized for these respondents. They may have expressed a fellowship with Blacks which was more sociocultural or economic than political. It is also possible that the ANC was not clearly identified with Blackness, or that the NP was not clearly associated with an anti-Black identity. In other words, for half the respondents who felt closer to Blacks, there may have been no connection between race and political identity.

The ambiguity of the term *Black,* which has both inclusive (political) and exclusive (racial) potential meaning, also raises the possibility that the question may have been understood in different ways by different respondents.

Third, whether there is cultural, linguistic, or religious affinity between Africans or Afrikaners and Coloureds is not immediately or automatically relevant to political identity. In the 1980s it was possible for at least a significant minority of Coloureds to have a Black political identity that could coexist with Coloured social identity. The two were not mutually exclusive, which supports the contention that social and cultural identities need not bear on political identity. At the same time, distrust and enmity between Afrikaners and Coloureds has been much more politically salient in this century than the potential cultural and linguistic affinities political entrepreneurs appear now to be fostering. It was precisely because Coloureds were considered to be much more closely aligned, politically, with the opposition (dominantly English) United Party that the (Afrikaner) NP sought consistently to deny Coloureds the franchise. NP leaders then claimed that Coloureds, who had fought on the English side in the Boer War and voted consistently for British parties, had a stronger natural affinity for the English than for Afrikaners. In 1975 Richard van der Ross, an eminent Coloured political leader and long-standing commentator on Coloured politics, made the claim that Coloureds were very distant from Afrikaners and viewed them with a fair amount of trepidation: "The middle class Coloured person is inclined to be more than a little skeptical about the Afrikaner's religious integrity. . . . The general policy of separateness in the social sphere has succeeded in widening the gulf between the Afrikaner and the Coloured person even further."[58] Whatever affinity there may be between Afrikaners and Coloureds, it has not been much politically exploited in this century. Rather, such "natural" links are today being constructed for political purposes, mainly by NP leaders who seek to link Whites and Coloureds in a single political constituency.

Nevertheless, only 1 percent of Coloured voters identified with a party because of their membership in an ethnic or racial group.[59] When asked whether they believed that they belonged to a distinctive cultural, historical, or linguistic community, 47 percent of Coloured respondents said no. Among groups defined in racial or ethnic terms, Coloureds had the lowest rate of this type of identification in South Africa. Feelings of South African—ness, as a national identity, are highest among residents of the Western Cape, in general, and among Coloureds in particular.[60]

Additionally, surveys show that Coloureds do not claim to vote, or affiliate politically, because of racial identity. Seventy-six percent of Coloureds surveyed identified with a party because of its ideology, policy, performance, or competence. The concerns of Coloured voters seemed to be mediated by interests and preferences rather than race. Coloured ANC voters had the same value preferences as African ANC voters; Coloured NP supporters had the same concerns as other NP supporters. Half of all Whites believed that the ANC's affirmative action policy threatened their jobs. Forty percent of Coloureds agreed with this proposition, whereas 43 percent disagreed. Fifty-eight percent of Coloureds were concerned that housing invasions (such as the one at Delft) would increase under an ANC government. Of this group, 66 percent supported the NP and only 7 percent supported the ANC.[61]

Surveys demonstrate that even when confined to ascriptive possibilities, (such as language, race, religion, and so on) people formerly labeled Coloured self-identify along multiple spectrums. In November 1993 one survey showed that 54.6 percent of Coloureds in the Western Cape preferred to be known as South Africans. Only 30 percent preferred to be known as Coloureds. Nine percent preferred to be called Afrikaans-speaking Coloureds and 3 percent called themselves Brown Afrikaners.[62] Polling data indicate, further, that Coloureds' answers to the question "How do you identify yourself?" may have changed during and immediately after the transition. In a survey conducted eleven months later, 75 percent of Coloureds said that they did not mind being called Coloured, and only 22 percent said that they did.[63] Although the questions asked in the two surveys were not identical, one asking which identity the respondent preferred, the other asking which identity the respondent would accept, that discrepancy alone probably does not account for a 45 percent swing toward Coloured identification. *Coloured* seems to have become a more acceptable identity category than it was in the 1980s. *Coloured* is no longer preceded by the modifying "so-called," even by former UDF activists who never failed to use such terminology in the 1980s. Some activists themselves, who were Black as recently as a decade ago, are now Coloured.[64]

This postapartheid phenomenon, in which Colouredness has emerged as a distinctly more available identity, has not yet assumed an obvious political dimension. Although a 1994 survey showed that 44 percent of Coloureds in the Western Cape agreed that there was "a need for self-determination for Coloured people such as a political party or a resistance movement," other data contradict this result.[65] A poll conducted in February 1994 asked people why they supported a particular political party. "Will see to the future of my group" was the least common response among Coloureds. Although that response rated low among all racially defined groups, it was least common among Coloureds. As the ANC has learned as well, placing a Coloured person in a leadership position is not enough to garner the Coloured vote. The ANC's decision to elect Allan Boesak chairman of the Western Cape ANC backfired because Boesak, though Coloured, is unpopular among most Coloureds. Coloureds are apparently not prepared to back an individual merely on the basis of apparent racial likeness.

In the run-up to South Africa's second democratic elections in 1999, a number of Coloured politicians moved from the NNP to the ANC. The most prominent defector was the well-known NNP politician Patrick McKenzie. Polls indicate, however, that his defection did not have a significant effect on voter support.[66] The NNP nevertheless won only 38 percent of the vote, a 16 percent drop-off from its 1994 showing, ceding dominance in the Western Cape to the ANC, which won 42 percent of the vote, an increase of 8 percent over its 1994 results. Although many of the NNP votes were probably lost to nonvoters, polls and election returns indicate that the NNP also lost support among the working class and in rural areas to the ANC and the DP. The ANC and DP did significantly better and the NNP significantly worse in results that could not have been predicted by a divided-society "racial census" analysis of the 1994 election. After the election, the NNP and DP, which won 11 percent of the vote, united in a coalition to rule the province, because no party had won an absolute majority.

In addition, no nationalistic or racially exclusive Coloured political party or resistance movement has gained support or credibility in the posttransition era. The new Labour Party, which can best be described as Coloured nationalist, fielded its only candidate for local government elections in 1995 in Riversdale—a small town with a predominantly Coloured population in the eastern part of the Western Cape. The candidate was Dougie Joseph, the leader of the new Labour Party. Joseph and his wife were both born in Riversdale and have lived there all their lives. He is a prominent member of the community who was a LP member of Parliament in the Tricameral Parliament. Even his political enemies (former LP politicians now in the ANC or NP) described him as a popular and powerful political figure in his area.[67]

Joseph stood for election in the poorest ward in Riversdale. The constituency is 100 percent Coloured. His campaign platform was that there was no place in the new South Africa for Coloureds, that they were being squeezed by the White NP and the African ANC, and that the time had come for Coloureds to govern themselves in the land of their birth, the Cape.[68] Although Joseph had little organizational or financial backing for his campaign, he personally visited more than three-quarters of the homes in his district, was clearly well-known in his community, and had widely disseminated his message.[69]

He and his party lost the election dismally. In his ward he won only twenty-four votes. He told me, "I was totally rejected. I am leaving politics altogether. There is no place for the Labour Party in South Africa anymore." He admitted that he was shocked, although he did not concede that his message may not have resonated. Instead, he blamed his loss on the fact that the ANC (which won) had more money and more canvassers. Despite his protestations, the extent of his loss suggests that the "Cape for the Coloureds" theme did not resonate and that his constituency did not share his vision, despite his local popularity and obvious commitment. Although Colouredness may be an increasingly acceptable marker of identity, Coloured as a separatist, nationalistic identity with political content and partisan attachments does not appear to resonate for most Coloureds.

Other cleavages which cross-cut and differentiate a homogeneous Coloured racial category played an important role in 1994 election results. Voting patterns differed substantially along socioeconomic and demographic lines. The relation between income and party support among Coloureds in the Western Cape was curvilinear. Support for the ANC was higher among those in the poorest sector, lowest among people in the two middle-income groups, and strongest among those in the highest income category. Among the wealthiest Coloureds, in fact, support for the ANC nearly equaled support for the NP (at 39 percent and 40 percent, respectively). Support for the NP was highest among those in the middle-income brackets, and dropped off substantially (by 22 percent) at higher income levels. Similarly, the ANC was most popular among those Coloureds who were fully employed, whereas the NP had more support among the unemployed.[70] These results are essentially duplicated when education is substituted for economic cleavages, with the NP doing worst among those with postmatric education, and the ANC doing best among those with Standard 9 or higher education.

Coloureds identify differently along multiple cleavage lines. In 1993 a total of 55 percent of Coloureds surveyed preferred to be known as South African. Sixty percent of Coloureds between the ages of seventeen and twenty-four preferred to be called South African, as opposed to only 47 percent of those over fifty. Seventy-two percent of metropolitan dwellers, but only 22 percent of rural dwellers, prefer to be called South African. Eighty-two percent of those with Standard 9 or more education preferred to be called South African, as opposed to only 23 percent with Standard 4 education or less. Sixty percent of men and 50 percent of women preferred to be called South African.[71]

Coloureds also differ along informational and associational dimensions. Among Coloureds who received their political information from meetings and community organizations, the ANC did more than twice as well as the NP.[72] Many of the community organizations that mediated politics in Coloured areas in the 1980s, however, disappeared in the 1990s. Union membership also affected political affiliation for many Coloureds. Thirty-one percent of a Coloured sample surveyed in 1993 supported the NP, and only 13 percent supported the ANC. Among union members, though, 29 percent of respondents claimed to support the ANC, and 23 percent supported the NP. Although only 17 percent of Coloureds trusted COSATU leader and ANC member of Parliament Cyril Ramaphosa, 37 percent of Coloured union members trusted him.[73] The Cape Teachers Professional Association, which is the largest body of Coloured teachers, was also drawn into the ANC camp by Franklin Sonn, an influential Coloured leader who was induced to publicly endorse the ANC to help the party's election prospects. ANC support is clearly much higher among union members than among the Coloured population as a whole. Religion and church membership (which have organizational as well as cultural and religious dimensions), on the other hand, do not appear to affect political affiliation. Nor does Afrikaans language. Coloureds whose home language was Afrikaans, or who were members of the Dutch Reformed Church, were not more likely to vote NP than English-speaking Coloureds who belonged to different churches.[74]

An inclusive Black political identity, which unites non-Whites against Whites, has also disappeared as a political possibility, both because of a shift in the context of politics and because of partly deliberate and partly careless ANC behavior and statements. An Afrikaans-language identity appears mostly latent at this point: Afrikaans-speaking Coloureds did not vote for the NP more than Coloureds generally, but "Afrikaans-speaking Coloured" was still the third–most popular choice of identification among Coloureds surveyed in 1993.[75] Neither do White or Brown Afrikaner identities appear politically salient for any sizable segment of the Coloured population.

One identity which does appear to resonate among Coloureds implicitly rejects race as a defining feature of political identity. It is a national South African identity—an identity that Coloureds choose by a factor of almost two to one over any other identity. *South African* is inclusive and has domestic political meaning in the sense that it signifies, in the aftermath of an exclusive political system that denied citizenship to the majority of its inhabitants on the basis of race, a place in the nation as a citizen. It denotes belonging and attachment and has more national salience than "normal" nationalities forged and predominantly expressed in an international context, in the presence of other nationalities. South African–ness establishes not only a place in the world as a South African but also a place in South Africa as a citizen. Coloureds also demonstrate least attachment to their "racial" group, despite an increasing tendency to call themselves Coloured. It is probably true that although the bulk of those people who supported the UDF in the 1980s appeared to hold an oppositional Black political identity, most of those who support the ANC in the 1990s articulate a South African political identity which sidesteps race-based political classification altogether. Support for this proposition can be derived from the fact that the sectors in which South African identity is strongest—younger, better-educated men—coincide with those among whom support for the ANC is strongest. It does not follow, however, that South African–ness is a political identity that attaches exclusively to the ANC. A South African political identity could be as easily claimed by the NP voter who sees the NP as a multiracial party with a strong anticrime platform, for instance.

The collaborationist ideological baggage that attached to Coloured political identity during the 1980s, a decade of vocal and highly mobilized opposition to the apartheid government, rendered it mostly unavailable to the majority of Coloureds. In the 1990s, although Coloured identity shed its collaborationist markers, it remained, like other exclusive identities based on group recognition in South Africa, ideologically conservative. If Colouredness does grow politically salient, it will occupy a conservative ideological space, and is likely to find its political allies among groups like the Freedom Front and the IFP. Whether it resonates in the future will depend on shifts in perceived material conditions, organizational networks, and available ideology—none of which are conducive to the mobilization of Colouredness in the immediate postapartheid era.

Although Coloured identity in the twentieth century more or less consistently occupied a political space in South Africa, it was not usually salient for the majority of Coloureds. Moreover, the political meaning, boundaries, and commitments of Colouredness have shifted as a result of contextual shifts in the factors that affect the construction of political identity. The relation among conditioning and proximate variables, and the effects of these on the resonance of political identities, is complex. Because factors interact to include effects over time, the probability that identities will change, within evolving but nevertheless constraining parameters, is practically built into expectations. Although available ideology will constrain organization, the way in which people are organized subsequently affects what is ideologically available, for example. This dialectic relation informs change over time and difference across space as distinct sectors of a group occupy different structural positions within the grid of material conditions, organization, and available ideology.

In the 1980s Coloured politics operated within the institutional parameters of apartheid and the Tricameral Parliament. The institutions of apartheid structured the entire spectrum of Coloured political organization. The Labour Party was constituted by participation within the system, and the UDF was explicitly organized in opposition to the Tricameral Parliament. Starting in 1990 the repeal of the law forbidding political representation across racial lines enabled many Labour Party MPs to cross over to the NP, destroying the LP. The lifting of the ban against the ANC led to the dissolution of the UDF. The negotiation of a majoritarian democracy that did not include special rights for racially designated groups set the stage for the potential mobilization of fear and vulnerability among South Africa's racial minorities. The institutional commitment to individual and not group rights has played some role in determining that South Africa's dominant political cleavage would bridge the majority rule/minority rights debate.

The political organizations that mediated Coloured politics in the 1980s disappeared in the 1990s. Those groups that have replaced them, the NP, NNP, ANC, DP, and Coloured nationalist parties, mobilize a variety of identities, none of which includes Blackness prominently. Even the ANC, the simultaneous ancestor of and heir to the UDF, has largely ceased to define itself or its constituency in "Black" terms. As an oppositional text, Blackness disappeared when the White minority government was replaced by multiparty democracy. So long as *Black* was an inclusive term, "Black majority rule" included Coloureds. But as *Black* lost its oppositional quality, it also lost its availability to Coloureds. It has become more exclusive, referring increasingly to Africans, not all non-Whites.

In the postapartheid era, the NP has articulated racial-minority, Afrikaans-language, and inclusive non-African identities among its Coloured constituents. ANC political entrepreneurs articulate a nonracial political identity, African and South African political and national identities, a limited Black political identity, and various nonascriptive identities, such as labor, which leaders hope can cross-cut racial categories. Like the NP, the ANC owes an ideological debt to the paradigm it inhabited in the apartheid era but has also diverged from the principles that guided the UDF during the last decade of struggle. It has avoided mobilizing Coloured or other racial identities because of its historical commitment to nonracialism.

The NP and ANC have had varying degrees of success among a Coloured population highly segmented by material conditions, organization, and available ideology. Coloureds were deeply divided by class in the 1980s as a result of government reform efforts that raised the position of skilled and educated Coloureds, yet simultaneously weakened the position of the unskilled and unemployed by loosing restrictions prohibiting competition from Africans. In the postapartheid era it seems true that Coloureds (like many other South Africans) fear for their economic future and feel vulnerable in the face of an affirmative action program that may not include them, open competition without racial restriction for jobs and opportunities, and a persistently ailing economy. But Coloureds are differentially affected by these concerns, depending in part on their material position. Support for the ANC is strongest among the poorest and wealthiest Coloureds, while the employed middle class is most likely to vote for the NP. The NP probably lost some of this support base to the DP in 1999.

Many of the grassroots organizations that sustained the UDF during the 1980s were leveled by the state in the second half of the decade, or simply disappeared gradually after 1990. The ANC lacked either the capacity or the will to rebuild them in the 1990s and suffered electoral defeat in the Cape partly as a result. Coloureds who continued to be organized through ANC-affiliated trade unions and civic organizations in the 1990s, however, were more than two times as likely as nonaffiliating Coloureds to vote for the ANC. The ANC probably picked up some support among Coloured workers in 1999 and could do better among unionized workers if it turned its attention to organization.

The National Party was conversely strengthened in the early 1990s because it was able to muster a majority of Labour Party branches. The local branches of the LP were in many cases more than twenty years old and closely associated with community patronage and welfare from the days of the Tricameral Parliament. This link may have grown more tenuous by 1999.

Available ideology also interacts with material conditions to explain the Coloured vote. Education is closely correlated with wealth. Coloureds who are better off are more likely to have matriculated high school and to have attended university. In the last two decades of the apartheid era, high schools and universities were the primary site of mobilization and consciousness raising through the Black Consciousness Movement and later the UDF. For many, school might be the only access to sustained engagement with these ideological positions. In school, exposure and indoctrination were hardly escapable. Money therefore bought some Coloureds access to a set of liberation and opposition ideologies that were less accessible to those who were unable to complete a formal education. In many cases identities and commitments forged on the anvil of opposition against apartheid, high levels of political mobilization and solidarity, and real danger, persisted through a volatile transition period. The language of the struggle continued to inform many political identities molded in struggle.

Coloured identity is no more politically salient in the immediate postapartheid era than it was in the previous decade. The political identities of Coloured people are multiply constituted, and mostly do not appear racialized. In response to incentives generated by postapartheid political institutions, under constraints imposed by prior ideological commitments, political elites trying to gather support among Coloureds mobilize a variety of identities. Some succeed more than others, but none has emerged as overwhelmingly successful. In the postapartheid era, the political identities held by Coloureds are highly contingent, shaped by the ideologies available to them, their material conditions, and the organizational networks they inhabit. Political identities are not dependent on race. Colouredness has been harnessed to multiple political agendas, continues to shift in unpredictable ways, as yet contains no dominant political meaning, and operated within a substantially different range of political possibilities in 1999 than it did in 1989.

8 Slaying the Hydra

Political Institutions and the Manipulation of Identity

The ways we think about the origin and nature of politicized ethnic and racial identities affect how we understand politics in societies that have been classified as divided, and what solutions we propose for the achievement of peaceful and stable political systems that include respect for universal human rights. Drawing from evidence culled from three cases of ethnically mediated political identity in South Africa, I advance a causal framework that explains how and why identities become politically salient, why they are more or less salient for different group members, and under what conditions they are likely to change. Evidence suggests that political identities are more directly affected by conditioning factors (material conditions, organizational networks, and available ideology) than by proximate factors (political institutions and mobilizing discourse), with two implications. First, an exclusive focus on the design of constitutional and electoral systems is probably misplaced. Second, an emphasis on the constant negotiation and re-negotiation of conditioning factors is likely to promote more fluid political identities, which will in turn both minimize the possibility that divisions will atrophy into permanent groups and bolster the foundations of a pluralist civil society with room for cross-cutting cleavages.

The Derivation and Duration of Political Identity

In Chapter 1 I set out a framework for the investigation of political identity. Some identities achieve resonance among some people at some times as a result of the action and interaction of five variables: political institutions, mobilizing discourse, material conditions, available ideology, and organization. Political institutions and mobilizing discourse are proximate variables. They represent a distinct category of factors in the sense that they operate from the top down and are deliberately involved in the manipulation and mobilization of identities for political purposes. Conditioning variables are material conditions, organization, and available ideology. In addition to providing incentives of their own, they frame the cognition of those who are mobilized. Potential constituents are embedded in a network of relations, understandings, interests, concerns, engagements, and commitments that are structured by material conditions, available ideology, and organizational patterns. Conditioning variables form the fabric that makes mobilizing discourse more or less likely to resonate, among different people, at different times.

Proximate Factors

The call to "bring the state back in" has been heeded.[1] Since the notion was abandoned that ethnicity and race are primordial, the converse assumption has dominated the study of the derivation of collective identities. If identities do not bubble up from below, they must be imposed from above, an outgrowth of political institutions and policies. Put most succinctly by Anthony Marx, "States made race."[2] Marx explains the salience of race as a political cleavage in South Africa and the United States, and its political dormancy in Brazil, as the result of specifically racist and excluding state policies in the former and more ambiguous and ostensibly inclusive policies in the latter. David Laitin argues that democracies can be consolidated in multinational societies so long as institutional design, the sequencing of institutions and elections, and party formation are organized in ways that attenuate the centrifugal tendencies of cultural groups. He says "best answers to separatist challenges . . . can be found both in institutional arrangements and in political strategies."[3] Bates argues in a similar vein that ethnic politics are rational because "by delineating administrative boundaries along tribal lines, (colonial powers) made it in the interests of their subjects to organize ethnic groupings."[4] As a result, "efforts should be devoted to creating institutional environments which alter incentives so that persons organize coalitions of a different nature when in pursuit of their interests."[5] Mamdani similarly credits the "indirect rule" arrangements of colonial states in Africa with persistent postcolonial identities and alignments.[6]

Electoral systems are the political institutions most often attributed with affecting the political salience of particular identities. Electoral systems are presumed to create incentives for political entrepreneurs to mobilize some but not other types of identities. It is for this reason that much of the literature on ethnicity and democracy is focused on the manipulation of electoral systems to undermine the incentives of political entrepreneurs to mobilize allegedly ascriptive identities. Consociationalism is an electoral system that operates with the dual intention of keeping ethnicities apart and ensuring equal political representation for all groups. The alternative vote system is designed to create incentives for political elites to draw support across ethnic lines. Both solutions presume that race, ethnicity, language, and religion are the problem.

Consociationalism is an institutional device whereby political elites share power.[7] Political parties that win more than a certain threshold percentage of the vote jointly form an executive to govern the nation. Every political actor has a role in government and none is excluded from power. Decisions are reached by consensus. Formally, the four principal tenets of consociationalism are power sharing, segmental autonomy, proportionality, and minority veto. Power sharing includes executive, provincial, and local levels. Segmental autonomy means that groups are divided into separate, ethnically based electorates and vote on separate voters rolls for separate leaders. Proportionality applies to representation. Each segment is represented in proportion to its numerical strength. In addition, the civil service and armed forces reflect the ethnic composition of the nation.[8] Finally, minority veto means that "even relatively small groups should have an absolute veto on the most fundamental issues, such as cultural autonomy, and a suspensive veto on non-fundamental questions."[9] At its inception, the new South African democracy consisted of a Government of National Unity that included many consociational aspects.

Arend Lijphart has refined some of the general principles of consociationalism to finesse critiques leveled against him. Most important, he partially amended his recommendations regarding segmental autonomy to avoid "the entire vexatious and controversial issue of whether the segments should be defined in racial, ethnic, cultural, or some other terms." Rather, he now believes that "the segments should be allowed to emerge spontaneously by means of PR elections and corporate federalism instead of being predetermined."[10] Recently he has reiterated: "Self-determination works much better than pre-determination because it is a neutral and flexible method."[11]

Donald Horowitz's perception of what constitutes, and causes, a divided society is slightly different from that of Lijphart, so his proposed electoral solution addresses the problem in a different way. Horowitz believes that parties organized along ethnic lines have a centrifugal effect on national politics. Unlike nonethnic parties, which tend to converge as each party competes to attract the pool of undecided and moderate voters that lie between them, ethnic parties do not compete for the same pool of voters. Ethnic leaders compete only for votes from their own ethnic group. "The near impossibility of party competition for clientele across ethnic lines means an absence of countervailing incentives encouraging party moderation on ethnic issues."[12]

At the same time, Horowitz has no doubt that parties will organize along ethnic lines, particularly in the postcolonial regimes of Africa, Asia, and the Caribbean. He claims that "surveys show that ethnicity is the primary affiliative category in Africa and Asia."[13] He presents no sustained argument regarding why this should be the case, but he cites numerous examples of parties and politics organized along apparently ethnic lines to support his contention. How then, he asks, given that non-Western nations will persist in organizing along ethnic lines, can the tensions such organization would ordinarily engender be attenuated? How can the centrifugal force of ethnic politics be moderated, or even converted to a centripetal force?

Horowitz returns to his model of the nonethnic two-party system for inspiration. Nonethnic two-party systems tend toward moderation because they compete for the same votes at the center. Presumably then, ethnic parties would also converge if they competed for the same votes. Horowitz's institutional structure forces ethnically based political elites to seek votes outside of their ethnic constituency.

He proposes a variation of majority rule—the alternative vote system. Horowitz argues that majority rule is preferable to a proportional representation electoral system because it requires parties to pool votes, not just seats. In PR systems, parties pool seats in postelectoral coalitions when no single party wins sufficient seats to actually govern. If, however, victory can be garnered only by the party that wins a majority and not merely a plurality, then parties have incentives to reach beyond their ethnic constituent base (which Horowitz assumes will be a minority) to attract voters. Vote pooling is preferable to seat pooling because it makes coalitions transparent and occurs at the level of the voters.[14]

In order to ensure that vote pooling will occur, Horowitz proposes that voters be required to register first, second, and perhaps even third preferences. In an alternative vote system, "the second and subsequent preferences of those voters whose preference is not one of the top two candidates are reallocated until a candidate attains a majority." Unless a party wins an outright majority, it relies on the second and third choices of voters who prefer another party. Only a moderate party, with appeal to a broad constituent base, is likely to win alternative votes and thereby achieve a majority. Successful negotiations require, and yield, intergroup accommodation and compromise.[15]

As a solution to the pitfalls of politics in putatively divided societies, consociationalism has been roundly critiqued from multiple angles over the past two decades.[16] At the least it has been undercut; for many it stands entirely discredited.[17] The alternative vote mechanism has had less attention but has been implemented, most famously in Nigeria. Although Lijphart and Horowitz approach divided societies from distinct perspectives, have bitterly attacked each other, and propose different solutions to the problems of divided societies, they are in fact vulnerable to similar critiques because both fail to interrogate the nature of ascriptively mediated political identities. Consociationalism is antidemocratic, is more likely to reinforce than to cross-cut whatever identities it reifies, and ignores the potential for conflict within ethnic groups or along other cleavage lines. The alternative vote system is just as likely to create as to defuse potential conflict. Because consociationalism has been so amply criticized elsewhere, I focus here on a discussion of the alternative vote system.

Horowitz's instincts regarding changing the structure of incentives for political elites appear sound. It seems reasonable to expect that in a consociational system, where the power and place in government of political leaders depend on an ethnic base, elites will have incentives to mobilize ethnicity and seek to ensure that the segment they represent remains intact and stable. Political parties are forced to organize along ethnic lines, creating ethnically based structures which may order people's lives and make ethnic political identity and politics more tangible and rational to voters. In particular, if ethnic segments are divided into separate electoral groups, one might reasonably assume that ethnic identities may be reified in the political arena.

If on the other hand, as Horowitz suggests, the incentives for gaining power are shaped in ways that require appeals to the grassroots members of other groups, political elites may moderate their rhetoric in order to compete for votes from politicized groups other than their own.[18] They will not have incentives to indulge in exclusive and conflictual rhetoric and behavior that might alienate other groups. All of this is for the best and cannot be faulted as an organizing principle for politics in any nation, whether or not it appears to be divided along ethnic or racial lines.

Horowitz's specific proposals seem largely contingent, however, and are as likely to be ineffectual, or to engender other potentially conflictual cleavages, as to achieve the moderating purposes he envisions. Horowitz claims that the electoral system he proposes will encourage conciliation and moderation along whatever lines occur.[19] In fact, his system ensures only that elites of one party will attract the second-preference votes of the grass roots of one or more other parties. This would lead toward moderation and conciliation under only two circumstances. First, an alternative vote system might encourage a moderate party to cast a wide net and try to get as many votes as possible from as many groups as exist. Arguably, this was the strategy of the ANC in South Africa. But a moderate party will not mobilize exclusive ethnic identities anyway, and so the arrangement has not accomplished much. An alternative vote system would also have the desired effect if there were two and only two ethnic groups and two and only two political parties, one representing each segment. Under such circumstances, an alternative vote system would require elites of each party to bridge the single dividing cleavage to attract voters who vote primarily for the opposing party.

Horowitz advocates party proliferation, however, as a way of maximizing representation and participation. He argues that although a first-past-the-post system usually tends toward a two-party democracy, majoritarianism with the alternative vote amendment would not hinder party proliferation.[20] Horowitz wants both party proliferation, and to remain mute on the question of which cleavages are salient. The only way to make it likely that an alternative vote system will attenuate the relevant and potentially conflictual cleavage is to predetermine what that cleavage is and to require that political elites have incentives to attract grassroots support across that cleavage. If, for example, the relevant cleavage in South Africa is assumed to be that between Black and White voters, an alternative vote system would have to require parties to bridge the Black-White voter divide. If an ostensibly "Black party," such as the ANC, merely recruited the second preferences of PAC voters, absolutely nothing will have been accomplished in terms of attenuating the racial political cleavage. There is nothing wrong with the ANC appealing to PAC voters, but neither is there any particular reason for it.

Horowitz correctly resists predetermining the relevant cleavages, however, because he does not want to fall prey to the same criticism that he has leveled against Lijphart—namely that he risks reifying those ethnically defined segments his proposed electoral mechanism is designed to weaken. Predefining which groups are politically relevant and potentially conflictual is also a politically loaded exercise. Thus he wants to leave open the question of which cleavages are breached through the alternative vote system. But by leaving this question open, he undermines the centripetal potential of his electoral system.

If there are more than two ethnic groups and more than two ethnic parties, leaders have incentives merely to enter into coalitional arrangements with one or two other parties. Such arrangements are as likely as not to create a cleavage with equal conflictual potential as that which the alternative vote was meant to attenuate. For example, two or three ethnic parties might enter a coalition against two or three other ethnic parties. Alternatively, two ethnic groups, say from the northern part of the country, might enter into an apparently permanent alliance that in turn fosters an entirely new, and potentially conflictual, regional cleavage.

Another possibility is that the alternative vote system might strengthen more radical parties at the political extremes. In South Africa, for example, polls indicate that most ANC voters would choose the much less moderate Pan Africanist Congress as their second preference.[21] If political identity is as ethnically driven as divided-society theorists believe, voters for whom a moderate ethnic party is their first choice will probably make the more radical ethnic party their second choice. If voters actually choose the moderate party from the opposing ethnic group over "their own" flank party, as Horowitz believes they might, there is reason to doubt that these societies are divided at all, at least in the ethnic ways that analysts suggest they are.[22] Perhaps they are more accurately divided ideologically, between extremists and moderates, for example.

The central part of Horowitz's recommendation is to encourage different parties to vie for the same voters. He believes that such competition will encourage convergence through centripetal force. Another possibility is at least as likely, though. Such competition for the same pool of voters may lead to intraethnic conflict. Parties often reserve their most bitter hatred for those closest to them on the political spectrum, however it may be defined, who are therefore most politically threatening to their support base. In South Africa for instance, by far the worst political violence has been between the ANC and the IFP in the province of KwaZulu Natal over control of the Zulu vote. Such violence did not erupt until after 1984, when the United Democratic Front began to challenge Inkatha's political dominance among Zulus. Political violence was precipitated precisely by the central principle of Horowitz's recommendation: competition for the same pool of voters.

Lijphart and Horowitz agree that "the electoral system is by far the most powerful lever of constitutional engineering for accommodation and harmony in deeply divided societies."[23] Indeed, the electoral system is a powerful tool of constitutional engineering. But whether electoral systems can be manipulated to attenuate the potential for conflict, or to undermine the salience of particular political identities that may be incompatible with democratic politics, depends on the manner and extent to which political institutions operate to shape political identities. Neither Lijphart nor Horowitz explores this prior question.

In fact, evidence from six case studies of the politicization and depoliticization of ethnicity among three ethnic groups shows that the impact of political institutions is consistently filtered through other factors that more directly affect resonance. Although political institutions play some role in every case, the proposition that "states made race" cannot account for the fluid, indeterminate, and variable salience of identities over time and across space.

Democracy is an organized contest among political elites and their constituents for access to power located in the government. Subject to the constraints of the electoral system, political leaders with the most support win. Given that democratic power rests on the mobilization of constituencies, political institutions generate incentives for political elites to mobilize majorities. Because majorities may be constituted in different ways, electoral mechanisms include incentives for the mobilization of multiple identities. Unless the mobilization of a particular type of identity is explicitly suggested, as in some types of consociationalism, or prohibited, as was the mobilization of national identities in Yugoslavia in the era of Tito, and as is labor in South Korea today, political entrepreneurs are likely to make ethnic or racial appeals under two conditions. First, some people who are true nationalists rise to positions of power (for whatever reason). Second, people in power calculate, based on a number of variables (including their own predispositions), that ethnic mobilization will enhance their power base. Political entrepreneurs may be true believers or rational maximizers. If they are true believers, they will not respond to incentives of any sort. If they are rational maximizers, they will make strategic calculations based in part on such factors as district boundaries and magnitude, electoral systems, and the rules governing the organization of power. Structural constraints will recommend the mobilization of more or less centrist positions.[24]

The question of the role and place of political institutions in the construction of political identity can be viewed from another angle. The transformation of the institutions that governed South Africa was nothing short of revolutionary. In 1994 the South African political system changed from a racial oligarchy, in which more than 70 percent of the population was excluded from political representation on the basis of race, to semifederalist list system proportional representation with universal suffrage. South Africa's new electoral system apparently generated multiple incentives for the mobilization of political identity. The ANC constituted support on the basis of race, class, and South African nationalism. The National Party mobilized middle-class, capitalist, linguistic, and oppositional non-African political identities. The IFP articulated ethnicity, regionalism, and capitalism. The FF mobilized ethnic, socially and politically conservative, and occupational identities. The DP constructed support around liberalism and federalism. The PAC mobilized African nationalism and communism. The ANC and NP, employing very different discursive repertoires, garnered almost 83 percent of the vote. The FF and the IFP, both ethnic nationalist parties, won only 12 percent of the vote between them.

If it is true that incentives are likely to evolve over time, as politicians learn which identities are compatible with particular structural arrangements, then we should expect South African political parties to demonstrate tendencies toward convergence between elections. NP candidates canvassing support for local government elections in 1995 were somewhat less likely to play the race card among Coloured voters than they had been in 1994, though the party again focused on the negative impact of affirmative action in 1999. In other areas the NP mobilized a primarily oppositional identity, based on criticism of the ANC record. The ANC focused on its efforts to reduce crime, building a constituency around "law abiding citizens," and on its record of providing service. The PAC continued to stress its commitment to land redistribution. The IFP mobilized a regional Natal identity, in opposition to the ANC central government, and the FF focused on such issues as Afrikaans language and schooling.[25] Although the ANC again won a large majority in elections in 1999, increasing its share of the vote by 4 percent to 66 percent, there were some important shifts within the ANC base of support and considerable movement among the three main opposition parties. The liberal DP emerged as the official opposition, with almost ten percent of the vote, while the previously dominant National Party slipped to fourth place, just behind the IFP, which also lost support. The new United Democratic Movement gained an unexpected 3 percent of the vote, almost all culled from the ANC. In the Eastern Cape the UDM was the second-most-popular party, though with only 13 percent of the vote. The United Christian Democratic Party also siphoned regional votes from the ANC in Northwest province, where it became the official opposition. Each of these parties continues to mobilize a distinct set of issues and identities with varying degrees of success among different groups at different times.

The evidence suggests that although South Africa's nascent democracy is supported by a single set of political institutions, its institutions sustain the mobilization of multiple, partly overlapping, political identities. There are at least three reasons why this is true. The first is that parties came to, and through, the transition with prior histories, constituencies, ideological commitments, and strength. All the parties that successfully contested the 1994 elections had an apartheid-era history that constrained their freedom to reposition and reconstitute themselves. The second reason is that postapartheid political institutions are sufficiently indeterminate, complex, and multilayered to include incentives for political elites to generate constituencies around a variety of symbols. The third reason is that political entrepreneurs also respond to incentives generated by conditioning factors, and conditioning factors largely determine their success.

Conditioning Factors

Conditioning factors account in part for the contingent success of political entrepreneurs. Conditioning factors generate their own set of incentives and create the variable and shifting conditions in which political entrepreneurs are forced to operate, rendering uneven their capacity to imbue identities with political salience. Material conditions, organization, and available ideology create a social grid that political entrepreneurs, as well as their potential constituents, operate within. The success or failure of elite mobilization efforts depends largely on the composition of this social grid. Although some political entrepreneurs always try to mobilize ethnic or racial identities for political purposes, they probably fail more often than not. Whether political elites succeed or fail to infuse ethnicities with political meaning depends on the material conditions, organizational patterns, and ideological predispositions of those they are trying to mobilize. These three variables interact to compose the fabric of voters' cognition, their sense of political self and of political possibility. They make up the "frames" of the voters.

It is analytically impossible to separate the effects of these three factors in conditioning possibility. Each variable works in a number of ways, both on its own and in conjunction with other factors, to affect which identities are likely to resonate, among whom. Material conditions suggest patterns of affect and common interest that may be mobilizable under certain conditions. Unequal material conditions and access to resources partly precipitated violence eventually articulated in ideological terms in the townships around Durban. Although political affiliations clearly broke down along socioeconomic lines, at least initially, these cleavages coincided, not surprisingly, with connections to jobs and trade unions, on the one hand, and to rural areas and tribal authorities on the other. Material conditions affect access to political organization and ideology. These sets of connections insinuated distinct, and conflicting, political commitments.

The presumption that the correlation between economic status and identity is linear, and that poorer group members are more likely to be mobilized in group-centric ways because they are more vulnerable to out-groups, does not bear out. Polls show, for example, that Afrikaners of all socioeconomic levels feared the end of apartheid and felt seriously threatened throughout the 1980s and 1990s. Material conditions intersect with organizational patterns, however, to make it more likely that poorer and rural Afrikaners remain embedded in ties of affect that tend to reinforce their ethnic affiliations and connection to right-wing nationalist parties. Organizational ties make Afrikaner nationalism available.

A similar symbiosis describes the relation among the material, organizational, and ideological conditions that structure political life for many Coloureds. Coloureds in higher socioeconomic categories were more likely to vote for the ANC than the NP in 1994. Coloureds in higher socioeconomic categories were also more likely to have attended high school and university, where they were politicized through the liberation-oriented South African Students Organization and the National Union of South African Students. Coloureds whose political teeth were cut in the liberation movement and who were socialized through liberation ideology in the 1980s were more likely to vote for the ANC in 1994 than those who left school early. Material conditions therefore affected the availability of ideological paradigms.

The argument that individuals are embedded in conditioning variables that constrain the possibilities of resonance does not imply that conditioning variables are static. Conditioning variables change as a matter of course, on their own, and in dialogue with proximate variables. Material conditions fluctuate, both for entire countries, as GNP goes up or down, and for distinctly positioned groups within the country, as the value of exports rises, as droughts affect production, as wages in some sectors increase or decrease, or as industrialization progresses. Who benefits and who loses as a result is not a random matter, of course, but it does lead to shifting fortunes and, within limits, to shifting equilibria among groups.

The availability of ideology is also apt to fluctuate. A dominant ideology is accompanied by its opposition. Its dominance is always contested. People may respond in various degrees to one or the other. Ideologies may suddenly lose, or gain, currency as a result of external shock as well. The fall of the Soviet Union marked the sudden end of the availability of communism in most parts of the world, for example. A confluence of circumstances has driven the simultaneous rise of democracy as a legitimating discourse.

Organizational patterns also shift, both as individuals join, or are drawn into, new organizations and commitments and as organizations themselves change their focus and parameters. People who move enter new neighborhoods, join new churches, coach new Little Leagues, have access to new trade unions, and engage new concerns. All of these provide them with access to new patterns of interest representation and commitment. Even people who do not move find that the organizations to which they already belong shift in focus, membership, and salience.

Finally, it should be noted that the line dividing proximate and conditioning variables is permeable. Proximate variables may play conditioning roles. The possibilities of politics are constrained by political institutions, and new choices of political institutions often reflect old choices. Moreover, the possibilities for changing political institutions are limited. They can be designed at founding moments, as the result of a democratic transition, for example, or in moments of reform and expansion of the franchise. Because supermajorities are usually required to amend constitutional or institutional frameworks, such amendments are difficult to enact. Political institutions play a conditioning role insofar as they appear permanent and not malleable.

Mobilizing discourse behaves as a conditioning factor when the memory of discursive repertoires frames what will resonate in the future. Although political entrepreneurs can reinvent themselves almost infinitely under the right conditions, they may be limited by positions, and arguments, they have used before. They may believe that their legitimacy and credibility rest on the consistency of their message and political commitments. It seems likely, moreover, that identities that have been mobilized before may suggest themselves for remobilization.

Resonance

It appears that the incentives generated by political institutions for elites to mobilize identities for political purposes are multiple and generally vague. The same set of political institutions drive different parties to constitute their political bases in distinct ways. Political entrepreneurs may behave strategically, or they may be true believers. If they are true believers, they will consistently mobilize a particular identity regardless of incentives for maximizing power. If they behave strategically, whether rational maximizing political elites choose to mobilize allegedly ascriptive or associational identities for political purposes depends on incentives that derive from conditioning as well as proximate variables. Moreover, the extent and degree of their success depends on conditioning factors. The role of electoral rules in the construction of political identity is contextually circumscribed and vulnerable to conditions outside institutional parameters. The hypothesis that changing political institutions would have a determinant effect on the possibilities of political identities turns out to be true only within these constraints. Political identity is a function of resonance: that which is mobilized from above refracted through the frames of potential constituents.

Zulu political identity was the dominant and dividing cleavage of politics in Natal in the 1980s. Although almost everyone in Natal is Zulu, Zulu identity was attached to Inkatha political affiliation after 1982 or so, and was therefore shunned by supporters of the United Democratic Front. Inkatha's urban support base consisted mainly in recent rural migrants. Migrants lived in shacks on the periphery of established townships, retained primary ties in rural areas, competed with established urban dwellers for access to scarce resources, and were often unemployed and therefore lacked access to trade unions. Inkatha also had solid support in the rural areas controlled by Inkatha-affiliated chiefs. The UDF was supported by more firmly established urban dwellers organized through trade unions and township civic associations.

Widespread violence between ANC and Inkatha supporters continued through the 1994 elections, reinforcing cleavage patterns established in the 1980s. Since 1994, however, the IFP has toned down its Zulu rhetoric in an attempt to carve a broader party base, and the ANC has invoked its own Zulu credentials in order to solidify a Zulu support base and build national unity. In the run-up to national elections in 1999, KwaZulu Natal had the largest percentage of undecided voters. A significant drop in violence after 1994 helped to create a much more fluid political situation in the province than was imaginable in the previous decade.

The Freedom Front's efforts to politicize Afrikaner identity have had limited success. The recent history of the right wing, the apparent end of the era of White politics, and the attendant impossibility of a return to apartheid propelled the "White right" into Afrikaner nationalism almost overnight in 1992. The concept of a Volkstaat as a homeland for Afrikaners anchors the political discourse of the right wing in the postapartheid era. Yet the FF garnered the vote of only a minority of Afrikaners, and a majority of its own supporters reject the notion of a Volkstaat, or the prospect of moving there.

Afrikaners are politically divided along socioeconomic, organizational, and ideological lines that influence their political orientation. The majority of Afrikaners who have joined the ranks of the upper and upper-middle classes in the past forty years hold political identities mediated primarily by class and ideology, not by ascriptive group membership. The minority to whom Afrikaner identity is politically salient continue to operate within traditional ethnic social, religious, and political networks that have kept Afrikanerdom alive and potentially available for political mobilization. Upwardly mobile Afrikaners in the cities, on the other hand, have mostly shed these affiliations, which makes them less accessible to the right wing. In addition, the Afrikaner political project is tied to a reactionary conservative ideology that does not fit the lived experience of the majority of Afrikaners. Thus, although White conservative political elites have attempted to mobilize an ethnic identity in the postapartheid era, their success has hinged primarily on prior organizational networks and ideological commitments, mediated in part by wealth, and is therefore limited to a minority of their potential ethnic constituency.

Social and political life in Coloured areas was primarily structured around the church, the Labour Party, and the UDF in the last decade of the apartheid era. In the early 1990s both the LP and the UDF were dissolved. Most LP members of Parliament defected to the NP and took their branches with them. The ANC, on the other hand, failed to reconstitute an organizational base in Coloured areas after the UDF was disbanded. The ability of political entrepreneurs to mobilize Colouredness as a political identity has been constrained by preexisting ideological currents and the history of the idea of a Coloured group. "Coloured politics" has long included a dominant and consistent tendency to reject the externally imposed designation Coloured. By the 1980s radical and moderate Coloured leaders alike rejected Coloured as a relevant political category. Although Blackness, the oppositional political identity that both groups predominantly articulated in the 1980s, has been rendered obsolete by the end of White minority domination, it has not apparently been replaced by a politicized racial or linguistic identity.

Some Labour Party and National Party political leaders have tried since 1993 or so to mobilize political identities based on Coloured racial and Afrikaans language affiliations, but their success has been limited. Material conditions, organizational patterns, and ideology have interacted to ensure that racial and linguistic identities resonate among only a minority of Coloureds. Coloureds in higher socioeconomic groups were more likely to attend school, where they were politicized through left-wing student movements. They were therefore more likely than poor and less-educated Coloureds to vote for the ANC in 1994 and 1999. Although it appears that poorer Coloureds perceive a greater threat from affirmative action, which they conclude benefits Africans over Coloureds in a postapartheid system of justice, such threats appear only superficially based on material conditions. Poor Coloureds who work in the fishing industry, for example, voted for the ANC because they were successfully organized through ANC networks.

The only way to explain the change and difference that become evident on close inspection of politically mobilized ethnicity and race is to complicate the story of the construction of political identity. The argument that "states made race" may describe broad and sweeping historical trends with accuracy. But the image that emerges is one of a highly determinate state and overdetermined identities. The prism of the state has rendered practically invisible the complexity and variability of the interaction between ethnicity and politics. The institutions of state cannot explain the interaction of politics, race, and ethnicity in the day-to-day business of mobilization, demobilization, alliance building, boundary making, and ideological attachment. Institutions do not account for the fact that identities are contingent, layered, multiple, and fluid. Although the state is by no means irrelevant to the politicization of cleavage, it acts as one among a number of variables that interact to form identities.

One argument for a focus on the design of political institutions, and in particular on electoral rules, has been that even if the effects of political institutions are remote and exist primarily at the margins, they are a good place to start because we can at least do something about them. We know less about how to affect human nature, or historical animosity, or poverty. The fantasy that political scientists can devise electoral systems that will be used to particular conflict-attenuating ends, however, has been undermined by recent analyses of how electoral systems are in fact chosen.[26] Electoral rules are negotiated among those who expect to contest power under them. Parties calculate their source of strength and push for a system that will maximize their constituent base. Observers have no more control over the design of electoral systems than we do over the course of history or the allocation of resources.

The implications of the finding that ethnic and racial identities are potentially multiple and fluid for political purposes reinforces the presumption against re-designing electoral rules. It is doubly true that electoral rules might be inappropriate to the task if it is the case that the "problem" with "divided societies" is not ethnicity but the potential for conflict. If communal identities are not politically permanent or overdetermining, then it is at least theoretically consistent that they are not obviously more likely than associational identities to be mobilized in zero-sum or conflictual ways. The manipulation of electoral systems to attenuate one apparently overdetermining cleavage is as likely as not to generate another. If we cannot assume that ascriptive divisions are the ones to watch, then designing political institutions around cleavages is the constitutional equivalent of slaying the Hydra.

The relative fluidity of political identities depends primarily on shifts and inter-actions among conditioning factors. Political identities are more likely to change when conditioning variables change. Although it is only in political transitions that political institutions, and in particular electoral laws, are likely to be modified, conditioning factors are at least potentially in more or less constant flux. They have the potential to shift both slowly, in incremental ways that undergo semicon-stant renegotiation and interaction, and quickly, in response to external shocks or paradigm shifts. They also, however, have the potential to atrophy into apparently enduring systems of hierarchy and social organization. Though it is unlikely that political identities will ever actually be permanent, the appearance of permanence may be equally harmful to the democratic project and its electoral patterns.

Conditioning factors are likely to be most conducive to change when they are themselves fluid, and when they pull in conflicting directions: when the material conditions, organizational patterns, and available ideology that together constitute the frames of individuals do not overlap. If each or some of these factors suggest different sets of commitments, identities may change even if conditioning vari-ables appear static. Nevertheless, conditioning factors should also be expected to change, and so long as they do not move in ways that reinforce existing patterns, they may also lead to shifts in political identity.

It may be true that human nature is such that individuals will always organize themselves into in-groups and out-groups. There will probably always be factions, always some people who count as "us" and some who are only "them." But the more often the meanings, goals, and boundaries of "us" and "them" shift, the less likely it is that the existence of distinct and occasionally conflicting groups in a society will undermine the possibility for democratic consolidation and reasonably nonviolent coexistence. Whether the parameters of in-groups and out-groups shift depends less on whether countries adopt political institutions that can attenuate ethnic identities than on whether material conditions, organizational patterns and available ideology cross-cut in ways that make identities more fluid over time and heterogeneous across space.

The greatest danger apparently facing South African democracy is the possibility that the ANC majority will atrophy into a one-party state. Although the strength of the ANC is bolstered by rules that strengthen the party, its practically uncontested majority stems mainly from the material, organizational, and ideological configuration of South African society, itself a result of prior engagement between state and society. The prospects for change in political identity and party identification are more likely to stem from shifting patterns of civil alignment than from changing electoral rules. Although the ANC retains the support of the majority of the electorate, there were sufficient shifts in party affiliation between the first and second elections to suggest that conditioning variables are indeed changing in ways that may undermine the party configuration established in the first election. If the material, organizational, and ideological frames of voters continue to shift in ways that affect resonance, South African politics should remain fluid enough to support the institutionalized uncertainty democracy requires.

9 Every Journey Conceals Another Journey Within Its Lines

Political identities mediated by race, ethnicity, language, and religion can take many forms and conceal many possibilities. The symbols of race and ethnicity interact with social and political context to mold political identity in a practically infinite variety of ways. As a result, portraits of political identity are in every case particular. Nevertheless, they reveal trends and tendencies that suggest a framework for the systematic analysis of ethnicity and politics more generally. In the previous chapter I tried to make a general statement about the construction of political identity based on particular case studies. By treating politicized ethnicity as a dependent, not an independent, variable, I have in this book attempted to draw a more complex picture of the political behavior of groups mediated by ethnicity and race. Where political identity comes from has implications for what it looks like and how it behaves, which in turn should affect how we think of it in context.[1]

For analytical purposes, three dimensions anchor the ways in which we have thought of political identities and collective groups. Identities and groups may be more or less primordial or constructed, more or less permanent or fluid, and more or less ascriptive or associational. The position of a group on one spectrum has repercussions for its location on the other two.

The first dimension identifies the derivation of identity. If identities are primordial, they are designated by birth. The physical characteristics, family, and inheritance with which an individual is born determines identity through group membership. Identity precedes social interaction in the sense that a person comes to a situation with identity already in place, and scant room is left for choice.[2]

If identities and groups are constructed, however, there is nothing essential, or innate, about which emerge as salient. Groups are defined and infused with content under changing conditions and incentive structures that make some boundaries and meanings more likely than others. Whether groups develop political salience and how they articulate a political agenda are contingent, dependent on interaction in the political sphere itself. Ostensibly objective characteristics such as race or language say very little about what is possible.

This contention does not deny that people are born with apparently objectively identifiable physical, socioeconomic, or cultural characteristics that may be largely unalterable. Some people are born white and some people are born with blue eyes. But which of these myriad markers attain political value, which contribute to political identities or bind groups, and which remain latent and unsignified, depends on constructed, not natural, values. Although it is true that people are born with different skin colors, naming this distinction a "racial" difference and imbuing it with public meaning and value should be understood as the result of the self-conscious construction of significance and boundaries around some, but not other, symbols. Whether an individual chooses membership in one but not another of the many groups in which he holds apparent membership is also at least partly a matter of choice.

To what extent, then, is the primordial/constructed variant actually a spectrum? On closer inspection, it looks more like a dichotomous variable in which the primordial category is a null set. Groups are not more or less primordial or constructed. It seems more appropriate to say that all groups are constructed, but some are constructed around apparent or suggested physical markers, some are constructed around ideas, and some are constructed around class. Though the symbols themselves may appear variably rooted in birthright, their salience is not. What is political does not derive from birth.

The second dimension measures stability. How long do collective identities last? Identities and groups may be more or less static or fluid. Groups may be permanent, with consistent boundaries, self-understandings, goals, and commitments that persist over time; or these characteristics—the very elements that imbue a collective with "groupness"—may shift, in partial response to a changing context.

Whether identities are primordial or constructed has repercussions for whether they are static or fluid. The perspective that identities are primordial, that they derive from birth and exist inherently within the individual, presumes permanence. A person cannot change the attributes with which she was born. Unless the innate characteristics that make up the group, such as skin color and language, change, the group itself, and the identity it constitutes, cannot, by definition, change.

On the other hand, if identity and groupness are constructed and externally constituted through a changing environment, there must be a presumption of underlying fluidity. Apparent permanence is temporary, in degrees. Once the external, temporal origins of collective identities are exposed and the group ceases to be understood as derivative of internal and apparently innate "natural" attributes, it must change so long as its environment changes. If the group is constructed in and through a shifting context and exists in a dialectical relation with other groups and individuals and changing social, cultural, economic, and historical structures, the presumption must be that it is not permanent. It is because

Zulu, Afrikaner, and Coloured political identities are constructed through external referents that they changed, in more and less significant ways, in the fifteen years covering South Africa's extended transition to democracy.

The actual extent to which groups are fluid or static, however, is an empirical question dependent, in every case, on examination of the meaning, boundaries, and goals of groups over time and upon an understanding of the shifting contexts within which they operate. Some identities are more politically enduring than others. Some groups last for generations, some for months. In certain periods forces coalesce to keep political coalitions together for long periods; in other moments everything is in flux. Though groups may appear more or less enduring, they do not reach the endpoints of the spectrum. Groups that are constructed are never either wholly permanent or infinitely fluid.

So far, this account suggests the following hypothesis: groups are constructed around symbols such as race, ethnicity, ideology, and class in ways that make them more or less politically enduring.

Whether identities are primordial or constructed, permanent or fluid, in turn has repercussions for the third axis along which we may measure identities: as ascriptive or associational. How easy is it to join or leave the group? Ascriptive identities are those that are presumed to have been designated or ascribed rather than chosen. Associational identities are those involving memberships that individuals freely embrace and discard. It is mainly on the basis of the primordial and permanent qualities that some category of identities supposedly possesses that those identities are analytically distinguished as ascriptive.

Yet if there is no category of primordial groups, and all groups are constructed in ways which render identities fluid in some degree, it follows that we cannot discern the relative ascriptive or associational quality of political identity with reference to its mediating symbols. The extent of individual choice depends less on whether the group is constructed around race, ethnicity, ideology, or class than on how and under what conditions it is constructed as political. Any group can probably include both ascriptive and associational values. Some aspects of group membership are chosen and some are ascribed. How much choice is available, and how easy it is to leave a group, are the results of the context of mobilization. In violent conflict or political opposition, for example, group identities are more "tightly scripted," regardless of their mediating variables. In the 1980s the South African United Democratic Front, organized around an ideological commitment to overthrow apartheid, tortured and killed supporters it branded as collaborators because they failed to respect boycotts or appeared insufficiently committed to "the struggle." When the stakes of politics are high, and perhaps in particular when groups are in opposition, a single voice and tight boundaries are taken to be crucial to the establishment and maintenance of group legitimacy and strength, regardless of how the group is constituted.

The final proposition, then, is that groups are constructed around such symbols as race, ethnicity, ideology, and class in ways that make them more or less politically enduring, under conditions in which members will have varying capacity for exit.

The crucial aspect of this formulation is that there is nothing inherent in symbols. It is the manner of construction and the context of constitution that determine whether identities will take on more or less permanent, primary, and passionate characteristics. Politicized ethnicity is the highly indeterminate result of the manner and context of its construction; it can take many forms and conceals many possibilities. This, in turn, has repercussions for the way we think of societies that have been called divided, for the compatibility of ethnicity and liberal democracy, and for ethnic conflicts. It is because ethnic identities have been considered permanent that they allegedly divide societies. It is because they are imagined primary that they are incompatible with liberal democracy; and it is because they are allegedly passionate that they are presumed to be peculiarly prone to conflict.

Implications for Divided Societies

The perception that Western political institutions cannot work in some societies because they are fundamentally and irreconcilably divided permeates conventional understandings of the limits of democracy. Divided societies are those that include two or more politically salient racial, ethnic, religious, or linguistic categories. They are divided because the politicization of culture is presumed to yield politically homogeneous and permanent identities that threaten the integrity of the state, undercut a common national identity, and lead practically to permanent majorities and minorities. South Africa, with four official race groups, eleven ethnic and linguistic groups, and at least two politicized religious cleavages, has long stood as the paradigmatic case of a divided society. Analysts have focused tremendous energy on the question of how a postapartheid South Africa might reconcile the deep cleavages that allegedly divide its citizens.[3]

The divided-society paradigm has classified countries not on the basis of apparent internal conflict but on the basis of ethnic, racial, religious, or linguistic heterogeneity. The existence of multiple symbols alone is presumed capable of creating division. But if ethnicity is indeed the much less determinate, potentially fluid, and permeable category of political commitment set forth above, what are the implications for the divided-society paradigm? First, there does not seem to be a good analytic reason to aggregate groups on the basis of their mediating symbols. The sets of symbols that mark religion, language, ethnicity, and race are internally distinct and should not obviously constitute a category of symbols separate from class and ideology. It is not clear that race and language, for example, have more in common than race and class. Race or ethnicity and class often overlap or reinforce each other in ways that make it difficult to determine which is the salient and overdetermining aspect of identity. Language and ethnicity also overlap. Language and religion are hereditary but learned, whereas race depends in the main on ostensibly physical markers. Ethnicity may depend on physical, cultural, traditional, material, or linguistic markers. Class may also depend on any of these in the everyday practices of classification and discrimination. No symbol or set of symbols appears to have sufficient, or sufficiently consistent, traits and attributes to distinguish it from any other symbol or set of symbols. The presence of ethnicity and race, which moreover exist everywhere, do not appear capable of behaving as markers of difference between some societies and others.

The assumption that ethnicity and race are permanent has contributed most to their alleged divisiveness. The actual rate of change within and among groups should not count as the relevant measure, however, in particular because we have established that groups are more or less permanent under different conditions. In fact, the question that must be answered is not whether ethnic identities meet some threshold of fluidity beyond which they may be deemed acceptable, but whether they are more permanent than other affiliations. As we know from the history of party affiliation in the United States, generations of people may vote for the same party as their parents, and party affiliation may appear to be determined by birth.[4] Ideological affiliations may be quite enduring. So may the salience of ethnic group membership. But the political mobilization of racial or ethnic identities is not presumptively more enduring than the political mobilization of class or ideological identities. Historical and contextual particularities determined, for example, that class was practically permanent in feudal Europe. Class distinctions between serf and lord in the feudal era were sufficiently enduring and encompassing to overdetermine a range of social and political possibilities, leading Louis Hartz, for example, to attribute American exceptionalism to a lack of dividing cleavages, such as the European class cleavage.[5]

Similarly, this argument does not ignore the existence and persistence of power relations that may operate to fix hierarchical structures, accrete power, and solidify patterns of inclusion and exclusion. Power relations may operate to repeatedly marginalize what could otherwise be transient minorities. Neither groups nor the context within which they operate is so fluid as to make anything possible and everything mutable. But relations of power are not more likely to be stable when they are implicated with, or even buoyed by, ethnic identities and patterns of organization.

Many, and perhaps all, societies go through periods of division. Nevertheless, even in division they do not exhibit the characteristics described by divided-society theorists. Because ethnic and racial identities are constructed in dialectic interaction with a shifting context, they are much more politically contingent, indeterminate, fluid, and heterogeneous than the divided-society paradigm allows. Moreover, it will not do to distinguish divided from undivided societies on the basis of the existence of politicized ethnicity in one and not another. If ethnicity and race are fluid and heterogeneous and molded by context, they are closer in structure and operation to class and ideology than they are to the homogeneous and static groups that allegedly uphold the divided society. As it has been framed, the divided-society paradigm is ineffectual in part because any society may become divided, and any cleavage may divide it.

Implications for Liberal Democracy

At the end of the twentieth century, liberal democracy has spread beyond most expectations. As it slips the bonds of its common habitat in Western societies, and as Western societies are themselves transformed by new forms of political organization, the parameters of liberal democracy have become highly contested. Standard assumptions about the definition of liberal democracy are being challenged. On one side of the debate are those who maintain that the symbols and politics of identity should be excluded from the public arena in order that people with distinct primary commitments might live together.[6] On the other are those who argue that cultural groups must be included in the sphere of politics because it is only within the constitutive group that the individual can fully realize freedom.[7] Both rely on an implicit conception of ethnic, racial, and religious groups as primary, prior, and essential. Both the proposition that ethnic groups should be excluded in the public realm and and the proposition that they must be included rely on the single condition that these are the groups that inform our most basic understanding of the world and determine our most essential commitments.

The assertion that affiliations mediated by a particular set of symbols hold primary claim on an individual's identity, however, seems unsubstantiated. At the least it is oversimplified and understudied in political science.[8] Cultural, religious, and communal affiliations should be expected to compel the allegiance, actions, and beliefs of their members in an almost infinite variety of ways, and to greater and lesser extents. Perhaps this is particularly true when members are objectively defined and not self-affiliated. Some Catholics are deeply religious, some are lapsed, and some are profoundly disaffected. Some Catholics are partly shaped by Catholicism (either by belief or opposition); others are barely touched. People have predispositions and make choices that filter the influences that act upon them. Any account of primary identities must assume that what primarily mediates identity includes significant capacity for change over time and is different for individual members of any objectively defined group over space. Objective membership in a group—the fact that a person speaks Afrikaans, for instance—cannot be used as a certain marker of primary commitments or political identity.

Moreover, there is no apparent reason that religion or ethnicity, and not neighborhood, class, family, or profession, should act as the primary mediator of a person's identity in the political sphere. Every individual shares linguistic, religious, regional, class, gender, ideological, and a variety of other characteristics and commitments with others. Which of these primarily mediate a person's identity depends on the person herself and on the context. Any one or any combination of the multiple traits, networks, and loyalties that mark the lives of individuals can behave as the primary locus of identity. The shifting place, significance, and role of collective identities in politics suggests that the most that can be said is that sometimes race, ethnicity, or language act as the dominant mediators of identity, and sometimes they do not. Sometimes union affiliations and ideology do.

Ultimately, "primary" is whatever is political. The implicit, and sometimes explicit, presumption of liberalism is that cultural identities exist in a natural and overdetermining state prior to politics, and inform political identities. In fact, salience travels in the opposite direction. The primacy of identity, which characteristics of identities emerge as signified, and how boundaries incorporate and exclude members are not organic. The process of politicization itself changes cultural meanings, definitions, boundaries, and hierarchies. An individual's primary identity is the one that most relevantly distinguishes him or her from others.[9] Such cleavages are explicitly drawn in the public sphere in the context of contact and competition over resources. It is the process of politicization itself that makes a particular identity primary. Any symbol that stands as the salient marker of difference between people will behave for a time as a primary identity. Only this explains how primary identities may shift even if people do not abandon their cultural heritage. What is "primary," then, is deeply implicated with what is "political." As a result, no set of identities need be either privileged within or excluded from the political sphere because of their putatively primary status. Any identity may become primary through politicization.

A more complex and less determinate account of the political parameters of groups bound by ethnicity, race, language, and religion can serve to partially reconcile competing strands of liberalism. Regardless of their mediating symbols, all groups are constructed in ways that make them more or less contingent, variable, and primary. As a result, politically mobilized ethnic groups are functionally similar to other groups that mediate the political affiliations and commitments that people hold. This perspective suggests that the symbols of race and ethnicity should indeed be included in democratic politics, not because they are different but because they are the same. At the same time, because the boundaries and salience of ethnic and racial groups are shifting and internally differentiated, democracy should continue to treat individuals, and not groups, as the primary unit of politics.

Implications for Ethnic Conflict

Ethnic, religious, linguistic, and racial commitments are presumed uniquely capable of inflaming passion and motivating violent and irrational behavior. Violence everywhere is commonly attributed to ancient ethnic hatreds. Conflict arises as a result of "a feeling of dread and disorientation in the face of those who seem unintelligibly different." Emotional and moral conflict "ensues when differently socialized individuals clumsily rub shoulders and attempt to coexist."[10] Even those who do not believe that difference itself precipitates violence expect that violence once precipitated interacts differently with ethnicity. Ethnic violence lasts longer, includes more atrocities, and is impossible to reconcile without separating the warring groups.[11] Ethnic conflict is treated as a separate category of violence, and the solutions proposed for its resolution are different. Whether or not it is true that ethnic conflict is different is a simple empirical matter, though one that has not been adequately explored. Most systematic comparative studies of ethnic conflict take as their starting point conflicts that the researchers have predetermined are ethnic.[12] As a result, they cannot compare the characteristics of ostensibly ethnically driven and other conflicts.

In the absence of this type of research, are there good a priori reasons to presume that ethnic groups are prone to conflict? What initial assumption should guide the research and analysis of conflict and the choice of cases? Do the symbols of race, ethnicity, religion, and language consistently suggest articulation in passionate and unreasonable ways? Robert Bates, Russell Hardin, and others have established fairly conclusively that behavior and beliefs motivated by ethnic-group membership are both rational and logical.[13] This should qualify them as reasonable, or at least not obviously unreasonable. Are they then nevertheless articulated in more passionate terms than other identities, and do they therefore motivate more passionate behavior? If political entrepreneurs advance accounts of political identity that seek to naturalize those identities, that make them appear incontestable, derived from God, or the soil, or hereditary rights and powers, they may generate passionate behaviors and beliefs that are prone to violence.

What, then, is to count as passionate behavior, and how are we to know it when we see it? Presumably, violence counts. When Greenpeace blows up ships to prevent nuclear testing, that must surely count as passionate behavior, yet it has not led us to conclude that democracies cannot process environmentalists. Timothy McVeigh's decision to blow up the federal building in Oklahoma City was apparently also motivated by ideological passion. Ideology, in fact, often motivates passionate behavior that reasonable people might not agree to; witness the McCarthy era in American history. Religious affiliations also motivate passion, as when pro-life activists murder doctors who perform abortions. Yet ethnic identities can be negotiated in rational terms, as when Afrikaner and Zulu nationalist parties concluded a cooperative agreement to work toward common aims in South Africa's negotiated transition. The range of examples cited here, and many others that could be cited, suggest that any group may include extremists who act out their identities in passionate and unreasonable ways, but that no set of symbols necessarily suggests such passion.

There are other reasons to doubt whether ethnic affiliation is the cause of conflict. In a world that includes millions of people who consider themselves members of hundreds of thousands of groups, "differently socialized individuals clumsily rub shoulders" every day. And yet, as James Fearon and David Laitin point out, ethnic conflict is the exception.[14] If cultural attachments and group membership are universal, and yet violent conflict is occasional, the problem is not ethnicity but conflict.

If the problem is conflict, then the focus on ethnicity is misplaced. Institutional mechanisms designed to separate groups and attenuate ethnic sentiment are inappropriate to the problem. We must assume the universality of difference, not only because it exists everywhere, but because it can be manufactured out of whole cloth. This suggests that the interesting question to look at would be, for example, why the cultural cleavage in Canada is negotiated by referendum while the cultural cleavage in Rwanda is negotiated by genocide. The goal should not be to reduce cultural attachments or to minimize difference. The goal should be to ensure that when inevitable conflicts occur they take the form of Quebecois demands for autonomy and not the form of Hutu and Tutsi reciprocal mass murder.

Although institutions should not be used to attenuate ethnicity and separate groups, neither are they incidental to the matter of conflict and the organization of politics. Political institutions are potentially determinant in two senses. First, if it is true that political institutions always generate incentives for political entrepreneurs to mobilize political identities in ways that might be conflictual, under what circumstances does such mobilization actually engender violence? I speculate that violence results from the mobilization of political identities under circumstances in which political institutions and the government lack legitimacy and where there is insufficient respect for the rule of law.

A democratic system may lack legitimacy generally, or it may lack legitimacy among a particular group of people. For example, some nascent democracies may have a legitimacy deficit simply because they are new and untested. They have no record of successfully processing elites or of generating benefits for the governed.[15] In this case, if conflict arises, as it inevitably will in any society, a majority of people may not turn to the democratic system to resolve it. They may resort to violence. A democracy may also lack legitimacy among some of its citizens, even if it is old and established, if it does not appear to represent a particular group. It is probably true, for example, that democracy lacks legitimacy among many African Americans in the United States because it does not appear to represent their interests. One might presume that if conflict arises, African Americans would be more likely than other Americans to resolve it through violence because they have less faith that the democratic system will process conflict in a way that is fair to their interests.

Conflict may also lead to violence if the rule of law is inadequately entrenched. Many underdeveloped or poor countries lack the resources and sometimes the will to sustain effective, reliable, and nonpartisan police and military forces and systems of justice. If there are no routinized and entrenched mechanisms that people recognize as effective for dealing with conflict as it arises, then conflicts are more likely to be resolved in ad hoc, potentially violent ways. If the rule of law is subverted to the interests of one group over another, as it was in South Africa, for example, then the group against which laws and security forces are arrayed may resort to violence against the state.

It appears that the propensity of a society to resort to violence to resolve political disputes is a function not of the mobilization of particular types of identities around particular symbols but of the extent to which other mechanisms for processing conflict, such as democracy, are perceived as legitimate and effective. This suggests that although political institutions are crucially involved in a society's potential for violence, it is not electoral mechanisms and the incentives they generate to attenuate ethnic sentiment that foster or mute violence, but rather the structural context within which inevitable conflicts arise.

Based on evidence from South Africa, I have shown that ethnic and racial groups behave politically in ways that are more multiple, fluid, heterogeneous, permeable, and indeterminate than is normally assumed. As such, they more closely resemble the identities that mediate politics in "normal" democracies than the homogeneous and static pillars long presumed to characterize a divided society. And I have made an argument about the politicization of ethnicity that attempts to encompass and explain the multiplicity of possibilities ethnicity includes. It may be the case that race and ethnicity look like ideology and class because they are constructed politically in the same or similar ways. To the extent that groups exhibit different characteristics, these depend on the manner of construction and the context of constitution rather than on the symbols that mediate them. Like other identities, ethnicity and race take many forms.

The picture I have drawn of ethnically mediated political identity has normative implications. Labeling a set of identities as illegitimate, dangerous to public interaction, and unfit for political mediation is an inevitably value-laden exercise. Though it is not obviously the case that political scientists and others writing in this vein have purposely used the existence of cultural identities to exclude and "orientalize" some (mostly non-Western) societies, and some people's identities within Western societies, implicitly they have. By showing that the symbols of race and ethnicity behave in ways that more closely approximate the symbols of class and ideology, I have highlighted the arbitrary and political nature of the classification of societies and the exclusion of groups.

What I have attempted most explicitly is to suggest new ways of thinking about the identities that mediate politics for millions of people. By drawing an analytical distinction between political and other types of identities that people hold, I have been able to isolate the behavior of political identities and to show that they operate distinctly from apparently corresponding social identities. Zulu identity may not be politically salient to a person who nevertheless calls herself a Zulu. This perspectival shift is responsible for exposing a much more fluid, indeterminate, and heterogeneous angle of ethnically mediated political identity. At the least I hope to have extended the parameters of possibility.

It is particularly important to extend possibility as millions of people whose political identities are mediated by ethnicity embark on experiments with democracy at the dawn of the twenty-first century. If democracy cannot process politics along whatever lines occur, then it is unequal to the task of governance in most of the world. Democracy risks obsolescence if it operates only, or best, in homogeneous societies. If there ever were homogeneous societies (a doubtful proposition to begin with), they are disappearing fast.[16] Moreover, difference does not rely on objective conditions. Societies that are homogeneous today may develop salient subgroup cleavages tomorrow. Difference is the norm, and difference along politicized lines of ethnicity, race, language, and religion is practically universal. Tracing the origins and behavior of political identities is crucial to conceiving the place and possibilities of race and ethnicity in politics. Like other identities people hold, ethnicity and race take many forms, and conceal many journeys.

Notes

Introduction

1. Larry Diamond, Marc Plattner, Yun-Han Chu, and Hung-mao Tien, *Consolidating the Third Wave Democracies* (Baltimore: Johns Hopkins University Press, 1997), xvii.

2. See Robert Kaplan, "Was Democracy Just a Moment?" *Atlantic Monthly,* December 1997, 55–80, and Francis Fukuyama, *The End of History and the Last Man* (New York: Free Press, 1992), for opposing views on this question.

3. Donald Horowitz, *Ethnic Groups in Conflict* (Berkeley: University of California Press, 1985).

4. Paul Sniderman, Joseph Fletcher, Peter Russel, and Philip Tetlock, *The Clash of Rights: Liberty, Equality, and Legitimacy in Pluralist Democracy* (New Haven: Yale University Press, 1996), 6, 192.

5. Henri Tajfel, *Human Groups and Social Categories* (Cambridge: Cambridge University Press, 1981), 226, 268–276.

6. Henri Tajfel, "Experiments in Intergroup Discrimination," *Scientific American* 223 (1970): 96–102. This literature is summarized in Horowitz, *Ethnic Groups in Conflict,* 144–147.

7. Horowitz, *Ethnic Groups in Conflict,* 145.

8. Henri Lefebvre, *Critique of Everyday Life* (London: Verso, 1991).

9. When Natal was engulfed in violence in the 1980s, a village might be attacked because of the political affiliation of its chief, or villagers might be expected to fight for their chief.

10. During the 1980s the king was closely linked with Inkatha and was used as a politically unifying symbol, although in the preceding decades the monarch had been stripped of power and prevented from playing any politically important role.

11. The Reed Dance is an annual celebration that was imbued with political and unifying meaning during the 1980s when Inkatha reinvigorated the tradition with an infusion of money and organization. The Reed Dance spans a few days and includes Zulu maiden dancing, drinking, and feasting. Many guests were transported to the Reed Dance by buses paid for by Inkatha.

12. For a classic analysis of this type of political identity trajectory, see William Beinart, "Worker Consciousness, Ethnic Particularism, and Nationalism: The Experience of a South African Migrant, 1930–1960," in Shula Marks and Stanley Trapido, eds., *The Politics of Race, Class, and Nationalism in Twentieth Century South Africa* (Harlow: Longman, 1987).

13. During the 1980s, and in particular toward the end of the decade, Inkatha insisted that its followers attend party rallies with "traditional weapons," formerly consisting of a fighting stick. The definition of "traditional weapon" was broadened in this era to include anything that could maim or kill, and people carried weapons as assorted as baseball bats and clubs embedded with nails. They did not for the most part carry guns, which were as a result associated with UDF members and were by extension sometimes deemed anti-Zulu.

14. Kwame Anthony Appiah, "Identity, Authenticity, Survival: Multicultural Societies and Social Reproduction," in Amy Gutmann, ed., *Multiculturalism: Examining The Politics of*

Recognition (Princeton, N.J.: Princeton University Press, 1996). Appiah uses the term *tightly scripted.*

15. For example, Donald Horowitz, *A Democratic South Africa? Constitutional Engineering in a Severely Divided Society* (Berkeley: University of California Press, 1991); Arend Lijphart, *Power Sharing in South Africa* (Berkeley: Institute of International Studies, 1985); Timothy Sisk, *Democratization in South Africa: The Elusive Social Contract* (Princeton: Princeton University Press, 1995).

16. *The Law of South Africa,* vol. 21 (Cape Town: Butterworths, 1984), 404–412. These definitions come from the 1950 Population Registration Act.

17. Sheila Van der Horst, ed., *The Theron Commission Report: A Summary of the Findings and Recommendations of the Enquiry Relating to the Coloured Population Group* (Johannesburg: South African Institute of Race Relations, 1976).

18. *The Law of South Africa,* 21: 412.

19. Interviews with Stan Fisher, 2 February 1995, and Allan Hendrickse, 28 June 1995, both of whom have "White" and "Coloured" family members. All subsequent quotations of Fisher and Hendrickse are from these interviews unless otherwise specified.

20. Heribert Adam and Hermann Giliomee demonstrate that even Afrikaner intellectuals, who may be presumed to have benefited from the system, began to criticize the legitimacy of apartheid as early as the 1950s. Adam and Giliomee, *The Rise and Crisis of Afrikaner Power* (Cape Town: David Philip, 1979).

21. See Gail Gerhart, *Black Power in South Africa: The Evolution of an Ideology* (Berkeley: University of California Press, 1978), and Anthony Marx, *Lessons of Struggle: South African Internal Opposition, 1960–1990* (New York: Oxford University Press, 1992), for the best analyses of the Black Consciousness Movement and its influence.

22. Steve Biko, *I Write What I Like* (London: Bowerdean, 1978).

23. Robert Mattes, "The Role of Identity in Building a Common Democratic Culture in South Africa." Paper delivered at the National Identity and Democracy conference at the University of the Western Cape, March 1997, 26.

24. Horowitz, *Ethnic Groups in Conflict,* 297.

25. *Cape Times,* October 7, 1997. Support for the DP went from 1 percent in 1994 to almost 10 percent in 1999, propelling it into the role of official opposition.

26. Robert Mattes, *The Election Book: Judgment and Choice in South Africa's '94 Election* (Cape Town: IDASA, Public Information Centre, 1995), 85–87, 88.

27. R. W. Johnson and Lawrence Schlemmer, eds., *Launching Democracy in South Africa: The First Open Election, April 1994* (New Haven: Yale University Press, 1996), 147.

28. SABC Survey (12–16 March 1994) and MPD/M&O Survey (February 1994), both reproduced in Robert Mattes, "The Election in the Western Cape," unpublished, undated, 11–12. This evidence is compiled in Ian Shapiro and Courtney Jung, "South African Democracy Revisited: A Reply to Koelble and Reynolds," *Politics and Society* 24, no. 3 (1996): 237–247.

29. Johnson and Schlemmer, *Launching Democracy,* 41, 53–54.

30. Coloured identity, arguably one of apartheid's most successful constructions, persists in the postapartheid era, both politically and socially, although its meaning and boundaries are contested.

1. Born from Speaking
   1. The chapter title is derived from Mario Vargas Llosa's description of the creation myth of the Machiguenga Indians of Peru: "They were born speaking or, to put it a better way, they were born from speaking." The universe, that is, was created as a result of being named. Mario Vargas Llosa, *The Storyteller* (Penguin, 1990), 131.
   2. Fredrick Barth, *Ethnic Groups and Boundaries: The Social Organization of Culture Difference* (London: Allen and Unwin, 1969); Crawford Young, *The Politics of Cultural Pluralism* (Madison: University of Wisconsin Press, 1976); Aidan Southall, "The Illusion of Tribe," *Journal of Asian and African Studies* 5, nos. 1–2 (1970): 15–45; David Laitin, *Hegemony and Conflict: Politics and Religious Change Among the Yoruba* (Chicago: University of Chicago Press, 1986).
   3. Leroy Vail, ed., *The Creation of Tribalism in South Africa* (Berkeley: University of California Press, 1989); Ian Goldin, *Making Race: The Politics and Economics of Coloured Identity in South Africa* (Cape Town: Maskew, Miller, Longman, 1987); Shula Marks, *The Ambiguities of Dependence in South Africa: Class, Nationalism, and the State in Twentieth-Century Natal* (Johannesburg: Ravan, 1986); Shula Marks and Stanley Trapido, *The Politics of Race, Class, and Nationalism in Twentieth-Century South Africa* (Harlow: Longman, 1987); Mahmood Mamdani, *Citizen and Subject* (Princeton: Princeton University Press, 1997).
   4. David Snow and Robert Benford, "Master Frames and Cycles of Protest," in Aldon Morris and Carol McClurg Mueller, eds., *Frontiers in Social Movement Theory* (New Haven: Yale University Press, 1992). Snow and Benford use the concept of frames to explain individual cognition.
   5. See Aletta Norval, "Against a Theory of Ethnicity: Thinking Political Identities in a Post-Apartheid Context," paper presented at Ethnicity, Identity, and Nationalism in South Africa conference, Rhodes University, Grahamstown, 20–24 April 1993; Jan Nederveen Pieterse, "The Varieties of Ethnic Politics and Ethnic Discourse," paper presented at same conference.
   6. Ernesto Laclau, "Political Frontiers, Identification, and Political Identities," presented at Ethnicity, Identity, and Nationalism in South Africa conference. Laclau states: "I cannot assert a differential identity without distinguishing it from a context, and in the process of making the distinction, I am asserting the context at the same time. And the opposite is also true. I cannot destroy a context without destroying at the same time the identity of the particular subject who carries out the destruction," 8.
   7. Verta Taylor and Nancy E. Whittier. "Collective Identity in Social Movement Communities," in Morris and Mueller, *Frontiers in Social Movement Theory*, 105.
   8. "Ascriptive category . . . ascriptive group": Nelson Kasfir, "Explaining Ethnic Political Participation," *World Politics* 32 (1979): 365–388.
   9. See John C. Turner, *Rediscovering the Social Group: A Self-Categorization Theory* (Oxford: Blackwell, 1987), for an interesting and informative theory of how a collection of individuals becomes a social and psychological group.
   10. See Lloyd Sandelands and Linda St. Clair, "Toward an Empirical Concept of the Group," *Journal for the Theory of Social Behaviour* 23, no. 4 (1993): 423–458, for an excellent overview of the conceptualization of the group as both a multiple and an entity.

11. Taylor and Whittier. "Collective Identity," 110.

12. I am grateful to Alexander Wendt for discussing and clarifying this concept with me.

13. Kwame Anthony Appiah makes the point, for example, that the politics of identity transforms the identity of its members. Appiah, "Identity, Authenticity, Survival," in Amy Gutmann, ed., *Multiculturalism: Examining the Politics of Recognition* (Princeton: Princeton University Press, 1994).

14. See Shula Marks, *The Ambiguities of Dependence in South Africa: Class, Nationalism, and the State in Twentieth-Century Natal* (Johannesburg: Ravan, 1986); interview with Paulus Zulu, 25 April 1995. All subsequent quotations of Zulu are from this interview unless otherwise specified.

15. Crawford Young, correspondence, 1997.

16. The children's author Dr. Seuss (Theodor Geisel) makes a similar analogy and argument in *The Sneeches* (New York: Random House, 1961).

17. See results of Bosnian national election as reported in the *New York Times,* September 1996.

18. Interview with Pauls Zulu.

19. For evidence of this see Chapters 2 and 3, results of the Bosnian national election in September 1996, and the report in the *New York Times,* 3 March 1997, regarding attacks by the militantly separatist Kurdish Worker's Party against moderate Kurdish villagers in Turkey.

20. Courtney Jung and Ian Shapiro, "South Africa's Negotiated Transition: Democracy, Opposition, and the New Constitutional Order," *Politics and Society* 23, no. 3 (1995): 269–308.

21. Heribert Adam, "Engineering Legitimacy and the Politization of Ethnicity," conference paper, University of Natal, Durban, 20–23 April 1982.

22. Douglas Rae, *The Political Consequences of Electoral Laws* (New Haven: Yale University Press, 1971); Arend Lijphart, "The Political Consequences of Electoral Laws," *American Political Science Review* 84, no. 2 (1990): 481–497; Donald Horowitz, *A Democratic South Africa? Constitutional Engineering in a Deeply Divided Society* (Berkeley: University of California Press, 1991).

23. Perry Anderson, *Arguments Within English Marxism* (London: Verso, 1980) "History is not, as Althusser proclaimed, 'a process without a subject.' Part of it is the conscious human choice, value, action"; chapter 2, "Agency."

24. Among the people I interviewed, Ken Lategan of the Labour Party exemplified the former characteristic, Robert van Tonder of the Boerestaat Party the latter.

25. Johann Degenaar, "The Myth of a South African Nation," paper presented at Ethnicity, Identity, and Nationalism in South Africa conference, 2.

26. David A. Snow and Robert D. Benford, "Ideology, Frame Resonance, and Participant Mobilization," *International Social Movement Research* 1 (1988): 197–217; for example, see three core framing tasks, p. 199.

27. Pnina Motzafi-Haller, "Historical Narratives as Political Discourses of Identity," *Journal of Southern African Studies* 20, no. 3 (1994): 417–431.

28. George Fredrickson argues, for example, that during the 1950s and 1960s the Civil Rights Movement succeeded where Black oppositional mobilization in South Africa failed be-

cause the Civil Rights Movement was extensively organized through churches and other grassroots organizations that sustained it. Black political mobilization in South Africa was at the time orchestrated mainly by charismatic leaders, with little organizational base. Fredrickson, *The Comparative Imagination: On the History of Racism, Nationalism, and Social Movements* (Berkeley: University of California Press, 1997).

29. John Comaroff and Jean Comaroff, *Of Revelation and Revolution* (Chicago: University of Chicago Press, 1991), 24.

30. Although the South African Communist Party stands as one member of the ANC triumvirate, it has little influence. The ANC has apparently renounced the redistributive and egalitarian principles that anchored the party during the apartheid era, and the Pan Africanist Congress, which retains many communist principles, has a support base of 1.8 percent of the population.

31. Gail Gerhart, *Black Power in South Africa: The Evolution of an Ideology* (Berkeley: University of California Press, 1978).

32. A variety of methods for the study of social representations have been suggested and used. There is some agreement that any attempt to understand psychological activities, such as identity formation, must be contextualized, possibly approached ethnographically. The constructivist approach used in this project also privileges the deeply contextualized analysis. Gerard Duveen and Barbara Lloyd, "An Ethnographic Approach to Social Representations," in Glynis Breakwell and David Canter, eds., *Empirical Approaches to Social Representations* (Oxford: Clarendon, 1993), 90–91. Although all the measures I propose may be inexact, nothing other than the outward manifestation of identity can be relied on in making informed judgments about individual or collective identities.

33. R. W. Johnson and Lawrence Schlemmer, eds., *Launching Democracy in South Africa: The First Open Election, April 1994* (New Haven: Yale University Press, 1996) 147.

2. Black Against Zulu

1. Shula Marks, *The Ambiguities of Dependence in South Africa: Class, Nationalism, and the State in Twentieth-Century Natal* (Johannesburg: Ravan, 1986), 22.

2. Eileen Jensen Krige, *The Social System of the Zulus* (Pietermaritzburg: Shooter and Shuter, 1936), 218–223.

3. Norman Etherington, *Peace, Politics, and Violence in the New South Africa* (London: H. Zell, 1992), 147–162.

4. Nicholas Cope, "The Zulu Petit Bourgeoisie and Zulu Nationalism in the 1920s: Origins of Inkatha," *Journal of Southern African Studies* 16, no. 3 (1990): 431–451.

5. Marks, *Ambiguities of Dependence*, 28.

6. Max Gluckman, *Analysis of a Social Situation in Modern Zululand* (Manchester: Manchester University Press, 1968), 8.

7. Mahmood Mamdani, *Citizen and Subject* (Princeton: Princeton University Press, 1996).

8. Gluckman, *Analysis of a Social Situation*, 13.

9. Cope, "Zulu Petit Bourgeoisie," 433.

10. Marks, *Ambiguities of Dependence*, 60.

11. Thulani Mshengu, Jabu Ndlovu, and Jean Fairbairn, *Asinamali: The Life of Msizi Dube*

(Pietermaritzburg: Hadeda, 1992); Francis Meli, *South Africa Belongs to Us: A History of the* ANC (Harare: Zimbabwe Publishing House, 1988). On the traditional Zulu political structure, see Krige, *Social System of the Zulus,* 217–261. See also Mamdani, *Citizen and Subject* for an excellent treatment of the systems and ideologies that governed precolonial and colonial African societies, including Zulus.

12. Meli, *South Africa Belongs to Us,* 120.

13. Ibid., 122.

14. In 1955 the ANC sponsored the Congress of the People to unveil a "people's charter of rights" that had been compiled over two years in meetings with people all over South Africa. This document was called the Freedom Charter and became the founding document of the ANC. Other groups that adhere to its principles are described as Charterist.

15. Gerhard Mare and Georgina Hamilton, *An Appetite for Power: Buthelezi's Inkatha and the Politics of Loyal Resistance* (Johannesburg: Ravan, 1987), 32. Buthelezi's son, Joe Matthews, is now a member of Parliament for the Inkatha Freedom Party.

16. Mare and Hamilton, *Appetite for Power,* 32–33.

17. Marks, *Ambiguities of Dependence,* 116.

18. Ibid., 117.

19. Mare and Hamilton, *Appetite for Power,* 30.

20. Donald Horowitz, *A Democratic South Africa? Constitutional Engineering in a Severely Divided Society* (Berkeley: University of California Press, 1991), 49.

21. Mare and Hamilton, *Appetite for Power,* 42.

22. Interviews with Sibusiso Ndebele, 16 May 1995, and Paulus Zulu. All subsequent quotations of Ndebele are from this interview unless otherwise specified. Umkhonto we Sizwe, known as MK, was the armed wing of the ANC from 1960 until 1991.

23. Mare and Hamilton, *Appetite for Power,* 56.

24. Mshengu, Ndlovu, and Fairbairn, *Asinamali.*

25. Tom Lodge and Bill Nasson. *All, Here, and Now: Black Politics in South Africa in the 1980s* (New York: Ford Foundation Foreign Policy Association, 1991), 153.

26. Speech delivered by Buthelezi, KwaZulu Legislative Assembly Debates, 5 (1975): 134.

27. Mare and Hamilton, *Appetite for Power,* 57.

28. Mare and Hamilton, *Appetite for Power,* 7 (KwaZulu Legislative Assembly Debates, 8 (1976): 85–86).

29. Paul Forsyth, "The Past in the Service of the Present: The Political Use of History by Chief A. N. M. G. Buthelezi, 1951–1991," *African Historical Journal* 26 (May 1992): 84.

30. Ibid., 85.

31. Gerhard Mare, "Tradition and Control: The Presence of the Past in Natal," unpublished, University of Natal, 1992, 9.

32. Mare, *Tradition and Control,* 8; interview with Oscar Dhlomo, 1984.

33. Mare and Hamilton, *Appetite for Power,* 219–220 (speech given by Gatsha Buthelezi).

34. Paul Wellings and Michael Sutcliffe. "The Widening Rift: Buthelezi, Inkatha, and Anti-Apartheid Politics in South Africa," *Transafrica Forum* 3 (1986): 51–79.

35. Jeremy Baskin, *Striking Back: A History of* COSATU (London: Verso, 1990).

36. Jay Naidoo, "Building People's Power," in *The Crisis: Speeches by* COSATU Office Bearers (undated pamphlet).

37. Wellings and Sutcliffe, "Widening Rift," 61 (speech given by King Goodwill Zwelithini in 1984).

38. Mare, *Tradition and Control,* 5 (speech given by King Goodwill Zwelithini in 1986).

39. Forsyth, "Past in the Service of the Present," 89, 90.

40. This was true in the Transkei, for example, where the UDF worked in cooperation with Xhosa chiefs, and in the Northern Transvaal, where the party was active in places like KwaNdebele.

41. Elijah Barayi, COSATU president, speaking at the organization's inauguration, Durban, 1985.

42. "What Is Inkatha Up To?" undated UDF pamphlet [mid-1980s].

43. Paulus Zulu and Mary De Haas, "Ethnicity and Federalism: The Case of oKwaZulu Natal," *Journal of Southern African Studies* 20, no. 3 (September 1994): 433–446 (speech by King Goodwill Zwelithini, Durban Stadium Imbizo, November 1989).

44. *Guardian Weekly,* 12 May 1991.

45. Mshengu, Ndlovu, and Fairbairn, *Asinamali.*

46. *Race Relations Survey* (Johannesburg: South African Institute of Race Relations, 1983), 110.

47. Mare and Hamilton, *Appetite for Power,* 12; *South Africa's Nine Provinces: A Human Development Profile* (Development Bank of South Africa, April 1994), 107.

48. Mare and Hamilton, *Appetite for Power,* 11.

49. Mike Morris and Doug Hindson, *The Social Structure and Dynamics of Metropolitan Durban* (CSDS Working Paper no. 13, University of Natal, Durban, 1995).

50. Catherine Cross, S. Bekker, C. Clark, R. Richards. *Moving On: Migrations Into and Out of Inanda* (Durban: University of Natal Press, 1995).

51. Mare and Hamilton, *Appetite for Power,* 66.

52. There are more than three hundred chiefs in KwaZulu Natal. Only one is a woman.

53. Interview with Tobias Mngadi, Rural Urban Studies Unit, University of Natal, Durban, 5 May 1995.

54. Interview with Chief Xolo, one of a small minority of chiefs who oppose Inkatha in KwaZulu Natal, 5 December 1995. All subsequent quotations of Xolo are from this interview unless otherwise specified.

55. Discussion with Paulus Zulu, University of Natal, Durban, 15 May 1995.

56. Although it is unclear when this rule was implemented, it was true by the mid-1980s.

57. Mare and Hamilton, *Appetite for Power,* 65, 72.

58. Jeremy Seekings, "The United Democratic Front and the Changing Politics of Opposition in Natal, 1983–1985," unpublished, University of Cape Town, 1993, 8.

59. Bill Freund, "The Violence in Natal, 1985–1990," unpublished, University of Natal, Durban, 1991, 12; Wellings and Sutcliffe, "Widening Rift," 63.

60. See J. McCarthy and M. Swilling, "Transport and Political Resistance," *South African Review* 2 (1984): 26–44.

61. Seekings, "United Democratic Front," 7.

62. Wellings and Sutcliffe, "Widening Rift," 74.

63. Michael Sutcliffe and Paul Wellings, "Inkatha Versus the Rest: Black Opposition to In-katha in Durban's African Townships," *African Affairs* 87, no. 348 (1988): 325–360.

64. Seekings, "United Democratic Front," 8.

65. Interviews with Thomas Shabalala, 20 May 1995, and David Ntombela, 21 May 1995, In-katha "warlords" in Lindelani, near Durban, and Taylor's Halt, near Pietermaritzburg, re-spectively. All subsequent quotations of Shabalala and Ntombela are from these interviews unless otherwise specified.

66. Over the decade, UDF organization came to resemble Inkatha organization more closely as democratic lines of communication and input atrophied, and UDF "strongmen" emerged to control their own areas.

67. Communism was opposed by Africanists, who attacked it as a foreign ideology imposed by paternalistic Whites.

68. Ultimately, Africanist ideologues left to form the Pan Africanist Congress in 1959.

69. Tom Lodge, *Black Politics in South Africa Since 1945* (London: Longman, 1983).

70. Gail Gerhart, *Black Power in South Africa: The Evolution of an Ideology* (Berkeley: University of California Press, 1978).

71. Steve Biko, *I Write What I Like* (London: Bowerdean, 1978), 49.

72. Ibid., 37, 52.

73. Interview with Johnny Issel, 14 February 1995. All subsequent quotations of Issel are from this interview unless otherwise specified.

74. See Lodge and Nasson, *All, Here, and Now,* and Jeremy Seekings, *The History of the* UDF (forthcoming), for comprehensive examinations of the UDF in the 1980s.

75. Albert Luthuli, *Let My People Go: An Autobiography* (London: Collins, 1962).

76. *New Frontiers: The KwaZulu Natal Debates,* an *Indicator* (South Africa) Issue Focus, Indica-tor Project, South Africa, Centre for Applied Social Sciences, University of Natal, Dur-ban, 1988.

77. Horowitz, *A Democratic South Africa?* 63–65 (Human Sciences Research Council investiga-tion into intergroup relations, 1973–82).

78. Y. S. Meer and Raymond Mlaba, *Apartheid: Our Picture* (Durban: Institute for Black Re-search, 1982).

79. John D. Brewer, "Official Ideology and Lay Members Beliefs in Inkatha," *Politikon* 12, no. 1 (1985): 57–63.

80. Roger Southall, "Consociationalism in South Africa: The Buthelezi Commission and Be-yond," *Journal of Modern African Studies* 21, no. 1 (1983): 77–112.

81. Theodore Hanf, Heribert Weiland, Gerda Vierdag, Lawrence Schlemmer, Rainer Hempel, and Burkhard Krupp, *South Africa: The Prospects for Peaceful Change* (London: Collings, 1981), 355.

82. Lawrence Schlemmer, "Build-up to Revolution or Impasse?" *Journal of Asian and African Studies* 18 (1983): 60–81.

83. Ibid., 71.

84. Wellings and Sutcliffe, "Widening Rift," 64.

85. Ibid., 68.

86. Ibid., 73–74.

87. *Race Relations Survey* (Johannesburg: South African Institute of Race Relations, 1984).

88. Mark Orkin, *Disinvestment, the Struggle and the Future: What Black South Africans Really Think* (Johannesburg, Ravan, 1986), 40.

89. Hermann Giliomee and Lawrence Schlemmer, *From Apartheid to Nation Building: Contemporary South African Debates* (Cape Town: Oxford University Press, 1989), 167–168.

90. Ibid.

3. Of Kings and Chiefs

1. Interviews with Sibusiso Ndebele and Johnny Issel.

2. Which is, of course, at least part of the reason that the ban was eventually lifted and the party came to be widely perceived as the relevant negotiating partner.

3. *Weekly Mail,* 19–25 July, 1991.

4. Timothy Sisk, *Democratization in South Africa: The Elusive Social Contract* (Princeton: Princeton University Press, 1995), 111.

5. Among the parties pledging to boycott were the Pan Africanist Congress, which did in fact participate, and the Azanian People's Organization (AZAPO), which did not. The IFP demanded international mediation on provincial powers, the status of the king, and other issues it considered outstanding. The IFP finally agreed to participate in the elections after the ANC agreed to international mediation and offered the king a vast tract of land in KwaZulu. "We decided not to go into the elections until some of our constitutional guarantees were met. When finally, one week before the elections, the constitution was changed, not to our satisfaction, but it had moved sufficiently, we believed, to allow us to enter the elections." Interview with Arthur Konigkramer, IFP member of Parliament, chairman, IFP election committee, 23 May 1995. All subsequent quotations of Konigkramer are from this interview unless otherwise specified.

6. *Race Relations Survey* (Johannesburg: South African Institute of Race Relations, 1995–1996), 432.

7. *Race Relations Survey* (Johannesburg: South African Institute of Race Relations, 1989–1990), 565–566.

8. Notes from KwaZulu Natal Provincial Parliament debates, June 1995.

9. Interviews with Farouk Cassin, 12 May 1995, and Ziba Jiyane, IFP secretary general, 18 May 1995. All subsequent quotations of Cassin and Jiyane are from these interviews unless otherwise specified.

10. His threats were apparently unfounded, as the IFP did not withdraw even after the NP left the Government of National Unity to take up a position of loyal opposition.

11. Speech delivered by Buthelezi at King Shaka Day celebrations, September 1994.

12. Interview with Peter Smith, 26 April 1995. All subsequent quotations of Smith are from this interview unless otherwise specified.

13. *Natal Mercury,* September 1995.

14. Ibid.

15. Interview with Senzo Mfayela, 26 April 1995. All subsequent quotations of Mfayela are from this interview unless otherwise specified.

16. See, for example, Tom Lodge, *Black Politics in South Africa Since 1945* (London: Longman, 1983), chapters 1–3.

17. Address by Prince Sifiso Zulu, King's spokesperson and executive member of the King's council: University of Natal-Durban, June 1995.

18. Interview with Jacob Zuma, provincial minister of economic affairs, 28 May 1995. All subsequent quotations of Zuma are from this interview unless otherwise specified.

19. Development Bank of South Africa, *South Africa's Nine Provinces: A Human Development Profile,* April 1994.

20. Mike Morris and Doug Hindson, *The Social Structure and Dynamics of Metropolitan Durban* (CSDS Working Paper no. 13, University of Natal, Durban, 1995), 16.

21. Ibid., 13,15.

22. Ibid., 17–30.

23. Ibid.

24. Mike Morris, *Violence in Squatter Camps and Shantytowns: Power and Social Relations Governing Everyday Life,* unpublished, unpaginated, University of Natal, Durban, 1993.

25. Interview with Antoinette Louw, editor of *Conflict Monitor,* a publication that tracked violence in KwaZulu Natal in the 1980s and 1990s, 13 May 1995.

26. In the brutal practice of necklacing, employed mostly by the UDF to punish traitors and collaborators, a rubber tire was doused in gasoline and lowered over the victim's head to his torso, pinning his arms. The tire was then ignited.

27. This is so at least partly because the ANC, as the government, has committed resources to policing and stopping violence, whereas the NP used a double-pronged strategy of alternately ignoring and fomenting conflict between the UDF and Inkatha in the 1980s. Violence flared again, to a smaller degree, in the run-up to South Africa's second election in 1999.

28. I take as evidence the fact that the IFP did well only in those districts that included hostels in both national and local government elections. Andrew Reynolds, *Election '94 South Africa: The Campaigns, Results, and Future Prospects* (London: J. Currey; New York: St. Martin's, 1994).

29. Lauren Segal, "The Human Face of Violence: Hostel Dwellers Speak," *Journal of Southern African Studies,* 18, no. 1 (1991): 211–227.

30. Interview with Chief Xolo.

31. Interview with anonymous respondent.

32. Interview with Inkosi Ngubane, 30 May 1995.

33. Morris and Hindson, *The Social Structure,* 8.

34. The ANC won almost 50 percent of the urban vote, and the IFP won 12 percent. In rural areas, on the other hand, the IFP won 75 percent of the vote in local government elections; "Local Government Election Results," compiled by the Public Information Centre, IDASA.

35. Jonathan Klaaren, "Structures of Government in the 1996 South African Constitution: Putting Democracy Back into Human Rights," unpublished, February 1997; Courtney

Jung and Ian Shapiro, "South Africa's Negotiated Transition: Democracy, Opposition, and the New Constitutional Order," *Politics and Society* 23, no. 3 (1995): 269–308.

36. Information gleaned from interviews with IFP political elites who fell into almost all of these categories.

37. South African newspaper accounts from September to December 1995, and again in early 1999, including the *Natal Mercury,* the *Weekly Mail and Guardian,* and the *Star.*

38. This number can only be approximated, but polls indicate that a fairly large percentage of people likely to fall into this category were at least sympathetic to the IFP in the run-up to elections.

39. This is not universally true, however. Since 1998 there have been reports of violence between the IFP and the United Democratic Movement (UDM), a new political party that started to organize in Natal. A UDM leader was assassinated in Natal in 1999 in what appears to be a new round of political violence with at least one new protagonist.

40. Local government elections in KwaZulu Natal were not held until June 1996, some eight months after most local government elections, because of conflicts over district boundaries and chiefs.

41. Laurence Piper and Steven Piper, *Hit and Myth: Zulu Ethnicity and the 1994 Elections in KwaZulu Natal,* paper presented at SAPSA Conference, University of Stellenbosch, September 1995, 10.

42. Ibid.

43. Robert Mattes, *The Election Book: Judgment and Choice in South Africa's '94 Election* (Cape Town: IDASA, Public Information Center, 1995), 64.

44. Ibid., 63.

45. *Hearing the People: Natal, Coloured, and* PAC Focus Groups, 1994.

46. Mattes, *Election Book,* 48, 63–65.

47. Ibid., 136, 137.

48. Unpaginated Research Initiatives survey material.

49. Mattes, *Election Book,* 46.

50. *Hearing the People.*

51. Mary De Haas and Paulus Zulu, "Ethnicity and Federalism: The Case of KwaZulu Natal," *Journal of Southern African Studies* 20, no. 3 (1994): 8–12.

4. In Defense of Whiteness

1. See Hermann Giliomee, "The Growth of Afrikaner Identity," in Heribert Adam and Hermann Giliomee, *Ethnic Power Mobilized: Can South Africa Change?* (New Haven: Yale University Press, 1979), 103, for a good brief description of the origins of Afrikaner identity.

2. Dan O'Meara, *Volkskapitalisme* (Cambridge: Cambridge University Press, 1983), 68.

3. Dunbar Moodie, *The Rise of Afrikanerdom: Power, Apartheid, and the Afrikaner Civil Religion* (Berkeley: University of California Press, 1975), 73, 77. Emphasis mine.

4. Dan O'Meara has done the most comprehensive job of detailing the construction of Afrikaner political identity in the preapartheid era. See *Volkskapitalisme.*

5. Isabel Hofmeyr, "Building a Nation from Words: Afrikaans Language, Literature, and Ethnic Identity, 1902–1924," in Shula Marks and Stanley Trapido, *The Politics of Race, Class,*

and Nationalism in Twentieth-Century South Africa (London: Longman, 1987). See also O'Meara, *Volkskapitalisme;* Moodie, *Rise of Afrikanerdom;* Adam and Giliomee, *Ethnic Power Mobilized.*

6. D. J. Van Vuuren, Pieter Latakgomo, Jannie Marais, and Lawrence Schlemmer, eds., *South African Election, 1987: Context, Process, and Prospect* (Pinetown: Burgess, 1987).

7. Mainly miners and steelworkers. O'Meara, *Volkskapitalisme,* 226.

8. The NP won 126 of 166 seats in Parliament in the general election in 1966; Van Vuuren et al., *South African Election,* 6. At that point, it had the support of more than 80 percent of Afrikaners and had begun to make inroads among English speakers; Lawrence Schlemmer, "Ruling Party Politics," *Indicator* (South Africa) 4, no. 3 (1987): 12–17.

9. Adam and Giliomee, *Ethnic Power Mobilized,* 169–171, 174.

10. David Harrison, *The White Tribe of Africa* (Berkeley: University of California Press, 1981), 163.

11. The pillars of apartheid include the Group Areas Act and the Population Registration Act. Other apartheid legislation of this era includes the Mixed Marriages Act and the Immorality Act.

12. Van Vuuren et al., *South African Election,* 67.

13. Robert Schrire, *Adapt or Die: The End of White Politics in South Africa* (New York: Ford Foundation, Foreign Policy Association, 1991), 153.

14. From P. W. Botha's so-called Rubicon speech, reprinted in Schrire, *Adapt or Die,* 153. The *laager,* literally a circle of wagons defending against an enemy, became a metaphoric representation of Afrikaner response to the perceived threat of social change.

15. Schrire, *Adapt or Die,* 151.

16. From the Afrikaanse Handelsinstitut, quoted in Stanley Greenberg, *Legitimating the Illegitimate* (Berkeley: University of California Press, 1987), 397.

17. Schrire, *Adapt or Die,* 151.

18. In South Africa Parliament, House of Assembly, *Debates of the House of Assembly,* 1983–1985 (Cape Town: Printed for the Government Printer by Cape and Transvaal Printers, 1983–1985), 2 May 1984, v. 116, col. 36. All subsequent excerpts from House of Assembly debates are cited parenthetically in text.

19. Speech by Botha, reprinted in Schrire, *Adapt or Die,* 118.

20. Hermann Giliomee, "Broedertwis," in Norman Etherington, *Peace, Politics, and Violence in the New South Africa* (London: Zell, 1982), 176.

21. Interview with Louwrens Pretorius, UNISA sociologist, who claims to have attempted to advise CP leaders to mobilize class identity at the time, 30 September 1994.

22. Giliomee argues, conversely, that the CP presented itself as the "NP-in-exile," eschewing working-class or populist appeals and concentrating on ethnic symbolism and status concerns to mobilize support; Giliomee "Broedertwis." This does not seem to me to be the case.

23. *Debates of the House of Assembly.*

24. Corne Mulder, "The Soul of the White . . . Negotiables and Non-Negotiables," *Indicator* (South Africa) 7, no. 4 (1990): 1–4.

25. South Africa borrowed R1.24 billion from the IMF in 1982; *Race Relations Survey* (Johannesburg: South African Institute of Race Relations, 1983), 110.

26. For example, the government abolished job reservation, recognized Black trade unions, and opened apprenticeships to Africans.

27. William Munro, "Revisiting Tradition, Reconstructing Identity: Afrikaner Nationalism and Political Transition in South Africa," unpublished, Northwestern University (1995), 15.

28. *Race Relations Survey* (Johannesburg: South African Institute of Race Relations, 1981, 1986).

29. Craig Charney, "Class Consciousness and the National Party Split," *Journal of Southern African Studies* 10, no. 2 (1984): 269–282.

30. Ibid., 273.

31. Hermann Giliomee, *Parting of the Ways* (Cape Town: David Philip, 1982), 37.

32. The Carlton Conference in 1979, and the Good Hope Conference in 1981.

33. Janis Grobelaar and Simon Bekker, *The White Right,* an *Indicator* (South Africa) Issue Focus, Indicator Project, South Africa, Centre for Applied Social Sciences, University of Natal, Durban, 1989.

34. Schrire, *Adapt or Die,* 48.

35. Charney, "Class Consciousness," 273, 276, 278.

36. Grobelaar and Bekker, *The White Right,* 41.

37. Loun Alberts and Frank Chikane, eds., *The Road to Rustenberg* (Cape Town: Struik Christian, 1992).

38. Grobelaar and Bekker, *The White Right,* 42.

39. Charney, "Class Consciousness," 277.

40. Interview with Robert van Tonder, 13 October 1994. All subsequent quotations of van Tonder are from this interview unless otherwise specified.

41. Headquarters of the militant Afrikaner Weerstandsbeweging (AWB).

42. This was the position of Jaap Marais, who left the NP to form the HNP in 1969, and Robert van Tonder, who left in 1962.

43. Deborah Posel, "The Language of Domination, 1978–1983," in Marks and Trapido, *Politics of Race.*

44. Stanley Greenberg, "Ideological Struggles within the South African State," in Marks and Trapido, *Politics of Race.*

45. This is the persuasive argument of Greenberg, "Ideological Struggles."

46. The first is the position of Robert van Tonder of the Boerestaat Party. The second is that of many interviewees in the CP.

47. See O'Meara, *Volkscapitalisme,* for elaboration of this argument.

48. Janis Grobelaar, "The SA State in Transformation: The Impact of Afrikaner Nationalist Dynamics, Tensions, and Policy Divergences," diss. submitted to UNISA, 1994, 234.

49. Interview with Janis Grobelaar, 30 September 1994.

50. Theodore Hanf, Heribert Weiland, Gerda Vierdag, Lawrence Schlemmer, Rainer Hempel, and Burkhard Krupp, *South Africa: The Prospects for Peaceful Change: An Empirical Enquiry into the Possibility of Democratic Conflict Regulation* (London: Collings, 1981), 275.

51. Pierre Hugo, "Toward Darkness and Death: Racial Demonology in South Africa," *Journal of Modern African Studies* 26, no. 4 (1988): 567–590.

52. Schrire, *Adapt or Die,* 99, 126.

53. R. W. Johnson and Lawrence Schlemmer, *Launching Democracy in South Africa: The First Open Election, April 1994* (New Haven: Yale University Press, 1996), 47, 48.

54. Suzanne Booysen, "The Legacy of Ideological Control: The Afrikaner Youth's Manipulated Political Consciousness," *Politikon* 16, no. 1 (1989): 7–25.

55. Kate Manzo and Pat McGowan, "Afrikaner Fears and the Politics of Despair: Understanding Change in South Africa," *International Studies Quarterly* 36, no. 1 (1992): 1–24.

56. Hugo, "Toward Darkness and Death," and others interviewed farmers from the Transvaal border areas in 1979, and in 1984 they interviewed farmers and miners in two small towns in the Transvaal.

57. Interview with Willie Lewies, 11 November 1994. All subsequent quotations of Lewies are from this interview unless otherwise specified.

58. Manzo and McGowan, "Afrikaner Fears," and Hugo, "Toward Darkness and Death."

59. Another survey of elite Afrikaners conducted in 1988 indicates that the attitudes of elite Afrikaners did not differ substantially from those of the national sample of Afrikaners interviewed in 1987. Manzo and McGowan, "Afrikaner Fears."

60. Johnson and Schlemmer, *Launching Democracy,* 48.

61. Charney, "Class Consciousness," 271.

5. Jelly Bag Bones

1. Johann Van Rooyen, *Hard Right: The New White Power in South Africa,* (London: Tauris, 1994), 138.

2. *Argus,* 8 June 1990.

3. Robert Schrire, *Adapt or Die: The End of White Politics in South Africa* (New York: Ford Foundation, Foreign Policy Association, 1991), 139.

4. Van Rooyen, *Hard Right,* 136, 139, 140–150.

5. Ibid., 151. The record turnout was surpassed in the 1994 national elections.

6. This was true throughout the Cape, as well as in Coloured areas in the Transvaal.

7. *Star,* October 1995, various dates.

8. Election results demonstrate that up to two hundred thousand people who voted for the Freedom Front for provincial government chose the NP for national government; Andrew Reynolds, *Election '94 South Africa: The Campaigns, Results, and Future Prospects* (New York: St. Martin's, 1994), chapter 11, "The Results."

9. Results as reported in the *Star,* October 1995.

10. Interviews with Carel Boshoff IV, 30 January 1995, and Andries Beyers, 23 January 1995. All subsequent quotations of Boshoff and Beyers are from these interviews unless otherwise specified.

11. The supposedly liberal United Party had so imbibed apartheid ideology, for example, that it called only for a qualified franchise in the 1960s.

12. Dunbar Moodie, *The Rise of Afrikanerdom: Power, Apartheid, and the Afrikaner Civil Religion* (Berkeley: University of California Press, 1975). Interviews with Afrikaner nationalists also left me with this impression.

13. Interviews with Ferdi Hartzenberg, 19 October 1994, and Tienie Loots, 12 November 1994. All subsequent quotations of Hartzenberg and Loots are from these interviews unless otherwise specified.

14. Interview with Wouter Hoffman, 4 October 1994. All subsequent quotations of Hoffman are from this interview unless otherwise specified.

15. Interview with Koos de la Rey, 11 October 1994. All subsequent quotations of de la Rey are from this interview unless otherwise specified.

16. Interviews with Louw Hartzenberg, 11 October 1994, and Daan van der Merwe, 2 November 1994. All subsequent quotations of Hartzenberg and van der Merwe are from these interviews unless otherwise specified.

17. Interview with Fred Rundle, 16 November 1994. All subsequent quotations of Rundle are from this interview unless otherwise specified.

18. Interview with Joseph Chiole, 19 January 1995. All subsequent quotations of Chiole are from this interview unless otherwise specified.

19. From a speech by Eugene Terreblanche, Germiston (June 1995).

20. Interview with Joseph Chiole.

21. Interview with Carel Boshoff IV.

22. As evidenced by the fact that the CP contested, and did well in, by-elections in places like Umlazi, which are overwhelmingly English speaking. Until 1993 the CP newspaper, *Die Patriot,* was published in English and in Afrikaans. Starting in 1994 it was published in Afrikaans only, with occasional columns in English.

23. Interviews with Joseph Chiole, Andries Beyers, Wouter Hoffman.

24. The Zulu nationalist party Inkatha is actively recruiting support among Coloured nationalists; interview with Peter Smith, IFP member of Parliament.

25. *Race Relations Survey* (Johannesburg: South African Institute of Race Relations, 1993–1994), 372, 374.

26. In 1999 the South African economy began to recover from damage inflicted by the Asian crisis in mid-1998.

27. *Race Relations Survey* (1993–1994), 374, 375, 383, 385, 387.

28. Ibid., 236, 250, 387.

29. *Race Relations Survey* (1991–1992), 464, 465–466.

30. Ibid., 484, 486.

31. Janis Grobelaar, "The SA State in Transformation: The Impact of Afrikaner Nationalist Dynamics, Tensions, and Policy Divergences," diss. submitted to UNISA, 1994, 11. Grobelaar usefully divides the network into six distinct categories: political parties (CP, HNP), churches and religious groups (HK, APK), policy study units (SABRA, Afrikanervryheidstigting), paramilitary organizations (AWB, Boere Krisisaksie), civil society bodies (agricultural unions, school committees), and cultural political organizations (Afrikaner Volkswag).

32. The CP held thirty-nine seats, the Democratic Party thirty-three.

33. Janis Grobelaar and Simon Bekker, *The White Right,* an *Indicator* (South Africa) Issue Focus, Indicator Project, South Africa, Centre for Applied Social Sciences, University of Natal, Durban, 1989, and Grobelaar, "SA State in Transformation."

34. Van Rooyen, *Hard Right,* 144.

35. Interview with Wouter Hoffman. According to Hoffman and others, the fact that they did waver may have undermined their credibility and popular support for a No vote.

36. Interviews with Joseph Chiole, Wouter Hoffman, and Daan van der Merwe.

37. Based on interviews with both hard-liners and pragmatists.

38. Interview with Willie Lewies.

39. What else they were designed to accomplish is unclear and in any case probably differs by group. I speculate, however, that not all commandos had only protection in mind.

40. Interview with Fred Rundle.

41. Interviews with Wouter Hoffman and Andries Beyers.

42. Vekom was another new White right-wing group.

43. The results of the 1995 local government elections, in which the CP performed abysmally and the FF did about the same as it had in 1994, suggest the two latter interpretations of the FF's 1994 showing. The FF won 2.6 percent, and the CP won 0.78 percent.

44. The Afrikaner critique of apartheid gained momentum in the late 1960s and 1970s. By the 1980s a fairly mainstream critical voice existed. Hermann Giliomee, "Broedertwis," in Norman Etherington, *Peace, Politics, and Violence in the New South Africa* (London: Zell, 1982). During the 1980s Afrikaner intellectuals and businessmen twice traveled outside the country to meet ANC leaders in Zambia and Senegal to try to broker a rapprochement.

45. Loun Alberts and Frank Chikane, *The Road to Rustenberg* (Cape Town: Struik Christian, 1992).

46. Heribert Adam and Hermann Giliomee, *Ethnic Power Mobilized: Can South Africa Change?* (New Haven: Yale University Press, 1979).

47. It has been argued that the democratic transition was an agreement between the ANC and the NP whereby the latter agreed to relinquish political power in return for guarantees that Whites would retain economic power. For a valuable perspective on the repercussions of this, see Michael MacDonald, "The Siren's Song: The Political Logic of Power-Sharing in South Africa," *Journal of Southern African Studies* 18, no.4 (1992): 709–727.

48. The only real White violence directed against the transition occurred in the week before the election, when AWB members, apparently acting without official AWB sanction, detonated a series of bombs in downtown Johannesburg. Predictions that Whites would cling to power continued as late as 1992; Kate Manzo and Pat McGowan, "Afrikaner Fears and the Politics of Despair: Understanding Change in South Africa," *International Studies Quarterly,* 36, no. 1 (1992): 1–29.

49. R. W. Johnson and Lawrence Schlemmer, eds., *Launching Democracy in South Africa: The First Open Election, April 1994* (New Haven: Yale University Press, 1996), 305.

50. Robert Mattes, *The Election Book: Judgment and Choice in South Africa's '94 Election* (Cape Town: IDASA, Public Information Center, 1995) 24.

51. Johnson and Schlemmer, *Launching Democracy,* 80, 308.

52. Local government election results, as compiled by the Public Information Centre, Institute for a Democratic South Africa.

53. http://www/sabcnews.co.za/right.htm. Results of South African elections as reported

by the South African Broadcasting Corporation via Internet, 7 June 1999; no longer accessible online.

54. Johnson and Schlemmer, *Launching Democracy,* 255.

55. Mattes, *Election Book,* 85–87.

56. The DP won 430,000 votes in 1989 and 500,000 in 1994 provincial elections. The CP won 673,000 votes in 1989, and the FF won 640,000 in 1994 provincial elections, with at least some potential supporters boycotting elections altogether; Andrew Reynolds, *Election '94 South Africa: The Campaigns, Results, and Future Prospects* (New York: St. Martin's, 1994) 194–198.

57. Mattes, *Election Book,* 133, 134.

58. Ibid., 85–87.

59. Johnson and Schlemmer, *Launching Democracy,* 256.

60. Ibid., 255.

61. Conversation at December 1994 Day of the Vow ceremony at Wonderboom, Pretoria.

62. http://www.sabcnews.co.za/electionresults; no longer accessible online.

63. Johnson and Schlemmer, *Launching Democracy,* 47.

64. Robert Mattes, "The Role of Identity in Building a Common Democratic Culture in South Africa," unpublished, March 1997, 26. Mattes cites survey results showing that just under 96 percent of South Africans are "proud" or "very proud" to be called South African.

6. Then I Was Black

1. *The Law of South Africa,* vol. 21 (Cape Town: Butterworths, 1984), 404–412. Definition derived from the 1950 Population Registration Act.

2. In this chapter, I use *African* to refer to Black South Africans classified as African under apartheid laws. I use *Black* in its more inclusive sense to refer to Africans, Indians, and Coloureds, in keeping with the definition of the Black Consciousness Movement.

3. Gavin Lewis, *Between the Wire and the Wall: A History of South African "Coloured" Politics* (Cape Town: David Phillip, 1987).

4. Anthony Marx, *Making Race and Nation: A Comparison of the United States, South Africa, and Brazil* (Cambridge: Cambridge University Press, 1997). Marx makes the argument that the English were willing to reverse their commitment to Coloureds in order to solidify White nationalism and unity.

5. Ian Goldin, *Making Race: The Politics and Economics of Coloured Identity in South Africa* (Cape Town: Maskew, Miller, Longman, 1987).

6. Lewis, *Between the Wire and the Wall,* 32.

7. Ibid., 119–149.

8. Ibid., 162–175.

9. Richard Van der Ross, *Myths and Attitudes: An Inside Look at the Coloured People* (Cape Town: Tafelberg, 1979) 76.

10. Lewis, *Between the Wire and the Wall,* 223.

11. Sheila Van der Horst, ed., *The Theron Commission Report: A Summary of the Findings and*

Recommendations of the Enquiry Relating to the Coloured Population Group (Johannesburg: South African Institute of Race Relations, 1976), 101.

12. Ibid., 112.

13. Robert Cameron, "An Analysis of the Structure and Functioning of Coloured and Indian Local Authorities Since the Introduction of the Tricameral System," *Politikon* 18, no. 1 (1991): 28–45.

14. Ibid., 39.

15. Quoted in House of Representatives Debates, 1984–1989, *Proceedings from the House of Representatives Debates* (Cape Town: Government Printers, 1984–1989). All subsequent excerpts from House of Representatives debates are cited parenthetically in text. The speaker was identified only by office, not by name, in the source.

16. Speech by Allan Boesak, UDF launch, July 1983.

17. Interviews with Logan Wort, 17 January 1995, and Johnny Issel. All subsequent quotations of Wort are from this interview unless otherwise specified.

18. Interviews with Eugene Paramoer, 15 June 1995, and Logan Wort. All subsequent quotations of Paramoer are from this interview unless otherwise specified.

19. UDF News, Western Cape, vol. 2, no. 1, March 1984.

20. *The Citizen,* 22 April 1980.

21. UNISA acc. 100, memorandum submitted by Professor Cloete.

22. R. W. Johnson and Lawrence Schlemmer, *Launching Democracy in South Africa: The First Open Election, April 1994* (New Haven: Yale University Press, 1996), 116.

23. Ian Goldin, "The Poverty of Coloured Labour Preference: Economics and Ideology in the Western Cape," SALDRU Working Paper no. 59 (January 1984), 11, 13.

24. Van der Horst, *Theron Commission Report,* para. 5.107, n1; and Goldin, *Making Race,* 150.

25. H. W. Van der Merwe, ed., *Occupation and Social Change Among the Coloureds of South Africa* (Cape Town: Juta, 1976) 61.

26. Goldin, *Making Race,* 131.

27. Van der Horst, *Theron Commission Report,* 29; Goldin, *Making Race,* 175.

28. Goldin, *Making Race,* 131, 149.

29. Van der Horst, *Theron Commission Report,* 33.

30. Goldin, *Making Race,* 174.

31. Ibid.; Van der Horst, *Theron Commission Report*; Van der Merwe, *Occupation and Social Change.*

32. Illegal because the Western Cape was a Coloured Labour Preference Area.

33. Van der Horst, *Theron Commission Report,* 30.

34. Goldin, *Making Race,* 185.

35. Ibid., 195, 200.

36. See Goldin, "Poverty of Coloured Labour Preference," 24–26.

37. Interviews with Joey Marks, 24 January 1995, Logan Wort, Johnny Issel, and Eugene Paramoer. All subsequent quotations of Marks are from this interview unless otherwise specified.

38. Interview with Logan Wort.

39. Jeremy Seekings, "The UDF in Cape Town." Unpublished, 1994, 2–3.

40. Goldin, "Poverty of Coloured Labour Preference," 34–36.

41. One union organizer said, "Racial divisions vary to such an extent from factory to factory that it is not possible to make a valid general comment about them"; (UNISA Acc. 100, Evidence of the Cape Chamber of Industries). Goldin attributes the difference from factory to factory to the level and type of trade union organization; Goldin, *Making Race,* 243.

42. Goldin, "Poverty of Coloured Labour Preference," 37. Goldin does not name the secretary.

43. Interview with Allan Hendrickse.

44. Interview with Stan Fisher.

45. Cameron, "Analysis of the Structure," 34.

46. *Cape Times,* 24 June 1985, quoted in Cameron, "Analysis of the Structure," 34.

47. Cameron, "Analysis of the Structure," 35.

48. Lewis, *Between the Wire and the Wall,* 180, 186, 208.

49. The NEUM articulated a strong Trotskyite line that made class, not racial, identity politically salient.

50. Lewis, *Between the Wire and the Wall,* 215.

51. Steve Biko, *I Write What I Like* (London: Bowerdean, 1978).

52. Lewis, *Between the Wire and the Wall,* 278.

53. Interview with Johnny Issel.

54. One of the most important differences between Charterism and Black Consciousness is that Charterists interpreted apartheid and resistance as a class issue, whereas BCM adherents perceived it in racial terms.

55. See Seekings, "The Origins of the UDF, 1977–1982," unpublished, 1993, for a full explanation of this period.

56. J. J. Morse and S. Peele. "Coloured Power or Coloured Bourgeoisie? Political Attitudes Among South African Coloureds," *Public Opinion Quarterly* 38, no. 3 (1974): 317–334.

57. Lewis, *Between the Wire and the Wall,* 278.

58. Pierre Hugo, *Quislings or Realists? A Documentary Study of Coloured Politics in South Africa* (Johannesburg: Ravan, 1978), 173–5, 199–200; and Lewis *Between the Wire and the Wall,* 278.

59. Goldin, *Making Race,* 207.

60. From a survey conducted by the Human Sciences Research Council in 1982 on attitudes regarding social and political change among Whites, Coloureds, and Indians.

61. Mark Orkin, *Disinvestment, the Struggle and the Future: What Black South Africans Really Think* (Johannesburg: Ravan, 1986).

62. HSRC survey, 1982.

63. Seekings, "UDF in Cape Town," 5, 11–12.

64. Ibid., 19.

65. Ibid., 22.

66. N. J. Rhoodie, Chris de Kock, and Mick Couper, *Coloured Perceptions of Sociopolitical Change in South Africa: Findings of a Sample Survey Undertaken in March 1986,* research finding SN-258 (Pretoria: Human Sciences Research Council, 1987), 5, 15, 16, 19, table 3.2.

67. Seekings, "UDF in Cape Town," 22.

68. Rhoodie, de Kock, and Couper, *Coloured Perceptions,* 20.

69. Whereas voter turnout was less than 10 percent in the Cape metro area in the 1984 elections, in 1989 participation was roughly double that in most areas. Participation ranged

from a low of less than 10 percent to 30 percent, but still hovered between 10 percent and 20 percent for the most part; Cameron, "Analysis of the Structure."

70. Rhoodie, de Kock, and Couper, *Coloured Perceptions,* 10.

71. Although this had not always been true, and parties like the collaborationist FCPP existed as late as the 1970s, by the 1980s the political climate was such that only the oppositional LP and UDF had any political credibility.

7. Now I Would Say I'm a Coloured

1. *Race Relations Survey* (1991–1992), 38.

2. Interview with Ken Lategan, 16 February 1995. All subsequent quotations of Lategan are from this interview unless otherwise specified.

3. *Race Relations Survey* (1991–1992), 38.

4. Interviews with Willie Hofmeyr, 22 January 1995, and Johnny Issel. All subsequent quotations of Hofmeyr are from this interview unless otherwise specified.

5. Interviews with Logan Wort and Eugene Paramoer.

6. *Race Relations Survey* (South African Institute of Race Relations, 1995–1996), 432.

7. Interviews with Abe Williams, 29 June 1995, and Andries Beyers. All subsequent quotations of Williams are from this interview unless otherwise specified.

8. Interview with Gerrie Morkel, provincial minister of economic affairs, Western Cape, 27 June 1995. All subsequent quotations of Morkel are from this interview unless otherwise specified.

9. Interview with Lawrence Solomon, 24 January 1995. All subsequent quotations of Solomon are from this interview unless otherwise specified.

10. Interview with Shahiem Ismael, 14 December 1995. All subsequent quotations of Ismael are from this interview unless otherwise specified.

11. Hermann Giliomee makes the point about the political use of language in "The Non-Racial Franchise and Afrikaner and Coloured Identities, 1910–1994," *African Affairs* 94 (1995): 199–225.

12. Interview with Jan Kruger, 24 January 1995. All subsequent quotations of Kruger are from this interview unless otherwise specified.

13. Speech delivered to a crowded hall in the very poor Coloured township adjoining the small town of Laingsburg in October 1995.

14. Interviews with Logan Wort, Joe Marks, and Eugene Paramoer. Also in R. W. Johnson and Lawrence Schlemmer, eds., *Launching Democracy in South Africa: The First Open Election, April 1994* (New Haven: Yale University Press, 1996), (1996) 121.

15. Matthew Eldridge, "In Retrospect: A Collection of Interviews Conducted with Strategists, Organizers, and Candidates from the African National Congress's 1994 Western Cape Campaign," M.A. thesis, University of Cape Town, 1995.

16. Interviews with informants who wished to remain anonymous on this issue.

17. Interview with Themba Sikhutshwa, 14 June 1914. All subsequent quotations of Sikhutshwa are from this interview unless otherwise specified. According to Sikhutshwa, focusing on the oppressed in general and "Africans in particular" has long been a tenet of ANC policy.

18. Interview with Johnny Issel.

19. Johnson and Schlemmer, *Launching Democracy,* 122.

20. Chris Nissen, ANC provincial leader, quoted in *Sunday Times,* Cape Metro Region, 11 April 1995.

21. Unnamed source quoted in *Mail and Guardian,* 24 April 1995.

22. *Mail and Guardian,* 24 March 1995.

23. *Sunday Times,* Cape Metro Region, 16 April 1995.

24. Among these, one of the most voluble was Peter Marais, the National Party member of executive council for local government in the Western Cape legislature. Marais defected to the ANC in 1999.

25. Interview with Dougie Joseph, 26 June 1995. All subsequent quotations of Joseph are from this interview unless otherwise specified.

26. *Cape Times,* 13 September 1995.

27. Interviews with Joseph Chiole and Ken Lategan.

28. *Cape Times,* 4 September 1995.

29. *Africa South of the Sahara 1996,* 25th ed. (London: Europa, 1997).

30. *Race Relations Survey* (1995–1996), 7.

31. Wolfgang Thomas, "The Western Cape: A Leading Edge?" *Indicator* (South Africa) 12, no. 3 (1995): 59–63.

32. Jerry Eckert, "Rural Western Cape: Harvesting Growth?" *Indicator* (South Africa) 12, no. 3 (1995): 64–67.

33. Ibid.; *South Africa Country Profile, 1992–93* (London: Economist Intelligence Unit), 24.

34. *South Africa Quarterly Bulletin,* South African Reserve Bank, December 1994, no. 194.

35. Thomas, "Western Cape," 63.

36. Quoted in *Sunday Times,* Cape Metro Region, 11 April 1995.

37. Interview with Joe Marks. See also Johnson and Schlemmer, *Launching Democracy,* 121.

38. Interview with Logan Wort.

39. Johnson and Schlemmer, *Launching Democracy,* 121.

40. Interview with Logan Wort.

41. Johnson and Schlemmer, *Launching Democracy,* 123.

42. Ibid., 130.

43. Interviews with Themba Sikhutshwa, president of the ANC Youth League in the Western Cape, and Eugene Paramoer, head of the delegation that walked out of the conference.

44. Eldridge, "In Retrospect"; interview with Logan Wort.

45. William Finnegan, "The Election Mandela Lost," *New York Review of Books,* 20 October 1994, 34.

46. Interviews with Dougie Joseph, Abe Williams, and Stan Fisher.

47. Tom Lodge, "The South African General Election," *African Affairs* 94 (1995): 471–500, *Sunday Times,* 13 February 1994. The ANC did well in Gordonia and Namaqualand, for example, where LP branches became ANC branches.

48. Interviews with Stan Fisher, Abe Williams, and Allan Hendrickse.

49. Johnson and Schlemmer, *Launching Democracy,* 123.

50. Ibid., 150.

51. Interview with Johnny Issel; and Brian Williams, "The Power of Propaganda," in Wilmot James, Daria Caliguire, and Kerry Cullinan, eds., *Now That We Are Free: Coloured Communities in a Democratic South Africa* (Boulder, Colo.: Rienner, 1996), 26.

52. Interviews with Achmat Davids, 21 February 1995, Willie Hofmeyr, Johnny Issel, and Sibusiso Ndebele. All subsequent quotations of Davids are from this interview unless otherwise specified.

53. It is impossible to tell accurately who voted for whom because votes were not tabulated by race, and ballot boxes were sent from different areas to central polling stations to be counted. These figures are an approximation, taken from Johnson and Schlemmer, *Launching Democracy,* 145.

54. Coloured political leader Richard Van der Ross, quoted in *Die Burger,* 22 February 1994.

55. Giliomee, "Non-Racial Franchise."

56. Johnson and Schlemmer, *Launching Democracy,* 149.

57. Ibid., 147.

58. Richard Van der Ross, "The Afrikaner as Seen by the Coloured," in H. W. Van der Merwe and C. J. Groenewald, *Looking at the Afrikaner Today* (Cape Town: Tafelberg, 1975) 60, 62.

59. Robert Mattes, *The Election Book* (Cape Town: IDASA, 1995), 85.

60. Mattes, *The Election Book,* 37, 41.

61. Johnson and Schlemmer, *Launching Democracy,* 152, 155.

62. Unpaginated MPD Market and Opinion Surveys, November–December 1993.

63. *Weekend Star,* 15–16 October 1994.

64. Interview with Eugene Paramoer.

65. Quotation from *Weekend Star,* 15–16 October 1994.

66. Independent Newspaper Bishop Lavis-Bonteheuvel Survey, reported in http://www.sabcnews.co.za/oppos.htm June 7, 1999; no longer accessible online.

67. Interviews with Allan Hendrickse, Abe Williams, and Gerrie Morkel.

68. Campaign literature from the Joseph campaign.

69. I base this on interviews with Joseph and on an informal survey in which I asked random people on the street in Riversdale what they knew about Dougie Joseph. Many respondents had a fair idea of his platform.

70. Johnson and Schlemmer, *Launching Democracy,* 147–149.

71. MPD Market and Opinion Surveys.

72. Johnson and Schlemmer, *Launching Democracy,* 150.

73. Research Initiatives survey material, Western Cape, "Coloureds," 6, 30.

74. Johnson and Schlemmer, *Launching Democracy,* 146.

75. MPD Market and Opinion Surveys.

8. Slaying the Hydra

1. Peter Evans, Dietrich Rueschemeyer, and Theda Skocpol, eds., *Bringing the State Back In* (Cambridge: Cambridge University Press, 1985).

2. Anthony Marx, *Making Race and Nation: A Comparison of the United States, South Africa, and Brazil* (Cambridge: Cambridge University Press, 1998), 2.

3. David Laitin, "Transitions to Democracy and Territorial Integrity," in Adam Przeworski, ed., *Sustainable Democracy* (Cambridge: Cambridge University Press, 1995), 32.

4. Robert Bates, "Modernization, Ethnic Competition, and the Rationality of Politics," in Donald Rothchild and Victor Olorunsola, eds., *State Versus Ethnic Claims: African Policy Dilemmas* (Boulder: Westview, 1983), 157.

5. Ibid., 16.

6. Mahmood Mamdani, *Citizen and Subject* (Princeton: Princeton University Press, 1996).

7. Although Arend Lijphart has spent most of his career elaborating and refining his ideas about consociationalism, it seems fairest to characterize his understanding of the concept with reference to his book *Power Sharing in South Africa* (Berkeley: University of California Institute of International Studies, 1985). There he explicitly applies his ideas to the South African case. He also dedicates a full chapter to criticisms that have been leveled against consociationalism. He counters these criticisms and amends parts of previous writings to state more precisely what he means and to correct possible overstatements. Thus it seems likely that this book truly reflects Lijphart's understanding of the way consociationalism works and what it works for.

8. Arend Lijphart, *Democracy in Plural Societies* (New Haven: Yale University Press, 1977), 38, 41.

9. Lijphart, *Power Sharing in South Africa,* 81.

10. Ibid.

11. Arend Lijphart, "Prospects for Power-Sharing in the New South Africa," in Andrew Reynolds, ed., *Election '94 South Africa* (Cape Town: David Philip, 1994), 225.

12. Donald Horowitz, *Ethnic Groups in Conflict* (Berkeley: University of California Press, 1985), 346–347.

13. Ibid., 6.

14. Donald Horowitz, *A Democratic South Africa? Constitutional Engineering in a Deeply Divided Society* (Berkeley: University of California Press, 1991), 196–203.

15. Horowitz, *Democratic South Africa?* 89–90, 188, 189.

16. Almost all of the important critiques of consociationalism have been outlined by Lijphart himself (*Power Sharing in South Africa,* chapter 4). Michael MacDonald, whose argument is not covered there, suggests that power sharing under conditions of tremendous disparities of wealth entrenches inequality: "The Siren's Song: The Political Logic of Power Sharing in South Africa," *Journal of Southern African Studies* 18, no. 4 (1992): 709–727.

17. Although consociationalism has been fairly universally discredited in the academic world, it is still being implemented, briefly in South Africa, and recently in Bosnia.

18. Ian Shapiro, "Group Aspirations and Democratic Politics," *Constellations* 3, no. 3 (1997): 315–325.

19. Horowitz, *Democratic South Africa?* 197.

20. Ibid., 198.

21. R. W. Johnson and Lawrence Schlemmer, eds., *Launching Democracy in South Africa: The First Open Election, April 1994* (New Haven: Yale University Press, 1996), 256.

22. Horowitz, *Democratic South Africa?* 178–179, 190.

23. Arend Lijphart, "The Alternative Vote: A Realistic Alternative for South Africa?" *Politikon* 18, no. 2 (1991): 91–101, quoting Horowitz, *Democratic South Africa?* 163.

24. G. W. Cox, "Centripetal and Centrifugal Incentives in Electoral Systems," *American Journal of Political Science* 34 (1990): 903–929. This is true in particular if we avoid the mistake of conflating centripetal and centrifugal with moderate and radical. The dominant center of the political spectrum in the Serbian enclave of Bosnia is apparently more radically nationalist than its flanks, for example.

25. Based on posters, pamphlets, speeches, and television commercials circulated in the weeks before local government elections in November 1995 and April 1996.

26. "South Africa's Negotiated Transition: Democracy, Opposition, and the New Constitutional Order," *Politics and Society* 23, no. 3 (1995): 269–308; Donald Horowitz "Constitutional Design: An Oxymoron?" paper presented at the American Society for Political and Legal Philosophy, San Francisco, 5–6 January 1998).

9. Every Journey Conceals Another Journey Within Its Lines

1. The chapter title is taken from Jeannette Winterson, *Sexing the Cherry* (New York: Grove, 1989), 2.

2. Clifford Geertz has most famously anchored the primordial tradition. See "The Integrative Revolution," in C. Geertz, ed., *Old Societies and New States* (New York: Free Press, 1963).

3. Most prominently, Arend Lijphart, *Power Sharing in South Africa* (Berkeley: Institute of International Studies, 1985), and Donald Horowitz, *A Democratic South Africa? Constitutional Engineering in a Severely Divided Society* (Berkeley: University of California Press, 1991).

4. Angus Campbell, *The American Voter* (New York: Wiley, 1960), and Donald P. Green and Bradley Palmquist, "Of Artefacts and Partisan Instability," *American Journal of Political Science,* 34, no. 3 (1990): 872–887.

5. Louis Hartz, *The Liberal Tradition in America: An Interpretation of American Political Thought Since the Revolution* (New York: Harcourt, Brace, and World, 1955).

6. Stephen Macedo, "Liberal Civic Education and Religious Fundamentalism: The Case of God v. John Rawls?" *Ethics,* 105 (April 1995): 468–496; Stephen Holmes, "Gag Rules or the Politics of Omission," in Jon Elster and Rune Slagstad, eds., *Constitutionalism and Democracy* (Cambridge: Cambridge University Press, 1988); John Rawls, *Political Liberalism* (New York: Columbia University Press, 1993).

7. Will Kymlicka, *Multicultural Citizenship* (Oxford: Oxford University Press, 1995); Charles Taylor, "The Politics of Recognition," in Amy Gutmann, *Multiculturalism: Exploring the Politics of Recognition,* (Princeton: Princeton University Press, 1996).

8. The move to reify the importance of ethnicity to Africans by arguing that the ethnic group is an extension of the family unit, for example, is one that naturalizes the alleged primacy of the ethnic group. Robert Bates, "Modernization, Ethnic Competition, and the Rationality of Politics," in Donald Rothchild and Victor Olorunsola, eds., *State Versus Ethnic Claims: African Policy Dilemmas* (New York: Westview, 1983).

9. This explains the shifting identities of many Bosnians who identified quite strongly as Bosnians in 1991 and yet came clearly to identify as Muslims, Serbs, and Croats within two years. See Misha Glenny, *The Fall of Yugoslavia* (London: Penguin, 1992).

10. Stephen Holmes, "Liberalism for a World of Ethnic Passions and Decaying States," *Social Research* 61, no. 3 (1994): 599–610.

11. Chaim Kaufman, "Possible and Impossible Solutions to Ethnic Civil Wars," *International Security* 20, no. 4 (1996): 136–153.

12. Donald Horowitz, *Ethnic Groups in Conflict* (Berkeley: University of California Press, 1985), and Ted Robert Gurr, *Minorities at Risk: A Global View of Ethnopolitical Conflicts* (Washington, D.C.: United States Institutes for Peace Press, 1993). I can think of no systematic comparison of the relative passion or violence of ethnic versus class- or ideology-based identities.

13. Bates, "Modernization," and Russell Hardin, *One for All: The Logic of Group Conflict* (Princeton: Princeton University Press, 1995).

14. James Fearon and David Laitin, "Explaining Interethnic Cooperation," *American Political Science Review* 90, no.4 (1996): 715–735.

15. Although the opposite may be true, that new democracies have a legitimacy surfeit because they have not yet been tested and found lacking, the instability of many new regimes, and the legitimacy problems we know them to have when trying to implement harsh market reform programs, for example, suggest that they more often suffer from a tenuous hold on legitimacy. See, for example, Adam Przeworski, *Democracy and the Market* (Cambridge: Cambridge University Press, 1991), for a discussion of the legitimacy problems that face new democracies undergoing economic transformation.

16. Only twelve countries in the world currently count as homogeneous along ascriptive lines. In many of these, growing immigrant populations (as in many of the Scandinavian countries, for example) and powerful regional cleavages (as in South Korea) undermine apparent homogeneity. See Rita Jalali and Seymour Martin Lipset, "Racial and Ethnic Conflict: A Global Perspective," *Political Science Quarterly* 107 (1992–1993): 585–606.

Index

Communism, 33, 119–20, 204; and total onslaught, 120
Community Youth Movement (CYM), 215
Concerned South Africans Group (COSAG), 155
Congress for a Democratic South Africa (CODESA), 77
Congress of South African Trade Unions (COSATU): and ANC, 101; in Natal, 51; and UDF, 61; in Western Cape, 189
Congress of Traditional Leaders of South Africa (CONTRALESA), 100
Conservative Party (CP), 112, 117–18, 121, 122; and Afrikaner identity, 145–46; boycott, 140; organization, 125–27, 151–56; and referendum, 153; strategy, 151–55; support, 129–32, 135
Consociationalism, 27, 137, 200–201, 237–38, 239. *See also* Electoral laws
Constitution: interim, 78, 136, 200; permanent, 79, 200–202
Constructivist approach, 17–19, 25

De Klerk, F. W., 134–35, 147, 165, 198
Discourse, 28–30, 246; and mobilization of Afrikaner political identity (1980s) 118–23, (1990s) 137–49; and mobilization of Coloured political identity (1980s) 175–83, (1990s) 202–17; and mobilization of Zulu political identity (1980s) 49–55, (1990s) 80–90; and role of threat, 29–30
Divided societies, 10, 111, 229, 236, 239, 250, 255–57
Dube, John, 42
Dutch Reformed Church: history, 114; and National party, 125, 126, 157–58

Economy: demography of Durban, 56, 90–91; in the 1980s, 55–57; reform, 57; and Zulus, 55–57, 90–91. *See also* Material conditions
Elections: *1987,* 118; *1989,* 135, 160; *1994,* 13, 14, 15, 104, 140, 201, 226; *1999,* 15,
105, 159, 160, 163, 201, 229; by-elections, 135; and Freedom Front, 155, 159–60; KwaZulu Natal provincial *1994,* 78, 104; local government, 104, 137, 159, 162, 201
Electoral laws, 26, 79, 136, 200–201, 237–42, 249–50; political institutions and political identity, 26; and Zulus, 45–49
Ethnic conflict, 259–62

Federal Coloured People's Party, 172, 173, 223
Federalism, 27, 79; and Inkatha Freedom Party, 80, 81; and National Party, 207–8
Franchise Action Committee (FRAC), 172
Freedom Charter, 43, 64
Freedom Front, 139, 144, 146, 155; Labour Party, 217; and 1994 elections, 160–61; organization, 152–56

GEAR, 102
Generals (the), 155
Great Trek, 148, 156

Hartzenberg, Ferdi, 123, 140, 141, 145, 146, 154
Hendrickse, Allan, 190, 199
Herenigde National Party, 113–14
Herstigte National Party, 117
Hertzog, Albert, 113
Homelands, 26, 45
Hostels, 96; and Inkatha, 96; and violence, 96, 97
House of Delegates, 135, 174, 199
House of Representatives, 135, 174–75, 176, 196, 199

Ideology: and Afrikaner identity (1980s) 127–29, (1990s) 156–59; and Coloured identity (1980s) 191–93, 223–25; role in construction of political identity, 33, 246; and Zulu identity (1980s) 64–69, (1990s) 100–103